30 Piers's
   lit rep of Rom
47 Will intelligent
49 L's poetry operates w/in diff.
       discourses of poverty

51 PP places spec. emphasis on social
       condition of poverty - removed
       from polemics

81 labour as model for all professions
(B.6+7 + scripture)
142 fear of purgatory

dis. of salvation (Merchants)
could have engaged in debates
re unmerited salvation

161 Will is the unifying force of the poem
162 hermits anchorites + friars act as reps of 1
163-4 Will + modern theologians
   175 unholy hermit
   177 like the involuntary poor, Will so marginal
212 on C9 passage

Piers Plowman and the Poor

Ms HM 1088 folios 225v & 226. 'Christ carrying the Cross assisted by the poor'.
This illustration is included by permission of the Huntington Library,
San Marino, California.

Piers Plowman
and the Poor

Anne M. Scott

FOUR COURTS PRESS

Set in 10.5 pt on 12 pt Bembo for
FOUR COURTS PRESS LTD
7 Malpas Street, Dublin 8, Ireland
e-mail: info@four-courts-press.ie
http://www.four-courts-press.ie
and in North America by
FOUR COURTS PRESS
c/o ISBS, 920 N.E. 58th Avenue, Suite 300, Portland, OR 97213.

© Anne M. Scott 2004

A catalogue record for this title
is available from the British Library.

ISBN 1–85182–725–0

All rights reserved. No part of this publication may be
reproduced, stored in or introduced into a retrieval system, or transmitted,
in any form or by any means (electronic, mechanical, photocopying,
recording or otherwise), without the prior written permission of both
the copyright owner and publisher of this book.

Printed in Great Britain
by Antony Rowe Ltd, Chippenham, Wilts.

In memoriam

Dr Idelle (Suzy) Sullens

scholar, mentor and friend

Contents

	LIST OF ABBREVIATIONS	9
	ACKNOWLEDGEMENTS	11
	INTRODUCTION	13
1	Meanings of poverty: Langland's five distinctions	25
2	The life of the poor, the necessity of work and the exercise of charity	68
3	'Marchaunt3 in þe margyne': how can the non-poor be saved?	115
4	Voluntary poverty and involuntary need: Will's experience of being a poor man	156
5	Food of life and heavenly reward: a question of justice	193
	CONCLUSION	231
	BIBLIOGRAPHY	237
	INDEX	249
	INDEX OF AUTHORS	261

Abbreviations

The following abbreviations are used:

Chaucer	*The Riverside Chaucer*, ed. Larry D. Benson and others, 3rd edn (Oxford: Oxford UP, 1987)
EETS	The Early English Text Society
MED	*Middle English Dictionary*, ed. Hans Kurath and Sherman M. Kuhn (Ann Arbor: University of Michigan Press, 1952–*c*.2001)
Pearsall, *C-Text*	'*Piers Plowman' by William Langland: an edition of the C-text*, ed. Derek Pearsall (London: Edward Arnold, 1978)
PL	Migne, J.-P. *Patrologiae cursus completus: series Latina* (Paris: 1844–1891)
RES	*Review of English Studies*
S. T.	*Summa theologica* of St Thomas Aquinas (online). Available at http://www.newadvent.org/summa/
Schmidt, *B-text*	William Langland, *The vision of Piers Plowman: a complete edition of the B-Text*, ed. A.V.C. Schmidt (London: Dent, 1978)
YLS	*The Yearbook of Langland Studies*

For the spelling of names I have used modern forms wherever these exist, and have retained Middle English forms for names such as Coveitise, Rechelesnesse and Imaginatif, for which there is no suitable modern equivalent.

In making reference to Scripture, and to medieval Latin writers, Latin originals have been used whenever these appear to have relevance for Langland's text. Otherwise I make quotations in Modern English.

Scriptural quotations in Latin are taken from *Biblia sacra vulgata* (online). Available from: http://bible.gospelcom.net/bible?language=latin. As this edition is unpunctuated, I have inserted punctuation where I felt the sense required it.

Acknowledgements

This book began as a doctoral thesis of the same name which was completed in English, Communication and Cultural Studies, at the University of Western Australia, under the inspiring guidance of Andrew Lynch, whose understanding and respect have been sustaining forces during the past few years. He generously shared his phenomenal scholarship with me during our many discussions and helped me to tease out the ideas which have eventually developed into this book. My co-superviser, Philippa Maddern, gave invaluable help in directing me to the historical materials necessary for me to embark on a study of *Piers Plowman* in relation to its culture.

Many kindly critics have read parts of the work, listened to presentations, questioned my conclusions, discussed my findings, and extended my thinking. Foremost among these are members of English, Communication and Cultural Studies at the University of Western Australia: Chris Wortham, Bob White, Gail Jones, Judith Johnston, and Patricia Crawford and Pamela Sharpe of History. I am also grateful to the participants of Work-in-Progress seminars, especially Monica Anderson and Marion Austin-Crowe, whose lively criticism reminded me that medieval literature belongs to modern readers. Of the scholars outside the University of Western Australia, I owe a particular debt of gratitude to Margaret Kim who generously loaned me her unpublished doctoral thesis: 'Vision of theocratics: the discourse of politics and the primacy of religion', and spent many hours reading and responding to my work.[1] Equally generous were Andrew Galloway, James Simpson and Derek Pearsall, whose criticism of the thesis in its completed form have helped me turn it into this book. I must also mention the Second International Langland Conference in Asheville, 1999, which was a turning point for me. Part of this book's second chapter was trialled as a conference paper there, and subsequent discussions with Anna Baldwin, Mary Clemente Davlin, Kathleen Hewett-Smith, Joan Baker and Richard Newhauser led me to recognize the deep significance of poverty in *Piers Plowman*.

I am glad to have the opportunity of acknowledging the assistance of many librarians. Toby Burrows and the staff of the Scholars' Centre in the University of Western Australia simplified the arduous assembling of resources by their good

---

1 I wish to acknowledge the recent article of M. Kim, 'Hunger, need, and the politics of poverty in *Piers Plowman*', which came to my attention just as this book was going to print.

organisation and unfailing helpfulness. I never fail to be impressed by their speed in acquiring documents, and their willingness to take trouble on behalf of scholars. In this thanks I include the general staff of the University's Reid library. I must also thank Susi Krasnoo and the library staff of the Huntington Library, San Marino, who put themselves out so that I could examine a large number of medieval manuscript illuminations during a brief week's visit. I am grateful, too, to Oliver Pickering and the librarians of the Brotherton Collection at Leeds University for help in accessing early printed books. The friendly and efficient office staff of English, Communication and Cultural Studies at the University of Western Australia gave me strong support throughout my studentship, and critical reading, in the final stages, by Bob Rogers, John Conway, Liz Cicolini, and Bruce McClintock has helped get the work into print.

This work owes much to a love of all things medieval engendered in me by three great teachers at St Anne's College Oxford: Dorothy Bednarowska, Elaine Griffiths and Patricia Ingham. It owes more to my parents, Michael and Una Conway, who understood that the greatest inheritance they could leave their children was education. Because of their sacrifices, I have been able to grasp a treasure. But it owes most to the unselfish support of my husband, Joe Scott, who has always behaved as though my work is more important to him than his own.

Introduction

This study explores, in a medieval literary context, the relationship between the good order of society and how people deal with poverty. I suggest that a barometer of society's condition, moral as well as economic, is its evaluation of need and its response to the state of the poor. I try to show that the value of poverty as portrayed within medieval literature lies in helping readers and writers come to terms with what is important within their culture. Medieval literature largely appears to express the culture and philosophy of the wealthy and the educated. If we turn this literature on its head, so to speak, and try to read with some knowledge and understanding of what it meant to be poor in the middle ages, I believe we shall find that the poor, even in the very act of being an object to the rest of society – of charity, contempt, revulsion, or pity – are crucial to the definition of social and spiritual well-being. I argue that a medieval writer's representation of poverty and the poor becomes a touchstone of faith, of moral probity and of identity. In precise terms, I look at *Piers Plowman* as a literary text which engages directly with the world and which questions the practical implications of the call to follow Christ in this world. As I see it, the poem's involvement with issues of poverty provides us with a way of reading the text as a work that engages with its own culture and makes visible to us the ideology of the late medieval English world.

My principal interest is to examine the roles played by the concept of poverty and the actuality of poor people in Will's search for personal salvation within the socio-economic environment of fourteenth-century England. Though Will is the poem's unifying character, the moral requirements for salvation apply to all members of society, and I explore the way the poem represents the response of different elements in society to the poor. Anyone who studies a sociological phenomenon such as poverty quickly becomes aware that there is no such thing as one single concept of poverty; one is dealing with a web of historical events, economic effects, cultural attitudes and philosophical stances. Poverty and poor people are not exclusive to the middle ages, and neither is the Christian religion. Part of the interest of my project is the ongoing nature of problems both for the poor and for the sincere person who accepts some responsibility for other members of the human family. As Michael Ignatieff says, in his book *The needs of strangers*:

> Our needs are made of words: they come to us in speech, and they can die for lack of expression ... Without a language adequate to this moment we risk losing ourselves in resignation towards the portion of life which has been allotted to us. Without the light of language, we risk becoming strangers to our better selves. (p. 142)

Because *Piers Plowman* is a work of art which has a life beyond the time and space of its creation, some of the processes the poem goes through in addressing problems of the poor can be seen to relate to a modern understanding of charity. I suggest that this medieval text can assist modern readers to find the language we need to avoid 'becoming strangers to our better selves'.

My approach as reader follows that of a growing group of scholars who have set themselves the task of the historical analyst as well as the literary critic. In the field of Shakespeare scholarship, Leah Marcus and Alvin Kernan, among others, apply the findings of historians to Shakespeare's plays with illuminating results of interpretation.[1] Paul Strohm, Steven Justice and David Wallace achieve similar successes with medieval writing.[2] Strohm, Wallace and Justice all bring the skills of the literary critic to bear upon historical documents, as well on imaginative and creative literature of the late medieval period. These literary critics make detailed examination of the social, economic and political contexts of their texts' genesis, and their readings unpack meanings dense with political and social significance, adding complexity to our view of the texts and the historical situations they record. Reading their works encourages me to focus on Middle English literature through a particular lens, that of poverty, and to make a 'poor reading' of *Piers Plowman* in a manner similar to the approach of scholars who make gendered readings of texts.[3] My approach to *Piers Plowman* concentrates on the way poverty and poor people are represented; more particularly, I attempt to capture, through its representation of poverty, the poem's dialogue with the culture and ideology of fourteenth-century England. There are three elements to this approach which I enumerate here, not in order of priority. One is to take note of *Piers Plowman*'s historical context; another is to read it as an expression of its culture; the third is to see how the poem has its own distinct life which is nonetheless bound up with the cultural ideologies of its moment – not only the moment of composition, but of its reception, too. In the next few pages I elaborate on what this means for a reading of *Piers Plowman*.

A work of literature is as much a part of the culture in which it was produced as any political event or historical personage; it is shaped within a moment, or, to be more precise, several moments of history, and carries within itself the

---

[1] L. Marcus, *Puzzling Shakespeare*; A. Kernan, *Shakespeare, the king's playwright*.
[2] P. Strohm, *Hochon's arrow*; D. Wallace, *Chaucerian polity*; S. Justice, *Writing and rebellion*. Important writers such as D. Aers and A. Middleton who apply this approach to *Piers Plowman* will be dealt with in the main body of the work.
[3] I am thinking of a work such as C.W. Bynum's *Holy feast and holy fast*, in which her study of food reveals deeply felt experiences of and attitudes towards women.

Introduction

writer's conscious and unconscious responses to the forces of culture and environment. In his 'Letter on art in reply to Louis Daspré', Althusser distinguishes between the actuality of what is scientifically (or historically) *real*, and the work of art which is born within an ideology but which is not, in itself, that ideology:

> What art makes us *see*, and therefore gives to us in the form of *'seeing'*, *'perceiving'* and *'feeling'* (which is not the form of *knowing*), is the *ideology* from which it is born, in which it bathes, from which it detaches itself as art, and to which it *alludes*.[4]

Piers Plowman is a very good work of art from which to 'perceive' ideology, since its creator, Langland, is obviously steeped in his own culture; the work intersects with important contemporary issues and institutions and enables the reader to engage with them as mediated within the text. Literature is inevitably nuanced; the creation of both imaginative and documentary texts involves interpretation. The selection of some materials and the exclusion of others is, in itself a judgment presupposing a purpose for the completed work, whether this is defined by the requirements of its end use, as in, say, a deposition, or by the demands of the genre, such as a chronicle, or a literary complaint. Macherey explains the positioning of the modern reader in the face of a text's representation of cultural ideology:

> Science does away with ideology, obliterates it; literature challenges ideology by using it. If ideology is thought of as a non-systematic ensemble of significations, the work proposes a *reading* of these significations, by combining them as signs. Criticism teaches us to read these signs.[5]

Perhaps the best way to apply such theory to *Piers Plowman* is to illustrate how the text works through the contradictions and confusions that are inherent in traditional representations of poverty and the poor as they appear to be played out in the historical scene of fourteenth-century England. Although the language Langland uses is shared by contemporary institutions such as church and state, and his literary conventions are inherited from traditions which include those of Scripture, satire and complaint, his poetry goes far beyond their formulas. Within the category of beggars in post-plague England, the poem makes a clear distinction between those who are powerless to rectify their needy situation and those who beg by choice. The A-text already delineated these latter; the B and the C-texts take Langland's discussion to some apparently clear conclusions: that those who choose to beg when they can work are parasites depriving the genuinely needy, and should only be helped when the genuinely needy have been attended to. Yet, while the words make it very clear that unworthy

---

[4] In *Lenin and philosophy and other essays*, p. 204.
[5] P. Macherey, *A theory of literary production*, p. 133.

beggars are those condemned in the fourteenth-century labour ordinances, Christian integrity, as the poem works through all the implications of poverty, the poor and how Christians should treat them, leads to the conclusion that God alone can be the judge of a person's worth or unworthiness.

> Woet no man, as Y wene, who is worthy to haue;
> Ac þat most neden aren oure neyhebores, and we nyme gode hede.
> (C.9.70–1)

The corollary is twofold. On the one hand, the Christian should and must continue to regard all as 'blody brethren', regardless of their behaviour; on the other, the poem recognizes the individual's autonomy and dignity. It is for each person, beggar or magnate, to act in accordance with Christian principles, and to accept responsibility for all actions and activities. This is a brief illustration of how Langland moves within several contemporary discourses in the same section of the poem; here Scripture, in the implied reference to 'Who is my neighbour?' (Luke 10. 29–37), canon law in discriminating how one's nearest (*proxime*) are to have priority, and statutory law illuminate the problem of the itinerant poor. Modern historical studies verify the events out of which the poetry is created, but the poetry shows up the moral poverty of the institutions which cannot contain their social problem.

The modern reader of medieval literature is, of necessity, a critic who must look back to history and yet remain firmly in the present to read what Macherey has called 'these signs'. This means recognizing them as signs, and not attempting to read them merely as historical facts. It is tempting, for instance, to try and find voices of the poor in *Piers Plowman* and other late medieval literature which deals directly or indirectly with issues concerning the poor and poverty. This is not possible. Margaret Kim is a recent writer who has confronted the issue and says:

> In the medieval world of traditional social hierarchy and feudal organization, the experiences of the poor were mediated, and had to be mediated, by the dominant classes.[6]

We may find traces, echoes of where the poor have been, but their voices are inevitably mediated by non-poor writers whose view of them may be shaped by aims far from sympathetic to their actual situation.

There is plenty of late medieval literature which deals directly or indirectly with issues concerning the poor and poverty, and the poor are significant or sub-

---

[6] Kim attributes a dichotomy in the late medieval discourse of poverty to this mediation: 'Vision of theocratics', pp 21–2. While I agree with her understanding of mediation (and with much of her work) I shall take issue, in the course of the book, with the notion that the discourse of poverty is dichotomous, since I find it far more subtly distinguished, especially in Langland's writing.

Introduction

sidiary figures in many narratives. A vast body of exemplary, hortatory, moral and satirical writings reflects the afflictions and sorry conditions of poor people while developing didactic themes; and we can find numerous instances of poor people's political thoughts and impulses recorded, albeit by the slightly better-off, in poetry and song. Historians may make a valid reading of this material on one level, using it to corroborate what they have recorded as historical fact and event; this may be helpful to a historian, but does little to further literary criticism. Raymond Williams outlines some of the difficulties in reading literature this way:

> What is now felt as most difficult is the simple assumption that there is, on the one hand, a relatively unproblematic body of 'literature', with its own inherent and autonomous qualities, and on the other hand, a body of general and summary knowledge which is, correspondingly, 'history'. For if these two bodies existed, in simple ways, the study of 'literature and history' would be a matter of tracing and illustrating evident connections between them, in ways that illuminated both but altered neither.[7]

Piers Plowman is a goldmine of material used by historians to illustrate late medieval practices and one example will serve for all. Historians of late medieval eating habits and of domestic architecture regularly quote *Piers Plowman* to demonstrate that late medieval aristocratic households used a parlour for the lord and lady to eat in privacy:

> Elenge is þe halle, ech day in þe wike,
> Ther þe lord ne þe lady likeþ noȝt to sitte.
> Now haþ ech riche a rule – to eten by hymselue
> In a pryuee parlour for pouere mennes sake,
> Or in a chambre wiþ a chymenee, and leue þe chief halle
> That was maad for meles, men to eten inne. (B.10.96–101)

But the poem at this point is lamenting the increased alienation of the lord from his *familia*, the relegation of the poor to a place well outside the household, and the decay of charity. This is an elegy for good practices lost, not an endorsement of historical behaviour; criticism must, as Macherey says, read the signs. The varied experiences of poverty that emerge in the course of this study illustrate the point that the perceptions of poverty which find expression in literary texts have a complex life both within the text and within the culture in which the text takes its life.

In making our reading of medieval literature we have to avoid two dangers: reading imaginative literature as 'mere sources of social history'[8] and reading it

---

7 R. Williams in the Editor's introduction to J. Coleman, *English literature in history, 1350–1400*, p. 10.
8 Coleman, p. 46.

solely according to modern standards of literary judgment. Imaginative writers live within the same culture as those who draw up the rolls; in some cases they may well be the same people – Hoccleve and Chaucer, for instance, were both civil servants as well as poets; Usk was a scrivener as well as an under-sheriff.[9] They share the social experiences that give rise to prejudices, hopes, fears, and they write within the influence of these. As Strohm says of the texts he analyses in *Hochon's arrow*:

> Yet all are finally composed within history – if not within a sense of what did happen, at least within a sense of what might have happened, of what could be imagined, of what commonly held interpretative structures permitted a late fourteenth-century audience to believe. (p. 3)

In another context, Alastair Minnis writes of medieval writers' attention to the arrangement of books; Minnis' theory of authorship is as relevant to this study as it is to his work on medieval literary prologues; the positioning of the author is crucial to our understanding of the views he is presenting:

> For the historian of today, knowledge of how men conceived of their actions must be as important as what, when the physical evidence is examined, they appear to have done.[10]

In relation to this theory I have suggested that in order to make a 'poor reading' of literature the critic needs to combine the knowledge of the historian with the skills of the literary critic. To read a work of literature *in* history is not the same as reading it to learn *about* history. Wallace expresses the difference clearly:

> The aim here is not to create a vantage point above the text from which the text – and the struggles of its protagonists – can be explained, or explained away. The aspiration is, rather, to restore the text to the movement of history; to recognize its own sense of precariousness in occupying a time and place that shifts even at the instant of its own articulation (which speaks, at least for me, to our own unsettled experience as historical subjects).[11]

Modern readers are several centuries distant from contemporaries of medieval writers, influenced by all the changes in attitude which have occurred as cul-

---

9 A. Galloway, 'Private selves and the intellectual marketplace', p. 294.
10 Minnis continues: 'When late-medieval scholars thought about their methods for arranging books both 'ancient' and 'modern', when they came to rationalize their own practice in this area, naturally, their concepts and their idioms were, to some extent, determined by the same basic influences behind the vocabulary used in discussing the *forma tractandi*': *Medieval theory of authorship*, p. 145.
11 Wallace, p. xvii.

Introduction

ture, ideology, taste, education and experience have shifted over the intervening centuries. In order to 'restore the text to the movement of history' modern readers need, initially, to become very well informed as to the thoughts and attitudes of medieval writers and their audience; and even after thorough assimilation of those influences which might have stimulated a medieval writer, we will have an imperfect perception of the middle ages. Not least, we are restricted by the fragmentary nature of documentary evidence and by the incompleteness of the current state of research in all forms of historical and archaeological enquiry. At best our assessments will be limited, but this is no reason to flinch from the undertaking. As Janet Coleman has said:

> We can never become a fourteenth-century audience, but we can read fourteenth-century literature with an eye and ear better able to recognize the subtleties of stylistic experiments and to realize the significance of its subject matter.[12]

An understanding of the immediate context may give some pointers as to the impulses that inspired the original writing, but the texts are concerned with their own intersection with the ideology from which they are born. Wallace makes the point well:

> The most skilled narrators of the history of political thought, like the best historiographers, possess the skills and techniques of gifted literary critics. And this should encourage us, as literary critics, not to carry political schemata to the literary text but rather to read the text as if it were its own politics (developed through its specific envisioning of possible social relations). The chief subject of 'Chaucerian polity' then, is the poetry of and prose of Chaucer.[13]

This is not the same level of reading as that which, to quote Williams,

> looked to history as a 'background', against which, in a foregrounded emphasis, works of literature occurred.[14]

It is a reading which seeks to situate the text within its own cultural ideology, and demands that the reader, with considerable knowledge of the medieval environment, become sensitive to medieval resonances within the text.

My investigation into constructions of poverty in the late middle ages inevitably employs an element of historicism because an understanding of where the writer and the work stand in the 'movement of history' is crucial to any

---

12 Coleman, p. 17.
13 Wallace, p. 3.
14 Williams, in Coleman, p. 10.

judgment. Information must be as accurate as possible as a preliminary step, so that judgments are not culpably anachronistic. In this respect modern readers are fortunate in having access to a body of material which results from sociological enquiries into the condition of the poor in medieval Europe. Michel Mollat's students at the Sorbonne in the 1960s and 1970s produced seminal papers on poverty and charity; Rodney Hilton, Christopher Dyer and David Nicholas[15] have given us major works on social conditions, with useful information on the poor in England. Detailed studies such as those of Lawrence Poos, Miri Rubin, Marjorie McIntosh, Barbara Hanawalt and Elaine Clark[16] narrow the focus geographically. In short, there is a growing wealth of detailed historical research on which to draw when attempting to become familiar with conditions of the life of the poor in the middle ages.

Reading the works of the philosophers, teachers, and sermon writers, the handbooks for sermon writers, and the manuals for confessors provides a foundation of philosophy and the applied philosophical, ethical and religious concepts which inform Langland and other writers on poverty at this time. Consideration of the language of poverty and need helps the reader understand something of the way late medieval writers negotiated ideas of poverty. Rubin reviews scholarship on the development of medieval terminology as it relates to her study of charity in medieval Cambridge. She points out that, particularly in the urban society of the twelfth and thirteenth centuries, the conservative dualities – *potens/pauper, laicus/clericus, paradisus/infernum* – were being replaced by the more sophisticated vocabulary of a society which recognized increased differentiation. Discussions of charity, however, were slower in adopting the more sophisticated and complex views of society, and the language shows how society was increasingly polarized:

> In exhortation towards almsgiving the pair *dives et pauper* remained, unwittingly expressing the ever-growing gap separating those able and those unable to support themselves. By the thirteenth century, even this moral and economic opposition was questioned and qualified, but it served in the *exempla* of thirteenth-century mendicant preaching, which was the main tool of instruction and of dissemination of the charitable imperative.[17]

---

15 R. Hilton, *The English peasantry in the later middle ages*; C. Dyer, *Standards of living in the later middle ages*; D. Nicholas, *The later medieval city*.

16 L.R. Poos, *A rural society after the Black Death: Essex, 1350–1525*; M. Rubin, *Charity and community in medieval Cambridge*; M.K. McIntosh, *Controlling misbehavior in England, 1370–1600*. Of B. Hanawalt's many publications, those immediately relevant to this chapter are: *Crime and conflict in English communities, 1300–1348*, her edited essay collection: *Chaucer's England*, and, with D. Wallace, *Bodies and disciplines*. E. Clark has contributed numerous articles on social welfare in the middle ages, including: 'Some aspects of social security in medieval England', and 'Social welfare and mutual aid in the medieval countryside'.

17 Rubin, *Charity and community*, p. 9.

The notion of poverty that emerges from the literary representations of the late middle ages may appear limited or stereotypical, but a large part of the problem confronting a modern reader lies precisely in the medieval use of terminology. We seek ways of dealing with poverty that seem real to us but for which the medieval writer had no vocabulary partly because the language lagged behind the reality. Andrew Galloway advances the idea that, by developing 'gratitude' as one of the senses of 'kyndenesse', *Piers Plowman* develops 'a concept of social and economic relationships and community' that goes beyond the usage of his contemporaries, Chaucer, Gower and the homilists.[18] In this context, Langland is seen to be, not only an exponent of his culture, but an original thinker.

Taking all these resources into account, we can begin to perceive how Langland discovers the point at which literary conventions can transmit signs of the historical moment. For instance, we may ask how medieval thinkers could perceive poverty to be of value when the scriptural imagery of heaven is couched in terms of treasure and profit. The poetry tries to resolve such tension by using the imagery of wealth for poverty, in this repeating the very contradiction that Christianity itself sets up. Poor people take on all the importance associated with the rich by virtue of clothing when Christ is seen to wear their 'sute' (B.5.488); the sumptuary laws designed to keep people visibly within their station elevate the poor to the rank of Christ, in the same action marking him as one of the most humble.[19] The poor become as successful as a usurious merchant when God goes surety for them (B.7.80), and when they grasp the significance of the treasure in the field they become shrewd traders (C.5.94–101). Yet the language makes it clear that this importance is not something to be delayed until after death; the poor are important in the here and now, and the non-poor must recognize their value, giving charitable relief to them without discrimination. Not only does the poem explore the position of poverty in the religious scheme of things; it examines contemporary life to show how an appreciation of the dignity of the poor challenges established notions of status. Language and imagery are marshalled to drive home the point; the language is made to work very hard and there are no easy assumptions to be made. For example, putting some of the best arguments about poverty into the mouth of a character called Rechelesnesse (C.12.90–13.128) demands our constant critical attention. So does the changing of familiar quotation; it is deliberate choice, not carelessness that makes Langland alter quotation, and retell familiar Scriptural scenes.[20] I have earlier used the term 'dialogue' to describe the relationship of *Piers Plowman* with its culture because

---

18 A. Galloway, 'The making of a social ethic in late-medieval England', p. 379.
19 F. Baldwin describes the sumptuary law of 1362 which decreed that all the lowest members of society 'may not wear anything but blanket cloth and russet': *Sumptuary legislation and personal regulation in England*, pp 50–1.
20 A good example of Langland's wordplay with scriptural quotation is his treatment of 'Non de solo pane' (C.5.86–8). I discuss this fully in Chapter Four; Langland alters the text in order to play on the meaning of 'solum' as 'soil', 'Not by working the soil', ironically diverging from its scriptural meaning: 'Not by bread alone'.

I see Langland as a tenacious questioner as well as a major exponent of his culture's ideology.

In my study of the way *Piers Plowman* deals with and represents poverty I use both the B and the C-texts. I recognize that each text is a poem complete in itself and many scholars have acknowledged this by dealing with issues exclusively in one or other version.[21] The danger of studying a theme in more than one text of the poem is that the reader may conflate the texts, regarding them as variants rather than as separate poems. The advantage of choosing to study the theme of poverty as expressed in both the B and the C-texts is that we can follow both continuity and development of thought. Kerby-Fulton's description of the poem as a 'textual continuum' is useful here.[22] When material that has proved a problem for critical interpretation is carried over from the B to the C-text verbatim, it is clear that it is integral to the total poem. When an apparent contradiction in the B-text reappears in the C-text there can be no question of stylistic ineptitude or philosophical vacillation on the part of the poet; such contradictions emphasize how the poet interprets, poetically, problematic issues of his time. Finally, when there are significant additions to the later text, as is the case with the subject of poverty in the C-text, the reader may look for explicit treatment of ideas which were, perhaps, implicit in the earlier text. This study takes the B-text as its foundation and refers to the C-text only where there is a significant addition to discussions relevant to the theme of poverty.[23]

My method has two main features. One is to identify specific aspects of poverty as represented within the poem and set them in the context of medieval culture, drawing on historical research and contemporary texts to help establish the ideologies from which the poem takes its source. The other is to provide close readings of certain fairly lengthy sections of the poem which illuminate these aspects of poverty in dialogue with contemporary cultural experience and ideology. This methodology helps the reader to explore the poem as a work of art illuminating the ideology 'from which it is born'.[24] A common feature of all the chapters stresses Langland's technique of making distinctions, the peculiarly scholastic skill of proposing questions and counter-questions in order to explore all aspects of a problem and come to a conclusion that transcends the component parts of the argument. Throughout the poem there is a continuing tension between the traditionally idealized, transcendent notion of poverty as uniting the pauper with Christ and issues of need, want, work and commerce, all of

---

21 The recent reopening of the debate as to whether the poem has more than one author does not materially affect my handling of the different texts. What I am concerned with is the poem's representations of poverty rather than what the poem shows about the life of the author. See D.C. Fowler, 'Piers Plowman'.
22 K. Kerby-Fulton, '*Piers Plowman*', in D. Wallace (ed.), *The Cambridge history of medieval English literature*, p. 522.
23 All references to the texts of *Piers Plowman* are taken from A.V.C Schmidt, *'Piers Plowman': a parallel-text edition*.
24 See reference to Althusser at note 5 above.

which, in themselves, have a figurative value derived from the Scriptures, yet reflect contemporary conditions of suffering for the needy. Making distinctions is one important way in which the poem is in dialogue with its cultural ideology, reflecting Wallace's vision of the text as 'occupying a time and place that shifts even at the instant of its own articulation'. A reader alert to this aspect of literary technique becomes sensitive to differing philosophies of poverty and varying circumstances of poor and non-poor in relation to each other. Recognizing Langland's distinctions helps the reader appreciate aspects of the poem which may appear contradictory or inconsistent.

The aim of this study is to show the unique role a work of art such as *Piers Plowman* has in its ability to make visible the ideology of a former period. In medieval texts, the poor enjoy the doubtful privilege of being approved and disapproved, valued and demonized, respected and feared, noticed and ignored, often simultaneously within the one text. To make a 'poor reading' is a useful way to approach literature, placing a new emphasis on works which have already been well studied, deepening critical appreciation of them. To ascertain the role of the poor or poverty in the text and to see how their presence (or, indeed, absence) determines attitudes, is to establish the ethical stature of the text. It becomes evident as we pursue a 'poor reading' of *Piers Plowman* that the poor, far from being insignificant, are often a catalyst of action, a factor in polarizing attitudes, unwittingly political. Consciousness of the poor creates a moral dimension for the work, even when it is not overtly concerned with poverty. Issues of poverty go to the heart of the key terms of the poem, charity and salvation, which are, in themselves, key concerns of late medieval culture. The poem's involvement with issues of poverty provides us with a way of reading the text as a work that engages with its own culture and makes available to us what Strohm has called 'a sense of what might have happened, of what could be imagined, of what commonly held interpretative structures permitted a late fourteenth-century audience to believe'.

The poor are the dark shadows that highlight the brighter figures of church, state and the mercantile world. Writers cannot ignore them and their literature derives inner logic and tension as they negotiate the issues raised by the demands poverty places upon the whole of society. In his text, Langland comes remarkably close to achieving that 'public discourse about the needs of the human person' which Ignatieff defines as essential if society is to take responsible action for the poor:

> It is because money cannot buy the human gestures which confer respect, nor rights guarantee them as entitlements, that any decent society requires a public discourse about the needs of the human person. It is because fraternity, love, belonging, dignity and respect cannot be specified as rights that we ought to specify them as needs and seek, with the blunt institutional procedures at our disposal, to make their satisfaction a routine human practice. (p. 13)

My intention, in the chapters that follow, is to illuminate the text of *Piers Plowman* in such a way as to show that its discourse of need has a place even in modern discussions of belonging, dignity and respect.

CHAPTER I

Meanings of poverty: Langland's five distinctions

Although poverty and poor people manifest themselves in modes conditioned by their cultures, spaces and times, some experiences are common to the poor of all ages. These similarities justify my drawing upon modern as well as medieval and patristic sources to create a theoretical foundation for the discussion of poverty, and to arrive at an appreciation of the ambiguities that English medieval writing expresses with regard to poverty and poor people. In the course of this chapter I explore five ways of looking at poverty, all of which influence the text of *Piers Plowman* and, in varying degrees, reflect concerns of both medieval and modern society. These views may be summarized as first, that material poverty is the greatest of all evils and a state to be avoided; secondly, that it is a scandal which must be eradicated; thirdly, that riches are a corrupting evil and poverty is liberation from care: 'Cantabit vacuus coram latrone viator';[1] fourthly, that poverty is a virtue fundamental to Christian life; lastly, that it can be professed as voluntary Christian poverty in imitation of Christ. It is essential to recognize these distinctions of poverty within *Piers Plowman* in order to appreciate the poem's nuanced and practical calls for reform within the church and society.

Piers Plowman reveals Langland's alertness to the fine distinctions within medieval attitudes to poverty. The poem is written within a society that accepts poverty as inevitable, an unchanging and unchangeable part of the medieval social structure. Measures were taken throughout the middle ages to improve the lot of individual poor people, but there was no movement to eradicate the condition of poverty completely. *Piers Plowman* reflects the cultural tension brought about when an obvious Christian duty to care for the poor conflicts with the intractable condition of material poverty and the fact that the status of 'the poor' is integral to society. Additionally, in portraying both the spiritual value of poverty and the material scandal of the poor, the poem faces head-on the ambiguities thrown up in a society where the five categories of poverty exist uneasily together. It can be a temptation, when reading the poem, to think that Langland portrays practical worldly poverty with compassion and then, because he appears to offer scant solution to its problems, retreats into traditional teaching that spiritualizes the concept of the poor as blessed and closest to God. I want

---

[1] Juvenal, *Satire* 10. 22; the Hardy edition.

to suggest, in this chapter and at greater length later, that the poem differentiates clearly between involuntary need, for which it puts forward reforming solutions, and the spiritual value of poverty lovingly accepted in imitation of Christ. Although influenced by his culture which does not see poverty as something to be abolished, Langland has definite proposals for the relief of the poor within an essentially humane as well as Christian context.

My initial discussion ranges, briefly, into modern perceptions of poverty and relates these to medieval approaches. From the vast body of literature dealing with the socio-economic phenomenon of poverty I draw most heavily on two modern sources, Gustavo Gutiérrez on the theology of liberation[2] and material drawn from the online site of the World Bank: 'A world free of poverty'.[3] I look to the writings of Gutiérrez because they face, in his contemporary context, problems similar to those portrayed by Langland. Like Langland, Gutiérrez is committed to educating his readers in the concept of justice for the poor as a necessary expression of Christian faith and love. Like Langland, too, Gutiérrez finds much to criticize in the institutional church which professes to follow the poor Christ yet fails to engage with those who experience material want. The World Bank site gives statistical information about conditions of poverty in the developing world relative to the economically developed world, and records the experiences of contemporary indigent people in their own words, quoted from interviews with World Bank researchers. To hear the voices of the poor is rare; the medieval poor have left no autograph records, their experience is mediated through the written documentation of the non-poor. The verbatim interviews transcribed in '*Voices of the poor*' give us the opportunity to hear, at least in translation, the words of those suffering poverty; in the anthology of their writing they reflect on contemporary conditions. I make no apology for assuming that these modern poor are speaking of the same human reactions to their poverty as medieval people experienced, for I am not, in this first chapter, discussing what people need so much as their reactions to being in need. At the level of need under discussion, people are reduced to the essentials of a common humanity irrespective of the changing circumstances of geography and history. This view is endorsed by Ignatieff in his study of human need:

> In the end, a theory of human needs has to be premissed on some set of choices about what humans need in order to be human: not what they need to be happy or free, since these are subsidiary goals, but what they need in order to realize the full extent of their potential. There cannot be any externally valid account of what it means to be human. All we have to go on is the historical record of what men have valued most in human life. There does exist a set of words for these needs – love, respect, honour, dignity, solidarity with others. (p. 15)

2 G. Gutiérrez, *A theology of liberation*.
3 The World Bank Group 2003, Povertynet (online).

In the medieval Christian context, need in one section of humanity provokes responsibility in those who are not needy. As many scholars before me have done, I turn to patristic and medieval church sources to tease out prevalent medieval attitudes towards the involuntarily poor.[4] Linked to this is an appraisal of the Christian virtue of poverty, and particularly its expression in the monastic, fraternal and eremitical life of the later middle ages. The purpose of such study is to read *Piers Plowman* within its contemporary ideology, and the last part of the chapter discusses the work of modern scholars who have engaged in just such a task, specifically on the subject of Langland and poverty. All the discussions of the chapter lead to the conclusion that it is necessary for the reader to grasp, as the poet does, the distinctions between the five aspects of poverty in order to appreciate and not try to explain away the paradox that emerges time and again throughout *Piers Plowman*. This paradox lies in the poet's firm conviction of the need for poverty to provide a path to heaven, yet also his keen awareness of the tragic suffering of the poor.

In a religious context, discussions of poverty revolve around two poles: poverty as the greatest evil and poverty as a Christian virtue. Gustavo Gutiérrez pinpoints accurately the confusion perennially associated with the evangelical counsel of poverty:

> Christians ... often have a tendency to give material poverty a positive value, considering it almost a human and religious ideal ... This interpretation would mean that the demands of Christianity are at cross purposes to the great aspirations of people today, who want to free themselves from subjection to nature, to eliminate the exploitation of some people by others, and to create prosperity for everyone. The double and contradictory meaning of *poverty* implied here gives rise to the imposition of one language on another and is a frequent source of ambiguities. (p. 289)

The Latin America about which Gustavo Gutiérrez writes may seem a far cry from fourteenth-century England, yet some aspects of the culture within which and for the redemption of which he writes are remarkably similar to those of fourteenth-century England within which and for the salvation of which Langland writes *Piers Plowman*. Broadly speaking, both are economies whose population is defined by a relatively small number of people who enjoy the greatest proportion of the available wealth and a large number of very poor people whose standard of living falls below that which can be considered worthy of

---

4 The most thorough study of medieval theories of poor relief in patristic and medieval church sources is that of B. Tierney, *Medieval poor law*. M. Rubin prefaces her study of charity in medieval Cambridge with similarly useful material: *Charity and community*, pp 54–98; K. Hewett-Smith applies patristic and medieval church sources in her interpretation of the ploughing of the half-acre in *Piers Plowman*: 'Allegory on the half-acre'.

human dignity. The political situation of the church in contemporary Latin America and that of the fourteenth-century church differ; the modern church is politically contained within the world, whereas the medieval church was politically dominant in the world.[5] Maitland went so far as to say:

> The medieval church was a state. Convenience may forbid us to call it a state very often, but we ought to do so from time to time, for we could frame no acceptable definition of a state which would not comprehend the church.[6]

More significantly for my discussion, both Gutiérrez and Langland are concerned to reconcile the teaching of the Christian church with their contemporary political and economic conditions, anchoring their opinions in the text of Scripture, their common spiritual and literary heritage. Gutiérrez's plea for clear definition of evangelical poverty carries resonances for the student of poverty in *Piers*:

> What we mean by material poverty is a subhuman situation ... The Bible also considers it this way. Concretely, to be poor means to die of hunger, to be illiterate, to be exploited by others, not to know that you are being exploited, not to know that you are a person. It is in relation to this poverty – material and cultural, collective and militant – that evangelical poverty will have to define itself. (p. 289)

Langland intimates such extreme material poverty, particularly in the C-text, and contrasts it with a recognition that many of his contemporaries who profess voluntary Christian poverty enjoy a standard of living far removed from the painful reality of poverty. The ninth passus of the C-text contains new material not found in earlier versions, which directly contrasts the hand-to-mouth poverty of the urban poor, single mothers, with the easy life obtained by men who outwardly profess religious poverty but fulfil none of the spiritual requirements (C.9.70–104; 188–218).

Piers Plowman does not purport to be a poem about poverty, but because it is a poem about the pursuit of salvation it must inevitably deal with the Christian's attitude to poverty, for the way a person treats the poor is not only the matter of the Last Judgment but fundamental to the following of Christ. In the poem's central character, Will, we follow the development of a person who experiences the physical hardships of poverty in its many manifestations, the spiritual ideal of voluntary poverty, the political implications of poverty within the social order, and the complexities of the fourteenth-century anti-clerical poverty controversy. Will is engaged in frequent intellectual debate with allegorical figures, and gains spir-

---

5 An excellent discussion of the theocratic nature of fourteenth-century politics is given by M. Kim, 'Vision of theocratics', pp 1–51.
6 F.W. Maitland, *Roman canon law in the church of England*, p. 100.

Meanings of poverty: Langland's five distinctions

itual understanding through allegorical participation in the scriptural event of the passion, death and resurrection of Jesus. Yet the poem shows him operating in the everyday context of this world whose activities, influences and experience he interprets in the light of the next. The issue that Will works out by physical suffering and intellectual questioning is that the person who seeks salvation has to accept and make sense of need in the material world. In Will, Langland portrays the experiential reality of both voluntary and involuntary poverty.

Gutiérrez throws light on the dilemma this double experience entails. In common with modern commentators and medieval writers such as Chaucer, Langland, and antifraternal polemicists, he challenges the religious interpretation of poverty as an attitude of detachment from the goods of this world, which allows a person to possess material goods providing there is no attachment to them:

> This spiritualistic [sic] perspective rapidly leads to dead ends and to affirmations that the interior attitude must necessarily be incarnated in a testimony of material poverty. But if this is so, questions arise: What poverty is being spoken of? The poverty that the contemporary conscience considers subhuman? Is it in this way that spiritual poverty should be incarnated? Some answer that it is not necessary to go to such extremes, and they attempt to distinguish between destitution and poverty ... This is to play with words – and with people. (p. 290)

FitzRalph in *Defensio curatorum* makes a similar statement:

> [Oure] Lord Ihesus in his conversacioun of manhed, alwey was pore, nouȝt for he wolde oþer louede pouert by cause of hit silf; ... for it is wrecchednesse to be pore & no man loueþ wreccidnesse for hit-silf; þanne no man loueþ pouert for hit silf.[7]

This fourteenth-century churchman's matter-of-fact assessment of poverty makes a clear distinction between material poverty as an evil and the sacrifice of Christ who became poor. His sermon goes on to make the point that contemporary mendicant orders are deceiving themselves when they say from within the security of well-built and well-funded convents that they are poor. Their life of security demonstrates that they, too, regard material poverty as an evil which they are not ready to endure. The late nineteenth-century *Catholic encylopedia* endorses this attitude which makes voluntary poverty such an ambiguous concept:

> [R]eligious poverty generally includes those things the lack of which makes the other kind of poverty so undesirable, namely, the requisites of elementary health and comfort, and decent living.[8]

[7] R. FitzRalph, 'Defensio curatorum', in *Dialogus inter militem et clericum* by John Trevisa, 79–80.
[8] J.A. Ryan, 'Poverty and pauperism', p. 329.

Such confusion arises because the one word, 'poverty', carries many significations as I have suggested above: poverty as a scandal, a condition calling for reform, a religious virtue, an institutional vocation and a philosophical good. Reading *Piers Plowman* in the light of these five meanings of poverty shows that Langland is alert to their differences and able to distinguish between them. The many graphic accounts of the effects of poverty, such as the great famine on Piers' half-acre (B.6.174–300), the portrait of the clothworker (C.9.71–98), and the inability of the poor to obtain justice (B.Prol.211–16; B.7.39–59) demonstrate that Langland is keenly aware of the socio-economic scandal of fourteenth-century poverty. Some of his praise of religious poverty, notably in the discourse of Patience (B.14.203–319), but at several other moments in the poem, too, sets forth the spiritual benefits of practising poverty for the love of God and in imitation of Christ. Will's full acceptance of his poor condition in solidarity with other destitute beggars (B.20.1–50) makes his movement towards the reform of evil and injustice soundly political. Each of the meanings of poverty carries within itself the seeds of ambiguity which the poem addresses: the indigent can be equated with fraudulent, idle vagrants (B.6.115–128); the voluntarily poor may shelter behind a formulaic detachment from goods which they believe will fulfil their obligation to be poor in spirit (B.15.325–30); Will, the reformer, is himself a sinner (C.5.1–108). The poem engages with such confusing signals as it follows the character, Will, through his life of searching for the best way to live, the life of Dowel, Dobet and Dobest. As I suggested above, Langland's great contribution to the literary representation of poverty is in the carefully teased out distinctions he makes between the different strands of poverty. To appreciate the distinctions is to realize that the poet does not jettison his earthly compassion for the poor by exalting a notion of patient poverty with heaven promised as its reward; he keeps all the aspects alive from beginning to end of the poem, and exemplifies them in the life of Will.

HATEFUL POVERTY

Poverty is a condition that has existed always, and continues to exist, a state of material privation which, according to the researches of Michel Mollat, is the condition in which the vast majority of early peoples lived:

> Poverty, understood in the usual sense of 'destitution', was a permanent feature of the middle ages. From classical antiquity through the social and economic regression of more barbarous times, poverty was thought to be inescapable.[9]

---

9 *The poor in the middle ages*, p. 1. This view is also put forward by D.J. Constantelos, *Poverty, society and philanthropy in the late mediaeval Greek world*, and more recently by P. Freedman, *Images of the medieval peasant*.

Meanings of poverty: Langland's five distinctions

Although statistics cannot be produced for the numbers of medieval poor, Lis and Soly summarize the situation of early fourteenth-century Europe:

> Around 1300, 40 to 60 per cent of western European peasants disposed of insufficient land to maintain a family. Their holdings were seldom larger than two or three hectares and had to be cultivated by hand, with low yields ... Social inequality was no less pronounced in the towns. At the end of the thirteenth century, 44 per cent of Parisian taxpayers consisted of *menus,* who all told contributed barely 6 per cent of total taxation.[10]

Estimates made by Hatcher and Poos[11] suggest that up to 40 per cent of the population in post-plague England suffered poverty, and this concurs with Mollat's findings from taxation records of Italian and French cities which estimate the proportion of poor people in the range of 35 to 60 per cent of the population during the late thirteenth and early fourteenth centuries.[12] Proportionally, the poor have diminished in today's world, yet figures available from the World Bank suggest a considerable world population of poor:

> Extreme poverty declined only slowly in developing countries during the 1990s: the share of the population living on less than $1 a day fell from 28 per cent in 1987 to 23 per cent in 1998, and the number of poor people remained roughly constant, as the population increased. The share and number of people living on less than $2 per day – a more relevant threshold for middle-income economies such as those of East Asia and Latin America – showed roughly similar trends[13] ... Even if the most optimistic scenario is achieved, 2.3 billion people would still be living under $2 per day in 2015. Thus, the global war on poverty is likely to be with us well into the 21st century.[14]

This gives a solid basis for considering that the phenomenon of poverty is a significant and continuing part of human existence. Its inescapability in the middle ages and in modern developing countries comes from factors that recur with monotonous regularity throughout the ages. The unpredictability of agriculture and of other forms of livelihood, coupled with the effects of political and social unrest, ensure that the well-to-do live with the possibility of sinking into poverty. For the medieval person this proximity to poverty made for an attitude of keen self-preservation. Wealth won with hard work and risk could be lost in an instant

---

10 C. Lis and H. Soly, *Poverty and capitalism in pre-industrial Europe*, pp 15–16.
11 J. Hatcher, *Plague, population and the English economy, 1348–1530*, p. 33; Poos, p. 19.
12 Mollat, pp 174–6. The demographics of medieval poverty in England will be considered more fully in Chapter Two.
13 The World Bank Group, 2003. Poverty reduction and economic management.
14 The World Bank Group, 2003. Povertynet. Income poverty. Prospects for poverty reduction: Scenarios.

of political confiscation, unfortunate merchant venture, poor harvest. A chapter in the most up-to-date report on global poverty from the World Bank Group recounting interviews held with the poor in developing or war-torn countries deals with many issues relevant to the medieval experience of poverty. The poor, who work primarily in the informal sector, report experiencing life as more insecure and unpredictable than a decade or so ago. This is linked to unpredictability of agriculture, jobs that are unreliable and with low returns, loss of traditional livelihoods, breakdown of the state, breakdown of traditional social solidarity, social isolation, increased crime and violence, lack of access to justice, extortion, and brutality rather than protection from the police. Illness is dreaded and lack of affordable health care pushes many families into indebtedness and destitution.[15]

Each of the ills mentioned in this recent World Bank report can be found in the text of *Piers Plowman*, discussed in detail not once, but many times, demonstrating Langland's alertness to the material condition of poverty, to the responsibility of both individual and institution to give poor relief and to the many self-deceptions of those who profess to a life of poverty and charity. Unpredictability of agriculture is clearly delineated in the account of the famine (B.6.174–300); unreliable and low paid jobs are suggested when the C-text describes false hermits who have abandoned trades because they can earn more by begging than by working (C.9.203–10). Breakdown of traditional social solidarity is suggested by the many references to clerics abandoning the responsibility of their parishes, and to lords withdrawing from communication with their people (B.10.96–101). References to the casting out of beggars in favour of the more congenial jesters and minstrels exemplify at least one form of social isolation (B.9.90–1). Lack of access to justice is deplored early in the poem (B.Prol.211–16); crime and violence among the poor are suggested in the wasters who feign illness (B.6.121–8), and among the beggars (B.7.88–97) who copulate like animals, flouting church and State law, and mutilate their children. These symptoms of poverty will be explored in subsequent chapters as part of my ongoing study of the poem. In the present context, they suggest that the evils of poverty as Langland describes them are relevant to more than medieval society.

Traditional church teaching on poverty, still applicable in the twenty-first century, informs Langland's representations of poverty. A working definition is given by P.R. Régamey in the *New Catholic encyclopedia*:

> Poverty, properly so-called, may be defined as a pinching limitation in the possession of things necessary for human comfort or life. Every creature needs to have in order to be. It can realize itself only through the possession of things other than itself. For man, property is an extension of his person.[16]

---

15 *World development report 2001/2002: attacking poverty* (online), pp 15–29.
16 'Religious Poverty', in *New Catholic encyclopedia*, p. 648. Gutiérrez similarly describes poverty: 'The term *poverty* designates in the first place *material poverty*, that is, the lack of economic goods

Meanings of poverty: Langland's five distinctions

The basic needs of human beings are related, in this definition, to the needs of every creature. From earliest patristic writings, the human being's need for food, clothing and shelter was regarded as the ultimate, below which no-one could survive:

> God has ordered all things to be produced, so that there should be food in common to all, and that the earth should be a common possession for all. Nature, therefore, has produced a common right for all, but greed has made it a right for a few.[17]

But the definition goes further than the needs of material survival to the expression of property as a factor that determines the human person. 'For man, property is an extension of his person.' This leads to the consideration of two aspects of the issue: the right of people to hold property as their own, and the equal right of all mankind to have a share in the gifts of creation.

According to the perennial teaching of the church, and expressed succinctly in the Catholic Church's most recent Catechism, the possession of property is an inalienable right of man, but it is subsidiary to the primordial gift of the earth to the whole of mankind:

> The *right to private property*, acquired by work or received from others by inheritance or gift, does not do away with the original gift of the earth to the whole of mankind. The *universal destination of goods* remains primordial, even if the promotion of the common good requires respect for the right to private property and its exercise.[18]

This universal destination of goods was forcefully defended in the early church by St John Chrysostom:

> Not to enable the poor to share in our goods is to steal from them and deprive them of life. The goods we possess are not ours, but theirs.[19]

Later, St Gregory the Great re-emphasized the same concept:

> For, when we administer necessaries of any kind to the indigent, we do not bestow our own, but render them what is theirs; we rather pay a debt of justice than accomplish works of mercy.[20]

---

necessary for a human life worthy of the name. In this sense poverty is considered degrading and is rejected by the conscience of contemporary man': *A theology of liberation*, p. 288.
17 St Ambrose, bishop of Milan, *Three books on the duties of the clergy*, Book 1, Chapter 28, § 132 (online).
18 *Catechism of the Catholic Church*, § 2403, p. 514.
19 St John Chrysostom, *Hom. in Lazarum* 2, 5: PG 48, 992, translated in *Catechism*, p. 523.
20 St Gregory the Great, *Regula pastoralis* 3, 21 (online).

Both these maxims were incorporated into the Code of Canon Law under the Decretals of Gratian and became a fundamental part of the understanding of poverty and its position in the Christian life. They stress the right of all to possess property, and the injustice that occurs when some people experience lack. The presupposition behind both these authorities is that, when some people have much and others not enough, fundamental justice requires that goods are shared out. Aristotle sums it up:

> What is just in this sense, then, is what is proportional, and what is unjust is what violates the proportion. So one share becomes too large and the other too small. This is exactly what happens in practice: the man who acts unjustly gets too much and the victim of injustice too little of what is good.[21]

Aquinas, following Aristotle, emphasizes the medieval understanding of distribution:

> One man cannot overabound in external riches without another man lacking them, for temporal goods cannot be possessed by many at the same time.[22]

The common theme underlying all these writings, so distant from each other in time and space, is that although poverty is widespread, it is also an evil, an injustice and a condition which reduces a person to a state unworthy the dignity of a human being. By definition, to be poor is to live in conditions which fall below the norm, as Mollat illustrates when he considers the semantic development of the adjective 'poor':

> People spoke of a poor man, a poor woman, a poor peasant, a poor serf, a poor cleric, a poor knight, a poor journeyman (*compagnon*); though belonging to different social orders, all were in some way below the condition normally associated with their estate. (p. 2)

Modern poor people speak of the various kinds of pain and distress which their poverty causes:

> Illbeing was described in terms of lack of material things, as bad experiences, and bad feelings about the self ... Poor people spoke about loss, grief, anguish, worry, over-thinking, madness, frustration, anger, alienation, humiliation, shame, loneliness, depression, anxiety and fear.[23]

---

21 Aristotle, *The Nicomachean ethics*, trans. J.A.K. Thompson, p. 179.
22 *S. T.*, II–II, q. 118, a. 1.
23 'What the poor say', in *Poverty trends and voices of the poor*, p. 42 (online).

Meanings of poverty: Langland's five distinctions

In this quotation from the World Bank's research into contemporary poverty the repetition of terms to denote lack presupposes that the norm is not to lack, but to possess, not to suffer deprivation but to live in wellbeing. What should define the level of comfort to which a person is entitled must, inevitably, vary from one culture to another, because poverty occurs, not in a vacuum, but within a culture which has its own expectations of what constitutes the necessities of a dignified human life. It is in falling short of what is perceived to be the norm that human beings experience misery in their poverty:

> So far as this lack threatens an individual's human integrity, and so far as this insecurity jeopardizes his possibilities of a future, poverty becomes misery. The more complex the civilization, the more numerous are the ways in which mere lack is objectively an adversity, a misery, or is subjectively reacted to as such, and the greater becomes the difficulty of distinguishing poverty from misery.[24]

The sense of misery in poverty is well understood and portrayed by medieval writers, particularly those who follow in the tradition of Lotario dei Segni's (Innocent III's) *De miseria condicionis humane*. This work, which was intended to be one half of a dual treatise on both the dignity and the misery of human nature, was highly influential throughout the middle ages and up to the seventeenth century.[25] It emphasizes how the misery of the poor is not confined to their material state, but to their status among fellow human beings, to their human dignity. In addition to physical privations, the poor man experiences shame, anger and resentment:

> If he begs, he is confounded with shame, and if he does not beg, he is consumed with want ... He maintains that God is unjust because he does not dispense properly; he accuses his neighbour of being evil because he does not help fully. (p. 114)

In this context, material poverty is seen as unmitigated material and moral misery, and although Lotario goes on to describe the possession of riches as being attended by 'labour in acquiring, fear in possessing, sorrow in losing,' it is poverty that strips a person of everything that makes for human wellbeing, including the companionship of others:

> The brethren of the poor man hate him, and even his friends have departed far from him.[26]

Chaucer's Man of Law, in the prologue to his tale, follows Lotario closely in describing the 'hateful harm, condicion of poverte' as seen by someone who

---

24 Régamey, 'Religious poverty', p. 649.
25 L. dei Segni, *De miseria condicionis humane*, ed. R.E. Lewis, pp 2–3.
26 *De miseria*, p. 114, quoting Proverbs 19. 7.

is not poor and, with the love of material goods traditionally associated with lawyers, has no intention of ever being so. Envy of others is one of the sins he attributes to the poor man:

> Thow blamest Crist, and seist ful bitterly
> He mysdeparteth richesse temporal;
> Thy neighebor thou wytest synfully,
> And seist thou hast to lite, and he hath al. (106–9)[27]

The poet Hoccleve, a follower of Chaucer employed at the office of the Privy Seal, addresses in his later poetry deep-seated fears that the exchequer may neglect to pay his annuity when he is old.[28] The fear is not for the lack of money, but for the loss of life as he has known it; in his observation of society, one must have money to sustain one's station. The poor have no place in the world of affairs, no personal identity; they cannot even be generous. It is clear that Hoccleve regards the poor as other, and their life as a condition he cannot contemplate sharing without fear of going mad with melancholy (*Regement* 79–112).

Much of Lotario's account of poverty is based on the authority of Scripture which itself presents poverty as a scandal to be eliminated. To the writers of the Old Testament, poverty was largely an evil and a great misery, even though it might be turned to good by the faithful suffering of the few – the *anawim* who were the humble ones, close to God's heart.[29] Prophets and psalmists write with indignation about the fact of poverty as well as its causes: injustice, fraud and violent oppression:

> ... because he hath sold the just man for silver and the poor man for a pair of shoes.
>
> They bruise the heads of the poor upon the dust of the earth and turn aside the way of the humble ... flight shall perish from the swift and the valiant shall not possess his strength. (Amos 2. 6–7; 14)[30]

Old and New Testaments are unambiguous in declaring that injustice towards the poor is sinful and that the perpetrators will be eternally punished for it. For New Testament writers the fact of Christ's poverty is shocking; his human poverty is strongly contrasted with his divine majesty:

> Who, being in the form of God, thought it not robbery to be equal with God: but emptied himself, taking the form of a servant, being made in

---

27 *Chaucer*, p. 88.
28 *Hoccleve's works: the regement of princes*, ed. and trans. F.J. Furnivall.
29 *Jerusalem Bible*, 'Index of biblical themes': '**Poor**: *anawim*, meek, oppressed, poor in spirit', p. 492.
30 Scriptural quotations in English are taken from the Douai-Rheims translation of the Bible.

> the likeness of men, and in habit found as a man. He humbled himself, becoming obedient unto death, even to the death of the cross.
>
> (Philippians 2. 6–8)

Christ's emptying of himself to become like men and to suffer the effects of sin is, in St Paul's view, an amazing aspect of Christian faith. According to the commentator of the *Jerusalem Bible,* 'what Jesus freely gave up was not his divine nature, but the glory to which his divine nature entitled him, and which had been his before the Incarnation'.[31] For Christ to endure a life of poverty and ignominy, an unjust trial and eventual execution is profoundly shocking. For Saint Francis the most radical and fundamental text of the New Testament was 2 Corinthians 8.9:

> For you know the grace of our Lord Jesus Christ, that being rich he became poor for your sakes: that through his poverty you might be rich.[32]

The New Testament writers do not hold up poverty as good because it is Christ's way of life; rather, it is an evil which Christ has identified as such by enduring it, and which his followers must eradicate. In Gutiérrez's view, the gospel message tells Christ's followers to struggle against human selfishness and to work towards the overcoming of 'everything that divides men and enables there to be rich and poor, possessors and dispossessed, oppressors and oppressed' (p. 300). Langland is not quite so radical in that he accepts a world order which includes rich and poor as states within society. Nevertheless, as I discuss in detail throughout this work, he promotes poverty as a spiritual good but rejects need as a violation of human dignity.

A SCANDAL TO BE ERADICATED

The poverty of biblical times and of the fourteenth century is akin to that of the twenty-first century; it is lack and it is misery. That it must be relieved is not contested, though the manner of relief may differ. Material need is an economic fact; human dignity is a philosophical concept whose maintenance falls within the province of church, state and global community. The poor suffer not only in material deprivation but in powerlessness; they express their need to do something to improve their conditions, and to support themselves without needing to rely on aid. Misery comes when circumstances prevent them from doing this, as the modern poor confirm:

> Many spoke of how their poverty prevented them from participating fully in society, and the humiliation brought on by being unable to follow the

---

31 *Jerusalem Bible,* Philippians 2. 7, note g, p. 341.
32 This point is made by P. Hebblethwaite, 'Liberation theology', p. 412.

traditions and customs of their culture ... Loneliness, alienation and estrangement are a source of great distress. Middle-aged men in Bulgaria said, 'When you are poor, nobody wants to speak with you. Everyone's sorry for you and no one wants to drink with you. You have no self-esteem and that's why some people start drinking.' The poor also spoke about discrimination – that is, being denied opportunities – and humiliating treatment by officials.[33]

The modern approach to poverty on a global scale is to place responsibility for its eradication on the shoulders of world governments, with organizations such as the World Bank and the United Nations monitoring action. Modern structures are set up to eradicate material poverty, but their success in attending to people's deep-seated need for solidarity, dignity and respect is limited. In national terms, Ignatieff writes of how the welfare state ensures that 'those with resources and those with needs remain strangers to each other'. He identifies problems of definition – the needs of common humanity are not the same as the needs of the individual – and of solidarity:

> Many of those lucky or rich enough to be adequately clothed, fed and housed themselves feel the lack of these things among their fellow citizens as a blight upon their possessions. (pp 16–17)

Nevertheless, it is true to say that in theory, and to a certain extent in practice, official global and national policies regard modern poverty as a scandal to be eliminated. The World Bank report quotes an international development goal of reducing the share of people living below $1 per day by 2015 to half of what it was in 1990. This is not elimination, but the fact that targets have been set indicates the intention of working towards eradication.

The medieval attitude to relieving poverty was different. In the medieval Christian world responsibility for the poor took the form of relief, not of eradication, and it rested on the organized church and on individual Christian citizens. Church and state were interrelated; it was everyone's duty to give of their surplus to relieve the needs of the indigent. Yet to recognize that poverty is a great evil is not the same as wanting to eradicate it. When a medieval writer like Lotario describes the ills of poverty he expresses horror at the idea of falling into such a state; his logic does not go so far as to consider eliminating it. Most modern commentators agree that medieval thought accepted the existence of the poor as one of the necessary estates and justified in various ways the continuance of a condition that evidently involved great suffering. Mollat contends that eradication was a much later impulse:

> Not until the Renaissance and Reformation, when contemporaries began

---

33 'What the poor say', in *Poverty trends and voices of the poor*, p. 45 (online).

to feel ashamed at the sight of people living in a state considered unworthy of human beings, did anyone dream of eradicating it. (p. 1)

In a practical sense, the poor and the peasant were close, for many peasants were both materially poor and unfree. Images of the peasant in medieval Europe form what one writer has called 'an extensive imagery of contempt' characterizing them as ugly, dull-witted, coarse, materialistic and cowardly, attributes that justify their continued subordination.[34] Positively speaking, the poor were useful to the rest of society. Mollat explains the potential spiritual value of the poor whose suffering 'could be useful to the poor man as well as to the rich man, for whom it served as a means of sanctification' (p. 106).[35] In this tradition of thought, poor and non-poor enjoy a reciprocal relationship in which the rich can fulfil the corporal works of mercy by attending to the needs of the poor, and the poor can justify their existence by praying for the souls of the rich.[36] The sentiment is expressed in a sermon of Caesarius of Arles:

> If nobody were poor, nobody could give alms and nobody could receive remission of his sins.[37]

From a slightly different viewpoint, the existence of peasants, many of whom were very poor, was accepted as vital to the good order of society. Thomas of Wimbledon's sermon, preached in 1388 at St Paul's Cross, sums up in memorable terms the relationship of peasants to the established estates of priesthood and knighthood:

> And to laboreris it falleþ to trauayle bodily and wiþ here sore swet geten out of þe erþe bodily liflode for hem and for oþer parties ... And ȝif þe laboreris weren not, boþe prestis and knyȝtis mosten bicome acremen and heerdis, and ellis þey shode for defaute of bodily sustenaunce deie.[38]

The reforming bishop, Thomas Brinton of Rochester, expresses a late medieval rationale of poverty in a sermon probably delivered on 17 July 1377, the day following Richard II's coronation.[39] He gives three reasons for the existence of the poor, and these will be discussed in my second chapter as an essential part of understanding *Piers Plowman*. Brinton preaches that the rich need the poor to work, otherwise the world would decay; the poor exist so that God may

---

34 Freedman, p. 2.
35 The same view is advanced by C. Dyer, *Standards of living*, p. 236.
36 M. Moisa makes this point, taking Bromyard's *Summa praedicantium* as her reference, in her article: 'Fourteenth-century preachers' views of the poor', p. 165.
37 *Sancti Caesarii Arelatensis sermones*, ed. G. Morin (Turnhout: Brepols, 1953), vol. 1, p. 112 (ep. 25), quoted by L.J.R. Milis, *Angelic monks and earthly men*, p. 55.
38 *Wimbledon's sermon redde rationem villicationis tue*, ed. Ione Kemp, pp 63–4.
39 *The sermons of Thomas Brinton*, p. 194.

test the love of the rich; and the poor are poor so that they may earn merit (pp 194–5). Some of his material derives from a sermon on the parable of Dives and Pauper, attributed to Saint Augustine. In its original context, this sermon is addressed to the rich and stresses the spiritual benefits to them of giving to the poor in order to obtain a secure entry to heaven:

> Da petenti, ut possis ipse accipere: tribue pauperi, si non vis flammis exuri. Da in terra Christo, quod tibi reddat in coelo.
>
> (Give to the one who asks so that you, yourself, may receive: pay money to the poor, if you do not wish to burn in hell. Give to Christ on earth so that he may, in return, give to you in heaven.)[40]

Underlying this aspect of Augustine's thought is his practice of referring his hearers to the ideal beyond the temporal, described well by Margaret Kim in her assessment of why Augustine downplays the temporal losses sustained when Alaric sacked Rome:

> Augustine is not unaware of the human pain, suffering and trauma naturally involved in that loss, as his theology very much concerns human frailty and the fragilities of existence. But to him such emotions over temporal loss clearly reveal the foolishness of vested interests in this-worldly goods and way of life. (p. 36)

At its best, Augustine's emphasis on the spiritual is the same ideal that inspired subsequent church legislation about the necessity of almsgiving, the non-poor demonstrating their zeal for the kingdom of heaven by giving of their superfluity to relieve the needs of the poor. At its worst, to the modern mind at least, it leaves the way open for continued acceptance of the poor as a structural part of society, recipients of bounty from the pious. This underlines the difference between Gutiérrez's view of poverty as a scandal to be eradicated and the medieval view of it as a condition. Gutiérrez works to raise people out of poverty; the medieval writer works towards establishing each person's human dignity within an estate. For this reason I want to explore, briefly, the means by which late medieval people set about relieving subhuman suffering for their contemporary poor, conscious that, in doing so, I am considering only one side of the equation, the non-poor vision of what the poor require. In subsequent discussion, Langland will be seen to stand out against the norm in his attempt to understand the poor from their own standpoint. His poetry appears to endorse a traditional view of society as organized in orders each of which has its own function, that of the poor being to labour to provide the food on which the other orders depend.[41] Yet it faces, too, the intractable problems such a model

---

[40] PL 39, col. 1652.
[41] For a clearly stated account of this medieval doctrine, see Moisa (pp 160–4). For a description

of society raises, and examines them in the context of the fourteenth-century English socio-economic environment and in the light of scriptural authority. The action of Passus B.6 and B.7 portrays the uneasy operation of this society, and reaches the conclusion, not without considerable heart-searching, that, in the light of the Last Judgment, all must work in charity to provide for the needy, regardless of whether they appear to be deserving or not. The nature of that work is different for all, according to status, and each group in society is obliged to take moral responsibility for its own actions which should be informed by proper love for others as 'blody brethren'.

Almsgiving was a time-honoured way of fulfilling the Christian obligation of charity to the poor commanded by Canon Law, but social conditions in the fourteenth century made it hard to identify who should be the recipients of this charity. The difficulties for the poor were twofold. For one thing, charitable works were unregulated, left to the good will and generosity or parsimony of the donor who might impose conditions that excluded the neediest. Donors would often specify that recipients of charity should be of good character, or belong to the parish. Judith Bennett points out that the mutual self-help of charity 'ales' excluded strangers: 'Help-ales offered charity to worthy, not profligate neighbours, and certainly not to strangers.'[42] Secondly, although a third or a quarter of the parochial tithe was, according to canon law, supposed to be set aside for the poor, it was a problem to decide who qualified to receive relief. Because poverty carries the stigma of degradation, those who relieve poverty customarily assume the power to discriminate between the deserving and the undeserving poor. Writers as early as St Gregory, St Ambrose and St John Chrysostom express stringent views about the treatment of the poor, and their words became enshrined as authorities in the medieval Code of Canon Law. Chrysostom is vehement in advocating indiscriminate charity:

> Quiescamus ab hac absurda curiositate, et diabolica, et peremptoria ... Si vero pro nutrimento postulat, ne in his examines.
>
> (Let us put a stop to this ridiculous, diabolical, peremptory prying ... If someone genuinely asks for food, do not put him to any examination.)[43]

The *Decretum* enumerates the cases when discrimination is to be applied in cases of need. St Ambrose gives ten levels of response to poverty, starting with

---

of how the orders might be seen to operate in practice, see Dyer, *Standards of living*, pp 17–26; for their representation in literature, see J. Mann, *Chaucer and medieval estates satire*; and for full development of the three orders theory, see G. Duby, *The three orders*. The theory of the three orders in the context of other medieval images of trifunctionality, particularly as they apply within *Piers Plowman*, is given detailed consideration by L. Clopper in *'Songes of Rechelesnesse'*, pp 145–79.

42 'Conviviality and charity in medieval and early modern England', p. 30.
43 *Corpus iuris canonici*, ed. E. Friedberg; Dist. 42, C.2. p.152, col.2.

those closest, kith and kin, and Christians.[44] The texts abound in recommendations to give away that which is superfluous, and place a firm responsibility on those who have plenty to attend to the want of their indigent brethren. If the amounts for distribution are limited, then plain fare and clothing should be given, so that the distribution may cover as many of the needy as possible. The twelfth, thirteenth and fourteenth-century glossators and commentators go into some detail to distinguish the proportions which may be given in alms. No-one is expected to give away that which is necessary to maintain his station in life in an appropriate manner. St Thomas Aquinas says:

> it would be inordinate to deprive oneself of one's own, in order to give to others to such an extent that the residue would be insufficient for one to live in keeping with one's station and the ordinary occurrences of life: for no man ought to live unbecomingly.[45]

Most frequently eliminated from the list of the deserving poor are the 'unjust', those who would be led into greater wrong if their wants were supplied from the alms. This implies some serious critical appraisal of the poor. Augustine is adamant in excluding from almsgiving those who are unjust, lest they should be encouraged in their sin. St John Chrysostom recommends indiscriminate charity, and Langland quotes Jerome in the same vein. Rufinus, whose *Summa* was one of the first commentaries on the *Decretum*, writes:

> If the one who asks is dishonest, and especially if he is able to seek his food by his own labour and neglects to do so, so that he chooses rather to beg or steal ... nothing is to be given ... but he is to be corrected ... unless perchance he is close to perishing from want, for then, if we have anything we ought to give indifferently to all such ... But if the one who asks is honest, you ought to give to all of this sort if the resources available suffice ... But if you cannot give to all asking of you then you should give first to those close to you.[46]

[44] 'But first we must always see that we help those of the household of faith. It is a serious fault if a believer is in want, and thou knowest it ... And we, indeed, ought to show mercy to all. But as many try to get help on false pretences, and make out that they are miserably off; therefore where the case is plain and the person well known, and no time is to be lost, mercy ought to be shown more readily ... True liberality also must be tested in this way: that we despise not our nearest relatives, if we know they are in want. For it is better for thee to help thy kindred who feel the shame of asking help from others, or of going to another to beg assistance in their need ... In giving we must also take into consideration age and weakness; sometimes, also, that natural feeling of shame, which indicates good birth. One ought to give more to the old who can no longer supply themselves with food by labour. So, too, weakness of body must be assisted, and that readily. Again, if any one after being rich has fallen into want, we must assist, especially if he has lost what he had from no sin of his own, but owing to robbery or banishment or false accusation.' St Ambrose, bishop of Milan, *Three books on the duties of the clergy*, Book 1, Chapter 30, §§148–50 (online).
[45] *S. T.*, II–II, q. 32, a. 6.
[46] Rufinus, *Summa ad dist.* 42 ante c.1. Quoted in Tierney, p. 59.

Meanings of poverty: Langland's five distinctions

All this implies that the giver of alms has the authority to make a judgment about what is to be given and to whom. Langland repeats many of the axioms of the canonists, but insists, with Chrysostom and Jerome, that, ultimately, the decision as to who is worthy must be left to God:

> Woet no man, as y wene, who is worthy to haue.   (C.9.70)

This is not an evasion of a problematic issue; it is, rather, an affirmation of the pauper's autonomy; responsibility for begging honestly rests with the beggar. In *Piers Plowman*, refusal to attend to the needs of the poverty-stricken or the diversion of money which should have gone to them becomes the negation of all virtues and the one thing which can, single-handedly, cut a person off from charity. To contravene the natural law of kindness is to put oneself outside the bounds of the *Lex Christi*: charity:

> For þouȝ ye be trewe of yowre tonge and treweliche wynne,
> And as chaste as a child þat in chirche wepeþ,
> But if ye louen leelly and lene þe pouere,
> Of swich good as God yow sent goodliche parteþ,
> Ye ne haue na moore merite in masse ne in houres
> Than Malkyn of hire maydenhede, þat no man desireþ.   (B.1.179–84)

While it cannot be established that Langland owned or even used the *Corpus iuris canonici*, it is evident that he knew its teachings. When he quotes canonical authorities they are usually those of the Fathers, quotations which travelled well, were not impaired by time and could have been found in a concordance of the kind which, as John Alford has demonstrated,[47] provided a resource for Langland. The canonical discourse was one on which he relied to endorse his urgent pleas for the poor to be treated with dignity and compassion. Authorities on poor relief, on the forgiveness of sin and on charity, based on Scripture and tradition, were probably accessible to Langland in the *Glossa ordinaria* and in scriptural concordances.[48] 'Tradition', the body of non-Scriptural, but authoritative church teaching, included the Decretals and their glosses.[49] The medieval concordance was a resource which brought together, in the context of church teaching, references to the works of philosophers, writers of *summae*, and standard teaching texts such as Cato's *Distichs* and Peter Lombard's *Sententiae*. Judson Allen considers that the concordance of Hugh of St Cher was a definite resource for Langland, citing the many correspondences between the Pardon Scene (B.7) and the Psalter commentary of Hugh.[50]

---

47 J. Alford, 'The Role of the Quotations in *Piers Plowman*'.
48 See Alford, 'Quotations' and J. Allen, 'Langland's Reading and Writing', for discussion on Langland's use of concordances.
49 Tierney, pp 7–9.
50 Allen, 'Langland's Reading and Writing', pp 350–8. Allen's article traces the development of

The fact that these longstanding decrees and commentaries continued to be glossed and explicated throughout the medieval period suggests that the abuses and problems they mention are perennial. Brian Tierney makes the interesting observation that the twelfth and thirteenth-century commentators on canon law were vigorous thinkers, alert to the problems of their age, but that those of the fourteenth and fifteenth centuries appear to have been content to rehearse traditional material, particularly in their discussions of poor relief, raising questions and giving answers that had already been treated two centuries earlier, but avoiding issues that were newly specific to the fourteenth and fifteenth centuries:

> What was really needed by the fifteenth century was a kind of scholastic critique of employability in able-bodied vagrants. It was no longer enough to divide beggars into the impotent and the able-bodied; the real problem that was emerging was to distinguish among the able-bodied themselves. (p. 119)

This in itself suggests that those later scholars who framed and interpreted church law did not treat contemporary problems of poverty and need as significant, and it contrasts with the serious attention *Piers Plowman* gives to issues of relief for the indigent. Langland's views on almsgiving reflect some of the major teachings on the relief of poverty founded upon canon law. The poetry makes clear distinctions between types of beggar and types of worker, trying to address issues of need among the itinerants of the time. Marjorie McIntosh, in her analysis of the control of misbehaviour in the late middle ages, singles out the poem, commending 'Langland's painfully honest efforts ... to wrestle with the actual manifestations of poverty and the reasons for these problems' in contrast with the general scarcity of educated discussion on the subject (pp 192–4). Langland applies the teachings of the canonists to the problems of poverty and need which he sees in his contemporary situation and the subsequent precepts of late fourteenth-century statute to the problems of vagrancy and work.[51] In both these cases McIntosh's term 'wrestles' is an appropriate indication of the conflicts Langland sees between the terminology of his authorities and the contemporary application of charity.

In all the precepts I have been quoting the dominant theme is that the needy require help from above – a top-down approach that expresses itself in practical relief. A later chapter will consider *Piers Plowman* in relation to late medieval charitable activities; at this point I refer to a few representative medieval practices which support my premise that, although devout and compassionate people took steps to alleviate suffering, elimination of the state of poverty was not on the medieval agenda. From the study of wills and the foundation of charitable insti-

---

the Pardon passus through the Z, A, B and C-texts, and points out Langland's use, both as reader and writer, of Hugh's material.
51 See particularly B.6 and C.5.

tutions, it is evident that the poor were structural to society. People left money for them, both specifically and generally, intending to secure prayers and earn merit for the donor's soul. In some respects, the attitude taken towards to the involuntarily poor by the generality of the population was not dissimilar to their attitude towards the voluntarily poor. Both were dear to God's heart and, as such, their prayers were considered to have great efficacy before the throne of God. To the modern mind the establishment of a hospital for lepers or a maisondieu to house a pauper seems preferable to subscribing to the building of a church or the erection of a stained glass window. To the medieval mind the two acts were considered to have equal merit, tangible signs that the donor wished to secure prayers for salvation from those whose entry into heaven would be surer than most.

Geographically specific information about who makers of wills considered to be the poor and how they lived is found in Patricia Cullum's study of maisonsdieu in Yorkshire. She quotes evidence of direct concern for individual poor people, sometimes named, who are to be provided for, sometimes in a room, sometimes in a house, usually for a defined length of time, and with a clearly stated amount of money. Merchants or their widows established the harbour, or the lodging, and some form of wardenship, even if it was only the setting aside of a room in the family home for one or more poor people. Others then made bequests to these maisonsdieu, of food, clothing, ale, or a regular stipend. Sometimes an annual rent was stipulated – maybe 15d. a year. Sometimes the poor were named by the donor and given specific objects, such as a russet gown, and there is, in the reading of some wills, a feeling of familial attachment between a particular pauper and the deceased which suggests that a family servant was provided for after the donor's death:

> Alice de Bridford of York, widow (d. 1390), left a tunic to Magota de la maisondieu; Richard Ledys of York (d. 1390) left a gown, hose and shoes to Grogson de masyndieu; and in 1459 Joan Cotyngham left to Joan Day, a poor little woman in a certain maisondieu, a lined russet gown and a linen chemise.[52]

Glimpses of the transient poor emerge in the foundation acts of almshouses such as those established in 1400 in Walden, where the parish founders stipulate that they should give shelter:

> to 'ony stronge poure womman w^t childe or any othir pore stronge syk man or womman' passing through the town.[53]

If one is accustomed to interpreting Langland's strictures about able-bodied beggars as typical of a generally hostile attitude towards mendicancy, it may be sur-

---

52 P.H. Cullum, '"For pore people harberles"': p. 40.
53 Poos, p. 276, footnote 51, quoting 'Statutes of Saffron Walden almshouses', ed. Steer, pp 174, 178. In this context, 'stronge' is taken to mean 'strange', as in 'stranger', someone from outside.

prising to read that donors expected the inhabitants of the maisonsdieu to support themselves by begging from door to door:

> Alice de Bridford of York, widow (d. 1390), left 1*d*. to each infirm pauper in each maisondieu who was not able to beg. Bernard de Everton of York, chaplain (d. 1407), left 6*s*. 8*d*. to the poor in the *domus dei* of Thomas Howme, 4*d*. to each bedridden pauper unable to go out and beg within the parish of St Mary (within which Howme's maisondieu lay), and 2*d*. to each pauper who was able to go out and beg daily from door to door within the parish.[54]

The implication of these prescriptions is that the bequests were intended to supplement the daily income which the pauper was expected to achieve from begging, not to dispense with the need for begging.

While the provision of relief to the poor was not uniform, it was not left entirely to the goodwill of private individuals. City corporations were often responsible for the foundation of hospitals and took responsibility for emergency action in times of crisis. This might backfire upon them, as happened in Florence. The charitable company of Or San Michele set up ovens in 1347 to feed the starving poor who flocked to the city, bringing with them the plague which, by 1378, had devastated the city.[55] Miri Rubin's study of charity and community in medieval Cambridge gives a wide-ranging survey of English hospital foundations and confirms the sense of responsibility for the poor and the weak that caused local communities to establish hospitals both large and small.[56] In Judith Bennett's study of village help-ales, we are given an unusual insight into the self-help available for people in need within the village community which, in her view, 'probably provided much more immediate assistance than any charity offered by a monastery, almshouse or poor-law overseer' (p. 23). The small gifts of people with limited means are an indication of society's concern to relieve the sufferings of the indigent in specific circumstances and geographical locations, but there is nothing in them to suggest any movement towards eliminating poverty as a condition. The charitable activities of crown, nobility and gentry, though on a grander scale, go no further in principle.

There is no doubt that throughout the middle ages people considered the plight of the poor and took practical measures to alleviate suffering. On the whole such measures were reactive. Even in the Eastern Church, traditionally committed to philanthropy, there are few specific proposals or guidelines for social action to eradicate social ills.[57] As in the Eastern Church, so in the West, church teachers saw the social order as pre-ordained by the Creator. Calls to repentance

---

54 Cullum, pp 46–7.
55 Wallace, *Chaucerian polity*, p. 25.
56 Rubin, *Charity and community*, pp 99–147; 237–88.
57 Constantelos, pp 39–52.

Meanings of poverty: Langland's five distinctions

were used to alert people to the requirement of relieving the ills of the poor, suggesting that the unjust or the wealthy were expected to practise charity without being organized by state authorities. This, in itself, explains why Langland, so compassionate about the suffering of the poor, does not urge any blueprint for social reform by the state, even though he points out many specific instances of injustice. Yet although he accepts the organization of society into estates, he is far more concerned with the fundamental relationship of people as brothers:[58]

> [And] it are my blody breþeren, for God bouȝte vs alle   (B.6.207)

These words of Piers form one of the many instances when the poem confirms the brotherhood of man in the blood of Christ. In matters of need it is explicit that justice demands help for the poor as a criterion for salvation. This lifts the poem above simple issues of how much one should give to the poor to a perception of them as human beings whose dignity needs to be respected. Later chapters consider how Langland looks at society from the point of view of the poor, a 'ground-up' view. Unlike the poor of the charitable bequests who are frequently cast as passive recipients, the character of Will in particular represents a poor man who is a force to be reckoned with. Will is intelligent, sentient, proactive in his own destiny, a representative poor man who makes moral choices and has human dignity, issues I return to in later chapters.

PHILOSOPHICAL VIEWS OF POVERTY

Will makes sense of the harmful condition of poverty by seeing it as a means of following the poor Christ. In his condition of greatest need Will accepts his poverty with patience,

> Siþ he þat wroȝte al þe world was wilfulliche nedy,
> Ne neuere noon so nedy ne pouerer deide.   (B.20.49–50)

A strong element in the medieval thinking that maintained poverty as an estate is the spiritual and philosophical value attaching to it in both Christian and classical thought as a condition of liberation from worldly care. The Christian expression of this is based on Christ's teaching in Luke 12. 13–34, with its eminently quotable advice to trust in God's providence rather than store up treasure on earth. The gospel advice against solicitude is grounded on the belief that God, who cares for the birds of the air and the lilies of the field, will ensure that his faithful children

---

58 He reiterates the sentiment at several points in the poem, e.g. (B.5.591) Wiþ no leed but wiþ loue and lowe speche, as breþeren [of o wombe]; (B.11. 201) And blody breþeren we bicome þere, of o body ywonne; (B.11.199) And breþeren as of oo blood, as wel beggeres as erles. See also B.11.206–10; B.18.394–6; B.19. 254.

have the essentials for life, so that they can devote themselves, without distraction, to following his precepts and spreading God's kingdom on earth.

Disregard for wealth is, in this context, philosophically necessary, and similar to secular thinking on the dangers of property, though this lacks the spiritual dimension that poverty brings a person close to God. Seneca, Juvenal and Boethius, influential writers from the classical Roman world, promote the moral and practical advantages of not having worldly possessions. Their works found their way into medieval collections of *sententiae*, schoolroom primers, and florilegia, and ultimately became commonplace in literature, sermon and commentary.[59] For these writers, the advantages of being unencumbered by wealth are earthly, linked to peace of mind and lack of danger; one who is already low cannot fall from fortune. Juvenal's tag about the emptyhanded traveller who can sing because the highwayman will not trouble him[60] is based on a quotation from one of Seneca's letters. In it, Seneca advises against having too many worldly possessions in a social environment fraught with the dangers of envy and greed:

> Nudum latro transmittit; etiam in obsessa via pauperi pax est.
>
> (If you are empty-handed, the highwayman passes you by; even along an infested road, the poor may travel in peace.)[61]

Boethius' *Consolation of philosophy* is similarly written in the hostile environment of political exile. Philosophy teaches him that wealth militates against safety and peace of mind:

> My contention is that no good thing harms its owner, a thing which you won't gainsay. But wealth very often does harm its owners, for all the most criminal elements of the population who are thereby all the more covetous of other people's property are convinced that they alone are worthy to possess all the gold and precious stones there are. You are shuddering now at the thought of club and knife, but if you had set out on the path of this life with empty pockets, you would whistle your way past any highwayman.[62]

The ideas of Boethius were widely assimilated into medieval Christian thinking, coinciding, as they do, with Christ's counsel to be not solicitous. When

---

59 For a synopsis of the medieval influence of these authors see L.D. Reynolds, *The medieval tradition of Seneca's letters*; G. Highet, *Juvenal the satirist*, pp 197–205; and V.E. Watts' introductory remarks in his edition of Boethius, *The consolation of philosophy,* trans. V.E. Watts, pp 7–9.
60 See above, note 1.
61 Seneca's *Moral Epistle XIV* in Seneca, *Ad Lucilium epistulae morales,* ed. and trans. R.M. Gummere, vol. 1, pp 88–9.
62 (Tu igitur, qui nunc contum gladiumque sollicitus pertimescis, si uitae huius callem uacuus uiator intrasses coram latrone cantares.) Boethius, *The consolation of philosophy,* II. v, trans. V.E. Watts, p. 68. Latin text of the *Consolatio philosophiae*, with links to commentary by J.J. O'Donnell, 1990 (online).

Meanings of poverty: Langland's five distinctions

[margin note: Hoccleve]

Hoccleve portrays himself as languishing in melancholy because he fears the prospect of old-age poverty he grants himself a Boethian counsellor, an old man, who propounds Lady Philosophy's idealized views on poverty. This man has no name; as a beggar, his identity is defined by his dependence on the wealthy to provide alms; yet he describes himself as one who has once been rich and noble, fallen into indigence by a combination of Fortune and his own excesses. Although he has lost his former identity and station within the court, this beggar has gained a sense of personal worth in relation to eternal, spiritual values and, in his poverty, assumes the voice of authority, like a resident anchorite whose life, dedicated to prayer, solitude, and penance, gives him authority as a counsellor. He accepts his poverty as a direct punishment for the sins of his youth (*Regement* ll. 1324–30) and, while he never underplays the suffering he must endure, demonstrates to the younger man, Hoccleve, three ways to minimize such suffering. First, his present penance makes restitution for his sins, and brings him close to Christ who, while being the all-powerful God, endured poverty as man (1079–92). Secondly, following the counsels of Seneca and Boethius, he rejoices that, as a poor man, he is in no danger of violence from thieving attackers (1093–120). Thirdly, once he accepts that a poor man has no role in the world of affairs, he ceases to worry about the opinion of others and concentrates on aligning his will with the will of God (1329–30). Although the old man suffers the uncertainty of being dependent on alms, he is more like a conventional representation of virtuous poverty than a flesh and blood character. Hoccleve's suffering, by contrast, takes specific and clearly articulated forms, and this antithesis between the idealized proponent of poverty as a philosophical good and a real sufferer like Hoccleve who rejects it as a threat of future ills points up the diverse attitudes to poverty found in literature.

Langland's Rechelesnesse and Patience both expound on the concepts in terms that represent poverty as a blessed state, far removed from socio-economic horrors. Rechelesnesse likens Christian poverty to the ease of the messenger who travels light, carrying just his bag of letters, and avoids the dangers that beset the merchant with his chest of valuables (C.13.32–97). Patience shows how poverty helps a person withstand the seven deadly sins because he cannot afford to indulge in the occasions of sin (B.14.202–61). Such philosophy is attractive to the non-poor who have the liberty to choose a life that can lead them away from sin and close to God. It has nothing to do with living in indigence, and though medieval sermons were keen to point out the advantages of patient endurance for the involuntarily poor, it will be seen in subsequent discussion that Langland has a complex approach to their plight which recognizes their sub-human conditions and the necessity of reform. The point I stress here is that Langland's poetry operates within different discourses of poverty, keeping their terms of reference distinct, while exploiting their juxtaposition.

POVERTY, A CHRISTIAN VIRTUE

A modern theologian writing for general readership states that, when the precepts of Christianity are taken to their logical conclusion, poverty is a *sine qua non* of the Christian life lived in sincerity:

> It is impossible to take the Gospel seriously without becoming poor with a spiritual poverty that is translated into an effective destitution.[63]

Though practised within a different culture, voluntary poverty in medieval times was initially inspired by this same understanding. Its devotees put into practice five principles of poverty which emanate from the gospel teaching. These are: an awareness of the human being's indigence in the sight of the heavenly Father; a practical acceptance of God's solicitude for each creature; detachment from one's personal will and abandonment to the will of God; a recognition that the poor person is a sacrament of Christ;[64] and, finally, an understanding that to be a member of Christ is to be drawn actively into his work. Régamey considers these ideals to underlie the essential quality of Christian poverty:

> The five notions we have just recalled are so essential to Christianity that they also make poverty essential to Christianity.[65]

If we read Langland's Will as one who chooses to be poor, it will become clear that Régamey's five notions are exemplified in his life. The criticisms made of venal monks by reforming hermits, of slothful friars by Langland, and of religious who opt for comfort by Gutiérrez, all relate to an understanding of Régamey's ideals. They are, however, primarily spiritual ideals which devotees embrace with the aim of drawing close to God. Each new wave of spiritual reform has its own interpretation of Christian poverty, and medieval poverty movements, of which there were many, were influential in the move to recognize the human dignity of the poor. Ministering to their physical needs was important, but incidental.

As well as poverty being a social condition, it is an ideal of sanctity. Medieval thought developed a quasi-abstract concept of the poor as *pauperes Christi* who, because they share in Christ's poverty, are close to God and valuable intercessors. While the very fact that Christ, the Son of God, lived as a poor man has made the condition of poverty fundamental to Christian living, the interpretation of his evangelical poverty differs from culture to culture, as study of church history reveals.[66] Medieval laity and clergy recognized that it was easier for a

---

63 Régamey, in *New Catholic encylopedia*, p. 650.
64 St Francis considered the 'leper' to be the eighth sacrament of the church, while others, significantly, saw the rite of coronation as the eighth sacrament: Hebblethwaite, p. 412.
65 Régamey, p. 650.
66 Good general views of the theory and practice of Christian poverty in the middle ages can be

Meanings of poverty: Langland's five distinctions

camel to go through the eye of the needle than for a rich man to enter the kingdom of heaven (Matthew 19. 23–4). This prompted two reactions; some, from among the wealthy and the more ordinary classes, gave charity for the relief of the poor; others, both wealthy and poor, embraced a life of voluntary poverty in order to secure the kingdom of heaven. Laymen and clergy were attracted towards increasingly literal interpretations of the Gospel counsel of perfection:

> si vis perfectus esse vade vende quae habes et da pauperibus et habebis thesaurum in caelo et veni sequere me. (Matthew 19. 21)
>
> (If thou wilt be perfect, go, sell what thou hast and give to the poor, and thou shalt have treasure in heaven. And come, follow me.)

This Christian precept was the starting point of a number of poverty movements that included hermits, cenobites, mendicants and lay organizations. In the examples that follow I outline varying expressions of voluntary poverty within the medieval tradition. Given the many interpretations, it is not surprising that the concept stimulates controversy. Within the late medieval poverty controversy, *Piers Plowman* will be seen to place unusually specific emphasis on the social condition of poor people, a concern remote from the debates of polemicists.

VOLUNTARY RELIGIOUS POVERTY

The essential meaning of 'poor' in the early middle ages was 'weak'; *potens* was the opposite of *pauper*.[67] For early monasticism the concept of 'poverty' was not the divesting of worldly goods, but the relinquishment of personal power. While traditions of hospitality and care for the weak are written into the Rule of St Benedict (c.480–c.547), there are cogent arguments put forward by Milis to support the thesis that the involuntarily poor were only incidentally helped by charitable actions of the monasteries. The poor and the pilgrim were to be given hospitality because in them Christ is received, not for the persons in themselves. In the world view of monks, life was a pathway to heaven, and the works of mercy were a means of attaining life in heaven. The ritualized nature of charitable works towards those outside the monastery suggests that such activities were marginal to the monastic life.[68] The monks believed that they performed the noblest and most important function in their society. They were Christ's poor, the poor in spirit, because they willingly gave up ownership of personal property.[69] Poverty was a condition of spiritual simplicity, and the monks saw it as no contradiction for the monastery to own property:

   found in L.K. Little, *Religious poverty and the profit economy in medieval Europe*; G. Leff, *Heresy in the later middle ages*; M. Aston, 'Popular religious movements in the middle ages'.
67 Little, p. 68; Milis, p.18.
68 Milis, pp 17–18, 41–5, 53–62.
69 For a clear summary of St Benedict's Rule in this regard, see Milis, p. 17.

> The old traditions of offering precious gifts to the gods lived on ... in the altars with all their appurtenances: altar cloths, retables (sometimes of gold), candle holders, plates, pitchers, chalices, crosses, statues, books, and, above all, reliquaries.[70]

In the tenth and eleventh centuries a shift in attitudes changed the perception of money from valuable treasure, and therefore intrinsically beautiful, to filthy lucre and intrinsically evil. Avarice became the worst of evils, the besetting sin which sermon writers and satirists were to pillory for the remainder of the medieval period. For the new monks – the Carthusians, the Premonstratensians and, initially, the Cistercians – the search for poverty led them to remote locations; the Carthusians would not even give hospitality to night-time callers, but would send them to the town. They were there for the spiritual good of those who came to them, not to provide for their material needs.

By contrast, the hermit movements of the eleventh and twelfth centuries saw poverty as the rejection of ownership, the rejection of the profit economy, but not the rejection of urban life – for they saw their mission as being to the city and to the worldly aspects of the church. They were reformers who preached against avarice and what they perceived to be the luxury of the monastic life. The hermits rejected monasticism as they saw it because of the material wealth and property of the monks – even though the property was communal, not personal. Reginald the Hermit preached rigorous poverty and austerity in contrast to the monks:

> You know as well as I that cenobitic cloisters rarely or never include this standard of perfection ... because they exclude as much as possible the poverty that Christ the pauper preached ... The monks show deep concern for personal comfort, good food, and protection of their property, if necessary through litigation; in these and in other ways, they are clearly not imitators of Christ or the Apostles but of the Pharisees.[71]

The various lay organizations which practised voluntary poverty in the middle ages had their own individual interpretations of poverty. For some, like the thirteenth-century Flemish Beguines, it included the possession of property and the rejection of luxury, but even luxury would have to be defined each time, and would be subject to interpretation. For others, such as the Italian Humiliati who flourished between the twelfth and fourteenth centuries, property was not renounced, but used for the good of all, in imitation of the early Christians. Many members of these groups came from the poorest on the margins of medieval society. For them, the Christian lay brotherhood to which they belonged was their protection from destitution.[72]

70 Little, pp 66–7.
71 Translation by Little, p. 82.
72 Little, pp 113–45.

Medieval voluntary poverty was related to but not the same as the involuntary poverty which was unsought by its victims, uncontrollable and, in the view of St Bernard, unmeritorious.[73] The voluntarily poor recognized that material need should be relieved, and, in the act of divesting themselves of property, many of the hermits and early friars set themselves to relieve the needs that, in their opinion, were the worst. Lepers, orphans, prisoners, the sick, were all objects of their attention. Robert of Arbrissel (c.1047–1117) founded a double monastery with the intention of saving prostitutes, and established colonies for lepers.[74] Their approach was pragmatic, not political; they addressed need in the deprived and the weak in whatever form it presented itself; attending to the needy was not, however, their primary aim. The voluntary poverty movements took literally, though in varying degrees, the counsel of perfection: 'If thou wilt be perfect, go sell what thou hast and give to the poor ... and come, follow me.' The positive action here is in divesting oneself of property; giving to the poor is an adjunct to this. The prime beneficiary is to be the donor who gains spiritually in growth of the virtue of charity; any benefit to the poor is incidental. Systematic eradication of poverty was not on the social agenda.

In living a materially poor life, the medieval practitioners of Christian poverty share some of the principles of contemporary liberation theologians:

> Christian poverty, an expression of love, is solidarity *with the poor* and is a protest *against poverty*. This is the concrete, contemporary meaning of the witness of poverty. It is a poverty lived not for its own sake, but rather as an authentic imitation of Christ; it is a poverty which means taking on the sinful human condition to liberate humankind from sin and all its consequences.[75]

In Chapter 9 of *Regula non bullata* St Francis tells his brothers:

> they should be satisfied to be among the common and rejected people, the poor and the weak, the sick, the lepers and the beggars of the streets.[76]

St Francis and St Dominic were to live like the poor, not to relieve their needs but to promote the gospel message. Innocent III had called for a preacher to go among the Cathars:

> wearing wretched clothes but with a fervent spirit, so that, by the example of his deeds and the teaching of his works, the heretics might be recalled from their error.[77]

---

73 St Bernard made a higher order out of giving to the monks than to the involuntarily poor. 'It is one thing to fill the belly of the hungry, and another to have a zeal for poverty. The one is in the service of nature, the other the service of grace': quoted by Little, p. 95.
74 Little, p. 79.
75 Gutiérrez, p. 301.
76 Quoted in Hebblethwaite, p. 412.
77 Innocent III, *Ep.* ix. 185 (*PL* 215, col. 1025), quoted by Little, p. 154.

The charter that engaged St Dominic for the task in 1215 specified that the men would go about on foot, 'preaching the work of the true gospel, in evangelical poverty *(in paupertate evangelica)*'.[78] St Francis was essentially a preacher; he, too, adopted a life of utmost exterior poverty, going before his audience wearing rags, with a beard and dirty, unkempt hair. For both these founders, revolutionary though their mode of life was, poverty was to be practised so that their hearers might learn the principles of the gospels from their example. By practising extreme poverty they believed they were strictly imitating Christ. St Francis and St Dominic made their definitive contribution to the understanding of Christian poverty by what Mollat describes as:

> attentiveness to what we would nowadays call 'signs of the times,' which they called the will of God and the needs of their contemporaries. (p. 120)

Yet when Langland was writing, one hundred and fifty years after the foundation of the mendicant orders, their pristine ideals of living in actual poverty had been lost. Within the medieval religious orders and the medieval church in general, poverty and mendicancy were the subject of over a century of polemic, and new reforms were required to establish a new attentiveness to the signs of the times. Langland's poem is written in the climate of reform that sought to re-establish and redefine ideals of religious poverty which would enable the church to respond to the spiritual and temporal needs of the laity in an increasingly complex society.

Within this complexity, philosophical notions of poverty as a state which liberates a person from material anxiety are linked with the Christian precept of spiritual childhood, dependence on God to provide, the *ne soliciti sitis* of the gospels. Interpretations of this concept lead to differing lifestyles. Taken to its extreme, the concept of relying on God to provide stimulates a life of disciplined trust such as that practised by the early Franciscans and Dominicans who were enjoined to live by preaching, and to accept whatever sustenance they were given by way of charity:

> We may see St Francis's ideal as the liberation of the spirit from its earthly toils: at once a rejection of worldliness and of submission to the world. On the one hand it was a refusal to pander to carnal desires and to seek relief from sin by indulging its cravings; on the other, it demanded open confrontation with man's wretchedness and a turning to God for salvation.[79]

It did not extend to directly improving material conditions for the needy, though this activity might be stimulated as a result of their preaching.

---

78 Little, p. 157.
79 Leff, p. 60.

PIERS PLOWMAN'S PLACE WITHIN THE 'POVERTY CONTROVERSY'

It will be important to keep sight of this distinction when considering *Piers Plowman*, for Langland is aware of it. His poetry expresses impatience with the perceived contradiction that those who profess poverty within the regular state do not live the same poverty as those who are involuntarily indigent. It satirizes religious who live like secular lords and neglect their vow of poverty (B.10.305–10) and develops specific anticlerical criticism, not for its own sake, but because of the harm unfaithful, venal prelates and clergy cause for the weak and vulnerable. Langland does not ask that clergy and religious should engage in social work on behalf of the poor, but he does ask that that they should not, by their negligence and avarice, harm the poor.

I do not intend to repeat here the already fully documented debate concerning the antimendicant and anticlerical controversies of the late fourteenth century which revolve around this issue. But because Langland engages with the discourses of poverty in this debate, I make reference to the work of three modern writers on the matter. The significant exponents of the voluntary poverty debate in *Piers Plowman* are Szittya, Scase, and Clopper.[80] These critics expound from differing, though not opposing, viewpoints the inescapable fact that Langland was deeply concerned with the contemporary debates over *dominium*, the clerical, fraternal and monastic right of possession, mendicancy, and the observant practices of 'parfit poverte'.

Penn Szittya's valuable work outlines the history of antifraternalism from its thirteenth-century origins in the clashes between friars and secular Masters in the University of Paris, through the debate led by William of St Amour, into the satirical literature influenced by Jean de Meung's *Roman de la rose* to the formative polemic of FitzRalph in the mid-fourteenth century. Szittya finds literary and scholarly precedents for Langland's critique of the friars who have changed the sacrament of penance into a financial transaction. Antifraternalism becomes, in Szittya's view, a critique of mendicancy. Langland, he argues, has joined the debate between the secular priests and the regular friars as to who is entitled to have the cure of souls. By dramatizing friars as smooth-tongued flatterers who sell forgiveness in order to build up their temporal possessions, Langland condemns the financially oriented activities of fourteenth-century friars. Moreover, Szittya sees his condemnation of able-bodied beggars as including rejection of mendicant friars who, so the polemic went, had no right to embrace 'perfect poverty', since, in the terms expressed by Pope John XXII, Christ and the apostles neither practised nor recommended total lack of possessions.

Wendy Scase takes Szittya's arguments a stage further. Starting from her observation that the friars portrayed in *Piers Plowman* and other contemporary literature have few characteristics of earlier satirized friars, her meticulous study shows

---

80 P.R. Szittya, *The antifraternal tradition in medieval literature*; W. Scase, *'Piers Plowman' and the new anticlericalism*; Clopper, *Rechelesnesse*.

how the poem participates in the development of anticlerical stances in the fourteenth century:

> Anticlericalism raised the question of the state of poverty proper to the clergy, of whether clerics should own property – either personally or communally – and whether they should beg, or work. (p. 2)
>
> The laity, the crown and the papacy all had, in this period, a particularly intense interest in clerical questions. For the crown and the papacy, the clergy were an important source of revenue, via such mechanisms as taxation and subsidies. For the laity, the clergy were a drain on resources, as recipients of alms and tithes, as able-bodied who did not contribute their labour and as fellow-taxpayers who did not appear to pay a fair share to the crown, or who diverted much-needed resources abroad to the papacy. (p. 6)

Scase shows how Langland systematically uses terms which reflect what she has identified as the new anticlericalism. He presents poverty as an ideal for all the clergy; their ownership of possessions in excess of that which is necessary for the pastoral cure of souls is consistently denounced in the poem. Scase's work establishes Langland squarely in the mainstream of contemporary anticlerical criticism. She points out the political dimension to many of his terms, and shows that many of the C-text revisions point up the anticlerical tendency of the satire. For instance,

> Where the B-text has 'parson', 'possessioner' and 'beggar', the C-text has instead 'prelates' (C.6.119, 120), and links 'beggares and barones' (C.6.123). This is typical of how C-text revisions develop the broadly anticlerical tendency of the satire. (p. 22)

Still more politically hot, Langland's use of the restitution theme suggests an understanding of the debates on papal temporalities and on the dominion of lay authorities over clerical temporalities in England. Scase's work has implications for the understanding of Langland's criticisms of ecclesiastical wealth, since she demonstrates how they are founded in an ongoing controversy which was to culminate, eventually, in the English Reformation.

Lawrence Clopper's work adds to the discussion about the fourteenth-century poverty polemic in that he sees Langland as having a profound understanding of evangelical poverty through an affinity with Franciscanism. The thrust of Langland's criticism, as Clopper sees it, is towards an appreciation of the primitive Franciscan ideal of poverty such as was upheld by the strict Franciscans – the Spirituals. While not differing from Scase in his assessment of Langland's satirical and reforming impulse, he believes Langland expounds a polemic that establishes the spiritual value of poverty in terms of the primitive Franciscan rule and the ongoing rigorist ideal.

Meanings of poverty: Langland's five distinctions

While it cannot be doubted that Langland participates in the thinking, the terminology and the arguments of the anticlerical debate, I would like to add some observations that move the discussion towards his views on the relationship between the clergy and the involuntarily poor. A major aspect of complaint in the poem is not only about the spiritual decay of dedicated religious and clerics, but about the damage which their infidelity to the evangelical ideal inflicts on the powerless poor. Langland is impatient both with secular and regular clergy when they prefer material goods to those of the spirit, specifically because they injure the poor under the cloak of religion. For instance, the poem condemns appropriation of parishes. The ideal parson is a man who accepts his parish duties personally rather than taking all the parish revenues and hiring a curate, vicar or rector to minister to the laity. The proper activity of clerics, from bishops to doctors, is to:

> shryuen hire parisshens,
> Prechen and praye for hem, and þe pouere fede.   (B.Prol.89–90)

In enumerating these duties, Langland follows the precepts of Lateran IV [81] which itself legislated for the spiritual care of parishes in reaction to widespread pluralism born of simony. Betrayal of the poor is compounded by the fact that the appropriating priests take up residence in London in Lent as well as at other times of the year (B.Prol.91). 'Lent' makes for good alliteration, but, more significantly, it intensifies the sense of deviation from the responsibilities of parochial life. It is bad enough to leave their poor country parishes to live in London where they can sing masses for payment. It compounds the simony that the offence happens in Lent, when instruction on the Paternoster, the Creed, the ten commandments and the rest of the pastoral 'curriculum' should have been preached in preparation for the hearing of confessions in the parishes.

The poetry laments the diversion of priests from pastoral care of the poor to secular work for the aristocracy:

> Somme seruen þe King and his siluer tellen,
> In þe Cheker and in þe Chauncelrie chalangen hise dettes
> Of wardes and of wardemotes, weyues and streyves.
> And somme seruen as seruauntȝ lordes and ladies,
> And in stede of stywardes sitten and demen.   (B.Prol.92–6)

For the clergy to be engaged in secular duties was inevitable in centuries when there were few learned laymen. Langland, writing in the latter part of the fourteenth century, makes no concessions for clergy who serve in the Exchequer and the Chancery. Galloway identifies the importance of the *miles litteratus* in the fourteenth century, identifying a learned contingent of laymen which directly

---

[81] Fourth Lateran Council: 1215, *Constitutions,* §§21, 29, 31, 32.

served the king.[82] What might have been necessary and important political work at one time has degenerated into such trivialities as dealing with lost property – 'weyues and streyves' – counting the king's silver and chasing debts. For Langland, the proper business of clerics is the cure of souls. Once the church forgets its call to poverty and becomes involved with money, it is betrayed at its core. Man's court is seen as more important than God's court (B.Prol.95–9) and love of money tempts some clerics to accept sin-stained offerings from usurers:

> If preestes weren wise, þei wolde no siluer take
> For masses ne for matyns, noȝt hir mete of vsureres,
> Ne neiþer kirtel ne cote, þeiȝ þei for cold sholde deye,
> And þei hir deuoir dide, as Dauid seiþ in þe Sauter.   (B.11.281–4)

The obligation for the parish priest to support the poor was forcefully promulgated in local regulations. England in the thirteenth century enjoyed the patronage of several great bishops like Poore, Grosseteste, Cantilupe, Quivil and Peckham who left clear and detailed statutes for the conduct of their clergy, not least in respect of poor relief. Archbishop Stratford, in his provincial council of 1342, decreed:

> that the above-mentioned religious holding appropriated ecclesiastical benefices shall be compelled by the bishops to distribute each year to the poor parishioners of those benefices a certain quantity of alms to be assessed by the local bishops under pain of sequestration of the fruits and revenues of the benefices.[83]

Legislation was particularly necessary to ensure that appropriating monasteries did not siphon off all the parochial tithes and leave the vicar with insufficient to care for the poor. It seems clear from such legislation that Langland by no means exaggerates the harm to the poor caused by appropriation:

> In many places þer þei persons ben, be hemself at ese,
> Of þe pouere haue þei no pite – and þat is hir pure charite;
> Ac þei leten hem as lordes, hir lond liþ so brode.   (B.10.313–15)

Following the decretals, the poem stresses that the church holds in trust the patrimony of God's poor. Damnation is assured for those prelates who live off this patrimony and neglect to pass it on to the needy. Bishops who give jesters silver and send the beggars packing because of their rags are judged already to be worse than Judas (B.9.90–2) and Wit quotes Peter Cantor:[84]

---

[82] 'Private selves and the intellectual marketplace', p. 299.
[83] Tierney, pp 100–1.
[84] Compendium (verbum abbreviatum), *PL* 205, cols. 135, 150.

> *Proditor est prelatus cum Iuda qui patrimonium Christi*
> *minus distribuit. Et alibi, Perniciosus dispensator est*
> *qui res pauperum Christi inutiliter consumit.* (B.9.92 a,b,c)

This reference to the patrimony of Christ being that which is due to the poor forms a continued thread throughout the poem, especially exemplified when ministers of the church are seen to indulge in excess; the notion of waste is crucial to this aspect of justice.

Failure by churchmen, bishops, parish priests and religious to put into practice those responses to need prescribed in law becomes, in *Piers Plowman,* the measure of ecclesiastical corruption which presages destruction for the temporal church. Lester Little describes how avarice was widely condemned as the greatest sin of the high middle ages,[85] and Langland trenchantly defines avarice in terms of its effect on the poor. When he calls on the authority of church law he is, in effect, giving the poor a voice and power, for if their claims are ignored then the legal basis of the ecclesiastical institution is undermined. The poetry moves within the confines of established authorities, yet when *Piers* pinpoints abuses in those responsible for the poor it speaks on their behalf. The virulence of the imagery for parish priests – the ignorant Sloth who can hunt the hare but cannot sing office (B.5.416–19), the 'lewed lorel' who tries to interpret the pardon for Piers (B.7.135–8), the priests who accept prebends from Meed to support their concubines (B.3.150–2), the 'proude preestes' of Antichrist armed for the fight[86] (B.20.219) – highlights for the reader an impression of reprehensible behaviour on many fronts. Priests betray the poor by using the parish revenue for personal means, and the laity by spiritual laxity and neglect of pastoral duties. The point I draw from these instances of Langland's impatience is that he has practical and positive things to say about the rights of the poor, and the forcefulness with which he says them conveys a sense that reform is both necessary and possible.

POVERTY AND LANGLAND'S LITERARY CRITICS

Up to this point I have outlined five ways of looking at poverty and suggested that Langland is alert to the contemporary medieval expression of them all. In the last part of this chapter I want to look at some views of modern literary critics who suggest that the poem, not finding solutions to problems thrown up by the conflict between precept and practice in such matters as labour, wages and the sufferings of the involuntarily poor, 'retreats' into an interpretation of poverty

---

85 Little, pp 35–9.
86 The equipment of 'pisseris longe knyues' which the priests bear may have a sexual connotation. In *Omne bonum,* the illustration of *Arma clericorum* shows the sword as a phallic symbol. L. Freeman Sandler, *Omne bonum,* p. 106.

as a spiritual good. Ever since Mollat's ground-breaking studies of medieval European poverty, many critics have taken it as axiomatic that there is not only a dichotomy in the medieval view of poverty, but a confusion between the two approaches. On the one hand poverty is a condition of material privation and shame; on the other, it is the state of perfection that brings the person closest to God. The ambivalence pointed out by those who follow Mollat's conclusions on medieval poverty is born of a perceived dichotomy which some scholars, notably Shepherd, Aers, Pearsall, and Hewett-Smith,[87] see as a problem for Langland. Each, from a slightly different viewpoint, comes to the conclusion that, in the early part of the poem, Langland has great sympathy for and understanding of the material plight of poor people, but that, as the poem progresses, he retreats into a spiritual interpretation of poverty which seems to cancel out his earlier sensitivity to socio-economic problems:

> After the encounter with Haukyn, the central visions of *Piers Plowman* retreat from the material world into a fully spiritualized scheme of salvation. The episodes of the Tree of Charity, the crucifixion and Harrowing of Hell, and the founding of Holy Church offer no vision of poverty. Even the deserving poor have receded from view. The vast middle of the poem has successfully transfigured history and moved our hearts from outer to inner, from material to spiritual concern.[88]

I suggest that this dichotomy is more in the mind of the modern reader than in the thought and composition of the medieval poet, and believe that Langland is better served if we credit him with an ability to distinguish between different strands or levels of poverty rather than see him reduced to abandoning one conflicting interpretation for another. I have already characterized these levels as fivefold: poverty as an evil to be shunned, a scandal to be eradicated, a philosophical good, the imitation of Christ, and a religious vocation to be practised voluntarily and rewarded in justice. I devote some space to a consideration of the critics mentioned above because their view that Langland retreats into a spiritualizing of poverty has important implications for his consistency as a poet and as a moral thinker. My view is that Langland distinguishes the different strands within the medieval discourse of poverty and does not see them as conflicting with each other. His ability to make distinctions is evident throughout the poem, and we do him an injustice if we fail to be alert to this particularly medieval and scholarly approach.[89] The fact that poverty is praised as the greatest help to attaining salvation is not to be confused with Langland's very real understanding that

---

[87] G. Shepherd, 'Poverty in *Piers Plowman*'; D. Aers, *Community, gender, and individual identity*; D. Pearsall, 'Poverty and poor people in *Piers Plowman*'; and K. Hewett-Smith, 'Allegory on the half-acre' and '"Lo, here be lyflode ynow, yf oure beleue be trewe"'.

[88] Hewett-Smith, 'Allegory on the half-acre', p. 162.

[89] Judson Allen writes of Langland as the great distinguisher: 'Langland's reading and writing', pp 343; 353–9; 362.

Meanings of poverty: Langland's five distinctions

material and involuntary indigence is a state to be deplored and to be countered by the exercise of justice and charity.

One of the first writers to embark on consideration of the poor in the poem is Geoffrey Shepherd who considers that Langland, who is not poor but writes of and for the poor, 'is precocious in that often he presents the inner life of the unvocal unassertive people who live in powerlessness and poverty and he draws them into the cultural reality of his time' (p. 175). Shepherd writes of Langland as a poet who thoroughly sympathizes with the plight of the poor:

> The poet's sympathies are with the stable and industrious poor who survive among this frantic confusion. Of them he speaks in terms of affection such as popular preachers used. (p. 173)

> His interest in and sympathy for the honourable poor shines constantly and repeatedly through the poem. On this theme his verse often acquires a surge and tender rapture. (p. 175)

Shepherd is alert to the different meanings of poverty I have detected, and although he does not define them in this way, he distinguishes aspects of poverty as propounded by allegorical characters who speak very much as one would expect them to speak within the authority of their realm of discourse. Thus, Patience sounds like a Stoic philosopher; Rechelesnesse sounds like an early Christian disciple expecting the end of the world at any moment; Holy Church sounds like the practical preacher of basic truths and codes of behaviour that she proceeds to unfold. But Shepherd is convinced that Langland proposes no solution for the problems of the involuntarily poor:

> Langland knows that some virtuous form of poverty is enjoined by Scripture. He understands also very well that to be a poor man is a misery. He knows that it is an absolute Christian obligation to relieve this misery of the poor. Yet the poem gives the sense that Langland believes that poverty is permanent and the poor are always with us. Poverty is a mystery. (pp 176–7)

To choose 'mystery' to sum up the poem's representation of the suffering poor suggests that Langland's is a hopeless view of the condition of poverty, since it can never be removed. I argue that the poem distinguishes between poverty as a social state, and need which must be attended to as one of the criteria for justification at the Last Judgment.

Whilst Shepherd has suggested that, for Langland, poverty with its varying and apparently conflicting interpretations is a mystery, Aers sees it as an area of unreconciled ideological conflict. Aers's work is important because it considers the poem in the context of the political and social ideologies of the late fourteenth century, concentrating on struggles between social groups, the development of the market and profit economy and new concepts of community. In particular, it traces the hardening of attitudes towards the poor which critics and historians have detected as a trend in the later fourteenth century,[90] and suggests that Piers, in the ploughing of the half-acre, adopts such an attitude, although the poem as a whole rejects it. The conclusion Aers reaches, after considerable interrogation of the poem's dialogue with its contemporary situation, is that it withdraws from an involvement with the 'field of material production', because Langland 'cannot imagine an alternative social and ecclesiastical order to the dynamic, mobile, market society and culture he realizes so impressively in *Piers Plowman*.'[91] For Aers, the poem's revitalizing of the traditional attitude towards the poor through a spiritualizing of their condition, represents an evasion of the social issues it so clearly portrays. He sees Langland's use of the terms 'kindness' and 'fraternity' as socially and ethically empty in the context of the fourteenth century.

My discussion of the labouring poor in Chapter Two deals with the criticism that Piers adopts a harsh attitude towards them. At this point, I am concerned with the question of whether the poem's terms for dealing with poverty are 'plangent anachronism', and out of touch with the contemporary world.[92] I agree with Aers that Langland offers no concrete plans for the improvement of society. He delineates the problems that militate against charity, but does not describe, in terms of legislative social reform, what the new society should be. I cannot accept, however, that his terms are anachronistic and empty. The poem is firmly set in the world of the fourteenth century, unlike many contemporary moral writings whose locations are geographically general and whose characters are abstractions. Close reading of the entire poem would throw up many examples of Langland's direct involvement with the operation of commercial, political and ecclesiastical activities in his society. For instance, behind Piers' suggestion that idlers should work (B.6.117–73) is an understanding of the need for surplus to provide food for the poor who cannot work; behind Reason's utopian suggestion that 'Lawe shal ben a laborer' (B.4.147) lies the principle that the work of the lowest should be valued with the highest. It is true that the society envisaged is founded on traditional Christian principles; the poem's advocacy of these injects urgency into its accounts of the need for charity and fraternity, as later chapters discuss in detail. At this point, my response to Aers is that the terms of traditional Christian charity are only empty when society ceases to accept them as fundamental. Fourteenth-century England still accepted them, the reform of society required that they should be reinvigorated, and Langland's poem expounds them within the context of his culture. I see *Piers Plowman* as a very practical move to 're-establish all things in Christ', as St Paul advocates,[93] and

90 Lis and Soly, p. 52; Rubin, *Charity and community* pp 98, 293, 299; Mollat, pp 290–3.
91 *Community, gender, and individual identity*, p. 67.
92 Ibid. p. 70.
93 'In dispensationem plenitudinis temporum instaurare omnia in Christo quae in caelis et quae in terra sunt in ipso.' (In the dispensation of the fulness of times, to re-establish all things in Christ, that are in heaven and on earth, in him.) Ephesians 1. 10.

Meanings of poverty: Langland's five distinctions 63

argue that this is Langland's principle in writing a poem designed to move the reader's will and so to become instrumental in effecting social reform.

One of the temptations in writing about *Piers Plowman* and poverty is to assume that Langland must share the same attitude to what constitutes social improvement as oneself. We must be aware of a temptation to invest Langland with the social conscience that a twenty-first century reader might like him to have; Langland is not Gutiérrez. Derek Pearsall is conscious of this temptation:

> There is no sense that the contemplation of the miseries and indignities suffered by poor people provides the fuel for indignation at economic oppression and for programmes for reform ... It is not at all like *The Road to Wigan Pier*, nor indeed, in the end, like Blake, for Langland has no proposals to make, no plans for reform which will remove the problem.[94]

Pearsall gives an important survey of late medieval poverty and the life of the poor, and sets Langland's representation of poverty within it. His discussion parallels the researches of Mollat's team and demonstrates the dichotomy in attitude to poverty and to poor people which I have mentioned above. He commends Langland for his

> power of imagination, allied to an implacable honesty and urgent personal sense of impending disaster, [which] enables him to see more penetratingly than other men. (p. 175)

Nevertheless, Pearsall views the representations of poverty in the later sections of the poem as illustrating traditional praise for voluntary poverty. Poverty and wealth have been abstracted from the fourteenth-century economic context to be understood only in terms of spiritual reality. Like Hewett-Smith, Pearsall concludes:

> the scrupulousness of Langland's record of reality can end only, for him, in the necessity of raising the eyes to a higher reality. (p. 185)

In reaching this conclusion Pearsall recognizes Langland's practical awareness of painful economic circumstances but suggests that his only solution for the ills of the poor is to regard them as a spiritual benefit, something that will win salvation for their souls.

Hewett-Smith writes powerfully and sensitively about the problems experienced by the poor as Langland portrays them. Her valuable study is an exploration of the 'authoritative language of allegory'. She argues that Langland's concrete representations of the poor, which form the most vivid expression of circumstantial history in the poem, deny the force of allegory which, character-

---

94 'Poverty and poor people', p. 180.

istically, privileges the abstract over the concrete, 'literal over figural modes of understanding'. Her main premise is that Langland moves from an experiential representation of poverty as a socio-economic problem to

> a powerful, authoritative, and totalizing idealization of poverty in which all conflict is resolved through faith.[95]

In particular, she argues:

> The central visions of *Piers Plowman* retreat from the material world into a fully spiritualized scheme of salvation.[96]

Of Piers in the Pardon scene, Rechelesnesse, and particularly Patience, all of whom advocate unconditional trust in God to provide, Hewett-Smith concludes:

> Our sympathies are transformed once again by the easy orthodox notion that the poor will be rewarded in the next life for the hardships of this one.[97]

This conclusion that the poem abandons its involvement with the involuntarily poor accompanies an implied opposition between spiritual and material matters. Together with the conclusions of Shepherd and Pearsall above, it runs counter to those which I propose. I believe, firstly, that the poem is immediately and specifically concerned with how to put Christian principles into practice in the concrete experience of day-to-day life. Secondly, Langland has a direct, practical and ongoing concern for the material relief of the poor which he regards as fundamental to any individual's pursuit of salvation. I base my argument largely on the poet's portrayal of Will and his associated personae, Haukyn and Rechelesnesse, and continue to develop it in the course of subsequent chapters which consider the character of Will, the church, the rich and the labouring poor in their relationship to poverty and salvation. For the moment, I will sketch the outlines of my argument by dealing with two issues: whether Langland accepts the existence of poor people as a sad, but necessary part of God's inscrutable plan for the world, and whether the poem sublimates earthly suffering by suggesting that it is a requirement for heavenly reward.

Patience, who dominates Passus B.13 and B.14, is widely regarded as the character who, more than any other allegorical figure in the poem, appears to suggest that the promise of heavenly reward is a palliative for earthly poverty. But careful reading shows that the function of Patience is to lead both Will and Haukyn to understand the central role of poverty in Christian life.[98] In this,

---

95 Hewett-Smith, 'Here be lyflode', p. 140. But see p. 66 for note on a recent article.
96 Ibid. p. 162.
97 Ibid. p. 160.
98 See Chapter Three for an explication of Passus B.14.

Patience does not negate the sufferings of the involuntarily poor, since he is quite clear on the issue of justice, and in a lengthy section of over one hundred lines stresses how the rich are obliged to help the poor as their brethren (B.14.97–201). The involuntary poverty spoken of by Patience is acknowledged to be an evil, an injustice which demands the ultimate resolution of heavenly reward:

> Ther þe poore dar plede, and preue by pure reson
> To haue allowaunce of his lord; by þe lawe he it cleymeþ:
> Ioye, þat neuere ioye hadde, of riȝtful iugge he askeþ. (B.14.108–10)

Yet it is important to see that Patience does not regard the heavenly reward as a justification for poverty, but as a compensation for it. Something that needs compensation is an injustice in the first place. Recognizing, however, that it can be a virtue as well as a curse, Patience does not confuse poverty that should be relieved with poverty that is voluntarily accepted and taken up. He knows the difference, and at the end of B.14 his task is to exhort Haukyn and Will to clean up their lives by stripping away all that holds them back from goodness. In a social climate which shuns poverty as hateful, Patience highlights the intrinsic value of the poor. They have already been put forward as the sacrament of Christ, in their poverty making Christ visible in the world:[99]

> Why I meue þis matere is moost for þe pouere;
> For in hir liknesse Oure Lord ofte haþ ben yknowe. (B.11.230–1)

Patience's teaching is that for a person to avoid sin, poverty born of temperance and justice is the direct route:

> And if men lyuede as mesure wolde, sholde neuere moore be defaute
> Amonges Cristene creatures, if Cristes wordes ben trewe.
> Ac vnkyndenesse *caristia* makeþ amonges Cristes peple,
> And ouer-plentee makeþ pryde amonges poore and riche. (B.14.70–3)

Towards the end of the passus, Patience propounds the virtue of poverty, not for those who are already poor, but for those who place all their trust in material possessions and who must adjust their priorities to appreciate the importance of their spiritual need. He points out that the physical hardships of poverty counteract each of the deadly sins (B.14.215–60). Poverty, for example, has no big income to buy rich food or good ale for Gluttony; so Gluttony goes to bed in straw, sleeps twisted and wakes up too cold to lie there slothfully. Langland

---

99 Clopper's thinking (*Rechelesnesse*, pp 253–4) supports my view that Langland considers the poor to be a sacrament. 'The 'recheles' person, therefore, may be said to secure his salvation not merely as a consequence of his patient acceptance of his poverty but because his example reminds others of Christ's poverty and the contingency of human existence.'

insists that poverty, whether patiently borne, voluntarily chosen or endured as inevitable, has, in itself, the power to save. While Patience certainly speaks in praise of the spiritual virtue of poverty, he is addressing himself at this point principally to the rich who need to become poor by divesting themselves of whatever is superfluous, making use of poverty to help them fight sin (B.14.202–73). The powerless indigent must be relieved if the non-poor are to be saved, and the non-poor must respect the poor as a sacrament of Christ, giving them respect as brothers and, ideally, giving up reliance on earthly goods in preference for abandonment to God's care.[100]

Treatment of the powerless poor is, throughout the poem, consistently specified as a major criterion in defining the just at the Last Judgment. This must give pause to those who consider that the later passus show the poet retreating from concern with the practical plight of the poor. Pearsall, Shepherd and Hewett-Smith all consider that Langland redefines his concern for the contemporary, fourteenth-century poor and needy, concluding that, in the later passus, he reinterprets the actualities of distress, and spiritualizes them. On the contrary, I think that the character of Will, especially in the B-text, but also memorably in the C-text 'autobiography' (C.5.1–108), keeps before us the actuality of material poverty from the beginning to the end of the poem, and exemplifies the fact that to embrace poverty voluntarily for the sake of Truth is to endure real poverty and need. There is no retreat from the contemplation of indigence; Will's concerns are entirely material at the start of Passus B.20 when, destitute and starving, he encounters Need (B.20.1–50). Will also learns that charity is the only way to belong to God's kingdom, and that this charity is measured on earth by the love given to other human beings. The discourse of the Samaritan in Passus B.17 makes this concretely plain. 'Lerne to love' is the command to Will if he is to enter Holy Church, and love is defined and redefined throughout the poem as a practical care of one's fellow human beings. Will experiences the full effects of material poverty in the course of his progress towards salvation, and, like the character of Mankynde in *The Castle of Perseverance*,[101] is led into the Barn of Unity even while he is still a sinner.

What Hewett-Smith interprets as a 'retreat from the material world into a fully spiritualized scheme of salvation' is in fact an acknowledgment of the movement of Salvation History.[102] The episodes of the Tree of Charity, the Crucifixion and Harrowing of Hell, the founding of Holy Church and the final passus which she feels marks this retreat actually do the opposite. They situate the fourteenth-century church, with its considerable materialism, at the end of the historic line. In Passus B.19 Will witnesses the establishment of the infant church, under the guidance of the Holy Ghost, with Piers being given the task of procurator and reeve, the job he said he held from Truth when he appeared in Passus B.5. This commission to Piers at the founding of the church is the

---

100 One of the five criteria of Christian poverty. See above, p. 50.
101 *The macro plays*, pp 98–111.
102 Hewett-Smith's views with which I have engaged here are modified in a recent article, 'Nede

background to the role of Piers, the fourteenth-century ploughman. The imagery of ploughing makes a deliberate parallel with the start of pilgrimage towards Truth and the ploughing scene of B.5, B.6 and B.7. In the scheme of Salvation History, Piers as a ploughman is in direct line with that Piers who has been commissioned by Grace to protect the world against Antichrist. In Passus B.20 neither Piers nor Will retreats into a spiritualized world; on the contrary, Will becomes involved in the conflict with Antichrist. The poem expresses a clear perception of the ills of the church and the problems of the laity in finding Truth in late fourteenth-century England. Conscience and Repentance work to achieve a balance between the active life in the world and the spiritual calling of all Christians, both clergy and lay. Will, poor but close to Christ in his need, joins the rest of the poor in resisting the corruption he sees in the fourteenth-century institutional church.

Langland distinguishes and is not confused by the different strands of poverty. He is clear when he is writing about the scandal of poverty, the shameful, pitiful condition that must be relieved, the sinfulness that need forces on those who resort to crime, and he does not confuse it with the evangelical ideal of voluntary poverty. He does, however, acknowledge that both forms of poverty make the poor person the sacrament of Christ. He goes to some lengths to stress the human dignity of all the poor, even those who are sinful, and emphasizes that to embrace voluntary poverty is to place spiritual concerns above material ones while recognizing the condition of humankind who live in the world. He identifies injustice, extortion and rapine on the part of the clergy and of the wealthy, sins which attack the poor and cry to heaven for vengeance. At the end of the poem, Conscience goes striding out to find Piers Plowman because there is still endlessly repetitive work to do in a world where people endlessly and repetitively fall into sin. That is why confession, not the eucharist, is the final act of the poem. The poem leaves us on the earth where moral poverty and material poverty remain as scandals to be endlessly combated and countered by a right understanding of Christ's call to leave all and follow him. The first stages of my discussion on how *Piers Plowman* promotes Christ's ideals focus on the practical and moral condition of the working and non-working poor.

ne hath no lawe: poverty and de-stabilization of allegory in the final visions of *Piers Plowman*', which came to my attention too late for me to incorporate discussion of it into the main text. It is clear from this article that she recognises, as I do, Langland's full commitment to the poor in the world here and now, particularly as he expresses it in the final passus. See my Chapter Four, pp 187–92, Chapter Five, pp 227–9, and Hewett-Smith, 'Nede', pp 237–53.

CHAPTER 2

The life of the poor, the necessity of work and the exercise of charity

In its responses to issues of work and poverty in the social order of the fourteenth century *Piers Plowman* acts as a barometer of society's condition, moral as well as economic. I argue, in this chapter, that socio-economic conditions for the medieval poor are so harsh that basic survival occupies their lives; to work or to beg are stark alternatives for them. In addition to working for their own survival, medieval labourers carry responsibility for the rest of society, and, although contemporary images represent the peasant as inferior to the other estates, Langland elevates the ploughman, giving him moral leadership over the knight. By doing this, the poem suggests that the poor are a model for all orders of society, since their labours provide the material food society needs and the wherewithal to ensure that every member, whether able to work or not, receives what is necessary in a spirit of mutual cooperation. The success of the ideal social order depends on the reciprocal duties of the labourers to work and the non-labouring estates to deal justly and charitably with them. I argue that the poem demonstrates how this static ideal of society breaks down under the practical and historical reality of need and famine, both conditions experienced by the poor, both demonstrating that the poor do not receive their due from the rest of society. The other factor destroying the ideal is sin, and, after studying the scriptural basis of the two passus under consideration, B.6 and B.7, I conclude that the provision of food and care for the needy are directly linked with the terms of the Last Judgment when those who have cared for the needy will be saved, and those who have neglected them will be damned. This is a far larger context than that of fourteenth-century statutory prescriptions with their emphasis on wage relations and discrimination against the poor. Langland confirms the relationship of charity and reciprocal need as that which unites all members of society.

Piers Plowman is set in the secular world of the fourteenth century where involuntary poverty is a significant aspect of many people's lives. Because Langland sees the world of the spirit as a fulfilment of life in this world, not an alternative to it, it is necessary to explore something of the secular experience of poverty for those medieval people who are poor without any choice or hope of raising themselves out of poverty. While I cannot, nor would I try to, convey the full quality of life for the medieval poor, I can describe selected features that relate to the five meanings of poverty which underlie many crucial issues in the

The life of the poor, the necessity of work and the exercise of charity 69

poem. However much one might wish to gain a 'true' picture of poor life in the middle ages, one must rely on mediated information. Mine is mediated, in this chapter, by modern historians who have interpreted primary sources, in themselves already selective and possibly partisan. Their work enables me to read *Piers Plowman* with some appreciation of its historical moment.

PROBLEMS OF WORK AND SURVIVAL

Who were the poor in the middle ages? They were the people for whom the development of literature, theology, science, medicine and general culture had little or no meaning, for their lives were remote from these developments. We can meet representations of them in the sermons and teaching handbooks addressed to the laity or to the priests who needed such handbooks to help them preach to their illiterate flocks. They figure in exempla dating from the early collections of the Fathers and handed down with small topical adaptation in exempla collections. Their lives are encompassed in the regulations of canon law and of local ecclesiastical law which outline the duties of all Christians to alleviate the needs of the poor. They appear in court records, accused of crimes that arise out of their need to survive – theft, trespass, vagrancy, affray, murder. Their sufferings are noted in chronicles; literature takes many views towards them, but their voices are heard probably only in the political outbursts which gained momentum in the fourteenth and fifteenth centuries. The details which follow give some idea of the harsh quality of life for the very poor, which is characterized by an unremitting need to work for survival, or to beg. Medieval society relied on the poor to labour, first for the good of the rest of society, then for their own benefit. Assistance was only deemed necessary in cases when they were incapable of such work so that late fourteenth-century legislation made begging by the able-bodied a crime. These two methods of basic survival, work and begging, are aspects of the historical scandal of poverty that I examine first, in preparation for close reading of Langland's representation of poor workers and beggars, especially in the ploughing of Piers' half-acre and the Pardon scene.

Socially, politically,[1] and economically, the condition of the medieval poor was characterized by such hardship and lack of liberty that the non-poor, contemplating the condition from outside, considered it an appalling fate.[2] In Anglo-Saxon society the serf was part of the *familia* and shared whatever conditions prevailed therein. The 'poor' person was the one outside the protection of the lord.[3] This is poignantly and bitterly lamented in the ninth-century poems, *The Wanderer*

---

1 Kim points out that the medieval poor have traditionally no political role or systematic participation in political dialogue. 'Vision of theocratics', p. 21.
2 In Hoccleve's *Regement of princes* (pp 1–73, ll. 1–2016,) revulsion from the state of poverty characterizes Hoccleve's attitude and is representative of the general medieval reaction.
3 Rubin, p. 6.

and *The Seafarer*. The lament is not just that the exile is deprived of the comforts of the hall; it is also that, on his own, he is powerless, without the support of kin. The powerlessness of the poor person is implied in Jacques de Vitry's definition of the urban poor. Writing in the early thirteenth century, he said that the poor are those who, by working with their own hands for the whole day obtain their meagre daily bread and have nothing left over when they have had dinner:

> qui, propriis manibus laborando, victum tenuem omni die sibi acquirebat, nec ei plusquam cenaret quicquam remanebat.[4]

A life on the very edge of subsistence is implied by this, and by a similar view, in the later thirteenth century, of Thomas Aquinas who said:

> Workmen who offer their labor for hire are poor men who toil for their daily bread: and therefore the Law commanded wisely that they should be paid at once, lest they should lack food.[5]

In these two views, basic survival absorbs the poor person entirely, leaving no liberty to pursue any other aspect of life.

Most historians agree that the poor in the fourteenth and fifteenth centuries formed a high proportion of the total population.[6] Hatcher suggests that peasant farmers and farm labourers formed three-quarters of England's post-plague population.[7] Poos finds that in Essex at the same period nearly three-fifths of all tenancies ranked among the humblest levels of property-holders; the landless must be added to this number.[8] After three national outbreaks of plague (more in some localities), late fourteenth-century families were left without fathers and sons to farm the land; unable to pay rent they were cast unwillingly into the role of vagrant beggars. Old people, bereft of heirs to continue farming, were often reduced to unforeseen poverty.[9] The materially poor were the marginalized people whose life was taken up with the struggle to survive and who did not possess the four hectares of arable land which constituted the minimum necessary to support a family of four. Inevitably, therefore, they were wage-earners who supplemented the farming of their own smallholding by working for others and by carrying out

---

4 *The exempla or illustrative stories from the sermones vulgares of Jacques de Vitry*, p. 27, quoted by Rubin, p. 8, n. 29.
5 S. T. I–II q. 105. a. 2.
6 Lis and Soly, pp 15–16; Mollat, pp 174–6.
7 Hatcher, *Plague, population and the English economy*, p. 33.
8 Poos, p. 19.
9 C. Dyer, *Lords and peasants in a changing society*, p. 350. The peasantry probably formed three quarters of the fourteenth-century population; it is likely that, in some parts of England, the desperately poor were only a small proportion of these, especially in the late fourteenth century. Dyer's study of the bishopric of Worcester found only ten who, at their death, could not pay the heriot. This is not to suggest that the rest were wealthy; and it does not answer for the landless and workless wanderers that loom so large in *Piers*.

The life of the poor, the necessity of work and the exercise of charity 71

cottage industries: cloth-making, baking and the brewing of ale.[10] To live as a poor person in the fourteenth and fifteenth centuries was to find oneself on the lowest rung of a clearly articulated scale in society.[11] It was to have so little property as not to be liable for the lay subsidy imposed on anyone owning moveables worth over a specified amount. It was frequently to be homeless unless in employment as a servant where bed and board were part of the wage.[12] With equal frequency it was to be single because one had not enough in wage, property or land to set up a household. Other significant groups of poor include the sick, especially outcast lepers, prisoners, orphans, widows and the aged. Church decrees defined these last groups as the *miserabiles personae* who came under the jurisdiction of the Church court in cases of litigation, to protect them from injustice.[13] They exemplify the poor of the Gospel parable (Luke 14. 16–24)[14] and appear in an early sixteenth-century manuscript illumination elevating their suffering to spiritual status as they help Christ carry his cross.[15] As I have suggested, such identification with Christ made no difference to the practicalities of poor life; it was not a condition to be abolished, but a necessary component of society.

The prevailing acceptance of poverty as an immutable state is challenged in *Piers Plowman*. Langland expresses the condition of poor people in terms of the corporal works of mercy; his poor are hungry, thirsty, ill-clad: 'weetshoed þei gange' (B.14.161), sick, cold, shelterless in the summer rains and the winter cold, imprisoned in suffering: 'þi prisoners ... in the put of meschief' (B.14.174). Those who qualify for assistance are the sick, the blind, the old, young orphans and pregnant women (B.9.67–70), the conventional beneficiaries cited in wills, the *miserabiles personae* defined by Pope Innocent IV. Langland is not alone or even original in portraying the poor in these conventional categories, but, in addition, the poem has the words for real famine which it describes in vivid and circumstantial detail (B.6.174–301), and for real hard work such as the C-text clothmaker's hard struggles (C.9.71–95). Pearsall[16] comments that, in spite of the raw truth in its representation of material poverty, the poem 'has no proposals to make, no plans for reform which will remove the problem'. In his view, Langland ultimately makes sense of the sufferings of the poor by reinstating the traditional

---

10 'In medieval England, several historians have argued, a tenement of ten to fifteen acres in size would probably have been the minimum (depending of course, on the levels of rent, taxes and so on owed) for a "typical" villager's family to subsist upon agriculture alone': Poos, p. 12. Lis and Soly (p. 3) quote four hectares as the minimum necessary in the twelfth century; this is equivalent to ten acres.
11 Poos, p. 21.
12 Poos, p. 181.
13 Tierney, pp 13–18.
14 The relevant verse (21) says: 'Exi cito in plateas et vicos civitatis et pauperes ac debiles et caecos et claudos introduc huc' (Go out quickly into the streets and lanes of the city; and bring in hither the poor and the feeble and the blind and the lame).
15 Huntington Library: MS HM 1088, fols 225v and 226; Book of Hours, France 1513. See frontispiece.
16 'Poverty and poor people', p. 180.

spiritual ideal of poverty with its expectation of heavenly reward. In my reading of the poem, Langland engages directly with their plight by stressing material and present relief of the poor as a *sine qua non* of salvation. Failure to pass on God's gifts to the needy negates the spiritual effects of prayer (B.1.179–84; B.7.190–5; C.13.65–77) and this applies as much to the poor themselves as to the non-poor, as subsequent analysis of Passus B.6 will show. For Langland, as for his contemporaries, there is no opposition between the divine order and the human one. His belief that the poor will be rewarded with treasure in heaven is a statement about God's role in social justice; at no point in the poem does he suggest that God's heavenly reward exempts human beings from their responsibilities. Whether clergy or laity, those who fail on earth by neglecting the poor and needy will fail to qualify for eternal salvation. This is a social as well as a spiritual concern, and Langland's expression of it stems from his understanding of the poor in their fourteenth-century historical environment.

Crises such as the Black Death, failure of harvests and the aftermath of war were events which, as much as harsh legislation and the imposition of heavy taxes, shaped the experience of individual and collective poverty. Political and natural crises took their toll first upon the poor whose lives were permanently precarious. Conditions might be dire for a period of twenty or thirty years, then relatively bearable. Individual poor people had differing experiences of poverty, as had the writers who spoke to and about them. The wars in France might not have impinged so harshly on the English poor as on the French, but civil disturbances, raids from the Scots and the raids of warring gentry certainly affected the land. Dyer reports Scottish raids deep into northern England from 1320 and quotes fifty-four places in the Carlisle area as seriously impoverished after the Scottish raid of 1345.[17] The Lanercost chronicle records such problems:

> The nobles of that district, who took refuge in Richmond Castle and defended the same, compounded with them for a large sum of money so that they might not burn that town, nor yet the district, more than they had already done. Having received this money, the Scots marched away some sixty miles to the west, laying waste everything as far as Furness, and burnt that district whither they had not come before, taking away with them nearly all the goods of that district, with men and women as prisoners.[18]

Political power struggles among the nobility led to seizure of lands in actions often thinly disguised as lawful,[19] while violence and the threat of burglary and theft were ever-present dangers for the peasantry, victimized by outlaws who needed day-to-day supplies. A Wakefield indictment illustrates this tendency of thieves to victimize the poorer end of society:

---

17 *Standards of living*, p. 139.
18 *The chronicle of Lanercost, 1272–1346*, p. 216.
19 Hanawalt, *Crime and conflict*, pp 214–15.

Richard de Wyndhill taken as a suspected thief because he came with a message from several thieves to the wife of the late William de Stodlay (begging) victuals for the said thieves and because he threatened the woman to burn her unless she sent food and money by him, and fled when the Earl's foresters tried to attach him for this. He shot at the foresters.[20]

Although peasants and paupers are not the same, the landless labourer was the nearest to the pauper and was likely to be the poorest member of working society, often drifting into begging between spates of seasonal work. It is often said that the late fourteenth century was 'the golden age of the peasant' because land was available and labour scarce. Before the Black Death had caused population reduction, the experience of poverty in the pre-plague years was of desperate poverty in an overpopulated country, with dire land shortage and severe outbreaks of famine after drought, flood and cattle murrain. The labourer in pre-plague years was in the most precarious position of all, because, without land to fall back on for sustenance, begging was his only recourse in time of dearth. Even in the post-plague years the labourer's situation could be similarly precarious, as Poos and Dyer show. In reviewing food benefits and rates of pay for harvest workers, Dyer points out that beneficial conditions were specific to the harvest season, when it was crucial to have plenty of workers well-nourished to bring in the harvest quickly and successfully. This period of profitable employment might be followed by lengthy periods of unemployment for the day-labourers who were, in the long run, worse off than the peasant whose normal diet did not come near that of the harvest worker, but whose life was more secure and regular than theirs.[21] Poos confirms the discontinuity of labourers' employment.[22] Hatcher concurs that 'life, even in an age of labour scarcity could sometimes be precarious for the industrious as well as for the impotent', citing harvest failures and bad weather as causes, but he argues that opportunities for work and rates of remuneration in cash and in kind improved after the Black Death. To this he attributes the much deplored tendency of labourers to work only when they decided, and to take leisure even when work was offered.[23] However, in spite of the movement towards higher wages, Hatcher admits that they were not on offer at all times and in all places, and that poverty remained a real possibility even for willing and able-bodied labourers.[24] Langland knew that prosperity was slippery, and he understood the direct relationship between labour and survival. It is important to bear this in mind when reading the ploughing of the half-acre (B.6) because it underlies his insis-

20 Ibid. p. 204.
21 'Peasants were better off than harvest workers overall because of the relative security of their source of income, while the harvesters taken on in August would not all have had a guaranteed job from October to July:' C. Dyer, *Everyday life in medieval England*, p. 90.
22 Poos, p. 181.
23 J. Hatcher, 'England in the aftermath of the Black Death'. See also Aers, *Community, gender, and individual identity*, p. 42, and Dyer, *Everyday life*, p. 179.
24 Hatcher, 'Aftermath', pp 31–2.

tence that all should work, not for the benefit of the landowner, but for the immediate benefit of the poor who would otherwise starve.

Even for those poor who had a home and land there was insufficient to support a family without supplementing what the land yielded, by working for a wage, and by exercising a trade such as brewing, spinning or weaving.[25] Though servile obligations, and the proportions of serf tenantry, were declining in the later middle ages, poorer tenants, whether serf or free, found it necessary to work either for the lord or for richer peasants, in order to supplement the meagre return from their smallholdings. These nearly landless peasants were essential to the system of manorial production. Moreover, the earlier practices of personal service had been commuted into the payment of cash rent which forced them to sell off part of their surplus, frequently at a time when the market price was unfavourable. In addition to paying rent and amercements to their lords they were obliged to give tithes of their earnings and their produce.[26] Any incapacity to work, such as sickness or old age infirmity, had to be made good by family or neighbours; there was no question of the lord's land being left untilled. Elaine Clark reports cases of village women 'worn-out by age and declared mentally incompetent' where the lord ordered the next of kin to work their land and use its crops to provide for the widows' necessities. This included paying their dues to the lord.[27] Many people were too poor to buy themselves out of service; they worked for a wage and therefore had insufficient time to work their land effectively; they could not afford technical aids unless they took on loans; in short, they were roundly disadvantaged.[28]

The rural poor were at the mercy of the market and the climate; a poor harvest could mean starvation; a good one could mean low market prices. In this respect most rural areas were controlled by city demands for supplies; during the thirteenth century many northern European cities had been given princely grants of privilege giving them control over the markets in their environs. As these cities would also import foodstuffs from distant areas the peasants were often undersold, compounding their problems of survival.[29] The early part of the fourteenth century was characterized, in the whole of North-West Europe, by a succession of bad harvests; rain ruined crops for several years and famine struck with depressing frequency, the most severe being over the years 1315–17.[30] Whole villages could be affected simultaneously; crisis on the land often led to the destitution of the rural poor who would then be homeless and condemned to vagabondage and beggary. Records confirm the desertion of villages.[31] The urban poor were in an equally deprived state; artisans flocked to the growing cities where there was little to be found by way of housing, adding squalor to their

25 Poos, pp 157–60.
26 Dyer, *Standards of living*, pp 135–9.
27 'Some aspects of social security', pp 310–11.
28 Lis and Soly, pp 3–8.
29 Nicholas, p. 12.
30 Poos, p. 13.
31 Mollat, pp 242–3; Dyer, 'The English medieval village community and its decline', pp 424–7.

impoverished conditions. They lived in the marginal areas, in the suburbs, outside the city walls, in the moats, and in the cellars and basements of city houses, or in the yards at the back.[32] Migrants who went from the country to the city hoping to find employment were feared by the townspeople who were themselves suffering unemployment.[33]

While the appearance of many beggars and vagrants was a European scandal throughout the later middle ages, a less obvious, though arguably greater scandal was the existence of vast numbers of working poor, those whose life of continuous labour did not bring them enough to live on, but who, because they were in work, were not entitled to the relief available to the idle.[34] Stratification of society became increasingly marked with the development of the later medieval city. The rise in the importance of money is, in itself, a crucial factor in the creation and demarcation of a poor class. Some people grew very wealthy, but the poor became increasingly poor and the divide grew ever wider. Towns that had numerous poor craftsmen felt the divisions most. York is an example of a city which, in 1327, had few citizens wealthy enough to pay the subsidy; later records, however, show that the number of very wealthy and very poor had increased; those previously in the middle had been absorbed one way or the other.[35]

Upward mobility was difficult even for those who were skilled craftsmen; journeymen found it hard to become masters because there was not enough work in the cities for the masters themselves, or alternatively, the latter were unwilling to pay the additional wages required by the journeyman – half that of the master – and preferred to employ the apprentice who was half as cheap again.[36] Guilds had strict conditions of entry and only masters could be admitted, but to become one required the co-operation of an existing master who would employ the journeyman for the qualifying period. For economic reasons masters were unwilling to add to their own number, and journeymen remained, on the whole, insecure:

> Together with the totally indigent, many females who had no professional training, some servants, orphans whose relatives would not or could not care for them, the physically disabled, and recent migrants with few employable skills, they constituted an impoverished underclass of late medieval urban society that tax records suggest included as many as half the inhabitants of most large cities by the fifteenth century.[37]

32 Nicholas, p. 9. Geremek, too, elaborates on the dwellings of the poor: 'In densely populated cities, the appearance of many-storeyed houses was soon followed by the building of lodgings adapted to the social position of their future inhabitants. Workers' lodgings, cramped and meanly equipped, began to appear as early as the fifteenth century ... It was in the middle ages that slums first made their appearance, and continued, throughout the various stages of urban development, to characterize the living conditions of the poor:' B. Geremek, *Poverty, a history*, p. 70.
33 Nicholas, pp 244–5.
34 Mollat, p. 244.
35 Nicholas, p. 194.
36 Ibid. pp 244–5.
37 Ibid. p. 248.

It is clear that, while work is essential for survival, the poorest faced constant obstacles in finding and keeping employment, and their chances of improving their economic conditions were slight. This is the grinding poverty that sets the poor apart from the rest of society and provokes writers to speak of it as one of the worst of all ills.

THE PROBLEMS OF VAGRANCY

The line dividing the impoverished underclass of medieval society from the marginal vagabonds is a fine one. The insecurities outlined above led, at times, to destitution and contributed to the contemporary perception of vagabonds and beggars roaming England in huge numbers, refusing to work even though able-bodied. The facts are harder to quantify, but there is no doubt that there were more vagrants and beggars than society wanted. Chronicles, statutes, sermons and poetry of the fourteenth century reflect this view of poor people who not only suffer the harmful state of indigence but are in some way morally culpable for having fallen into it. Work is the primary duty of the poor; not to work is a sin. Langland is concerned about vagabondage, and so are the chroniclers and the compilers of statutes, though their approach is different. As I hope to show, whereas the statutes arose from the need to compel labour, Langland is concerned with the moral as well as the material welfare of the poorest in society.

The principal statutes designed to combat transience and idleness were enacted in the wake of the labour shortage created by the Black Death in 1348. The 1349 labour ordinance which became statute in 1351, as well as fixing wages and prices, legislated that all able-bodied lay people under the age of sixty should accept work from the first employer who offered it. The contract was to last one year. Punishment for infringement by workers was imprisonment or the stocks. Another clause designed to increase the pool of available labour was that which forbade people to give alms to able-bodied beggars.[38] By 1359 the special Justices for the enforcement of the statute had established its norms and their role was subsumed by the Justices of the Peace. Nevertheless, employers continued to feel threatened by what they perceived as increasing idleness and vagabondage among the able-bodied. In 1376 a Commons complaint asked for powers to combat those wandering labourers who had become mendicant, potentially criminal beggars:

> Many of them become 'staff-strikers' and lead an idle life, commonly robbing poor people in simple villages by two, three, or four together, so that their malice is very hard to bear.[39]

---

38 25 Ed. III, Stat. 2, in *Statutes of the realm*, vol. 1, pp 311–13. See also B. Putnam, *The enforcement of the Statute of Labourers during the first decade after the Black Death, 1349–1359*, pp 71–6.
39 The Commons Petition, 1376, in *The Peasants' Revolt of 1381*, p. 73.

The Commons recommended that they should be put in the stocks or gaoled until they submit and return to work in their own area. Many of the requests in this complaint became statute in 1388, when even those with a recognized craft were obliged to work in the harvest. Able-bodied beggars came under this liability to forced labour, and those who could not work were banned from travelling from place to place.[40]

The language of these official documents conveys a general impression of widespread abuse in terms of mobility, refusal to work and crime among transients, yet a variety of evidence suggests that local people did not consider every mobile person to be an idle vagabond or criminal. Poos, in his work on Essex after the Black Death, suggests that mobility of labourers had been a longstanding structural feature of rural Essex life, even before the Black Death struck,[41] and Dyer describes large numbers of workers on building sites in the late thirteenth century as migratory.[42] The poorest were the young who were starting out in their employment and often went into service, usually changing masters after a year. Equally poor were the single, including large numbers of labourers who had to travel for their work which would be seasonal, poorly paid and inadequate to provide for a household and family; labourers were late in marrying, or they did not marry at all for this reason.[43] The same applies to women who were also often single, in service and poor. All these people would be moving from village to village in search of work.[44] Hanawalt's study of crime in English communities in the half-century before the Black Death shows that vagabonds and 'outsiders' certainly did commit crimes by twos and threes; but so did many other individuals and groups, including the nobility and the gentry, and burglary was just as likely to be committed by a neighbour as a stranger.[45] In her research at the level of local courts McIntosh shows that crimes which she designates as 'the poverty cluster' – hedgebreaking, vagrancy, and subtenanting – were only sporadically presented at local court level in the period 1370–1425, compared with a huge rise during the fifteenth and early sixteenth centuries. She concludes that the late fourteenth-century poor were more generally tolerated at local level than by the makers of the statutes.[46] Putnam, in reviewing the most common infringements of the 1351 statute, comments that:

> except for the prohibition of almsgiving to the able-bodied, the justices were taking cognizance of every clause of both ordinance and statute; and it is very likely that just at this crisis employers were not very likely to be guilty of almsgiving.[47]

40 12 Ric. II. 1388, in *Statutes of the realm*, vol. 2, pp 55–60.
41 Poos, p. 160.
42 Dyer, *Standards of living*, pp 225—6.
43 Poos, p. 179.
44 Ibid. pp 131–2; 157.
45 Hanawalt, *Crime and conflict*, pp 184–216.
46 McIntosh, *Controlling misbehavior*, pp 81–96; p. 192 n. 20.
47 Putnam, p. 77.

The alternative may be that the able-bodied who refused to work were not begging. Dyer and Hatcher both posit the view that, once the late medieval labourer had earned sufficient for his needs, he was unwilling to work and preferred to take his leisure.[48] Such findings suggest that the actuality of able-bodied idleness or vagrancy in later fourteenth-century England may have been less pernicious than the language of the statutes suggests.

Statute-makers were employers who wanted labour to be plentiful and cheap. It is also possible that, aware of the 1358 Jacquerie rebellion in France, English lawmakers needed to prevent the poor having time to foment disturbance. Workers' infringements of the statutes reflect increasing insubordination among the peasants which the governing classes interpreted as a threat to political stability.[49] Moreover, the 1388 statute was made with hindsight gained from the English peasants' rising against the Crown in 1381 where one of the petitions was that 'no man should serve any man except at his own will and by means of regular covenant.'[50] Vagabonds were the obvious target for punitive legislation because they were the most obviously unstable, living outside recognized order and contravening the status description of the poor as *laborator*.[51] Parisian records give evidence for prosecution of beggars and vagabonds as scapegoats for disaster. In one incident, three beggars were accused of poisoning the springs around Chartres in the summer of 1390 and executed for treason.[52] The practice of beggars mutilating children to elicit sympathy when begging is attested by Parisian chronicle and records of Parliament. In 1396, a woman petitioned the municipal authorities to take her son into their care because his father wanted to take the child begging with him, brutality being a potential danger as the following case shows. In 1449 a band of highwaymen and beggars was arrested. The records confirm that they stole children; one of them put out a child's eyes, a second cut off another child's two feet.[53] Such activities horrified public imagination, and helped to generate language of scorn, contempt and exclusion against beggars in general. Their crimes and misdemeanors, whether perpetrated by many or few, well attested or alleged, influenced legislators to make vagrancy in itself an offence. Not to work is a crime recognized in English official language, parallelled by French and other European ordinances of the same period.[54]

Although I have no such records for London, beggar folklore was certainly present in the language. Sturdy beggars are conventionally satirized as keenly as other groups in medieval sermons and poems. *Jacob's well* warns against

---

48 Dyer, *Standards of living*, pp 223–5; Hatcher, 'Aftermath', pp 27–8.
49 Putnam, pp 98–208.
50 'Et qe nulle ne deveroit servire ascune homme mes a sa volunte de mesme et par covenant taille.' *The anonimalle chronicle, 1333 to 1381*, pp 144–5.
51 Moisa, pp 166–7.
52 B. Geremek, *The margins of society in late medieval Paris*, pp 200–2.
53 Geremek, *Margins*, pp 202–4.
54 Ibid. p. 31.

[C.9 on false beggars]

faytours, that getyn mete and monye of pyteous folk wyth wyles, as to makyn hem seme crokyd, blynde, syke, or mysellys, and are noȝt so.[55]

Handlyng Synne portrays beggars basking in the sun, their hats on their chests, well able to field a loaf thrown by a rich man, smart enough to sell a kirtel received as charity.[56] Most memorably, in *Piers Plowman*, the idle able-bodied pose a threat to the orderly and productive members of the community and Langland's poem shows them violating the moral status of poverty in all its five expressions. His beggars who feign illness portray the degradation of scandalous poverty (B.7.92–7), but instead of eliciting sympathetic assistance from the pious their fraud provokes scepticism and confusion in would-be donors. The wasters who sing in the alehouse while the rest work with Piers to avert famine (B.6.115–20) are a travesty of Juvenal's carefree traveller; they sing in drunken idleness whereas he sings because he does not rely on material goods for happiness. Men who dress as religious mendicants without ever having been consecrated mock the vocation of faithful religious and pervert the image of Christ who is seen in the poor (C.9.203–54). The poem recreates their behaviour in dramatic detail. The voices and actions of Langland's beggars, wasters and false hermits afford a glimpse into the world of poverty-generated crime which reveals, more clearly than any moral exhortation, the scandalous nature of poverty and the deceptive lengths to which some people go in order to survive. Even if such practices are not universal, their possibility needs to be recognized and in condemning them, Langland identifies the worst sins of the poor as being against the poor. They are especially harmful, not to the landlords for whom they refuse to labour, but to the other poor whose unavoidable suffering they ape, whose alms they divert and whose honesty they taint. In this assessment I agree with Anne Middleton who describes fraudulent beggars as corroding the community's 'shared premise of mutuality in charity'.[57] False beggars destroy the trust that should exist between the almsgiver and the needy person and Langland is at pains to point out that their sin is not in being needy but in deceiving.

It is undeniably distasteful for a modern reader to find such repellent images of beggary in the poem.[58] But two things must be kept in mind. First, the poem portrays aberrations, not as the whole picture of poor people, but as their sins. Secondly, while the language here is in the same vein as that of the statutes its spirit is different. In Langland's economy of salvation, deception and fraud are primary sins; for beggars to pretend they are deformed is as bad as for Meed to lay plots with her Friar confessor. Langland's generic idle wasters have to be con-

[apology]

---

55 *Jacob's well*, p. 134.
56 Robert Mannyng of Brunne, *Handlyng synne*, ed. I. Sullens, pp 140–3 (ll.5581–622; ll.5697–710).
57 A. Middleton, 'Acts of vagrancy', p. 242.
58 Shepherd (p. 171) calls the relevant section 'as hateful a passage as any in the poem;' Kim (p. 96) refers to 'the insensitivity and ignorance that many modern readers perceive at the heart of the poem's contradictions on poverty.'

demned, just as the seven deadly sinners, simoniac prelates, money-loving mendicants and high-living monks are condemned; yet his rhetoric of poverty is tolerant of individual cases. The poetry demonstrates the vices attendant upon the condition of poverty, while portraying the material and ethical problems faced by the individual poor person. As for the spirit behind the language, the statutes, concerned to ensure a reliable body of labour for the landlords, characterize labourers as owing them a duty of service; able-bodied, non-labouring itinerants are, without differentiation, classed as wilfully perverse. *Piers Plowman*, by contrast, constantly differentiates, recognizing that even sinful poor people are brothers and deserving of charity. The requirement to work is part of their duty to help other poor, and if they beg the onus is on them to do so honestly. The relationship of work and charity will be the main concern of the rest of this chapter.

THE ROLE OF THE POOR AS LABOURER AND PRODUCER

Langland inherits a language for discussing society in which each estate has its function and all are mutually dependent. My previous chapter and the historical survey above show that the poor, whether labouring or not, have the lowest and least enviable position in society's hierarchy. So when Langland chooses a labourer as the paradigm of all work and the ploughman as moral leader, he is making a deliberate reversal of current values, presenting an imagined social order in which the poorest and the lowest become the exemplar for the best. This point needs to be established before examining the two passus, B.6 and B.7, which portray troubled economic relationships between members of society, and I first devote some space to appraising the poem's early references to the role of the labourer both as paradigm of work and as producer of grain. This will lead to a discussion of the workers' role in the scene where Piers ploughs his half-acre, since understanding the importance of grain as livelihood, and the worker as the producer of that 'liflode', gives a foundation for examining the contentious events when workers refuse to work and hunger afflicts the community. In the ploughing episode the opposition of need and plenty is made most forcefully. Langland sees the worker as the direct producer of grain, and the fundamental necessity of growing grain lies behind Piers' insistence that all should work. I argue, contrary to a number of critics, that although Piers may seem to adopt the language and even the work ethic of the statutes and the employers, he is anxious that all should work, not in order to produce profit, but to advance towards the stage when there shall be no more need. More than any other activity, production of surplus will ensure that the poor can be cared for with justice.[59] To appreciate this is to understand the poem's criticism of fraudulent, non-labouring poor.

---

59 Dyer reminds us that the ploughman is an independent peasant with his own draught animals, whose social role is to provide for his own needs and to create a surplus that supports others: '*Piers Plowman* and plowmen', p. 161.

The life of the poor, the necessity of work and the exercise of charity 81

The traditional 'three orders' model of society recognizes how dependent each order is upon the work of the other two, and I have already made reference to Brinton's well known sermon at St Paul's Cross in which he stresses the mutual need of rich and poor: 'For if all were poor, nobody would support anyone else. If everyone were rich, nobody would work and the world would decay'.[60] In this context, it is the duty of the poor to labour, and it is a short step from this to the notion that to be poor and not to work is a sin. Increasingly in the fourteenth century, to preachers like Thomas of Wimbledon and Bishop Brinton who propounded the doctrine of the three orders in their *ad status* sermons, work was the defining factor which gave status to the poor:

> To prestis it falliþ to kutte away þe voide braunchis of synnis wiþ þe swerd of here tonge. To kny3tis it falliþ to lette wrongis and þeftis to be do, and to mayntene goddis lawe and hem þat ben techeris þer of, and also to kepe þe lond fro enemyes of oþer londes. And to laboreris it falleþ to trauayle bodily and wiþ here sore swet geten out of þe erþe bodily liflode for hem and for oþer parties ... And 3if þe laboreris weren not, boþe prestis and kny3tis mosten bicome acremen and heerdis, and ellis þey shode for defaute of bodily sustenaunce deie.[61]

Piers Plowman seems to be going beyond the idea of mutuality suggested in this sermon; the poem portrays the labourer's work, direct production of food, as the most important as well as the most necessary.

In proposing the labourer as the model to which all professions will be assimilated in a utopia, Langland places the highest importance on the lowest member of society who is a labourer but may also become a beggar, moving in and out of indigence according to how much work is available. Although the labourer is not invariably to be equated with 'the poor', labourers are usually poor and potentially 'the poor' by the precariousness of their existence. Always on the lowest social rung, the labourer is next in line for poverty, for when the harvest fails, the labourer and the peasant will experience the effects of famine directly, whereas members of the other orders will not starve. If a poor person does not work, the alternative is to become a beggar;[62] and, in *ad status* sermons, work is the defining characteristic of the poor. *Piers Plowman* acknowledges how closely the labourer is related to the poor, proposing work as necessary for the labourers' own and their neighbours' good, and promoting charity as mutual concern which the labourers who shirk are negating. Although the poem works on an allegorical level, it is also firmly rooted in contemporary culture, and Dyer, in describ-

---

60 'Nam si omnes essent pauperes, nullus alium supportaret. Si omnes essent diuites, nullus laboraret, et sic deficeret statim, mundus.' Brinton, p. 194.
61 *Wimbledon's sermon redde rationem villicationis tue*, pp 63–4.
62 The same is true of modern poor people in developing countries. An Argentinian man says: 'You have work and you are fine. If not, you starve. That's how it is.' *Poverty trends and voices of the poor*, p. 16 (online).

ing the many examples of Langland's specialist knowledge of agriculture, manorial administration and rural labour comments on 'his ability to view society from a remarkably low level'.[63] In presenting the poorest of society as the models to which all should aspire, *Piers Plowman* gives the poor a presence and a voice.

The rural labourer becomes the paradigm of work in the utopian community which Conscience and Reason advocate to the king in the *Visio*, notwithstanding the fact that, after the absolute beggar, the labourer is the poorest member of society:

> Ac kynde loue shal come ȝit and Conscience togideres
> And make of lawe a laborer.   (B.3.299–300)

Passus 4 deals with the setting up of an ideal kingdom, where Meed shall have no influence. Reason proposes a list of impossibilities – restoration and reparation of wrongs perpetrated by every branch of society – which will validate the king's justice in line with that of the Last Judgment:

> For '*Nullum malum þe man mette wiþ inpunitum*
> And bad *Nullum bonum be irremuneratum.*'   (B.4.143–4)

Labour is proposed as the model of true living, replacing the need for law; if all the abuses of office, profession and station are corrected, then the utopia where law shall be a labourer will come to pass:

> Late þi confessour, sire Kyng, construe þis [on] Englissh,
> And if ye werchen it in werk, I wedde myne eris
> That Lawe shal ben a laborer and lede afeld donge,
> And Loue shal lede þi lond as þe leef likeþ.   (B.4.145–8)

Although Piers does not appear until the end of the fifth passus, intimations of the ploughman are made at several earlier points. In the fair field full of folk ploughmen are the first to be mentioned, and their life is work: '[they] swonken ful harde'; play is something they seldom do. We are here looking at a postlapsarian community in which work is opposed to play and is the moral norm; it is also opposed to waste and gluttony with their pejorative overtones. Early in the Prologue, ploughmen are established as the foundation of the ideal society:

> And for profit of al þe peple plowmen ordeyned
> To tilie and to trauaille as trewe lif askeþ.   (B. Prol.119–20)

In Passus 3, using the imagery of a prophetic and biblical utopia,[64] the poetry establishes the ploughman as the model of all work:

63 '*Piers Plowman* and plowmen', p. 156.
64 The poetry makes direct reference to Isaiah 2. 4 which proposes the utopia of peace which will herald the Messianic Age.

>   Ech man to pleye with a plow, pykoise or spade,
>   Spynne, or sprede donge, or spille hymself with sleuþe.   (B.3.309–10)

Conscience's theory is that there will be no need of law or law enforcement because there will be no crime or conflict. In his peaceful commonwealth, heavy manual labour is defined as 'pleye', and sloth is self-destruction, reversing the temporal attitudes of the postlapsarian world. Work is not the curse of God upon Adam, which Piers in B.6 refers to, but something pleasurable. Medieval teaching on life in the garden of Eden suggested that prelapsarian man worked without hardship. A graphic illustration of this paradisal concept of labour is found in the image of Adam being taught by an angel how to dig, now in Museu Nacional d'Art de Catalunya, Barcelona, restored from a thirteenth-century ceiling painting in the Monastery of Sigena, Aragon.[65] Langland is here proposing that the man with the plough and the spade is the one to recreate the paradisal community and resolve the problems of society. In traditional religious thought, the monk was the custodian of the paradisal community. He cultivated his monastic garden and conquered his wilderness set apart from the rest of humanity, creating an earthly version of the heavenly paradise. In appropriating this imagery for the labourer and ploughman, Langland boldly stresses the poor layperson's value both in the sight of God, and as founding God's social order in the here and now.

It would be wrong to suggest that Langland is unique in using the ploughman as leader. The status of the plough as sanctuary, and the ploughman as an example of leadership justified by personal righteousness are attested in biblical, classical and medieval tradition.[66] Piers himself incorporates many aspects of the medieval ploughman, who, in the later fourteenth century, had an unfixed socio-economic status. He might be reasonably wealthy as the owner of the draught animals and equipment required to till the soil, but in the late fourteenth century, his annual wage of 7s. in cash with four-and-one-third quarters of grain could make him poorer than the day labourer who earned £3.0.0d. a year.[67] Whatever his economic status, the ploughman was an essential person in the community without whose cooperation the harvest could not be achieved.[68] Piers adds moral leadership to practical importance. Even though he is not among the poorest, the thrust of his emphasis on labour is towards providing for the poorest in society. The food he eats, at least in famine, is the same as that given to paupers (B.6.280–6). This is not a comment on Piers' diet as such – it reminds us that Piers is to be understood within the context of the poor and that he carries a community significance. The

---

65 Images of Adam being taught by an angel how to labour are discussed by Freedman (pp 28–9).
66 James Morey gives a multitude of examples that show the ploughman's authoritative role to be well-attested in literature and custom. 'Plows, laws and sanctuary in medieval England and in the Wakefield *Mactatio Abel*', pp 46–9.
67 Dyer, '*Piers Plowman* and plowmen', p. 159.
68 Ibid. p. 161.

leader eats like a poor person, even while exercising a role as leader. His poverty is responsible; he provides for the community in need, and when he has achieved the cultivation of the half-acre, he expresses his desire to live as a poor man (B.7.118–21). Piers is not indigent, but has a reasonable subsistence and appropriate means of earning his living, as the poor should have. He is therefore able to represent the poor as they should be, rather than in the state of indigence Langland deplores.

To choose the labourer and ploughman as fundamental models for society is to make a radical statement that values in the ideal community are the opposite of those proposed by Meed and her powerful followers (B.3.284–330). Dyer suggests that Langland is almost unique among poets in his ability to grasp the tensions within the village community that were exacerbated in the years after the Black Death.[69] Setting Piers the ploughman above the knight reverses the accepted medieval pattern of social and moral leadership. Traditionally, those outside the labouring classes exercised keen antipathy towards the manual worker required to provide 'liflode'. Elizabeth Kirk reminds us that the biblical figure of the ploughman carried unfavourable associations with Cain.[70] Hilton speaks of 'the sharpness of antagonism between lord and peasant in the second half of the fourteenth century', an antagonism engendered by uneasy relationships with regard to wages, labour, rent and tenancy agreements.[71] Jill Mann's work on estates satire reminds us that although, conventionally, love and fidelity were the traditional virtues of the labourer and the ploughman, and physical labour their primary duty, their quarrelsomeness, idleness and failure to observe Sundays and religious festivals are among the satirists' most frequent complaints.[72] To this may be added a traditional literary and exemplary view of the peasant as boorish and unpleasant, in some cases almost bestial, naturally lowly, unintelligent and only fit for subjugation and physical toil.[73]

Langland's idealized labourer is the force for good order whereas his wasters exhibit the vices satirized by other writers as characteristic of labourers. Throughout the *Visio* the ploughman or labourer is referred to as the model of the productive life, the direct producer who wins food in contrast with gluttonous wasters; the ploughmen win, the gluttons waste. When Langland identifies all good and virtuous work with that of the labourer he is making the labourer himself an image. Essential to our reading of this image is an understanding of the qualities Langland attributes to the labourer, who is associated with nature, with love and with Conscience (B.3.299–300). This early portrayal of the labourer and ploughman in the poem prepares for the appearance of ploughman leader

69 '*Piers Plowman* and plowmen', p. 156.
70 'Langland's plowman and the recreation of fourteenth-century religious metaphor', p. 3.
71 Hilton, p. 69.
72 Mann, *Chaucer and medieval estates satire*, pp 67–74.
73 See Freedman, *Images of the medieval peasant*. This is a thoroughgoing study, as its title implies, of medieval representations of peasants. It provides numerous examples taken from literature and art of the sometimes favourable, but largely unfavourable images of peasants.

whose task it is to make distinctions between types of work and their mutual value, and whose call to work reinstates the importance of charity as the foundation of social relationships, including that between poor labourer and poor beggar. This appreciation of the fundamental value of labour in the ideal society contrasted with the prevailing cultural disdain for manual labour[74] sharpens Langland's subsequent satire of the wasters and 'faitours', and stirs his alter ego, Will, into debate over the value of his intellectual and spiritual labour (C.5.1–109).

PIERS' ROLE IN FOOD PRODUCTION

Piers emerges from the crowd as a postlapsarian labourer, employed in the service of a good lord (B.5.537–55). His directions are given in the knowledge that utopia is not yet in existence, and the perils of the journey to the good lord Truth are moral hazards. Langland has, already in the first four passus, pointed to the significance of the labourer who represents honesty, *leautee*, hard work and virtue. However ideal his concept of labour may be, Piers' interaction with the people on the half-acre demonstrates unmistakeably the importance of work as survival. In this, Langland makes a distinction between a prelapsarian view of labour, and the historical reality of fourteenth-century conditions. The poetry is forceful in proposing the poor person as the model for all to follow, yet Langland's poor on the half-acre enact the harsh reality that underlies their necessary function in the traditionally ordered society; if the poor do not work to cultivate food materials, famine will overtake them.

The main work of Piers' enterprise is to till, plough and sow the field in preparation for starting out on pilgrimage, and he calls upon all elements of society to attend to their own discrete tasks – the ladies to work with their sewing, spinning and weaving, and to see that food is provided for the workers (B.6.9–20), the knight, whose work is validated in reference to ploughing (B.6.21–32), to perform his duty of protection and law-enforcement. The rest must assist in the ploughing, seeding and weeding. While many commentators rightly take this to be an allegory of the standard medieval social hierarchy,[75] it must be noted that Langland has shifted the emphasis. In the traditional order, the value of labour is that it produces what is necessary to support the aristocracy, whereas Piers relates mutual obligations directly to the labourers' work; ladies and knights do their tasks so that the food production may be done with workers well fed and protected, not exploited, by the knight's operation of law (B.6.37–45). Langland, looking forward to Judgment Day, reminds the knight of the essential dignity of all:

---

[74] 'In the middle ages ... it was possible to hold conflicting opinions of labor and to praise or belittle it for different reasons': see Freedman's discussion of some of these attitudes, *Images of the peasant*, pp 24–33.
[75] Hewett-Smith, 'Allegory on the half-acre', p. 5; Aers, *Community*, p. 41.

> Thouȝ he be þyn vnderlyng here, wel may happe in heuene
> That he worþ worþier set and wiþ moore blisse:
> *Amice, ascende superius.*
> For in a charnel at chirche cherles ben yuel to knowe.   (B.6.46–8)

It is, to use Simpson's analysis, 'a redefining of the essential relationships of feudal society based on "truthe"',[76] and it echoes a similar definition of essential human equality expressed by St Ambrose:

> A narrow mound of turf is enough for rich and poor alike; and a bit of land of which the rich man when alive took no heed now takes in the whole of him. Nature makes no distinctions among us at our birth, and none at our death. All alike she creates us, all alike she seals us in the tomb. Who can tell the dead apart? Open up the graves, and, if you can, tell which was a rich man.[77]

Running counter to the obviously idealized labourer and ploughman is the poem's representation of those called 'wasters' who disturb the ideal nature of the allegorical society by refusing to work, preferring to sit in the alehouse singing 'How trolly-lolly'. Piers' wrath on encountering them may seem excessive if we read the passus literally; after all he invited help only from those who wanted to go with him on pilgrimage. But this is a question of necessity; if the seed is not sown, there will be no harvest. If these wasters idle about there will be nothing for anyone to live on.

It would be difficult to overestimate the importance of grain cultivation, particularly in the medieval rural economy characterized by grain production, animal husbandry and trade.[78] Undoubtedly, the peasant's survival depended on his ability to make his land yield. Dyer relates the yield from the peasant holding to that of the demesne, and suggests that if a peasant renting five acres grew crops on the whole holding every year, he might be expected to harvest ten quarters, or enough 'to provide next year's seed and most of his family's food needs'.[79] Grain was often part of the pension arrangements made for the elderly and of the liveries granted to manorial servants. A Norfolk widow's holding of three acres was assigned to two local men 'on condition that they seed, plow, and harvest the land, using its crops to provide the widow with "all her necessities"'.[80] A

---

76 J. Simpson, *Piers Plowman: an introduction to the B-Text*, p. 70.
77 St Ambrose, *De Nabuthe Jezraelita*, quoted by Arthur Lovejoy, 'The communism of St Ambrose', p. 299.
78 For varied aspects of grain production in the economy and daily life of the fourteenth century see the following works: Dyer, *Standards of living*, pp 128–34; E. Clark, 'Some aspects of social security', p. 309; M. Murphy, 'Feeding medieval cities', pp 120–1; J.A. Galloway, 'Driven by drink?', pp 87–100; B. Campbell, 'Land, labour, livestock and productivity trends in English seigneurial agriculture, 1208–1450', pp 144–82.
79 Dyer, *Standards of living*, pp 127–9.
80 NRO 12475. St Matthew 19 E III, quoted by Clark, 'Some aspects of social security', p. 310.

dying husband's will left an arrangement for his widow that, among other things, provided her with sixteen bushels of malt annually, and the stipulation that the new owner of the land was to cultivate and seed an acre of arable in every season of the year for her use.[81] Grain was also used for charitable giving, as the example of Alice de Bryene illustrates. She made an annual gift averaging four bushels to each of the three orders of friars who frequently came to dine: the Austin Friars of Clare, the Franciscans from Babwell and the Dominicans from Sudbury. Paupers from the estate were also occasionally granted corn; and twice note was made of quantities of grain given by Alice to help fund the repair of the bell tower at Acton church.[82] The town pre-eminently depended on the cultivation of the land. Medieval townspeople were largely dependent on the labours of others for their daily food and drink, and grains provided most of the daily nutritional needs of rich and poor alike.[83] One study traces the impact of London's increasing demand for ale in the latter part of the fourteenth century, and concludes that such a demand changed both the face of the agrarian landscape and the London-centred distributive systems. Barley and dredge outstripped wheat as the main grain crop and, perhaps because they were relatively easy to transport when malted, became widely cultivated in counties not in the immediate vicinity of London: Hertfordshire, Buckinghamshire, Cambridgeshire, Huntingdonshire, Bedfordshire and Northamptonshire.[84]

To recognize the significance of grain production is to appreciate with an added force Langland's choice of a ploughing episode to be the focal point of Piers' leadership. Grain was food when turned into bread, drink when malted as ale and the means of economic survival when sold at market. The peasants who formed the demographic majority of medieval European society were its producers. Piers' insistence on the necessity of all working for the harvest recognizes the centrality of grain, and to appreciate this helps to rationalize the issues of work and idleness, exploitation and begging, hunger and charity, reward and punishment that dominate the two passus that conclude the *Visio* of the poem. Piers is a more complex character than the simple ploughman. Cast in the role of a tenant-farmer with too much land to work on his own, needing the help of others, Piers recognizes the direct relationship between sowing grain, reaping the harvest and 'liflode'. This is a term for material necessities of life, and belongs to the world of profit and loss as well as to the world of reliance on God to provide. On the one hand, 'liflode' comes from God; on the other, it must, in justice, be worked for. Langland is able to make a clear distinction between necessary work for material sustenance and Christian reliance on God to provide for his faithful. His use of the word 'liflode' illustrates his perception of this distinction.

In Passus 1 Holy Church proclaims that God has created the earth with the ability to provide enough for all if its resources are used with 'mesure':

---

81 Clark, 'Some aspects of social security', p. 311. See also examples on p. 315.
82 ffiona Swabey, 'The household of Alice de Bryene, 1412–13', p. 142.
83 Murphy, 'Feeding medieval cities', pp 120, 131.
84 J.A. Galloway, 'Driven by drink?' pp 98–9.

> And þerfore he hi3te þe erþe to helpe yow echone
> Of wollene, of lynnen, of liflode at nede
> In mesurable manere to make yow at ese.   (B.1.17–19)

Piers acts as an intermediary between God and man; in distributing duties to those who are to help him plough his half-acre he undertakes to provide the food:

> For I shal lenen hem liflode, but if þe lond faille,
> As longe as I lyue, for þe Lordes loue of heuene.   (B.6.17–18)

Hunger extends this usage to emphasize that unless the people work the land they will not receive their 'liflode' (B.6.231–6), a concept echoed in Need's scathing words about the friars in the final passus:[85]

> For lomere he lyeþ, þat liflode moot begge,
> Than he þat laboureþ for liflode and leneþ it beggeres.
> And siþen freres forsoke þe felicite of erþe,
> Lat hem be as beggeris, or lyue by aungeles foode!   (B.20.238–41)

That Langland distinguishes between working as a matter of justice and relying on God to provide one's 'liflode' becomes very clear at the start of the *Vita*, when Thought first introduces the triad, Dowel, Dobet and Dobest:

> Whoso is trewe of his tunge and of his two handes,
> And þoru3 his labour or þoru3 his land his liflode wynneþ,
> And is trusty of his tailende, takeþ but his owene,
> And is no3t dronkelewe ne deynous, Dowel hym folweþ.   (B.8.80–3)

The essentials for the life of the spirit are the same as for a well-ordered society: each estate must perform work appropriate to its station, in this fulfilling the prescriptions of Dowel.

The centrality of food provision to the whole poem reflects the significance of food production in the medieval economy and highlights the position of the poor both as producers of food and its most needy consumers. The contexts of 'liflode' show that its terms of reference go beyond what is necessary for bare subsistence. Famine reduces the poor to eating the barley bread and coarse beans usu-

---

[85] This last use of the word in the poem yokes together the spiritual 'liflode', so frequently identified with the spiritual sustenance given to those who concentrate on God, and the temporal food which should be gained as a result of work. At the end, the Friars are accused of perverting the concept of spiritual food by undertaking the cure of souls only for money. In this case, Need says, they should be forced to take God at his word and literally wait for the angels to feed them. The ironic overtone is that God's angels fed Elijah who was God's faithful prophet, whereas there is little hope of such miraculous food being given to the venal friars.

ally fed to horses. When the dearth has abated and the crops have been sown, the allegorical feeding of Hunger with peas, beans and apples reflects the well-documented 'hungry gap'. This regularly occurred, for the poorest of the peasantry, when the previous year's produce of grain, bacon and cheese were running low, and there would be nothing more until the new harvest brought grain to mill and to trade for other foodstuffs.[86] 'Liflode' refers to that which is necessary for life to be human, not simply survival. Piers, in the face of famine, knows the difference and is concerned that people should work productively to provide surplus, so that need can be overcome.[87] It has been suggested by Hatcher that the much deplored tendency of labourers to refuse to work once they had earned enough for their immediate needs is plausible in the light of the improved wages and food that labourers could command after 1349. Labour was unrelieved drudgery, and, if they had satisfied their subsistence needs, labourers might well purchase a break from toil by foregoing wages. Such an attitude would certainly give rise to the repeated complaints about idle peasants, of which Gower's is representative:

> The servant of the plough, contrary to the law of the land, seeks to obtain a hereditary obstacle [to taking up ploughing]. These men desire the leisures of great men, but they have nothing to feed themselves with, nor will they be servants.[88]

It would also run counter to Piers' efforts to provide for the most vulnerable. Piers' anger and frustration with the able-bodied idlers underline the value of the labourers who are essential to the success of the ploughing episode. The poorest labourers are here the models to which all should aspire and the idlers' subversion of the established order is a violation of the laws of charity in two ways. First, the presence of able-bodied wanderers choosing leisure rather than work jeopardizes the success of the ploughing venture which depends on the efforts of all to produce sufficient to ward off dearth and provide a surplus. Secondly, when able-bodied beggars, whether religious or lay, take alms they do not need they are exhibiting the same gluttony, waste and unnaturalness as the selfish rich and creating an injustice towards those incapable of work who depend upon the alms for their 'liflode'. This point is well made by Middleton who regards it as a contributory factor to the corrosion of society's goodwill towards all poor.[89]

Critics, most notably Aers,[90] have accused Langland of endorsing the language of the draconian statutes which stereotype all mobile labourers as idle and,

---

86 Dyer, *Standards of living*, p.160; J. Masschaele, *Peasants, merchants and markets*, p. 41.
87 Frank's view that Langland, in his lifetime, witnessed the ravages of famine, endorses my feeling that Piers is more concerned about producing plenty for the needy than producing surplus for the sake of profit. 'The hungry gap: crop failure, and famine', pp 88–95.
88 'Sic famulus sulci contrarius ammodo legi / De patria patriam querit habere moram. / Ocia magnatum cupiunt hii, nil tamen vnde / Se nutrire queunt, ni famulentur, habent.' Gower, *Vox clamantis*, V. 9 (ll.585–8), in *The complete works of John Gower*, p. 217.
89 'Acts of vagrancy', p. 241.
90 Aers, *Community, gender, and individual identity*, pp 47–9, and 'Justice and wagelabor after the

90   Piers Plowman *and the poor*

in this, aligning himself with the 'wage-fixing employers' who are only looking to their own economic interests. Such language, as Hatcher demonstrates, is used recurrently throughout the centuries from the fourteenth onwards, especially by employers and rulers, as a justification for the necessity of labour in a society that depends on labourers to produce the goods that generate the wealth and incomes 'of the fortunate few'.[91] Piers does indeed, as Kim points out, seem to urge the people to work in order to produce more. Her analysis of the biblical texts behind Hunger's dialogue with Piers finds that they justify the hunger for acquisition: 'what first starts out as an argument for honest manual labor steadily turns into one in support of the hunger for gain and accumulation'.[92] Kim sees Hunger as promoting to the poor the benefits of working hard to gain and accumulate material goods and Piers as endorsing this attitude. So too does Hewett-Smith: 'Piers' compassion for the starving laborers turns to a kind of self-interested vision of worldly gain as he begins to see economic advantage in the worker's fear of need'.[93] In this, the poetry uses language that was an integral part of statute, complaint and sermon of the period, as indeed it was of later periods.[94] Hunger attacks the poor at Piers' behest, and Kim describes how the twists and turns of Hunger's arguments are led by him. 'Hunger's agenda concerns the policy of containment and order in the political management of the needy – from the top down'.[95] Kim's overall analysis of Hunger's dialogue with Piers and his ultimate transformation into Gloton gives a clear appraisal of Piers' attitude to labour and labour enforcement which she equates with that of the statutes. Her cogent arguments demonstrate the dangers inherent in Piers' invocation of Hunger who is 'a deadly killer'.[96] Yet, persuasive though her analysis is, she has omitted to credit Piers with an understanding that charity requires him to produce surplus so that the needy may be cared for. For these critics, Piers begins to look like an inconsistent representative of the poor person.

 I would not want to explain away such readings, for they emphasize that the scene on the half-acre grows from its contemporary ideology. In restoring this section of the poem to 'the movement of history' we encounter the very precariousness 'in occupying a time and place that shifts even at the instant of its own articulation' which Wallace identifies as part of the reading process.[97] Aers, in particular, has highlighted the fact that Langland's vision of traditionally organized

 Black Death', p. 171.
91 'Labour, leisure and economic thought before the nineteenth century', p. 64.
92 Kim, p. 88. And see also her more recent article, 'Hunger, nede', pp 151–7.
93 Hewett-Smith, 'Allegory on the half-acre', p. 12.
94 Hatcher quotes from writings of the 17th, 18th and 19th centuries which reiterate the same ideas, for example, Thomas Mun, 1664: 'Penury and want do make a people wise and industrious'; William Temple, 1770: 'Idling the whole day together ... never happen[s] when wheat and other necessaries are dear'; Thomas Pennant, 1772: 'until famine pinches they will not bestir themselves': 'Labour, leisure and economic thought', pp 76–80.
95 Kim, pp 86–8.
96 Ibid. pp 92–3.
97 Cf. Wallace, quoted in my Introduction, p. 18.

society cannot find solutions for the problems thrown up by demands of contemporary wage-labourers, whether they are clerical or lay. He rightly concludes that these problems of justice continue to haunt the poet as he revisits them.[98] Moreover, Piers has more than one function, even within these two passus, shifting from being a poor ploughman to exercising control over the people of all estates; the workers and the non-workers have varying motivations; the poor appear in many guises. Initially portrayed as a ploughman, Piers is pressed into the role of a leader (B.6.1–2). As such he experiences the conflicts that any leader experiences; a 'top-down' approach is inevitable, for by virtue of the role, the led, or the organized, impose upon the leader a distance born of their expectations. It takes more than one harvest, and more than words, for a leader like Piers to convince the led that his agenda is different from those of the wage-fixing employers. Yet Piers is precisely different in his efforts to distinguish the various demands of Hunger, the differing requirements of the people for subsistence and consumption, and the demands of justice and charity. Where Kim detects Hunger as shifting in his perspectives while Piers leads him through various sets of questions, I regard him as responding to *quaestiones*, and making a series of distinctions.

Langland sets his critique of idlers, expressed in language so like that of the statutes, in the context of charity. The wasters and the labourers have the same obligation as the wealthy to care for the needy, and their apparently selfish attitude to the taking of leisure is part of Langland's criticism. Piers is acutely conscious of the perils of not making the land yield sufficiently – the poorest will be the first to suffer; he hopes the brush with famine will alert the labourers to the same danger. He also knows about poverty and how hard the poor have to work in order to keep hunger at bay.[99] With his angry accusations and invocation to Hunger Piers imitates Christ's righteous anger (Matthew 21. 12–13).[100] It is amply clear that the effect of idleness is social as well as individual; without sufficient labour there will be insufficient food; Hunger will not need to be invoked, it will be inevitable, and the poetry links work directly with the good order and stability of society. As someone intimately involved in the production of food, Piers understands clearly the relationship of effort to result. In condemning able-bodied beggars as fake cripples (B.6.121–2) and phoney hermits (B.6.187–8; C.9.188–218), Langland stresses the injustice they perpetrate on the really helpless poor. Yet he uses the language of the Church decrees which call for the poor to be relieved as a matter of justice, leaving the matter of discrimination to God. What he asks is that all orders of society work, justly, so that each may able to support the other: 'Alter alterius onera portate.'

98 'Justice and wagelabor', pp 176–82.
99 This point is also made by Hewett-Smith, 'Allegory on the half-acre' (p. 11), and by R. Frank who points out that Langland had lived through a number of famines in his early life. 'The hungry gap: crop failure, and famine', pp 91–2.
100 J. Bowers, who equates the ploughing scene with the wandering of the Israelites in the desert, compares Piers' anger with that of Moses who smashed the tablets of the ten commandments on finding the Israelites singing, dancing and worshipping the golden calf: *The crisis of Will in 'Piers Plowman'*, p. 127.

When Piers has sought to discriminate who should receive alms, he is told by Hunger, the allegorical embodiment of every human being's basic need to consume, that God is to be the arbiter, and that it is his responsibility to assist all who are in need, without reference to their moral state:

> And alle manere men þat þow my3t aspie
> That nedy ben and nou3ty, [norisse] hem wiþ þi goodes.
> Loue hem and lakke hem no3t – lat God take þe vengeaunce;
> Thei3 þei doon yuele, lat þow God yworþe:
> *Michi vindictam et ego retribuam.* (B.6.222–5a)

Piers' concern is always for charity which is to be interpreted through *mesure* and justice. Any form of immoderation inevitably leads to injustice and must therefore be outlawed. Some of the non-workers on Piers' half-acre pretend to be blind and crippled, adopting the role and the words of traditionally legitimate beggars; unable to join in the work, they promise to pray for the workers in exchange for receiving alms:

> Ac we preie for yow, Piers, and for youre plow3 boþe,
> That God of his grace youre greyn multiplie,
> And yelde yow of youre almesse þat ye 3yue vs here. (B.6.125–7)

Piers applies the rules of discrimination; only the traditional categories of beggar – the old, the sick, the blind, the crippled, the prisoners, faithful anchorites and hermits, accredited mendicant friars – are eligible for alms. The others, able-bodied beggars, men who dress up as hermits and friars but have no religious commitment, vagabonds too idle or lecherous to work, should not receive the alms intended for the poor. Such fraudulent beggars are condemned more fully in Passus B.7 where, in addition to faking disability themselves, they are accused of maiming their children in order to make them eligible to beg.

In Passus B.7 Piers receives from Truth a document of Pardon – an indulgence – which makes explicit distinctions[101] as to who is eligible for salvation (B.7.1–104). Once more, as in Passus B.6, false beggars are condemned, and once more the donor is warned against making judgments. Excluded from the pardon are the able-bodied, idle poor whose begging deprives the helplessly needy of alms they would otherwise have received. Fundamental to this is the notion that there is only a limited amount of food and property available for distribution, and that the greed of one part of society, by definition, deprives others of their livelihood.[102] Langland cites Cato and Peter Comestor as supporting authorities (B.6.71–3).

---

101 The discussions by Allen, 'Langland's reading and writing', and Alford, 'The role of the quotations in *Piers Plowman*', have stimulated my thinking here.
102 Langland refers to this specifically in B.14.70–3.

To discriminate in almsgiving was not a new phenomenon in the fourteenth century. St Ambrose's ten principles were accepted as standard in the decretals and glossed frequently. Piers' problem of what to do with the ribald, idle and sinful had long ago been addressed by St Augustine who excluded from almsgiving those who were unjust, lest they should be encouraged in their sin.[103] Another dictum of Augustine seemed to endorse condemnation of able-bodied idlers:

> The Church ought not to provide for a man who is able to work, ... for strong men sure of their food without work, often do neglect justice.[104]

On the other hand, Langland quotes St Gregory – the reference is actually from Jerome – advocating no discrimination in giving. Langland endorses those powerless poor for whom begging is a necessity; elsewhere he calls them the image of the needy Christ who, in his poverty, is most powerful.[105] Here, he invokes the gospel in support of their beggary which is seen to be a transaction for which God undertakes to stand surety; the gift will grow with divine interest:

> For beggeres borwen eueremo, and hir borgh is God Almyȝty –
> To yelden hem þat yeueþ hem, and yet vsure moore:
> *Quare non dedisti pecuniam meam ad mensam, vt*
> *ego veniens cum vsuris exigissem vtique illam?* (B.7.80—1a, b)

Those who give to the poor table – the *mensa* which was one of the ways of donating food directly to the poor – are said to avoid the punishment of the unprofitable servant who hid his talent in a napkin. To give to the poor, even in such a minimal investment *ad mensam*, the table of the moneylenders in the parable, is a sure way of making restitution for sin. There is a distinct suggestion here that the recipient may be a sinful and fraudulent beggar, and that the donor may also be sinful, indulging in a usurious transaction. This makes Langland's point still more forceful: it is for God to be the judge of sin or merit, it is for man to practise charity, even if it appears to arise from an unworthy motive.[106] While at other points in the poem Langland condemns usury, here he recognizes that even a poor intention – giving for the sake of gaining a reward of interest from God – will be enough to indicate pity for the poor, the primary condition for forgiveness. *Handlyng synne* has a similar case of the rich usurer who wanted to throw a stone to get rid of a beggar; no stone was to hand, so,

---

103 He drew specific parallels with gladiators, fortunetellers, actors, prostitutes and other ribald entertainers who received money for that which was most sinful in them. This is the authority behind Langland's frequent strictures against bishops and lords who pay minstrels and jesters for sinfully entertaining them while they neglect the poor (B.9.90–2).
104 *Glossa ordinaria ad dist.* 82 *ante* c.1., in Tierney, p. 59 n. 39.
105 B.11.184–6; B.11.230–1.
106 See also the words of Repentance to Coveitise, when he recommends him to practise mercy by giving his ill-gotten gains to the bishop for charitable works (B.5.285–92).

instead, he threw a loaf of bread at him; that loaf appeared on the scales as his only good act, and outweighed the pile of evil acts he had done in his lifetime.[107]

In this important section of the poem, the one who begs is credited with some responsibility as an active moral subject, not just a passive case for the discrimination of the donor:

> For wite ye neuere who is worþi, ac God woot who haþ nede.
> In hym þat takeþ is þe trecherie, if any treson walke. (B.7.76–7)

Langland condemns the sinfulness of the wildly promiscuous beggars who deform their children (B.7.88–95), and exalts the helpless need of the old, weak and powerless; but his discussion recognizes that donors and recipients have reciprocal responsibilities: the donor to give and the recipient to be honest. With its careful distinctions of deserving and undeserving, supported by reference to the authorities of Scripture, the Fathers and the glossators, this section is constructed like a scholastic commentary which evaluates and distinguishes all aspects of the question.[108]

Not only does Langland employ *distinctiones* within the passus, he also makes clear distinctions between the episodes. Passus B.2, B.3 and B.4 deal with the dislocation of the social order by Meed and her money-loving wasters; Passus B.5, B.6 and B.7 show this dislocation caused further down the social scale by the sins of the lower orders of peasantry and the very poor. Langland shows the orderly society in which all estates work together for the mutual good of the whole community to be an ideal which is shattered, as ideals must be shattered, by the all too real apathy, greed and sloth of recognizably real and historically attested human beings. Like a series of *ad status* sermons preached to defined social groups,[109] the poetry successively dramatizes the sins of each element of society.

Another shattered ideal is Piers' hope of a straightforward pardon. It seems that, in spite of opposition from the non-workers, Piers had hoped that, following the great confession (B.5), if good order could be established in the context of all fulfilling their reciprocal duties (B.6), and the obligations of their station in life (B.7), then pardon for sin would be assured. When the pardon is opened, however, there is no hint of an organizational forgiveness of sin, but a reiteration of the gospel maxim that those who do good will be rewarded and those who do evil will be punished eternally. I deal more fully with this pardon below; in the present discussion I see this lack of a conventionally expressed pardon as another factor forcing Piers to continue his pilgrimage. Just as the

---

107 *Handlyng synne*, pp 140–2 (ll. 5571–674).
108 A similar inclusivity is endorsed by St Ambrose in his sermon *De Nabuthe*: 'You are not to ask what each man's deserts are. Mercy is not ordinarily held to consist in pronouncing judgment on another man's deserts, but in relieving his necessities; in giving aid to the poor, not in inquiring how good they are.' Translated and quoted by Lovejoy, p. 301.
109 Moisa (p. 168) draws attention to Owst's contention that preachers were not to stress the vices of one group before an audience consisting of other groups.

advent of Hunger seemed to restore the harmony of the working community but was only a temporary solution, so in this context Langland makes a deliberate statement about the inadequacy of institutional formulas.

The *Visio* has explored large issues of sin and repentance in relation to the fourteenth-century society of Langland. The labourer has been typified as the paradigm for the utopian society – honest, industrious and poor. Mendicancy has been allowed only for the élite – those who are incapacitated, Christ's poor, blind, halt and bedridden, and those who perform spiritual duties on behalf of others and earn their 'wages' of charity by virtue of being 'voluntarily' poor. Dishonest idlers and wasters are as guilty as any other group of sinners, yet, as the inspired 'lewed vicory' concludes, in B.19, they are equally worthy of salvation after repentance:

> Right so Piers þe Plowman peyneþ hym to tilye
> As wel for a wastour and wenches of þe stewes
> As for hymself and hise seruauntʒ, saue he is first yserued.
> [So blessed be Piers þe Plowman, þat peyneþ hym to tilye],
> And trauailleþ and tilieþ for a tretour also soore
> As for a trewe tidy man, alle tymes ylike.
> And worshiped be He þat wroʒte al, boþe good and wikke,
> And suffreþ þat synfulle be til som tyme þat þei repente. (B.19.438–5)

Langland insists that God's charity is applied to all, and that human beings should be no less discriminating in their practice of this virtue.

The issues of work, charity and of trust in God to provide, form a continuing thread of exploration in the poem. The fact that Piers, once he has read the terms of the pardon, decides to 'cessen of my sowyng' does not mean that his previous concerns for the provisioning of his people and his anxiety about false beggars have been cancelled. Those problems are examined in B.6 and B.7, and Langland returns to them in the revision of C.9, with a fuller definition drawn, perhaps, from his observation of contemporary labourers and mendicants. When, at the end of Passus B.7, Piers decides to leave the plough and cease being solicitous about his 'bely ioye' it is not to have greater leisure, like the wasters, but to spend time in making provision for soul as well as for body. Having stressed the crucial importance of working for the harvest which requires hard physical toil, Piers asserts the still greater necessity of concentrating on spiritual nourishment, with equal, though different labour:

> Of preieres and of penaunce my plouʒ shal ben herafter. (B.7.120)

The two passus under discussion develop elements of the provision of 'liflode' and distinguish them as both/and, not as either/or. This means that work is interpreted as positive and good, rather than a punishment, and Piers' insistence on the necessity of work relates directly to the appropriateness of time and place.

When it is time to do the sowing, that is what should be done. When the work has been done it is time for Piers' pilgrimage.

A RATIONALE FOR PASSUS B.6 AND B.7 GROUNDED IN SCRIPTURE

The social order that Piers espouses in which each person carries an assigned function is an established medieval model; the poem's analysis of how it works in practice is the poet's admission of its inadequacy as a model. Only when the social model is informed by the Christian ideal of love can it lead to any politically sound order and Langland reinforces this message by his use of scriptural authority. In concluding this chapter, I offer an analysis of both passus in the light of their scriptural quotations, adopting a methodology of reading *Piers Plowman* developed by John Alford and Judson Allen which follows what they consider to have been Langland's method of composition. Alford describes how Langland, in quoting from Scripture, relies on the reader's knowledge of the complete Biblical context from which that passage comes, together with its glosses such as can be found in medieval biblical concordances. Both he and Allen have explicated a variety of passages starting from consideration of the quotations and, in doing so, have produced some illuminating readings which underline the continuity in the poem's structure. My analysis differs slightly from theirs in that they have referred primarily to the concordances which must have been available to Langland whereas I have addressed the immediate scriptural context, searching Jerome's Vulgate translation of the Bible for the quotations of Passus B.6 and B.7. I have found that the technique throws into relief contextual material that develops consistent themes which I have already discussed in their historical context. The biblical quotations are the necessary foundation for understanding Langland's attitude to these issues. Making Scripture his starting point, Langland conducts a dialogue between the historical here and now of Piers' half-acre and issues concerning the provision of both material and spiritual food, harvest as a literal and an allegorical experience and suffering which leads to eternal vindication. His confident understanding and use of the texts leads him, through Piers, to reinterpret issues of his historical moment in the light of an underlying belief in charity. The repeated expression, 'alter alterius onera portate' (bear ye one another's burdens), is the scriptural theme that gives a rationale for care of the poor and needy as brothers (Galatians 6. 2).

Familiarity with Scripture is a fundamental quality of *Piers Plowman*. The poem is grounded in Scripture, and allusions are as significant as direct quotations, many of which are abbreviated, suggesting, as scholars have pointed out, that Langland was drawing upon material he expected to be entirely familiar to his audience. To simplify my reading of Passus B.6 and B.7, I will first list the relevant scriptural allusions and quotations in Passus B.6 before drawing conclusions for the interpretation of the poem from their context in the Vulgate.

The life of the poor, the necessity of work and the exercise of charity 97

i) 1–56, allusion: Piers' distribution of duties within society relates to Luke 3. 7–14, John the Baptist's preaching to all orders of society prior to the start of Christ's public ministry.

ii) 47a, quotation: '*Amice ascende superius*' derives from Luke's parable of the invited guests at a banquet, Luke 14. 12–14, and illustrates the significance of the lowly in God's scheme.

iii) 57–78, allusion: there is a verbal echo between Piers' approach to sowing his seedcorn and the words of Christ in John 4. 35–8, which refer to a spiritual harvest.

iv) 75, 76a, quotation: '*Deleantur de libro viuencium ... quia cum iustis non scribantur*', Psalm 68. 29, relates Piers in his leadership of the labourers to the Christ-figure foreshadowed in the full text of this psalm.

v) 105–70, allusion: Piers' trouble with the idlers relates to the parable of the labourers in the vineyard, Matthew 20. 1–16. The scriptural context of this parable, the imminent passion and death of Jesus, a debate as to seniority among his disciples, and an affirmation of the place of beggars in Jesus' order of priority, colours the contentious issues addressed by Piers at this point in the poem.

vi) 221a, quotation: '*Alter alterius onera portate*', Galatians 6. 2. Coming, as it does, towards the end of the account of Hunger's punitive attack on Piers' people, this quotation and its scriptural context emphasize the importance of charity in human relations, and the necessity of leaving judgment to God alone.

vii) 225a, quotation: '*Michi vindictam et ego retribuam*', Romans 12. 19, develops this theme.

viii) 227a, quotation: '*Facite vobis amicos de mammona iniquitatis*', Luke 16. 9, demonstrates, in relation to the parable of the Unjust Steward and its context in Luke 16, how God's justice is different from and more tolerant than man's. Piers learns, through these scriptural associations, that charity to the needy is the overriding principle of God's justice.

ix) 232, quotation: '*In sudore* and swynk þow shalt þi mete tilie' derives from Genesis 3. 19 and is the traditional justification for work as punishment for sin. It is closely linked with the next quotation, 235–6: '*Piger pro frigore* no feeld wolde tilie – /And þerfore he shal begge and bidde, and no man bete his hunger.' This is a rendering of Proverbs 20.4, used in the poem with proverbial force.

x) 237–45, allusion: this paraphrase of Matthew's parable of the talents, which in its scriptural context (Matthew 25. 1–46) directs the reader to contemplation of the Last Judgment, underlines the link between work and providing for the needy (pp 41–2).

xi) 250–1a, quotation: 'The freke þat fedeþ hymself wiþ his feiþful labour,/ He is blessed by þe Book in body and in soule./ *Labores manuum tuarum* ...', Psalm 127. 1–2. This quotation links work in the harvest with the blessing of food and with spiritual nourishment.

Passus B.6 plays out in dramatic form concepts which are further developed in the next passus. Contemporary problems of social order, labour, wages, poverty and famine are explored as part of the overall eschatological picture. Langland recognizes the status quo of an ordered society and the problems caused by those who are not willing to work. His explication of the Hunger allegory demonstrates concern for the social plight of his contemporaries and shows him attempting to work out a logic which will account for the problems, put them in place in the earthly as well as the supernatural scheme of things, and see them as contributing to salvation. Passus B.7 discusses who is to benefit from the pardon sent to Piers by Truth. This is a manifesto of Langland's social norms and expresses his attitude towards work, trade, law, begging, almsgiving, what is enough; what is need, who may beg; and who may not beg. Like the previous passus, this one examines all in the light of the Last Judgment which is intimated throughout the passus but plainly referred to in the two lines of the Pardon:

> *Et qui bona egerunt ibunt in vitam eternam;*
> *Qui vero mala, in ignem eternum.* (B.7.110 a, b)

For ease of discussion I divide Passus B.6 into three rough divisions: first the division of labour and Piers' preparation for his pilgrimage; second, the ploughing of the half-acre and the laziness of the wasters; and third, the Hunger episode. The biblical texts which the passus uses as commentary are themselves commented upon in terms of the historical and social contexts of the two passus. They connect in a dialogue on the themes of the Last Judgment: the reciprocal responsibilities all Christians have for one another, themes of tilling, sowing, reaping, harvest; and the overarching power of God who wields the vengeance and makes the judgments. The scriptural quotations make an array of distinctions upon which are superimposed the exemplified distinctions of the false, the hungry and the needy. The duty of charity overrides all others, and the importance of giving to the poor, even those who may be deceitful, is plainly stated.

The opening section (1–56) in which Piers gives each group work to do according to its estate makes a clear statement that care for the needy is integral to every person's work. It is reminiscent of John the Baptist in the wilderness, preaching to the people and telling them, in their discrete estates, that they must work according to their station – in preparation for the coming of the Messiah. In the context of Luke (3. 7–14) this was the prelude to the public life of Jesus; Piers adopts a similarly prophetic role in terms of the Second Coming, the Last Judgment, which is the context in which the two passus work out the contemporary social issues. The ladies have a relationship with the poor in the traditional context of the works of mercy on which they will be judged:

> The nedy and þe naked, nymeþ hede how þei liggeþ,
> And casteþ hem cloþes, for so comaundeþ Truþe. (B.6.15–16)

The knights have a duty to treat the poor, including their own bondsmen, with charity and justice; the puns are well chosen: 'tene no tenaunt,' 'þouȝ ye mowe amercy men, lat mercy be taxour', 'þouȝ pouere men profre yow presentes and ȝiftes' (38–41). For the knight to take gifts proffered by the poor is for him to earn purgatory (44), for in canon and civil law it was forbidden for anyone to take gifts from the poor in exchange for justice.[110]

The first quotation: '*Amice, ascende superius*' (47a) immediately goes to the heart of why the poor are to be cared for: they have an intrinsic value. It comes from a parable whose context is of eating bread and healing the sick (Luke 14). Jesus has entered the Pharisee's house 'manducare panem' (to eat bread), and appeals to the assembled guests to know if it is lawful to heal on the Sabbath or not. Piers has just mentioned law: right law whereby the knight should govern justly and not charge the poor. Jesus heals the dropsical man and proves by action, not by theory, that charity to the poor must come before law. Immediately Luke's gospel moves to Jesus' parable of the wedding feast at which the humble guest was invited to go up higher, while the proud guest was displaced from his high position. In basing his discussion of the knight's justice to his bondman and to the poor on this parable, Langland links the knight's justice with God's justice to be awarded at the wedding feast, another scriptural figure for the Second Coming. The chapter in Luke goes on to advise the listeners of their duty to give a banquet for the needy: 'sed cum facis convivium voca pauperes debiles claudos caecos' (Luke 14. 3), (but when you make a feast invite the poor, the sick, the crippled and the blind), raising them to their own level. This reflects back on Piers' words to the knight:

> Thouȝ he be þyn vnderlyng here, wel may happe in heuene
> That he worþ worþier set and wiþ moore blisse.   (B.6.46–7)

Further, in Luke there follows the parable about the wedding feast to which the invited guests did not come, and to which the irate lord then invited all the poor, sick and vagabonds from the highways and the byways:

> Tunc iratus pater familias dixit servo suo 'exi cito in plateas et vicos civitatis et pauperes ac debiles et caecos et claudos introduc huc'. Et ait servus 'domine factum est ut imperasti et adhuc locus est'; et ait dominus servo 'exi in vias et sepes et conpelle intrare ut impleatur domus mea'.
> (Luke 14. 21–3)

(Then the master of the house, being angry, said to his servant: Go out quickly into the streets and lanes of the city; and bring in hither the poor and the feeble and the blind and the lame. And the servant said: Lord, it is done as thou hast commanded; and yet there is room. And the lord said

---

110 Tierney, pp 12–15.

> unto the servant: Go out into the highways and hedges, and compel them to come in, that my house may be filled.)

In this situation, not only are the traditional poor raised to the level of the invited guests, but they supersede them, and are brought to the banquet. Significantly, this story of the banquet is the biblical source for the standard categories of the poor which are so frequently quoted by Langland, and which were conventionally referred to by Lollard preachers in their reformist sermons: the poor, the sick, the blind and the lame.[111] In view of Piers' later problems with vagabonds, it is useful to note that contextually, even vagabonds are forced into the banquet. The gospel connects ideas about status, law and feeding the needy; the parable foreshadows the Last Judgment, which is clearly in Piers' mind as he speaks of the hour of death:

> For in a charnel at chirche cherles ben yuel to knowe,
> Or a knyȝt from a knaue þere – knowe þis in þyn herte.   (B.6.48–9)

At this point in the passus, the poor are singled out as worthy of respect in their own right. Piers makes explicit their essential human dignity which makes them indistinguishable from the rich in death and potentially worthy of a higher place in heaven.

As Piers prepares to go on pilgrimage (57–78), he sets about sowing the seed-corn, in terms reminiscent of Christ's words about planting the seed of the heavenly harvest in John 4. This helps to establish the allegorical position of Piers as preparing himself and his fellow workers for Christ's judgment:

> And whoso helpeþ me to erie or sowen here er I wende,
> Shal haue leue, by Oure Lord, to lese here in heruest
> And make hym murie þermyd, maugree whoso bigrucche it. (B.6.65–7)

> et qui metit mercedem accipit et congregat fructum in vitam aeternam
> ut et qui seminat simul gaudeat et qui metit   (John 4. 36)

> (And he that reapeth receiveth wages and gathereth fruit unto life everlasting: that both he that soweth and he that reapeth may rejoice together.)

His mind is on thoughts of Judgment and he makes an array of distinctions as to who are the just and the unjust, placing himself in opposition to those practitioners of unjust occupations, the ribald, dice-playing, thieving deceivers that Augustine had condemned. Psalm 68, from which the next two quotations come, begins with the psalmist in deep and threatening waters and oppressed by many;

---

[111] They were also used as categories by polemicists such as FitzRalph who disputed whether the poor should be a separate category, and argued that Christ's word for poor was to be an adjective, thus eliminating the possibility of someone who was able-bodied being accepted as validly poor.

he is an alien to his brothers and a pilgrim, because the zeal of God's house has eaten him up:

> alienus factus sum fratribus meis et peregrinus filiis matris meae
> (Psalm 68. 9)
>
> (I am become a stranger to my brethren, and an alien to the sons of my mother.)

This pilgrim is mocked by idlers 'in the gate' and drunkards (Psalm 68. 13) who give him vinegar and gall to drink – a symbol of Christ's passion; he feels that their 'mensa' (banquet table) should be turned into a trap for them. The implication is that they are feasting while they revile and persecute the psalmist who calls forth God's vengeance to fall upon them in the shape of loss of food, blindness, lameness and loss of home:

> sit mensa eorum coram eis in laqueum et in retributiones ad corruendum; contenebrentur oculi eorum ne videant et dorsum eorum semper incurva; effunde super eos indignationem tuam et ira furoris tui conprehendat eos; fiat commoratio eorum deserta in tabernaculis eorum non sit qui habitet.
> (Psalm 68. 23–6)
>
> (Let their table become as a snare before them, and a recompense, and a stumbling-block. Let their eyes be darkened that they see not: and their back bend thou down always. Pour out thy indignation upon them: and let thy wrathful anger take hold of them. Let their habitation be made desolate: and let there be none to dwell in their tabernacles.)

These are the conventional problems of the poor, and the psalmist here presents them as punishment for persecuting God's follower. The pleas for them to be removed from the book of life are a result of their injury to God's beloved, who, immediately designates himself as 'pauper et dolens' (poor and sorrowful), (Psalm 68. 30). The psalm ends with an affirmation of God's salvation for the poor and the humble who are in chains:

> quoniam exaudivit pauperes Dominus et vinctos suos non dispexit.
> (Psalm 68. 34)
>
> (For the Lord hath heard the poor, and hath not despised his prisoners.)

The vehemence of this psalm is reflected in Piers' rejection of the ribald ones; and there is more than a hint that he sees himself as the righteous one, experiencing the suffering, derision and rejection of the poor Christ. It is as though Langland, in making his commentary on election and justification, chooses the scriptural passages, and then dramatizes them in terms of his contemporary society and his concerns about it. As Alford comments:

The quotations are the points *toward which* as well as from which the preacher is constantly working.[112]

In the next scene of the passus (B.6.105–70), Piers and his helpers set about ploughing and sowing, and Piers encounters a threat to the project from those who will not work. The choice of scriptural texts reminds us that God's ways of judging merit are not man's ways. Piers begins to labour in his field with echoes of the biblical parable, the labourers in the vineyard. In Matthew 20. 1–16, the lord of the harvest asks each time: 'Why stand ye here all the day idle?'

> et egressus circa horam tertiam vidit alios stantes in foro otiosos ... circa undecimam vero exiit et invenit alios stantes et dicit illis 'quid hic statis tota die otiosi?' (Matthew 20. 3, 6)

> (And going out about the third hour, he saw others standing in the market place idle ... But about the eleventh hour he went out and found others standing. And he saith to them: Why stand you here all the day idle?)

The gospel story is an image of election – 'many are called but few chosen' (cf. Matthew 20. 16) – and of the ordering of heavenly society: 'So shall the last be first and the first last' (Matthew 20. 16). In the gospel context, this parable is immediately followed by the journey to Jerusalem for the final time, and Jesus' premonitions of his death. It is at this point that the mother of the sons of Zebedee makes her request for rank for her two sons in the new kingdom. This whole passage is a reaffirmation of the heavenly order of things:

> non ita erit inter vos sed quicumque voluerit inter vos maior fieri sit vester minister et qui voluerit inter vos primus esse erit vester servus.
> (Matthew 20. 26–7)

> (It shall not be so among you: but whosoever will be the greater among you, let him be your minister. And he that will be first among you shall be your servant).

The sons ask for power, and Jesus offers to share his chalice with them: 'calicem quidem meum bibetis' (Matthew 20. 23); the next moment, in the gospel narrative, Jesus cures two blind men who are making a nuisance of themselves, and whom the disciples want to silence and ignore.

> Et ecce duo caeci sedentes secus viam audierunt quia Iesus transiret et clamaverunt dicentes, 'Domine miserere nostri Fili David'; turba autem increpabat eos ut tacerent at illi magis clamabant dicentes, 'Domine miserere nostri Fili David'. Et stetit Iesus et vocavit eos et ait, 'Quid vultis

---

112 Alford, 'The role of the quotations in *Piers Plowman*' (p. 86); emphasis in the original.

> ut faciam vobis?' Dicunt illi, "Domine ut aperiantur oculi nostri'; et confestim viderunt et secuti sunt eum. (Matthew 20. 30–3)
>
> (And behold two blind men sitting by the way side heard that Jesus passed by. And they cried out, saying: O Lord, thou son of David, have mercy on us. And the multitude rebuked them that they should hold their peace. But they cried out the more, saying: O Lord, thou son of David, have mercy on us. And Jesus stood and called them and said: What will ye that I do to you? They say to him: Lord, that our eyes be opened.)

At this point in the poem Piers is worried by the slothful and by the infirm, unable to distinguish between those who are truly incapable of work and those who simply want to sing 'trolly-lolly', relying on others to find food for them. Piers' wrath and pain are Langland's pain; they are in concordance, too, with the lack of understanding of Jesus' disciples. The disciples judged the clamorous beggars to be a nuisance and wanted to get rid of them; instead, Jesus healed them of their blindness. In his own context of hiring labour Piers encounters people whom he judges to be idlers and clamorous beggars. The gospel associations of labourers and beggars link, in context, with the work of Piers and raise doubts as to whether his beggars are to be punished as deceivers or not, since God operates on a different scale.

Langland makes the *distinctio* between the hard-working labourers who are busy about their rural tasks, the genuinely sick or imprisoned who will be given a eucharistic feast of wheaten bread and drink with Piers, and the deceitful beggars who are on their way to the devil. Their deception is to adopt both the form, actions and words of those genuine beggars who offer to pray for the work of the able-bodied, and who promise to pray to God for a blessing on the giver of alms (B.6.124–8). Piers' wrath is directed against the idleness of the slothful whose penalty will be to get no grain from the planting in which they did not take part. Yet, though some of the beggars live in lechery, deceit and sloth, God's longsuffering has not wrought vengeance on them. Piers, at this point, is more like the psalmist who wanted total vengeance, as described above; that is the law of justice:

> Ac Truþe shal teche yow his teme to dryue,
> Or ye shul eten barly breed and of þe broke drynke. (B.6.134–5)

But God's law is of love:

> In lecherie and losengerie ye lyuen, and in sleuþe,
> And al is þoruʒ suffraunce þat vengeaunce yow ne takeþ! (B.6.143–4)

Langland is here making a distinction between an Old and a New Testament approach: vengeance or forgiveness. This is a suggestion that links this passage with earlier discussions on giving to the poor, that God's generosity is to be the ultimate model for man's assessment of his fellows, regardless of how unrighteous they may appear.

In the final section of the passus, Piers' invocation of Hunger is used as an exemplum; the historically imagined event of famine is given tropological significance (B.6.171–329). Through all the twists and turns of Piers' dialogue with Hunger, the contextual force of the scriptural quotations stresses that charity must be shown to all whether they appear to be sinful or not, and that God alone is the judge of a person's moral state. Events that represent an actual experience of famine are transmuted in Piers' reading of them as a direct punishment for the wasters' sloth. The two are linked; lack of work in tilling the ground will bring dearth. Yet that, in itself, is insufficient to account for this natural disaster, so it is attributed to a force above nature that has intention – the intention of correcting sin. In terms of correcting the idlers' tendencies to sloth, the visitation of Hunger proves to be hugely, if temporarily, successful, but Piers' compassion extends to the moral welfare of his brethren, 'for God bouȝte vs alle' (207).

Piers expresses his concern for all the beggars, both genuine and fake, because they are his 'blody breþeren' (B.6.207), asking Hunger for a solution to the problems of 'beggeris and of bidderis' (B.6.203). Hunger makes the same *distinctio* that Piers had made earlier, advocating minimal rations for 'bolde beggeris and bigge þat mowe hir breed biswynke' (B.6.213), and generous almsgiving to those 'þat Fortune haþ apeired' (B.6.218). The full context of the quotation from Galatians (Galatians 6. 2), however, situates it within the discussion of God's ability to judge each one. 'Alter alterius onera portate' (Bear ye one another's burdens) is a summative quotation from a passage in which Paul is teaching about both spiritual and material mutual assistance. Christians ought to correct, with gentleness, those found guilty of some fault. Paul's text advises against the passing of judgment, but recommends the correction of faults. The spiritual collapse of the deceitful beggars has been Piers' concern. Unlike the statutes of labourers which deal with the immediate symptoms of idleness, errancy and dishonesty, Piers is committed to helping those on the half-acre to understand their moral obligations in charity. The verses that follow in Galatians consider both spiritual and material sustenance, once more drawing upon the imagery of sowing and harvest:

> Nolite errare Deus non inridetur. Quae enim seminaverit homo haec et metet quoniam qui seminat in carne sua de carne et metet corruptionem; qui autem seminat in spiritu de spiritu metet vitam aeternam. Bonum autem facientes non deficiamus tempore enim suo metemus non deficientes; ergo dum tempus habemus operemur bonum ad omnes maxime autem ad domesticos fidei. (Galatians 6. 7–10)

> (Be not deceived: God is not mocked. For what things a man shall sow, those also shall he reap. For he that soweth in his flesh of the flesh also shall reap corruption. But he that soweth in the spirit of the spirit shall reap life

The life of the poor, the necessity of work and the exercise of charity 105

everlasting. And in doing good, let us not fail. For in due time we shall reap, not failing. Therefore, whilst we have time, let us work good to all men, but especially to those who are of the household of the faith.)

Hunger's advice to Piers to tell the strong ones to go and work exonerates Piers from any wrong if he subsequently gives to the undeserving. The judgment is left to God. 'Theiȝ þei doon yuele, lat þow God yworþe' (225). Piers had earlier said that 'Truþe woot þe soþe' (130); and here in Galatians Paul says 'Deus non inridetur' (God is not mocked). In Galatians, the sowing and reaping refer to the practice of good works towards other people, and this must be considered in a reading of Piers' words and actions. Any generous works will reap an eternal reward and will become a spiritual harvest.

The context of the next quotation 'Michi vindictam et ego retribuam' (Romans 12. 19) reinforces the notion that each person must do good to all, even to those who are hostile, because God alone makes the judgments. Paul's quotation is from Deuteronomy and he links it with another from Proverbs 25:

> Sed si esurierit inimicus tuus ciba illum si sitit potum da illi; hoc enim faciens carbones ignis congeres super caput eius. Noli vinci a malo sed vince in bono malum. (Romans 12. 20–1)

> (But *if thy enemy be hungry, give him to eat; if he thirst, give him to drink. For, doing this, thou shalt heap coals of fire upon his head.* Be not overcome by evil: but overcome evil by good.)[113]

The preceding verses in Romans 12 expound the well-known figure of Christians forming one body:

> Ita multi unum corpus sumus in Christo singuli autem alter alterius membra. (Romans 12. 5)

> (So we, being many, are one body in Christ; and every one members one of another.)

The verbal echo of 'alter alterius' with Galatians 6. 2 links the sense of the two passages in Langland's scheme. It is followed by discussion of the individual gifts which each one must practise according to his station; this reflects on the start of the passus where Piers exhorts each person to work as befits his or her estate. There is a significant exhortation against idleness:

> Sollicitudine non pigri spiritu ferventes Domino servientes.
> (Romans 12. 11)

> (In carefulness not slothful. In spirit fervent. Serving the Lord.)

---

113 Italics in the original.

which, by association, reinforces Piers' calls for work. There are further recommendations on charity and hospitality, an exhortation to sincere love:

> Necessitatibus sanctorum communicantes hospitalitatem sectantes.
> (Romans 12. 13)
>
> (Communicating to the necessities of the saints. Pursuing hospitality.)

But the clear statement of charity (Romans 12. 20) gives a firm foundation to what Hunger is telling Piers to do about almsgiving. Romans prescribes that even enemies are to be given food and drink; Hunger has also specified that all the needy, even the ones who do evil, are to be helped:

> And alle manere men þat þow myȝt aspie
> That nedy ben and nouȝty, [norisse] hem wiþ þi goodes.
> Loue hem and lakke hem noȝt – lat God take þe vengeaunce;
> Theiȝ þei doon yuele, lat þow God yworþe:
> *Michi vindictam et ego retribuam.* (B.6.222–5a)

The full context of the quotation fits with Piers' compassion for his 'blody breþeren' and the necessity of leaving judgments to God. It is also closely linked with the provision of food and drink: the New Testament insists on giving food and drink even to one's enemy. In the context of famine, and before the powerful figure of Hunger, Piers is forced to reappraise all his preconceptions in the light of the *lex Christi*:

> [And] it are my blody breþeren, for God bouȝte vs alle.
> Truþe tauȝte me ones to louen hem ech one
> And to helpen hem of alle þyng, ay as hem nedeþ. (B.6.207–9)

No-one is to be excluded from Piers' charity; his words are inclusive: 'God bouȝte vs *alle*'; 'louen hem *ech one*'; 'helpen hem of *alle þyng*'; '*ay* as hem nedeþ'. In terms of the employer/employee relationship he is not limited by the statutes and their discrimination; he has put human needs into a far larger context than that of fourteenth-century work and wage relations.

In the process of dealing with the perplexing problem of what to do with undeserving beggars, Hunger quotes from the equally perplexing parable of the Unjust Steward (Luke 16. 1–9), reinforcing, as he does so, the legitimacy of giving to all without discrimination:

> *Facite vobis amicos de mammona iniquitatis.* (B.6.227a)
>
> (Make unto you friends of the mammon of iniquity.)

This is a parable in which prudence is commended in terms of the world's goods. The servant was a waster:

The life of the poor, the necessity of work and the exercise of charity 107

> Hic diffamatus est apud illum quasi dissipasset bona ipsius. (Luke 16. 1)
>
> (And the same was accused unto him, that he had wasted his goods.)

and he was a deceiver; but he was prudent in looking after the debtors – the powerless ones, who were in the power of his master. Even in the Gospel context a deceiving waster can be saved. The false and idle beggars whom Piers thinks he should condemn are, by association with the steward of the parable, accepted into the kingdom. As for Piers, the giver, all that matters is that he practises charity so that, in time of judgment, he will qualify for the kingdom:

> Et ego vobis dico facite vobis amicos de mamona iniquitatis ut cum defeceritis recipiant vos in aeterna tabernacula. (Luke 16:9)
>
> (And I say unto you: Make unto you friends of the mammon of iniquity: that when you shall fail, they may receive you into everlasting dwellings.)

Within a few verses of this parable, Luke recounts the story of Dives and Lazarus (16. 19–31) which was emblematic of the neglect of the poor and the reward or punishment related directly to endurance or rejection of poverty. The contextual emphasis on giving to all who are needy is overwhelming.

The last four scriptural quotations of Passus B.6 revert to Piers' anxious discussion on work. Hunger refers first to the origin of work as mankind's duty in the Genesis story, where work is Adam's punishment for sinning:

> *In sudore* and swynk þow shalt þi mete tilie,
> And laboure for þi liflode. (B.6.233–4)

The full quotation describes the consequences of sin: work followed by death:

> In sudore vultus tui vesceris pane donec revertaris in terram de qua sumptus es quia pulvis es et in pulverem reverteris. (Genesis 3. 19)
>
> (In the sweat of thy face shalt thou eat bread till thou return to the earth, out of which thou wast taken: for dust thou art, and into dust thou shalt return.)

Hunger uses this quotation with a double implication: tilling the ground will produce food. It is arduous, but it is the punishment for sin, measure for measure. By implication, the one who does not work for his bread remains in sin. Next, the macaronic quotation from Proverbs points out that the logical consequence of sloth at ploughing time is dearth at harvest time; lack of food leads directly to begging which will go unrelieved. The sin of sloth and begging are linked verbally here:

> Propter frigus piger arare noluit; mendicabit ergo aestate et non dabitur ei. (Proverbs 20. 4)
>
> (Because of the cold, the sluggard would not plough: he shall beg therefore in the summer, and it shall not be given him.)
>
> *Piger pro frigore* no feeld wolde tilie –
> And þerfore he shal begge and bidde, and no man bete his hunger.
> (B.6.235–6)

Hunger's synopsis of the parable of the talents reinforces another hard saying of the gospels:

> He þat haþ shal haue and helpe þere it nedeþ;
> And he þat noȝt haþ shal noȝt haue, and no man hym helpe,
> And þat he weneþ wel to haue, I wole it hym bireue. (B.6.244–5)

Because the servant 'wolde noȝt chaffare' (238) the master confiscates his talent and gives it to the one with ten. In its gospel context (Matthew 25. 14–29) this is one of the eschatological parables, following that of the ten virgins and immediately preceding the story of the Last Judgment where the judgment of each person depends on the practice, in life, of the corporal works of mercy. The servant in the parable is castigated for his slothfulness in not at least giving the money to the bankers – the usurers:

> Dominus eius dixit ei, 'serve male et piger'. (Matthew 25. 26).
>
> (And his lord answering said to him: Wicked and slothful servant.)

'Piger' applied to the servant concords with the 'piger' of the previous quotation and echoes, too, the exhortation in Romans 12, against slothfulness in the service of God. Hunger's choice of authority directs Piers to the necessity of work both as the rough and ready measure of survival and as part of each person's duty in the light of the Last Judgment, where providing for the needy is the ultimate criterion of salvation.[114]

The final quotation takes a positive view of work and portrays the blessings that accrue to the industrious man. 'Beati omnes' (Psalm 127. 1) states:

> The freke þat fedeþ hymself wiþ his feiþful labour,
> He is blessed by þe Book in body and in soule. (B.6.250–1)

---

[114] In the case of Luke, the parable follows the account of Zacchaeus who gave up his tax-collecting and fraud, and promised to give half of his goods to the poor: 'stans autem Zaccheus dixit ad Dominum "ecce dimidium bonorum meorum Domine do pauperibus et si quid aliquem defraudavi reddo quadruplum"' (Luke 19. 8). The following lines link with the quotation from Galatians 6. 7–10, in which each one has to reap what he sows. Teachers are to have a share in all that their disciples have to bestow.

The life of the poor, the necessity of work and the exercise of charity 109

This is one of the gradual psalms. Like all Jews going up to Jerusalem for the Passover, Jesus and his disciples would have sung these on their way, in preparation for their final Passover together, and his passion. Here, the ideal of a happy life is of a family where the father has toiled to win his food and his wife and children surround him like vines and olives:

> Laborem manuum tuarum cum comederis beatus tu et bene tibi erit.
> (Psalm 127. 2)
>
> (For thou shalt eat the labours of thy hands: blessed art thou, and it shall be well with thee.)

Happiness is equated with a sufficiency that is won by fruitful labour, and it is the sure path of ascent, the road to Jerusalem.

At this point in the debate, Hunger has outlined for Piers the necessity of work for survival. The case of those unable to work is not under discussion, and the scriptural texts demonstrate a similarly single-minded approach. The scriptural quotations and Hunger's application of them are a description of what is the case when people refuse to work rather than a prophecy of punishment for moral failings. They provide *distinctiones* to balance those used in the earlier analysis of charity. Indeed, the whole passus proceeds by means of distinctions: those derived from Scripture and those played out by the false, the idle, the hungry and the needy poor of Piers' half-acre. Piers acts as the husbandman who employs the labourers and feeds them as part of their hire. The terms in which he speaks of feeding them are harsh, but the fact is likely that the food was the same for the strong as for the weak beggars in time of famine, and Piers is the distributor of that which he has available – peasepudding and bran and beans.

The essence of Langland's reforming satire is to attack falsehood in all its forms, here in the social form of the undeserving beggar. This had always been a category – in Roman law an able-bodied beggar who took the dole could be enslaved, and the church, as study of the Decretals shows, had always recognized it. Piers appears to make distinctions between beggars, yet learns, in the course of the passus, that he is not in a position to determine who is deserving or not, while Hunger stresses that all beggars, like all doctors, lawyers and knights, are answerable to God individually. The onus is on the receiver. It is clear, then, that the distinctions are made only from externals, and that God is the judge. The important thread through all the scriptural quotations is that of charity, solidarity and openness to God's distinguishing judgment. This takes the poetry far beyond the limiting social view of Piers as an enforcer of contemporary feudal law.

Passus B.7 is, in many respects, a doublet of Passus B.6; the one allegorizes the Christian's life as employment in the ploughing of Piers' half acre; the other considers who is to be saved in the light of the Last Judgment, which was itself traditionally and scripturally allegorized as the harvest. The similarity of theme is established in the first few verses. Where, in Passus B.6, those who helped Piers to plough were promised rights of gleaning at harvest (B.6.66) (judgment-time), in B.7 they are promised pardon with Piers Plowman (B.7.8). Where B.6 opens with a list of different members of society and an outline of the work that is their duty, B.7 starts with a parallel list of people who are to be pardoned if they have lived out their calling in life according to the rules of their estate. There is a complex interrelationship in these two passus, in both of which images of feeding, harvest, and judgment come together to form a tapestry of meanings. The biblical quotations concord on the word 'bread'; the poet is concerned with both earthly and heavenly food, and those who are to be fed encompass the whole of society. Images of food have already been distinguished in Passus B.6: bran and beans are opposed to wheat bread. In B.6 Piers would have given the coarse bread to the 'faitours' (B.6.135) and reserved the wheat bread for those he considered to be genuinely needy (B.6.137), giving them of his own 'catel' (B.6.220) on the recommendation of Hunger. In B.7 he is personally prepared to surrender the wheaten bread in exchange for the food of prayer and penance:

> 'I shal cessen of my sowyng,' quod Piers, 'and swynke noȝt so harde,
> Ne aboute my bely ioye so bisy be na moore;
> Of preieres and of penaunce my plouȝ shal ben herafter,
> And wepen whan I sholde slepe, þouȝ whete breed me faille.'
> (B.7.118–21)

Images of judgment set out an array of those eligible for salvation and conditions of salvation for the unlikely: merchants, lawyers and cheating beggars. The poetry works through the difficult cases of contemporary society. There are good and bad merchants who must give to the poor in order to be forgiven the sins that are endemic to their calling. There are lawyers who, to be saved, must serve the poor without charging them legal fees.[115] True and false beggars are defined. Finally the poetry arrives at the terms of the pardon itself. This, when it is opened, turns out to be not an indulgence that will guarantee forgiveness at the hour of personal judgment at death, but another *distinctio*: a statement from the Athanasian Creed that sums up the Last Judgment itself:

> *Et qui bona egerunt ibunt in vitam eternam;*
> *Qui vero mala, in ignem eternum.* (B.7.110 a, b)

When a priest in the crowd offers to read the Latin for the ploughman and construe it in English, his amazement at the brevity of the document, and the fact that it is not a conventional indulgence, but a declaration of the essential good work needed for salvation, becomes the catalyst for Piers to tear the pardon 'atweyne'. This reaction of Piers has been wittily, and I think convincingly, explicated by David Lawton as an action which tears the pardon horizontally, separating the two lines in an action which foreshadows the Last Judgment:

---

115 Tierney, p. 13.

it divides those who do well from those who do ill, the right hand from the left, the sheep from the goats. It forcefully forecasts the Last Judgment by stressing the terrible finality of its criteria.[116]

In support of this interpretation I offer further observations. This quotation echoes Matthew 25 and John 5. In the context of Matthew 25, the parable of the sheep and the goats, the two lines declare that judgment will be made on how well or badly a person has treated the hungry, thirsty, homeless, sick and imprisoned; in other words, care of the poor and needy is the criterion of salvation. The second context, John 5, recounts how Jesus heals a cripple and tells him to sin no more. In the ensuing debate with the Jews Jesus reaffirms that, as the Son, he will preside on Judgment Day when those who have performed good deeds will be saved, and those who have done evil will be damned:

> Et procedent qui bona fecerunt in resurrectionem vitae; qui vero mala
> egerunt in resurrectionem iudicii. (John 5. 29)

> (And they that have done good things shall come forth unto the resurrection of life: but they that have done evil, unto the resurrection of judgment).

In telling the healed cripple to sin no more Jesus equates physical healing with forgiveness of sin. Similarly, Langland implies that the crippled beggars are sinful, just as, a few lines earlier, he has outlined the sins of lawyers and merchants. Like the cripple at the pool of Bethesda, Langland's cripples must take moral responsibility for their lives, recognizing what is sin for themselves according to their own state. When Langland quotes the scriptural reference to the Last Judgment, by contextual association the poor are suddenly thrust into the forefront of the pardon, and given full moral responsibility for their behaviour. All this is in the light of his reiterated conviction that other people must attend to their duty of poor relief, and leave the moral assessment of sinful beggars to God:

> For wite ye neuere who is worþi, ac God woot who haþ nede.
> In hym þat takeþ is þe trecherie, if any treson walke;
> For he þat yeueþ, yeldeþ, and yarkeþ hym to reste. (B.7.76–8)

In this respect, while it is true that Langland represents lazy beggars and vagrants in the same terms used by the statutes which condemn the able-bodied poor as idle and culpable, he never loses sight of society's responsibility of charity towards all poor, and rejects any facile dismissal of their needs on the grounds that they may be undeserving.

The final parallel to be drawn between the two passus surrounds the response of Piers to intimations of the Last Judgment which the terms of the Pardon have

---

116 D.A. Lawton, 'On tearing–and not tearing–the pardon', p. 420.

introduced into the immediate present. In Passus B.6 he has already made his last will and testament in preparation for going on pilgrimage, a practice often undertaken as a final penitential act by medieval people setting their moral affairs in order in contemplation of death which might occur on a pilgrimage, or on a sea-voyage.[117] The Pardon's quotation from the Athanasian Creed contrasts the ultimate 'bona', salvation, with 'mala', damnation; in a quotation from Psalm 22, '*si ambulavero in medio vmbre mortis /Non timebo mala, quoniam tu mecum es*' (B.7.116–17), Piers avers that he fears no 'mala' because the Lord is with him. The full psalm evokes the context of the eschatological banquet, the messianic dream of the Jews, Christian heavenly bliss. The Lord prepares the spiritual food of the banquet, anoints the head with oil and the psalmist's cup, the 'calix' prepared by the Lord, is overflowing. In the immediate quotation, the Lord leads him through narrow pathways and through the shadow of death. In Passus B.6, an underlying gospel passage from Matthew 20 refers to the 'calix' that Jesus must drink and his disciples, too, if they are to experience their passion, trial and identification with Christ (Matthew 20. 22–3). If we read B.7 in tandem with B.6, as I think we must, then Piers, on pilgrimage through the valley of the shadow of death, drinking from the chalice offered to him by God, accepting a life of poverty, is joining Christ on the road to Calvary. He is prepared to fast without wheat bread, that bread which earlier he had promised to the genuine poor; like the prophets and the psalmist, his tears have become his bread; he chooses to live a life of sorrow and penance.

From a practical concern with providing food for the needy, Piers now moves to the practice of another form of poverty, conscious dedication to a life in which he plans to follow the Gospel injunction to 'be not solicitous' (B.7.127). This does not negate the practical requirement of all to work in order to stave off hunger; rather, it upholds the moral value of the choice made by those who concentrate on following Christ and who give up attachment to material goods, contrasting starkly with the hypocrisy of those who wear hermits' and friars' clothes as a cover for parasitical sloth. In its context immediately following the highly charged psalms, the quotation 'Ne soliciti sitis' suggests that relying on God to provide does not remove the suffering of walking through narrow paths, under the shadows, drinking the tears of penitence, but it guarantees God's protection to the poor as part of their condition.

When we look at 'be not solicitous' in its gospel context (Luke 12. 22), we find that Luke places it immediately after the story of the rich man who had gathered in his harvest and was then called, unprepared, to judgment (Luke 12. 21). It is followed by the injunction to sell what you have and give alms, in this acquiring 'bags which grow not old, a treasure in heaven which faileth not' (Luke 12. 33). In Matthew it is preceded by this section. Both contexts establish poverty as a medium of exchange which will purchase heaven, for, as James Simpson has clearly argued, the good life must be observed before the hour of death:

---

117 P. Heath, 'Urban piety in the later middle ages', pp 209–13.

> The words of this document are of no use to the sinner looking for forgiveness; instead, as words with any practical force, they are of use only if they *precede* the act of sin. If they are read after the act of mortal sin , they do not absolve the sinner from that sin or pardon him from the penance pertaining to it – on the contrary, they simply insist on the inevitability of punishment.[118]

Langland outlines a scenario in which Piers progresses from an anxious assessment of his contemporary society in terms of labour and sufficiency to an acceptance of the insufficiency of purely temporal food. Piers' decision to 'cessen of my sowyng' (118) comes in contemplation of the Last Judgment, and we must regard it as the positive embracing of the next stage in his pursuit of perfection rather than the rejection of the active life that has gone before. Coming as it does at the close of two passus which deal with the situation of the involuntarily poor, as well as those who choose a life of poverty, it marks the importance of the poor person who must not be ignored and whose poverty is a qualification for salvation. The harsh life of the poor is, by the end of Passus B.7, embraced by Piers with no illusions as to its severity. In B.6 the full impact of famine and the hardships endured by all beggars has been set within the context of a political and economic order that is clearly not coping with problems of labour, mobility and want. By identifying himself with the poor in this way, Piers gives them both a voice and an authority that their social condition would seem to belie.

Where Passus B.6 ends with the triumph of the demon-god, Hunger, and the anarchy of the wasters, Passus B.7 ends with a grasp of the need for attention to the spiritual, in imitation of Joseph who was a holy dreamer, as well as being a legendary provider of food in famine, (B.7.160–7).[119] Nabuchodonosor, rejecting the warnings of the prophet Daniel, reverted to eating the grass of the fields,[120] food fit for horses, only able to concentrate on his 'bely ioye' (305–7). The pardon of Piers is directly associated with the Last Judgment, and contrasts with the inadequacy of pardons purchased by earthly wealth. The sterility of earthly wealth in terms of the kingdom of heaven has been stated early on, and is now reiterated at the end of the *Visio*. The close of Passus B.7 (180–95) insists that no amount of money can purchase forgiveness in the light of the Last Judgment which will be conducted on the basis of what works people have done on a day-to-day basis:

> How þow laddest þi lif here and hise lawes keptest,
> And how þow didest day by day þe doom wole reherce.   (B.7.190–1)

'Works', as the two passus have demonstrated, are twofold; each person must be individually responsible for undertaking the tasks particular to his or her sta-

---
118 Simpson, *Piers Plowman: an introduction*, pp 73–4.
119 Genesis 41–5.
120 Daniel 5. 30.

tion and, in addition to this, relieve the needy. These appear in many guises: obvious, as in the traditional forms of poor, sick, blind and lame; hidden, like the poor described in C.9, who live permanently on the verge of destitution; and apparently undeserving, like the beggars who seem to be strong enough to work. While he satirizes characteristic vices in conventional terms, Langland is passionately concerned about salvation for the particular poor person. His acceptance of beggary in the poem and strong perception of the harmful condition of poverty reveal his clear understanding of the hardships all the poor endure, whether the indignity of being hounded and scorned (B.10.58–65), the discomfort of being homeless, the distress of being too ashamed to beg from a neighbour, or the misery of working day and night with hungry, crying children to support (C.9.70–95). In stressing these hardships of poverty, Langland insists that poverty, whether patiently borne, voluntarily chosen or endured as inevitable, has, in itself, the power to save. Characters in the poem like Haukyn and the idle, sinful vagrants, demonstrate that poverty can lead people into all the sins, yet they may be saved, in spite of themselves, because they wear Christ's livery:

> And þouȝ Sleuþe suwe Pouerte, and serue noȝt God to paie,
> Meschief is his maister, and makeþ hym to þynke
> That God is his grettest help and no gome ellis,
> And is seruaunt, as he seiþ, and of his sute boþe.   (B.14.254–7)

This is the case whether they consider themselves God's servants or not, because they are wearing the badge of poverty:

> And wher he be or be noȝt, he bereþ þe signe of pouerte,
> And in þat secte Oure Saueour saued al mankynde.   (B.14.258–9)

Christ will be a 'good lord' to the poor marked out as his own, beyond human society's estimation of their deserts. Though Langland adopts the language of statute, church law and Scripture, and writes within the conventions of estates literature, allegory and sermon, he constantly explores the issues thrown up by his historical moment. His method is always to make distinctions; these do not resolve the problem of poverty, but they make it a central concern for the person who recognizes charity as the overriding principle of salvation. The next chapter will elaborate further the role of the non-poor in creating a society of justice and love.

CHAPTER 3

'Marchaunt3 in þe margyne': how can the non-poor be saved?

> The marchaunt is no more to mene but men þat ben ryche
> Aren alle acountable to Crist and to þe Kyng of Heuene,
> That holde mote þe hey way, euene the Ten Hestes,
> Bothe louye and lene lele and vnlele,
> And haue reuthe and releue with his rychesse by his power
> All maner men yn meschief yfalle...
> *Alter alterius onera portate.* (C.13.65–70, 77a)

These words of Rechelesnesse express succinctly the poem's response, in its contemporary context, to the much quoted Gospel passage of Matthew 19, the teaching that underpins the medieval view of the spiritual value of poverty:

> si vis perfectus esse vade vende quae habes et da pauperibus et habebis thesaurum in caelo et veni sequere me (Matthew 19. 21)

> (If thou wilt be perfect, go sell what thou hast and give to the poor and thou shalt have treasure in heaven. And come follow me.)

Less frequently quoted in modern commentaries on medieval attitudes to wealth and poverty is the continuation of this gospel story. The rich young man could not bring himself to abandon his goods and turned away in sorrow from the Saviour who then likened the difficulty of the rich in attaining heaven to the problems experienced by a camel in going through that narrowest of Jerusalem gates, nicknamed the eye of the needle. The disciples, astonished that riches could be so pernicious, asked the obvious question: 'Who then can be saved?' and received the classic answer:

> Apud homines hoc inpossibile est: apud Deum autem omnia possibilia sunt. (Matthew 19. 26)

> (With men this is impossible: but with God all things are possible.)

Where the previous chapter focused on the essential production of food and the moral requirement that all should work in order to provide enough for the poor, this chapter will concentrate on *Piers Plowman's* insistence that the goods of the earth must be shared. The poem works through two issues, worldly and spiritual. From a spiritual standpoint, it faces the dilemma of how to reconcile a life of worldly affairs with Christ's injunction to sell all and give to the poor. Haukyn is the character who, more than any other, experiences this dilemma, particularly because he is so thoroughly materialistic. He demonstrates, too, the second issue which I have classed as worldly, that the rich have more than they need, often gaining it by sinful means, while the poor are in want, frequently because of direct exploitation by the rich. The moral implications of this make it immediately obvious that both worldly and spiritual issues are interwoven. I argue that the poem grounds its ideas on principles of justice and charity and that its recommendations of charity to the poor show up the inadequacies of contemporary medieval poor relief. The poem takes a realistic view that the wealthy can be saved provided they associate themselves with the poor. This must be done by seeking out the genuinely needy and using material goods to relieve their suffering. The danger to be avoided is a formulaic manner of charitable giving which donates to already wealthy religious orders instead of to the indigent (B.15.331–40). More subtly, the rich can associate with the poor by taking care to treat them with justice. Otherwise they run the risk of a double sin in extorting money from the needy which they then give in alms to those religious who are not poor (B.15.309–12). The final way in which poverty can redeem the rich is for them to put the love of God before love of material things. This, as Patience expresses to Will and Haukyn, demands a readiness to relinquish worldly goods, thus abandoning solicitude. This last condition is the one that allows them to possess and enjoy their goods while being, like Job, ready to lose all with patience for the love of God (C.13.14–19).

To follow the nuances of the poem's arguments about the spiritual difficulties of the rich this chapter first examines the poem's prescriptions on poor relief in the light of two aspects of medieval thinking: views on the moral problems faced by merchants and practical approaches to the relief of the poor. Next, an appraisal of Haukyn in his context as a merchant/provider shows how the poem focuses through this character on the conflicts between doctrine and practice, ideal and reality. As representative of those who spend their lives in the pursuit of this world's goods, Haukyn experiences huge problems in accepting the philosophy of *ne soliciti sitis*.[1] I examine how the poetry sets him in parallel with Piers as it explores the difficulties and the consequences of putting this gospel counsel into practice. The wealthy are in a unique predicament which *Piers Plowman* recognizes and explores in the light of the widely held medieval belief that the poor exist in order that the rich may have the opportunity to redeem their sins. The poem engages with this approach and confronts, head-on, the notion it implies: that the poor have no value in themselves. A 'poor reading' of the poem leads to the conviction that the poor not

---

1 Matthew 6. 25–34; *Piers Plowman* B.14.34–6; 319–32.

only have a value by virtue of their condition, but that they are the paradigm of true Christian life:

> Forþi be noȝt abasshed to bide and to be nedy,
> Siþ he þat wroȝte al þe world was wilfulliche nedy,
> Ne neuere noon so nedy ne pouerer deide. (B.20.48–50)

This chapter develops such a reading of Patience's discourse on the poor and the rich (B.14.99–201), arguing that Langland's poor achieve salvation simply by virtue of being poor, whereas his rich must identify themselves with the poor by recognizing their need and sharing their goods with them in the practice of charity. Langland knows, as does Jesus in the Gospel incident, that the rich can be saved, although with difficulty; his poetry wrestles with the question of how this salvation can come about, concluding that only by lightening the burdens of the poor can the rich settle their account with God. Finally, the chapter demonstrates the poem's original insights into the seldom-asked question of how the involuntarily poor, who have nothing to give up in order to follow Christ, can themselves earn salvation.

THE DILEMMA OF MERCHANTS

Langland's portrayal of the problems faced by the non-poor in attaining salvation shows him to be as alert to ethical dilemmas faced by the wealthy as he is to those of rural labour relations. The paradox underlying the gospel quotations on riches is fundamental to an understanding of why poverty, socially so undesirable, should have assumed such conceptual importance in the fourteenth-century scale of values. To reconcile counsel with practice, evangelical poverty with day-to-day life in the world of affairs, is a difficulty that seems intractable in the context of conflicting late medieval attitudes. At one extreme people give up property to live a life of voluntary poverty and, at the other, they cultivate a life of conspicuous consumption as if it were a virtue.[2] Between these poles lie many gradations within a society which shares the conviction that salvation is the ultimate goal of humankind and that Christ's counsel of poverty is the straight road that leads to salvation.

The history of the development of commerce and exchange demonstrates the importance of medieval merchants. On their shoulders rested the prosperity of gentry and aristocratic primary producers, and peasant agricultural and industrial workers (some of whom were part-time merchants themselves). On them, too, depended the conspicuous consumption of gentry and nobility which was a mark of social worth.[3] Scholastic theologians recognized society's need for

---

2 For a discriminating approach to the critique of consumption in *Piers Plowman*, see Kim, pp 97–169.
3 Masschaele, *Peasants, merchants and markets*, gives a thoroughgoing analysis of the medieval merchant.

merchants to stimulate trade and satisfy the requirements of its citizens. Aquinas describes man as a social animal who needs his fellows to supply those aspects in which he is deficient. This, he says, underlies the social order that recognizes people as endowed with different aptitudes for work or office,[4] an idea that *Piers Plowman* sets out on a number of occasions when discussing the mystery of why there are rich and poor (B.11.196–7; B.14.166–7; C.16.19–21). Yet in official church teaching developed by the scholastic doctors of the middle ages, trade is regarded with distrust because, though not wicked in itself, it can be the occasion of sin.[5] A canon of the *Decretum*, falsely attributed to St John Chrysostom,[6] but influential, nonetheless, states that 'qui emit et vendit sine mendacio et perjurio esse non potest' (one who buys and sells cannot be free from lying and perjury).[7] All the more interesting, therefore, is the positioning given to merchants by Langland. In the preamble to Piers' pardon, merchants are annotated in the margins:

> Marchaunt3 in þe margyne hadde manye yeres,
> Ac noon *a pena et a culpa* þe Pope nolde hem graunte.   (B.7.18–19)

Some of the sins the poem attributes to merchants are conventionally associated with them. San Bernardino urged merchants to be 'punctual in the discharge of their religious duties, refrain from trading on Sundays and holy days, and confess their sins at least once a year to a devout and God-fearing priest'.[8] The perennial danger to truth and justice in merchants' transactions has already been noted from the *Decretum*. Langland comments on their sins:

> For þei holde no3t hir haliday as Holy Chirche techeþ,
> And for þei swere 'by hir soule' and 'so God moste hem helpe'
> Ayein clene conscience, hir catel to selle.   (B.7.20–3)

It becomes clear that, while Langland shares the traditional view of merchants, he does not reject the possibility that they can be saved. The poem does not condemn the practice of making profit, but, like the scholastic doctors who recognize the constant danger of sin for the merchant, offers methods of practising charity that are directly related to merchants' trade. For those who were unable to avoid the practice of usury, restitution was to be made to the family of the

---

[4] Several works of Aquinas state this idea, as quoted by de Roover, 'The scholastic attitude toward trade and entrepreneurship', p. 337 n.8.

[5] 'Qualitas lucri negotiantem aut excusat, aut arguit, quia est honestus quaestus, et turpis ... difficile est inter ementis vendentisque commercium non intervenire peccatum.' *Decretum*, II Pars. dist. V. *de poenitentia*, c. 2. *PL* 187, col. 1635

[6] The real author is probably a heretical writer of the fifth or sixth century, as de Roover points out (p. 336 n.4).

[7] *Decretum*, canon *Ejiciens Dominus*, dist. LXXXVIII, c. 11, *PL* 187, col. 0419.

[8] de Roover, 'The scholastic attitude toward trade', p. 344.

'Marchaunt3 in þe margyne': how can the non-poor be saved

person from whom illicit interest had been taken, or to the poor.[9] This is implied in the poem's suggestions as to how merchants should justify their habitual getting and spending:

> Ac vnder his secret seel Truþe sente hem a lettre,
> [And bad hem] buggen boldely what hem best liked
> And siþenes selle it ayein and saue þe wynnynges,
> And amende mesondieux þerwiþ and myseisé folk helpe.   (B.7.23–6)

We must read the poem's debates on wealth in the context of ideas about justice. Early in the poem, Holy Church establishes the concept which is at the root of the contemporary controversy about *dominium*,[10] that goods originate from God and that people are stewards of that which they have been lent by God. Concerning this principle, St Ambrose writes:

> [The Stoic philosophers] considered it consonant with justice that one should treat common, that is, public property as public, and private as private. But this is not even in accord with nature, for nature has poured forth all things for all men for common use. God has ordered all things to be produced, so that there should be food in common to all, and that the earth should be a common possession for all. Nature, therefore, has produced a common right for all, but greed has made it a right for a few.[11]

While this is not an original concept in *Piers Plowman*, Langland develops it with considerable force. Neither rich nor poor have a right to goods; they are lent by God, and all have an obligation to use them with charity and justice. 'Loue hem and lene hem' (B.6.221) is a phrase reiterated by many speakers in the poem who contrast generous giving with the customary self-interest of worldly practice. Dame Study praises theology because, in contrast with the teaching of secular sciences, it expounds charity and advocates practising it even towards those such as enemies from whom no benefit may be derived:

> He kenneþ vs þe contrarie ayein Catons wordes,
> For he biddeþ vs be as breþeren, and bidde for oure enemys,
> And louen hem þat lyen on vs, and lene hem whan hem nedeþ,
> And do good ayein yuel – God hymself it hoteþ.   (B.10.198–201)

In B.15 Anima speaks passionately about the need for justice, and particularly about the injustice that occurs when the wealthy give alms to already rich religious orders from money they have obtained by extortion from the needy:

---

9 *S. T.* II–II q. 78, a. 3; see also Jacques le Goff, *Your money or your life*, pp 43–5.
10 See Little, p.176.
11 St Ambrose, bishop of Milan, *Three books on the duties of the clergy*, Book 1, Chapter 30, §132 (online).

> And þanne wolde lordes and ladies be looþ to agulte,
> And to taken of hir tenaunt3 moore þan trouþe wolde,
> Founde þei þat freres wolde forsake hir almesse
> And bidden hem bere it þere it [haþ ben] yborwed. (B.15.309–12)

The poem moves beyond a conventional critique of mercantile ethics to express the overriding principle of charity as it applies to those involved in the material business of profit. Strictly speaking, merchants do not qualify for the full pardon *a pena et a culpa*, a term that refers to a plenary indulgence which gives full remission of the sin and guilt which remains after the sin has been forgiven. The merchants' forgiveness is qualified; they are given an indulgence which has a temporal limit, and a marginal note suggests they may be pardoned on some conditions. Their expression of charity has to be as material as their mercantile activities: good works to help the needy. Merchants are not the only rich people portrayed in *Piers Plowman*, but their positioning in the margins of the pardon provides a useful sidelight on the rich in general.

By contrast, Langland moves the poor to the centre of his argument, confirming that their heavenly reward is guaranteed by virtue of their poverty. The poetry considers the construct of the poor as *impotens* and the rich as *potens* and reverses it, pointing out that the poor have value precisely because they are poor. They go easily to heaven, overtaking the rich who walk gingerly, encumbered by their wealth (B.14.211–21):

> Ther þe poore preesseþ bifore, wiþ a pak at his rugge …
> Batauntliche, as beggeris doon, and boldeliche he craueþ,
> For his pouerte and his pacience, a perpetuel blisse. (B.14.213–15)

While recognizing the suffering and powerlessness of the poor in economic and social matters the poetry brings out clearly their considerable power in terms of gaining the kingdom of heaven. This power is theirs by association with their lord whose livery, 'sute', they wear. Poverty is that livery. The response of Patience to Haukyn, the merchant, sets out the ideal of poverty as a condition which counteracts all the deadly sins; Rechelesnesse, in the C-text (C.13.32–77), allegorizes the merchant as subject to danger and violence, in contrast to the simple messenger who runs lightly, unencumbered by property. Close reading of Patience's disquisition on the poor and the rich shows that he makes poverty an attractive ideal for the non-poor person. Patience stresses the duty of the rich to give to the poor both in restitution for their sins and to impose upon themselves some material suffering to compensate for their life of ease which militates against the life of the spirit.

LATE MEDIEVAL FORMS OF POOR RELIEF

For Langland, relief of the poor is a *sine qua non*; failure to pass on God's gifts to the needy negates the spiritual effects of prayer (B.1.179–84; B.7.180–95). This is a social as well as a spiritual concern. For him, as for his contemporaries, there is no opposition between the divine order and the human one; his belief that the poor will be rewarded with treasure in heaven is a statement about social justice. People who fail in social justice on earth by neglecting the poor and needy will fail to qualify for eternal salvation. Langland is explicit in placing the needy and indigent in the forefront of his exhortations to charity. In this, if we are to follow the conclusions of modern commentators on medieval charitable practices, Langland was unusually uncompromising. For many medieval people, the act of giving was more important than the effect of the gift on the recipient:

> The act of giving the gift – be it money, goods, or land – formed the essence of the charitable activity, the social exchange. The act of giving was what impressed the medieval donor. The medieval mind (and social conscience) made no distinction between an eventual sacerdotal and a social end of charity.[12]

Studies of charitable giving in the fourteenth and fifteenth centuries suggest that patterns of giving placed gifts to the actual poor and needy fairly low in the scale of priorities; if this is so, Langland's insistent promotion of the needy goes against the contemporary trend. Fear of purgatory dominated popular religious thought and practice. From his study of the wills of the nobility over the period 1307–1485 Rosenthal reached the conclusion, confirmed by a number of later historians, that fear of purgatory prompted much spending on the provision of intercessory prayer and considerably less on direct poor relief:

> Popular religion largely focused on this one chapter in the entire corpus of Christian belief. As well as occupying the time and efforts of the clergy, the concern with purgatory consumed a considerable part of the laity's money and spiritual enthusiasm. (pp 11–12)

Langland's poetry clearly and repeatedly counters habits of thought that exalt the act of giving as sufficient in itself, and stresses how important it is for donors to face and deal with the material needs of poor people:

> For þouȝ ye be trewe of youre tonge and treweliche wynne,
> And as chaste as a child þat in chirche wepeþ,
> But if ye louen leelly and lene þe pouere,
> Of swich good as God yow sent goodliche parteþ,
> Ye ne haue na moore merite in masse ne in houres
> Than Malkyn of hire maydenhede, þat no man desireþ.   (B.1.179–84)

Modern studies make it clear that, though all classes in society paid attention to the need for charitable giving, the poor were not regarded as first priority; *post obit* provision for the benefit of the donor's soul was considered much more pressing. In this context the researches of Clive Burgess into wills and pious pro-

---

12 J.T. Rosenthal, *The purchase of paradise*, p. 10.

vision in Bristol reveal an interesting and opposing view to that of Langland. For Burgess, wills express the belief in purgatory and an understanding of the need for prayers after death:

> Long-term post obit arrangement was two-fold, providing for donation or for services. Donation might take the form of benefaction to the parish church or largesse to the poor. Services were commemorative or discharged by stipendiary priests.[13]

Long-term *post obit* provision could be of either movable or immovable property. Although the following example is a century later than Langland's poem, Burgess believes that it represents a longstanding convention:

> The All Saints' Church Book, however, reveals that Henry and Alice gave the parish property in Broad Street. Deeds substantiate the Book; Alice enfeoffed parishioners with the property in 1477 and a lease of 1486 reveals an annual rent of £5. It was a valuable benefaction and was to furnish two services in All Saints – a weekly Jesus Mass and anthem on Fridays, and an anniversary perpetually observed on the date of Henry's decease, 14 February. Later a second anniversary was added, observed on 4 March. The weekly service cost 32s. 6d. annually and the anniversaries 14s. 2d., leaving the parish an annual revenue of 4 marks [53s. 4d] – although it was obliged to keep the property in repair.[14]

A second example illustrates the practice of leaving real property to the church in exchange for masses. In 1440 Agnes Fylour had acquired a house in the High Street. According to the All Saints' Church Book, the vicar, Maurice Hardwick, 'procured, moved and stirred Agnes' to give her house to the parish. With some resistance from her son, and by a compromise which saw the house revert to the parish only after the son's and daughter-in-law's deaths, the parish was enhanced and the liturgies required on Agnes's anniversary perpetually secured.[15]

Langland considered money given for indulgences was money lost to the poor.[16] What, then, about gifts given to the friars who had adopted poverty for Christ's sake? As far as Langland's poem is concerned, only works of almsgiving which directly assist the needy are eligible activities in the procurement of salvation:

> And amende mesondieux þerwiþ and myseisé folk helpe;
> And wikkede weyes wiʒtly hem amende.

---

13 C. Burgess, 'Wills and pious provision in late medieval Bristol', p. 841.
14 Ibid. p. 843.
15 Ibid. p. 844.
16 'For the parisshe preest and þe pardoner parten þe siluer / þat þe pouere [peple] of þe parissche sholde haue if þey ne were:' (B.Prol.81–2)

> And do boote to brugges þat tobroke were;
> Marien maydenes or maken hem nonnes;
> Pouere peple and prisons, fynden hem hir foode,
> And sette scolers to scole or to som oþere craftes;
> Releue religion and renten hem bettre. (B.7.26–32)

Yet historical studies bear out the enormous popularity of the friars in the minds of those preparing for death. Rosenthal finds plenty of evidence as to the popularity of the mendicant friars for bequests:

> The mendicants, as an order within the church, exceeded any other comparable sub-group in terms of attracting deathbed bequests. Almost every will of substance left something to the friars, though the amounts rarely exceeded £20 (unless it was a burial church or family pet project). (p. 121)

Anne Warren notes that, in her study of thirty-five wills written after 1368, twenty-three (65.7 per cent) made bequests for one or more groups of friars. In the interval between 1381 and 1408, twelve of thirteen wills (92.3 per cent) did so. Thompson notes a continuing trend in this direction throughout the extended period of his study: gifts for the friars were more common in 1529–30 than in 1401–49.[17] These practices suggest that reliance on the power of wealth to purchase paradise was not popularly regarded as sinful. It stemmed, in some degree, from the doctrine of purgatory, which prescribed the necessity of reparation for the stain of sin after the guilt had been forgiven. Intercession, almsgiving and the celebration of masses both in life and death were acknowledged forms of reparation:

> Thus to reduce as far as possible the rigours to be endured, individuals invested a considerable portion of their substance to their own and others' benefit, the rich naturally having more to redeem than the honest poor.[18]

Thomson suggests further that the mendicants' dedication to the ideal of poverty may lie behind their popularity for bequests, noting that the Observant houses at Greenwich and Richmond received a substantial number.[19]

In Langland's poetry, whenever the giving of gifts to the friars is mentioned in reference to the sacrament of penance it represents a perversion of the concept of restitution. By giving material gifts to the friars for their buildings to appear increasingly opulent, wealthy sinners can be misled into believing that they have bought forgiveness. Among the tasks that can be used for restitution,

---

17 J.A.F. Thompson, 'Piety and charity in late medieval London', p. 189.
18 Burgess, 'Wills and pious provision in late medieval Bristol', p. 838.
19 J.A.F. Thompson, 'Wealth, poverty and mercantile ethics in late medieval London', p. 270.

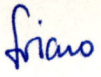

almsgiving to the poor is the one which Langland advances before all others. The support of the established church in building, liturgy or accoutrements does not figure, and gifts to the friars in exchange for prayers are portrayed both as stimulants to the friars' avarice and ineffectual substitutes for true repentance. The poem's only references to building contributions are to those made to friary churches. One appears when Repentance condemns the offerings of Coveitise to the friars, because they are ill-gotten gains (B.5.264–7), implying that the friars are indiscriminate in their acceptance of gifts. In the other, Langland condemns ostentation in almsgiving when Meed offers to pay for the stained glass window in the conventual church to be engraved with her name. Not only does Meed sin against humility here, but her gift is made on the understanding that she and other courtiers will continue sinning. Her friar confessor's knowing acceptance of this invalidates Meed's confession (B.3.35–75). The most pernicious effect of the friars comes at the siege of Unity when Frere Flatterer replaces the pains of repentance with the easy salve of silver for prayers:

> ... A pryvee paiement, and I shal praye for yow,
> And for al[le hem] þat ye ben holden to, al my lif tyme,
> And make yow [and] my Lady in masse and in matyns
> As freres of oure fraternytee, for a litel siluer.   (B.20.365–8)

To the conventional antifraternal satire of these examples Langland adds *saeva indignatio* at the harm to the souls of those rich for whom the sacrament of penance has become a money transaction instead of a spiritual renewal. That Langland should have written in such a vehemently critical manner about gifts to the friars suggests that he had an acute grasp of both the material needs of the poor and the spiritual needs of the rich. The difference in perception between testators and the poet reveals, too, the strongly anticlerical tendency of Langland's poem, as Scase has shown. Strictures against bequests both to possessioners and to the friars abound in the text, whose argument is part of the politically charged poverty controversy and hinges on the duty of the clergy to pass on alms to the needy poor.[20]

The other commonplace long-term provision for the benefit of the deceased was the maintenance of stipendiary priests, a practice fiercely criticized in the poem. Burgess produces evidence to show that the practice of establishing a chantry was overwhelmingly the preferred method of Bristol citizens for procuring long-term prayers for their souls; even those of apparently limited means endowed stipendiaries. These were of value, not only in saying masses, but in enhancing the liturgies by their participation in the parish music and singing, and in their probable educational role.[21] The chantry stipend – £5 or £5 6s. 8d.

---

20 The complexity of the arguments, and Langland's involvement in them, is minutely detailed by Scase, pp 97–119.
21 Burgess, 'Wills and pious provision in late medieval Bristol', p. 850.

'Marchauntz in þe margyne': how can the non-poor be saved

in the late fourteenth and fifteenth centuries – was usually close to the salary of the incumbent. The parish therefore benefited from 'free' services of an additional priest. As the fourteenth century progressed even the peasants came to have some surplus wealth and, within their limitations, they were as generous in endowing chantries as those with far greater wealth:

> The increasing size of the ceremonial fund is also indicated by the rising membership of religious fraternities, which many peasants joined by paying a few shillings entry fee. Richer peasants in East Anglia bequeathed in their wills sums of money (£5 for a year, in some cases) for a priest to pray for their souls.[22]

Unbeneficed clergy were useful, particularly to the less wealthy, because they could make what McHardy calls 'a more flexible response to the needs of the laity than could those tied to the fossilized parochial structure', offering masses and prayers in small quantities for those sections of the laity who wanted to be able to provide for their souls but lacked sufficient money to endow a full chantry.[23]

Why then should Langland be so opposed to chantry priests if the chantries could provide so many spiritual benefits? Once again, the problems are manifold. The poem criticizes chantry priests who treat their calling as a lucrative career and deplores the commercial connotations of their receiving money for masses:

> If preestes weren wise, þei wolde no siluer take
> For masses ne for matyns, noȝt hir mete of vsureres ...
> *Spera in Deo* spekeþ of preestes þat haue no spendyng siluer,
> That if þei trauaille truweliche and truste in God almyȝty,
> Hem sholde lakke no liflode, neyþer lynnen ne wollen.
>
> (B.11.281–2; 285–7).

At the same time, priests who leave their parishes to take up office in a chantry are abandoning the poor to whom they should minister (B.Prol.83–6). A chantry in one of the cathedrals or great London churches could carry a stipend of £10 per annum,[24] a handsome sum when some gentry families at the same time managed on a similar amount.[25] Ten pounds per annum for performing offices and singing mass daily is an attractive alternative to the parish priest's arduous pastoral task when the remuneration, at £5 per annum or less, is only half that of the London chantry priests. Chaucer's Parson comes to mind here. Like his

---

22 Dyer, *Standards of living*, p. 183.
23 A.K. McHardy, 'Ecclesiastics and economics', p. 136.
24 Rosenthal, pp 38; 45.
25 Dyer, *Standards of living*, p. 31.

ploughman brother, he is close to the soil in his far-flung rural parish. Trudging on foot to visit his parishioners in thunder and rain he is likely to become encumbered in the physical mire while he rescues his flock from their spiritual one.[26] The life of a rural parson was recognized to be far from easy.

The point made by Rosenthal in his survey of chantries helps to give some foundation to Langland's criticisms that chantries cause priests to neglect the poor. Rosenthal suggests that, at the hour of death, testators were concerned only with ensuring the wellbeing of their souls:

> Not that the nobles did not give to the poor. But when their thoughts turned towards their own chantries, they usually had no mind for eleemosynary considerations. They cared about themselves at that critical moment. (p. 51)

Langland's understanding of purgatory is more altruistic than this view. He argues that spiritual health is directly related to charity to the poor and expressly states that poverty borne patiently is the purgatory of the poor person:

> For loue of hir lowe hertes Oure Lord haþ hem graunted
> Hir penaunce and hir purgatorie vpon þis [pure] erþe. (B.7.103–4)

This is the further understanding of Patience's exposition of poverty, reflecting back on the danger of the practice which purchased prayers in preference to giving money to feed the poor. Langland also makes the specific point, frequently and in varied contexts, that unless the poor are directly cared for, in an ongoing manner, during the life of the rich, then salvation cannot be achieved. The strongest statement of this belief comes resoundingly at the close of the *Visio*, where Langland implicitly negates the value of bequests for chantries, insisting that no amount of money can purchase forgiveness in the light of the Last Judgment. Then the judgment will be about what works the rich have done on a day to day basis:

> How þow laddest þi lif here and hise lawes keptest,
> And how þow didest day by day þe doom wole reherce.
> A pokeful of pardon þere, ne prouincials lettres,
> Theiȝ ye be founde in þe fraternite of alle þe fyue ordres
> And haue indulgences doublefold – but Dowel yow helpe,
> I sette youre patentes and youre pardon at one pies hele! (B.7.190–5)

Piers' pardon, which quotes the concluding lines of the gospel account of the Last Judgment (Matthew 25. 46), is made dependent on charitable treatment of the poor. At the Last Judgment the poor are led to the centre of the stage and

---

26 Chaucer, *Canterbury tales*, General prologue, ll.491–514, in *Chaucer*, p. 31.

identified with Christ in their physical need: hunger, thirst, nakedness, sickness, homelessness and imprisonment. The judgment will be made on the practice of the works of mercy – masses, pardons and bulls have no validity. *Piers Plowman* demands more than the parade of works of mercy at death. For any pardon to be valid, it must be written on the parchment of poverty:

> Ac þe parchemyn of þis patente of pouerte be moste,
> And of pure pacience and parfit bileue.   (B.14.192–3)

It is the day-to-day practice of charity that gives both rich and poor their identification as of the 'secte' of Christ, the only identity that will bring them to salvation.

Langland's understanding of the doctrine of purgatory is detached from the purchase of prayer and directly focused on repentance which must be shown in good works, charity to the poor being pre-eminent among these. Unlike Mannyng and sermon writers who pepper their teaching with exempla of the antics or activities of suffering souls, cautionary tales to underscore the value of religious observances, Langland is more inclined to indicate the uselessness of mechanical reliance on the customary aids to the souls – indulgences, prayers and pilgrimages – if they are not based on a firm foundation of day-to-day good works (B.14.192–200; B.7.174–95; B.11.150–2). Piers embraces a life of pilgrimage and penance and Will lives a life of solitude, travel and prayer, but neither relies on purchased intercession. It is noteworthy, too, that the penances enjoined upon Langland's deadly sinners do not include making donations for prayers. In fact, this practice is considered by Langland to be the very opposite of salvific; it is downright harmful. Langland goes to the heart of the issue of salvation; it has to be earned by rich and poor, and specifically by the practice of charity towards the needy. The sufferings of the poor are to be alleviated directly, not by indirect gifts.

Yet in an autobiographical interlude in the C-text Langland represents Will as a mendicant who prays for his benefactors in exchange for being found by them. The prayers are the standard ones stipulated in wills of the time:[27]

> The lomes þat Y labore with and lyflode deserue
> Is *Pater-noster* and my prymer, *Placebo* and *Dirige*
> And my Sauter som tyme and my seuene psalmes.   (C.5.45–7)

Clearly Langland does not criticize the practice of giving payment for spiritual services. Will, however, while he makes a living from praying, does not make any money out of it. His intention is single-minded – to apply his intercession to the benefit of the souls who find him, and to accept only the minimum necessary for survival, 'liflode':

---

27 'Beyond these detailed stipulations governing prayers, scores of wills at least mention a "Placebo, Dirige, and Requiem", or "a mass of Our Lady", or a "Trental of Gregory"': Rosenthal, p. 28.

Withoute bagge or botel but my wombe one. (C.5.52)

Pearsall suggests that Langland's Will has no alternative, being unbeneficed. He leaves no sheep 'encombred in the myre', and he wins only enough for his daily sustenance.[28] I think that this is likely to be the case, but it is also yet another example of Langland making distinctions between apparently opposing attitudes in his text. In this case Will is the poor person who is given relief by benefactors, and in return prays for them. Will's acceptance of payment is different from a gift or bequest made for masses irrespective of the recipient's need. It is vastly different from the begging of those false mendicants, whether friars or hermits, who go about with bags, collecting more than they need and neglecting their duty of prayer (C.9.98; C.9.139–58; B.Prol.41–6). And it is different from the cringing of the beggars who, instead of helping with Piers' ploughing, pretend to be weak and promise prayers for Piers' success (B.6.121–8). Will is a poor man whose honest labour is prayer; the gift of his prayer is the reward his benefactors gain for relieving his poverty. Venality is not an issue.

Will explicitly fulfils the bargain implicit in the relationship of beggar and donor: that the poor person will pray for the spiritual health of the benefactor. The fact that the poem gives vivid and circumstantial detail about the sufferings of the poor, coupled with its insistence that they should be the first, not the last recipients of charity, raises questions about the poem's response to circumstances of contemporary poor relief. Certainly there was relief, and on the evidence of wills, household and monastic books and records, and parish books, the responses to the poor took standard forms. The poem enumerates some of them as conditions of forgiveness for the sins of merchants: provision of almshouses, repair of roads and bridges, endowment of young women too poor to marry, feeding poor people, relieving prisoners, and educating the young (B.7.26–32). The question implied by the poem's recurrent descriptions of suffering poor is whether contemporary response was directed towards relieving real poverty or satisfying the need of the non-poor to make restitution.

Rosenthal makes the point, mentioned above, that the medieval mind made no distinction between gifts given to the church and those given for philanthropic purposes. In the light of this statement, Langland's insistence on the direction of charity to the poor is perhaps different from the understanding of his contemporaries. It is understood that gifts were channelled through the church, and that the church had the responsibility for the care of the poor. Langland therefore directs criticism at the clergy for their failure to care for the poor. His strictures against the prelate who 'biddeþ the beggere go, for his broke cloþes' (B.9.92) suggest that the church did not always live up to its duty of providing for the poor; and the monasteries who do not care 'thouȝ it reyne on hir auters' (B.10.312) may well have been diverting the funds bequeathed by parishioners. The poor definitely suffered from monastic appropriation of parishes, a

---

28 Pearsall, *C-text*, p. 99 nn. 46–7.

widespread system which stripped the parish of all its revenues and returned a vicar who would manage the parish on a small stipend:

> And if parishes could be stripped of all their funds on the pretext that monastic houses needed additional income to maintain hospitality, that was a real abuse. Monastic charity was likely to be more indiscriminate and less effective than alms administered by priests on the parochial level, and, even if the appropriating monasteries (or other absentee parsons) did give generously to the poor around them, there would still have been no provision for the destitute of the parishes that actually provided the funds.[29]

Although there were laws to govern the payment of tithes, and those which decreed the responsibility of the clergy to support the poor, the methods of practising direct charity were not subject to law, and people interpreted their duty of charity on a voluntary basis. Studies of wills reveal the accepted methods of ensuring that prayers were said after death for the repose of the souls of the faithful departed; and they also reveal time-honoured methods of practising charity. It is this freedom that lends urgency to Langland's writing; he interprets some of the testamentary and charitable practices as simoniac and sinful, and sees an imbalance between the needs of poor people and the distributions made by voluntary givers. Through the voice of Anima he castigates rich people for giving to religious who live in comfort, from whom they can expect reciprocal benefit, and condemns religious in similar terms for their hospitality to the well-to-do, rather than to beggars who can give nothing in return:

> Right so ye riche, ye robeþ and fedeþ
> Hem þat han as ye han – hem ye make at ese.
> Ac religiouse þat riche ben sholde raþer feeste beggeris
> Than burgeis þat riche ben, as þe book techeþ.   (B.15.339–42)

His poetry seeks to act as a corrective, placing the needy centre-stage, where they belong in the drama of the Last Judgment, not on the margins where their poverty normally places them: in the lanes and round the edges of the fields, gleaning at harvest time, outside the gates waiting for the daily basket of leftovers from the monastic or lordly table. One of the few times when the poor are historically recorded as entering centre-stage is, ironically, at the death of a wealthy person; then they are dressed in warm, if distinctive, robes, and become identified as belonging to the household for this fleeting occasion. Some benefactors gave copiously and thoughtfully – forty lined robes and forty pairs of shoes, bread for a hundred paupers. One York testator left

> one hundred shillings to the poor, blind, lame, weak, and sick on his burial day, with forty shillings more to be distributed on the octave; fifty

---

29 Tierney, p. 82.

shillings for ten chaldrons of sea-borne coals to be given to the poor and needy in York and its suburbs, with a further 6s. 8d. allotted for their delivery to the homes of the poor; twenty shillings for wood – fallen branches – to be distributed to the poor, especially those in his parish of St. Saviour; twenty shillings for forty pairs of men's shoes and ten shillings for twenty pairs for women; and lifetime pensions of one pence per week for five poor widows.[30]

Cullum and Goldberg give examples from some York wills which stipulate that the paupers on the funeral day should be selected in numbers to represent the thirteen who were present at the Last Supper, the five wounds, the ten commandments. Benefactions were also tailored to correspond with and fulfil the seven corporal works of mercy. Poverty, like leprosy, was in some respects a living death, and this association with death as they took their place in the funeral procession was a dramatic statement of their function in terms of the Last Judgment.[31] Symbolically they were enacting the corporal works of mercy as they accompanied the donor to meet God, and the framing of some wills in devotional terms was a picturesque acknowledgement of this. By seeing that the works of mercy were practised on their behalf after their death, the testators believed they were ensuring a reciprocal benefit to their souls.

It cannot, however, be assumed that funerary doles were sufficient to meet all requirements for poor relief. Some studies of wills suggest that the poor and needy were placed last in the order of benefaction. Anne Warren's research on wills leads her to conclude that extensive charitable giving was not widespread. Her interest is in the support of anchorites and she observes that those who gave to anchorites were likely also to be generous to other needy groups:[32]

> If we look at the fourteen Roos, Scrope, Beauchamp, Stafford, and Lancastrian wills that benefit anchorites in the period 1392–1480 (nine written by men and five by women), the following patterns emerge: nine made bequests to the poor, thirteen to convents, and twelve to friars ...

---

30 A.K. Warren, *Anchorites and their patrons in medieval England*, pp 253–4.
31 P.H. Cullum, and P.J.P. Goldberg, 'Charitable provision in late medieval York,' pp 25–30.

32
Recipient	Hustings wills with anchorite grants (1342–1413)	Marche and Luffenam (1401–49)
Poor in hospitals	54.9%	23.4%
Lepers	63.3%	
Prisoners	47.2%	29%
Public works	32.1%	15%
Friars	56.6%	30%
All conventual orders	90.6%	25.8%

Warren continues (p. 228): 'If the data relative to burial day disbursements also had been available, the 'poor statistic' probably would have approached the 100 per cent mark, for that information typically provides the nucleus of grants to the poor in a statistical analysis of medieval wills.'

> In comparison with the wills of other members of the aristocracy, in which only one in three left money for alms,[33] this group of testators is significantly more sympathetic to the needs of the poor. (pp 207–8)

Warren makes the specific point that those London merchants who were good to anchorites were also generous to the poor, sometimes naming these specifically in their wills, but more usually leaving them anonymous, to be assisted by a general donation administered by the hospitals.[34] Analysis of York merchants' wills reveals a similar commitment to the poor in those who made grants for anchorites, and a similar anonymity in the giving:

> The poor are disembodied even when living in maisondieux (the name given to poorhouses in the North) of a testator's own establishment. Lepers are in their hospitals, prisoners in their cells, anchorites by parish churches.[35]

Such findings accord with the way Langland credits those who exercise charity to the poor with an appreciation of the value and demands of dedication to the inner life.

York itself had a number of maisonsdieu; fourteen were suppressed at the Dissolution. Robert de Howm founded a house for twenty people of both sexes and, on his death, endowed it with enough funds to pay each of its inhabitants one penny per day for one hundred years.[36] John de Craven, a testator who did not endow anchorites,

> left arrangements in his 1416 will for his paupers on Layerthorpe Bridge: thirteen persons were to receive weekly grants, twelve of them at three pence weekly and the thirteenth at four pence in return for morning and evening prayers.[37]

Malcolm Vale[38] finds that in the wills of one hundred and forty-eight members of the Yorkshire gentry who died between 1370 and 1480, only forty-seven, one in three, show any provision for the poor. Of these, only thirty-four provided for poor other than their own tenants or servants, and most of these bequests were to paupers gathered at their funerals. Evidence from a variety of sources

---

33 See also Rosenthal, p. 103.
34 Warren concedes (p. 230) that a few testators made bequests to named individuals or establishments, but usually the poor, lepers and prisoners were treated generally: 'Most donors made grants to a great many units, many of which must have been relatively unknown to them but which were part of their gift-giving consciousness. The anonymity of the city is felt in these wills.'
35 Warren, p. 242.
36 Ibid. p. 249.
37 Ibid. p. 249.
38 *Piety, charity and literacy among the Yorkshire gentry, 1370–1480*, p. 24.

suggests that charity to the poor came only when other obligations had been met. Only a third of the peers' wills analysed by Rosenthal contained any provision for the poor. The laity further down the social scale than merchants – yeomen and artisans – were less likely than merchants to make numerous charitable bequests. Of two hundred and sixty-four wills written by residents of St Albans between the years 1416 and 1451, one-hundred-and-three left no charitable bequests. Of the rest, ninety-eight wills considered their 'charitable gifts' to be covered by gifts to a cleric or the local parish church, to its lights, fabrics, chapels, vicars and chaplains. Only fifty-six wills dispensed other gifts, for bridge repair, the upkeep of anchorites, the repair of roads. As an indication of the relative importance of the poor, it is chastening to note that the poor were mentioned only twice for other than burial-related gifts in the wills analysed by Warren.[39]

Burgess's research on pious provision in Bristol questions whether bequests show only the tip of the iceberg in demonstrating the extent of charitable donations. He considers that a neglect of the poor in wills need not mean that they were neglected during the testators' life, and points to some notable hospital and almshouse foundations in Bristol to illustrate this idea.[40] Some merchants who appear not to have left wills were responsible for important almshouses, yet there is no paper record of the charitable gift. Some wills are minimal and conventional; Burgess suggests that meaningful disposals had been made before the hour of death.[41]

In terms of regular charitable practices, we know that the distribution of alms through the household officials was a regular part of an aristocrat's life, and that of many of the gentry, too:

> In the house of a lord, after every meal a basket filled with fragments of food not eaten was taken to the poor at the gate.[42]

John of Gaunt gave away on average £50–£75 per annum, and it can be expected other nobles and gentry emulated this practice according to their means. Monastic houses were so precise in drawing up regulations about food distribution that Tierney believes food in excess of the monks' daily needs was prepared expressly for the benefit of the poor who were to be given the leftovers (p. 80). Funerary doles of food and clothing generally provided short-term benefit, but sometimes testators ensured the distribution of largesse for long periods or in perpetuity.[43] The distribution of a robe and a pair of shoes may have been intended to clothe a poor person for a year, if we consider that elderly people arranging pensions often required an annual new robe and a pair of shoes as part

---

39 Warren, p. 262.
40 Burgess, 'Wills and pious provision' (pp 845–6) mentions two benefactors who, during their life, established three almshouses, none of which is well-documented.
41 Burgess, 'Late medieval wills and pious convention', pp 14–33.
42 F. Harrison, *Medieval man and his notions*, p.101.
43 Burgess, 'Wills and pious provision', pp 845, 848.

'Marchauntʒ in þe margyne': how can the non-poor be saved

of their allowance.[44] On the other hand, it is unlikely that funerary gifts answered the needs of all local paupers. Did the gift of forty lined gowns and forty pairs of shoes for men and twenty for women represent the actual numbers of paupers, or a ceremonial number who would be the lucky ones to benefit on the funeral day? In some instances, neither the funeral dole nor the almshouses catered for the non-local, destitute poor, since the terms of the donor specifically discriminated against them. Itinerants were similarly excluded from the type of self-help gained from the community 'help-ales' which Judith Bennett considers to have been more significant and reliable than any other medieval form of poor relief.[45] Nor is it known how faithfully or otherwise the clergy, who were so often the recipients of the laity's charitable donations, attended to the needs of the poor from their income as they were obliged to do. When economies had to be made, the poor might readily have been the first to suffer. Dyer recounts incidents of Yorkshire monasteries laying off servants in time of famine:

> In extreme shortages like in the great famine of 1315–17 in Yorkshire, monastic employers did not scruple to lay off servants to save cash and grain.[46]

This suggests that some monasteries were prepared to treat the poor as expendable; the charity they may have given out in food at the monastery gate would be cancelled out by the lack of charity shown to these servants who were likely to starve without work. At least one historian of monasticism argues that monks did not consider themselves responsible for the involuntarily poor in anything approaching a modern view of social security and that they gave to paupers in a ritualized way.[47] They themselves were the poor, and the quantities of food distributed to paupers would have made no impact on the number of needy nor would it have alleviated their hunger and physical want:[48]

> To what extent for instance was the recurrent risk of starvation attacked by the solemn supper which charitable institutions traditionally offered to twelve poor old men on Maundy Thursday? ... That their feet were washed and a meal served to them had no meaning save as a liturgical commemoration of Jesus' humility and his Last Supper.

Milis argues cogently that analyses of the expense patterns of later medieval monasteries confirm that the almoner of Christ Church Canterbury was not unusual in spending only half of one per cent of his income on external poverty relief in the period 1284–1373.[49]

44 Clark, 'Some aspects of social security', pp 311–12.
45 Bennett, 'Conviviality and charity', pp 38–41.
46 Dyer, *Everyday life*, p. 91.
47 Milis, pp 53–62.
48 Ibid. pp 54–5.
49 Ibid. p. 57, especially n. 25.

It appears from the information reviewed above, contradictory though the findings sometimes are, that *Piers Plowman* quite validly castigates many of the non-poor for neglecting the poor. The research suggests that while there was, indeed, a care for the poor shown in funerary arrangements and bequests, day-to-day alms-giving and the foundation of charitable and educational establishments, the details of these charitable works varied from donor to donor and place to place. As Elaine Clark comments, 'the information we have about charity and mutual aid in the middle ages is more often descriptive and personal than quantitative.'[50]

The experience of those poor who did receive food is twice reflected in the poem in a way which suggests that Langland believed the poor should be treated with the dignity of being given good food, rather than stale leftovers. One is the distinction made by Piers (B.6.136–8) who promises to feed the poor on wheaten bread which, throughout the fourteenth and fifteenth centuries, formed only a small proportion of the cereal consumed by peasants.[51] The other occurs when Patience and Will are eating at a side table, watching the Great Doctor eat gluttonously while he and Patience eat sour bread and water:

> 'By þis day, sire doctour,' quod I, 'þanne be ye noȝt in Dowel!
> For ye han harmed vs two in þat ye eten þe puddyng,
> Mortrews and ooþer mete – and we no morsel hadde.'   (B.13.106–8)

Will reacts against the hypocrisy of the Doctor's actions which contrast with the words of his earlier sermon when he preached of penance. In both these instances, the food has a symbolic significance, representing the moral superiority of the poor. The symbol is, however, drawn from the perceived actuality of a provision which regarded the poor person as an anonymous recipient of charity whose terms are defined by the donor's wish rather than the pauper's need. In Will, Langland has given us the opportunity, rare in medieval literature, to witness a poor pilgrim with identity, intelligence and emotions, who thinks about the implications of his position relative to his host, and, like many another beggar, becomes a nuisance. The strong overtones of anticlerical satire in his *sotto voce* response to the friar:

> *Periculum est in falsis fratribus*   (B.13.70)

link indignation at the neglect of the needy with well-documented clerical abuse of the ideal of poverty. It is clear that Langland values the poor in more than a conventional manner. He is acutely aware of the imbalance which appears to exist between material provision for the poor and a more selfish attitude which believes that prayers applied directly to the donor's soul will be more productive of eternal peace, and the poem uses satire to advocate specific reform of perceived contemporary neglect of the poor.

---

50 'Social welfare and mutual aid', p. 382.
51 Dyer, *Everyday life*, pp 93–5.

Langland's poem is a corrective to attitudes in giving; the poor are entitled to relief, and it is a scandal when they go unrelieved. In spite of the effectiveness or inadequacy of contemporary charitable provision the poem remains uncompromising in its requirement that care of the poor must be tackled constantly as the pre-eminent method of practising the life of 'Dowel'. At the same time, the poem develops a rationale of charity to the poor as leading to love of God, and positively promotes Christ's philosophy of not being solicitous about material possessions as the best way to develop the inner life. The health of the inner life depends on the practice of good works, and works do not end with themselves, but lead to the conversion of the sinner. Langland's clear commitment to this belief will emerge in close textual analysis of Patience's words to Haukyn and Will (B.14.103–201). Concerned, as he is, with spiritual well-being, Patience concentrates as much on the hard task facing those rich who want to fulfil the life of Dowel as he does on the harsh practicalities of a pauper's existence.

HAUKYN'S DIFFICULTIES: WHAT DOES 'NE SOLICITI SITIS' MEAN?

The church has always considered the practice of poverty to be fundamental to the following of Christ, an ideal that should govern the lives of all. Although the extreme that Christ asked of the rich young man is recognized to be a counsel of perfection, not a commandment, all the rich – gentry, aristocracy and merchants – are urged in penitentials, sermons, and in *Piers Plowman* to place love of God above love of money. The practical difficulties this entails are most forcefully expressed in the character of Haukyn, who is the embodiment of the non-poor way of life in its worst aspects. Haukyn is a sinner not because he is a merchant, or because he lives in the world, but because he has no better goal in life than worldly gain. He is represented not as a rich man, but a man in the perpetual pursuit of riches. The poem does not condemn riches as such; it condemns the fallacy of placing the attainment of material goods first in life, and to show Haukyn as forever trying and failing to achieve worldly wealth demonstrates forcibly the corrosive effect of living with the wrong priorities. Haukyn demonstrates vividly the moral failure that occurs when material gain is placed before love of God and one's fellow human beings. He sins like a merchant, small trader and rural land-grabber for, like those who understand what want can be, he never tires of working to avoid the trap of poverty. Much of the time this involves exploiting other people.

The rest of this chapter considers how Patience gives Haukyn something nobler to work for. It is important to recognize that what follows in Passus B.14, though an exposition of the value of poverty, is carefully directed towards Haukyn and is not simply praise of poverty in a vacuum. This is a view of poverty for the non-poor whose life of business in the world is fraught with moral danger, and the help offered by Patience is specific to Haukyn, the baker. Haukyn bakes wafers, delicious treats, and Patience offers him a piece of God's daily bread, the

Paternoster. Like a good spiritual director, Patience helps Haukyn recognize the sinfulness of his life and gives him guidance in three stages: leading Haukyn to recognize his sins; offering him spiritual food; and guiding him through a process of repentance. Everything Patience proposes about poverty is directed towards changing Haukyn's priorities so that he will stop devoting his whole attention to material gain and adopt a way of life that will free him from sin. I start the discussion pointing out similarities between Haukyn and the Piers of B.6 and B.7,[52] recognizing that they are both practitioners of the active life and face similar experiences and problems. Haukyn's responses to the demands of his worldly life lead him into sin, whereas Piers has his mind fixed on heavenly goals. Studying the kind of 'liflode' that Patience can provide leads me to conclude that Patience's offer of food to sustain Haukyn in performing the will of God is an antidote to his empty concern about making profit from material provisioning.

Haukyn is called the active man, and Piers' man. Both he and Piers are committed to the world of work, but whereas Piers works as a servant of Truth, Haukyn has worked for a succession of worldly goals which have betrayed him into the seven deadly sins. Where Piers is the direct producer of the grain, Haukyn is the baker. Piers undertakes the active life of ploughing and dealing with all kinds of people; Haukyn works hard to provision the city, the court and the papal palace. Piers appears in the rural setting of the manorial fields; Haukyn is part of urban life, baking his bread to sell in the city and at court. Haukyn refers to himself as Piers' man, one who hates idleness and looks to Piers' profit (B.13.235–8).[53] With regard to beggars and to jesters, Haukyn accepts his duty to provision all without regard for their moral probity, and Piers works out his responsibility to include all in his alms, leaving the moral responsibility with the poor themselves to be genuine in their begging. Both know what dearth means and evince genuine concern to feed the people. Both require the services of a 'clerc þat couþe write' (B.13.248), Piers to read the terms of his pardon, Haukyn to write an application for a pardon that will bring spiritual healing. Hard work is their vocation, and both are brought to understand the meaning of *ne soliciti sitis*. The verbal similarities are unmistakable:

Piers	Haukyn
And *alle kynne crafty men þat konne lyuen in truþe,* I shal *fynden hem fode* þat feiþfulliche libbeþ. (B.6.68–9)	For alle *trewe trauaillours and tiliers of* þe erþe, Fro Mighelmesse to Mighelmesse I fynde hem wiþ wafres.

---

[52] Aers also makes this connection, calling Haukyn 'a follower of the *earlier* Piers': *Community, gender, and individual identity*, p. 58.
[53] The C-text, at this point, refers to Actyf as 'his man'.

Alle *libbynge laborers þat lyuen wiþ hir hondes,*
That treweliche taken and treweliche wynnen,
And lyuen in loue and in lawe, for hir lowe herte
Haueþ *þe same absolucion þat sent was to Piers.*
Beggeres ne bidderes ne beþ noȝt *in þe bulle*
But if þe suggestion be sooþ that shapeþ hem to begge. (B.7.60–5)

Beggeris and bidderis of my breed crauen,
Faitours and freres and folk wiþ brode crounes.
I fynde payn for þe Pope and prouendre for his palfrey,
And I hadde neuere of hym, haue God my trouþe,
Neiþer prouendre ne personage yet of þe Popes ȝifte,
Saue a pardon wiþ a peis of leed and two polles amyddes! (B.13.240–7)

The ostensible similarities between them point up the contrasts. Haukyn provides material food for all with the primary goal of material advancement; he would like to have a prebend or a parsonage from the Pope. Having lived a life of worldly sin, Haukyn wants to buy himself into eternal salvation, but the pardon which ought to be of spiritual benefit is just a leaden seal, spiritually worthless: 'a peis of led and two polles amyddes'. Ironically, Haukyn has not achieved his worldly ambition either, since the Pope is as much use to him as the Pope's horse. He feels he has been cheated on both material and spiritual counts. Piers' provision is of material food from the harvest to provide for rich and poor and spiritual food from the heavenly harvest, symbol of the Last Judgment, for all who have worked loyally, according to their estate. Piers' pardon, which is taken by the priest to be worthless (B.7.111), turns out to be a promise of salvation for those who are merciful to the needy. This, in itself, involves material provisioning – the needy must be clothed, fed and sheltered. In this portrayal of Haukyn and Piers as busy provisioners the poem recognizes the problems faced by those who want to conduct their worldly enterprise according to God's principles. Haukyn demonstrates that it is not easy, Piers shows that it is possible.

Careful reading shows that Patience's view of poverty is not a rejection of wealth, but a reappraisal. The overt parallels between Piers and Haukyn connect in their preoccupation with work in the world of material needs and with repentance. Piers' penitence is to be a pilgrimage, and before setting out he makes his will, preparing himself to meet his maker as was customary when medieval people went on pilgrimage.[54] The 'pilgrimage' becomes conflated with the ploughing of the field in two passus which deal with the necessities and vicissitudes of work and survival in the active life. Clearly, Piers is preparing for heaven by carrying out his earthly responsibilities and, as a diligent agricultural producer, by striving to produce not only that which is needed for subsistence, but surplus

---

54 Merchants, too, made their wills before going on voyages, as Heath describes in his study of Hull wills, 'Urban piety', pp 209–13.

that will make for profit. The profit Haukyn hopes to amass from trade does not materialize of itself, and he resorts to repeated, urbanized, everyday sin, as his stained coat reveals. On one level, the poem draws upon convention in polarizing the traditionally virtuous agrarian life and the traditionally vice-prone mercantile life.55 Though Haukyn's coat is stained with all kinds of sin, including those of false religion, it is as a merchant, primarily concerned with amassing earthly treasure, that Patience addresses him. Yet the poem is not concerned with contrasting the work of Piers and Haukyn but with pointing up the necessity of right intention whatever their occupation. Langland's vision recognizes that society comprises rich and poor, and also recognizes that, as farmers make surplus, merchants must make profits. Patience's role is to persuade the non-poor, in Haukyn, to share their God-given goods with those in need, and to value goods as secondary to the 'liflode' that nourishes the spirit and raises the mind and heart to God in acceptance of his will.

Both Piers and Haukyn are led to 'be not solicitous' in the context of the Last Judgment, worked out through association with parables. Piers' resolve to 'cessen of [his] sowyng' (B.7.118) comes after Hunger has assaulted him and his 'blody breþeren'. Piers has been brought to a practical understanding of the essentials of life, especially when seen in the context of the Last Judgment, which is adumbrated by the words of the pardon. Haukyn, too, has experienced the difficulties of feeding his people in time of famine. The lessons of Patience, given in the presence of Will, become part of his understanding of the value of poverty. For Piers it seemed to be a simple matter to turn towards penance once he had encountered the Last Judgment in the pardon. For Haukyn, busy about urban and financial considerations, the understanding of God's providence requires lengthy tuition. By the evidence of his heavily soiled coat, Haukyn's life has been an exploration of sin and he is invited by Patience to have his coat of sin transformed by the sacrament of penance into a heavenly garment, as Alford points out in his analysis of the scriptural connotations of Haukyn's coat.56 Alford links the promise of Patience, 'Shal neuere my[te] bymolen it, ne moþe after biten it' (B.14.23) with its source in Matthew 6. 19–21 which recommends laying up treasure in heaven.57 The previous instance of this scriptural quotation occurs in Haukyn's admission of the avarice he practises as a merchant: 'Vbi thesaurus tuus, ibi et cor tuum' (B.13.399a), falling into the danger of believing that material gain is an end in itself.

This coat recalls the parable of the wedding feast which, in turn, is linked to the Old Testament concept of the messianic banquet, itself a type of the eucharist. Haukyn, too, as a provider of bread, wafers, has potentially eucharistic signifi-

---

55 'Following in the steps of the church fathers, the scholastic doctors of the middle ages looked with favor upon husbandry but regarded trade with distrust because it was an occupation which, although not wicked in itself, nevertheless endangered the salvation of the soul': de Roover, p. 336.
56 'Haukyn's coat'.
57 Alford, 'Haukyn's coat', p. 135.

'Marchaunt3 in þe margyne': how can the non-poor be saved

cance. In his life of activity, Haukyn seems to have had the chance, as Piers' 'man', to do all the right things but, like the rich young man, he has neglected the one thing which is alone is necessary – he is not wearing the wedding garment. By setting his heart on earthly treasure he has diverted himself from the heavenly treasure and is in danger of being cast into the outer darkness (Matthew 22. 13). Patience will demonstrate for Haukyn and Will how poverty earns heavenly treasure, but first he must give him 'liflode' which, by association with other uses of the word in the poem, carries both material and spiritual meanings.

Before commenting on these, I need to point out how Patience's teaching about setting life in the correct perspective is supported by three scriptural references which recur throughout *Piers Plowman* and whose original scriptural contexts resonate through the poem. The first, *Non in solo pane* has two sources, Christ's words when tempted to turn stones into bread (Matthew 4. 4) and Deuteronomy 8. 3, from which Christ derives his statement. Deuteronomy relates to the trials of the Chosen People when they are fed with manna from God. Both references relate to material want, specifically hunger, that helps a person turn the mind towards God and accept whatever he provides by actively embracing his will. The trial of the Chosen People in Deuteronomy is a prelude to their reaching the promised land of material plenty, just as the forty days of Jesus in the wilderness are preparation for an active life in his contemporary world. I think it is important to remember this when we consider Patience's words about poverty, so that they do not assume an absolute status. His poverty is a means to an end, a way of coming into line with God's will, so that active life in the world may be conducted according to God's principles. It is not something to be valued for its own sake alone.

The second quotation, *Fiat voluntas tua*, is the third petition of the *Paternoster*, the acquiescence of the Virgin Mary in her role as mother of God, and the words of Christ in Gethsemane, accepting his forthcoming passion and death. This is a direct prayer that the will of God may be done, and, in its most frequently used context of the *Paternoster*, links closely with the next petition, 'Give us this day our daily bread'. Together they confirm that material food is important, and that there is no conflict between seeking material provision and attending to the things of God. What matters is conformity to God's will. The third reference, *ne soliciti sitis,* is the one which, most of all, relates to the state of mind of the sincere follower of Christ. In its gospel context it contrasts with the anxious greed that stores up corruptible earthly treasure. Treasure in itself is not condemned; Christ condemns hoarding that which is not needed.

It is important to recognize how insistent the poem is on the possibility of the rich being able to attain to the poverty of spirit that will gain salvation for them. There is a network of references in the poem to the *Paternoster* and *fiat voluntas tua*, linked with *non in solo pane* and *ne soliciti sitis*. They occur when poverty is under discussion, and keep the provision of daily bread firmly in the context of the Last Judgment and God's will, which is precisely where Piers' pardon takes us. Patience gathers up the concording references:

Ne soliciti sitis ... Volucres celi Deus pascit ... Pacientes vincunt ...

(B.14.34a.)

echoing in them the scene where Piers, having contemplated the Last Judgment in the terms of the Pardon, leaves his sowing. Patience teaches Haukyn that God's 'liflode' is all that is necessary, and shows him how to practise poverty by giving up the anxiety that leads him to sin rather than risk being poor. Even one who wants to remain in the mercantile world can adopt the right practices providing he keeps sight of the Last Judgment which assesses people on how well they have cared for the needy.

Patience does not deny the importance of material sustenance, but, using terms of striking similarity to those of Piers and of Anima in the following passus, urges Haukyn to get his life into perspective:[58]

PIERS:	We sholde noȝt be to bisy aboute þe worldes blisse.	(B.7.126)
PATIENCE:	We sholde noȝt be to bisy abouten oure liflode.	(B.14.34)
PIERS:	Haue þei no gerner to go to, but God fynt hem alle.	(B.7.130)
PATIENCE:	Alle þat lyueþ and lokeþ liflode wolde I fynde.	(B.14.32)
ANIMA:	Antony on a day, aboute noon tyme,	
	Hadde a brid þat brouȝte hym breed þat he by lyuede;	
	And þouȝ þe gome hadde a gest, God fond hem boþe.	(B.15.283–5)

At another point in the poem, Will, in his C-text apologia, validates his work of prayer and penance in similar terms, pointing out that the *fiat* will provision him:

'*Non de solo*,' Y sayde, 'for sothe *viuit homo*,
Nec in pane et in pabulo, the *Pater-noster* wittenesseth;
Fiat voluntas Dei – þat fynt vs alle thynges.'   (C.5.86–8)

Like Haukyn, Will has squandered his life yet comes to recognize that the will of God provides all he needs, the scriptural treasure hidden in a field which replaces all any sincere merchant can want.[59] Will expresses the hope that he will be given a drop of God's grace with which he can turn his time into profit (C.5.92–101), an audacious use of mercantile imagery, for making profit of time

---

58 Clopper, *Rechelesnesse* (pp 241–3), discusses Patience's call to Haukyn to give up labour and live 'rechelesli'. While I agree that Patience proposes poverty as an ideal that may lead to perfection, I think he treats the encounter with Haukyn as something in the nature of a spiritual 'retreat' for him, during which Haukyn will have to work out his priorities in the light of Patience's guidance.

59 'The kingdom of heaven is like unto a treasure hidden in a field. Which a man having found, hid it: and for joy thereof goeth and selleth all that he hath and buyeth that field. Again the kingdom of heaven is like to a merchant seeking good pearls. Who, when he had found one pearl of great price, went his way and sold all that he had and bought it': Matthew 13. 44–6.

'Marchauntz in þe margyne': how can the non-poor be saved

is the sin of usurers.⁶⁰ Will is determined to put as much effort into doing the will of God to make spiritual gain as earthly merchants invest in their money-making. This mercantile image is another of those scriptural images drawn from earthly commerce to represent heavenly good. Its position after the *Fiat* and the *nec in pane* links it with the *ne soliciti sitis* of B.14. The imagery suggests that commerce is not evil in itself, but the merchant must work hard to keep his actions in line with the will of God, and in case of conflict, put God's principles of justice and charity above those of material gain.

Another significant reference to the *Fiat* is made in Passus B.15 when Anima speaks about Charity, who is never without someone to provide for him in response to his charity to others:

> Of rentes ne of richesse ne rekkeþ he neuere,
> For a frend þat fynt hym, failed hym neuere at nede:
> *Fiat-voluntas-tua* fynt hym eueremoore. (B.15.177–9)

Essentially Charity is provided for by aligning his will with the will of God. Doing the will of God does not mean doing without, or abandoning material things, nor does it means giving up mercantile activity; it means putting God first.

First Piers, later Haukyn, and finally Will learn the essentials of obtaining spiritual 'liflode'. Piers has recognized that worry about physical food distracts the soul from seeking God's nourishment,⁶¹ and Patience has to teach Haukyn the overriding importance of the 'vitailles of grete virtues ... *Fiat voluntas tua*' (B.14.38, 49). This corresponds to the sustenance of God: *non in solo pane* (B.14.47a, b) which, with its overtones of the promised land in Deuteronomy, seems to be food that will win everlasting life. It will nourish Haukyn spiritually once he repents of the sins his active life has led him to commit. The food which Patience offers Haukyn is also identified as the piece of the *Paternoster* that will bring Haukyn through all tribulations:

> 'Haue, Haukyn,' quod Pacience, 'and et þis whan þe hungreþ,
> Or whan þow clomsest for cold or clyngest for drouȝte;
> And shul neuere gyues þee greue ne gret lordes wraþe,
> Prison ne peyne – for *pacientes vincunt*.' (B.14.50–3)

Such tribulations inevitably echo those endured by the poor in the parable of the Last Judgment:

---

60 See le Goff, *Your money and your life* (p. 39), quoting Thomas of Chobham's *Summa confessorum*.
61 'I shal cessen of my sowyng,' quod Piers, 'and swynke noȝt so harde, / Ne aboute my bely ioye so bisy be na moore; / Of preieres and of penaunce my plouȝ shal ben herafter, / And wepen whan I sholde slepe, þouȝ whete breed me faille ... / That loueþ God lelly, his liflode is ful esy.' (B.7.117–20; 123).

> Esurivi enim et dedistis mihi manducare; sitivi et dedistis mihi bibere; hospes eram et collexistis me; nudus et operuistis me; infirmus et visitastis me; in carcere eram et venistis ad me. (Matthew 25. 35–6)
>
> (For I was hungry, and you gave me to eat: I was thirsty, and you gave me to drink: I was a stranger, and you took me in: Naked and you covered me; sick, and you visited me: I was in prison, and you came to see me.)

Linked with Deuteronomy's evocation of the promised land,[62] they place Haukyn in the context of the Last Judgment, a scene foreshadowed by the parable of the wedding banquet, for which Haukyn is unprepared, not wearing a suitable garment (Matthew 22. 1–14). His coat is covered in sin, and only acts of charity to the needy can make amends. Haukyn cannot see how being patient and unsolicitous can help, but the underlying economic of Patience's concept of society is like that of Holy Church in Passus B.1:

> And if men lyueded as mesure wolde, sholde neuere moore be defaute
> Amonges Cristene creatures, if Cristes wordes ben trewe.
> Ac vnkyndenesse *caristia* makeþ amonges Cristes peple,
> And ouer-plentee makeþ pryde amonges poore and riche. (B.14.70–3)

If moderation were practised there would be sufficient for all. The words of Patience, as the passus proceeds, relate the state of poverty to justification at the Last Judgment, showing how it prevents, rather than stimulates, the seven sins (B.14.202–61). The life of trade and merchandise has led Haukyn into all the sins; poverty will lead him out of them.

In this important lesson given by Patience, the rationale behind *ne soliciti sitis* is thoroughly explored. Haukyn has the same attitude to material life as those in the tavern (B.5.307–57), busy about their 'bely ioye', unregenerate, but not subversive. Patience offers him 'liflode' as spiritual food, *fiat voluntas tua*, a bread which will rival Haukyn's delectable wafers. This will protect Haukyn against all the ills that can afflict mankind, which have been elaborated by Paul. Patience's disquisition of an ideal must be read in the light of Hugh of St. Cher's gloss on Matthew 6. 25–34, in which he quotes St John Chrysostom on three types of solicitude:

> The first is for our spiritual needs and is commanded; the second is for the necessities of life and is allowed; the third is for superfluity and is condemned.[63]

---

62 'For the Lord thy God will bring thee into a good land, of brooks and of waters, and of fountains: in the plains of which and the hills deep rivers break out. A land of wheat, and barley, and vineyards, wherein fig trees and pomegranates, and oliveyards grow: a land of oil and honey. Where without any want thou shalt eat thy bread, and enjoy abundance of all things: where the stones are iron, and out of its hills are dug mines of brass. That when thou hast eaten, and art full, thou mayst bless the Lord thy God for the excellent land which he hath given thee': Deuteronomy 8. 7–10.
63 Alford, 'The role of the quotations in *Piers Plowman*', p. 92.

Haukyn is exhorted, not to give up work, but to recognize the value of poverty, to put spiritual food before physical bread.[64] The exempla from the lives of Elias and the Israelites in the wilderness suggest that, at this point, Patience likens Haukyn's life to a pilgrimage or to a sojourn in the desert. Both exercises are symbolic of Lenten penance which will prepare him to return to his active life regenerated by the sacraments of penance and the eucharist, with his will re-educated to place spiritual needs before material gain and to share his goods with the poor.

HOW THE RICH CAN BE SAVED

Haukyn's problems in living without solicitude are equalled by the rich who do not practice charity. I have already described how, in practice, medieval charity was voluntary and varied. Will, speaking to Anima in Passus B.15, declares that he has never witnessed the kind of charity St Paul speaks of, where people give without expectation of return:

> Men beþ merciable to mendinauntʒ and to poore,
> And wollen lene þer þei leue lelly to ben paied.   (B.15.154–5)

In a continuation of Haukyn's education, Patience now turns to consider the second aspect of poverty for the non-poor – their obligation to share their goods with the needy. The detailed argument proceeds within a series of metaphors that show how all must earn heaven – the poor by their lives of earthly suffering, the rich by sharing their wealth with the poor. The imagery insists that strict justice governs all, rich and poor alike, and that reward will only be given for work done. A passage of extended imagery represents God as a lord who pays day-labourers for work well done and who demands a strict account from his servants (overseers as well as workers) on the day of reckoning. In Patience's celebration of poverty (B.14.99–201), both rich and poor have to do their 'deuoir', their 'dayes journee', in order to earn the hire that is heavenly bliss. The sheer length and complexity of the argument here demonstrates the moral urgency of Langland's message conveyed in poetry designed to move the will, not just of Haukyn, but of the reader.[65]

Much of Langland's concern about reward in the *Visio* is closely related to theological discussions about merit. Simpson has pointed out the distinction drawn between *meritum de condigno* and *meritum de congruo* and Langland's use of these concepts:

> *Meritum de condigno* is an absolute, strict merit, whereby men can be said justly and absolutely to merit reward. Congruent merit, on the other hand,

---

64 This idea is expressed in very similar terms by A. Baldwin: 'Patience intends to reform Hawkin's sinfulness by an internal and an external transformation'. This is in the context of her article 'The triumph of patience in Julian of Norwich and Langland', p. 82.
65 See Simpson, 'From reason to affective knowledge', pp 5–9.

is relative and conditional, whereby man receives reward out of the giver's generosity. When we look to the images used by theologians to describe these two kinds of reward, we see that they describe condign reward as wages, whereas congruent reward is described as a gift.[66]

I wish to extend Simpson's consideration of merit to analyse the social and spiritual importance of poverty as presented by Patience in his response to Haukyn's crucial question:

> 'Where wonyeþ Charite?' quod Haukyn. 'I wiste neuere in my lyue
> Man þat wiþ hym spak, as wide as I haue passed.'
> 'There parfit truþe and poore herte is, and pacience of tonge –
> There is Charite þe chief, chaumbrere for God hymselue.'(B.14.97–100)

Patience has just recommended penance as the only way for Haukyn to cleanse himself of the sin which, as his life-story has demonstrated, is inseparable from the active life of commerce and trade. Charity is the one solution, but it must be practised trusting in God to provide what is necessary and not taking more than 'mesure' allows. Haukyn has, initially, expressed reservations about Patience's idealistic picture:

> Thanne lauȝed Haukyn a litel, and lightly gan swerye,
> 'Whoso leueþ yow [eiþer], by Oure Lord, I leue noȝt he be blessed!'
> (B.14.35–6)

Aers comments pointedly:

> Perhaps thinking about the current labour legislation, certainly secure in his own culture of discourse, Haukyn laughs at this teaching, promising that whoever followed it would be far from blessed, a view that FitzRalph, vagrancy petitioners and many others would share.[67]

Patience is about to propose a view of society equally practical and far more positive than that of Haukyn, FitzRalph and the anti-poverty legislators. What follows (B.14.99–201) is a minutely worked out disquisition on the concepts of merit, justice, reward, and labour in which Langland presents an incontrovertible case for the value of poverty as, in itself, fitting a person for the reward of heaven. At the same time, the duty of the rich to share their goods with the poor is set out as a clear requirement under natural law. Langland, in this passus, expresses his social vision in both practical and ideal terms. Throughout the passage his thought proceeds by means of wordplay: verbal echoes, puns, synonyms

---

66 Simpson, 'Spirituality and economics in passus 1–7 of the B-text', pp 93–4.
67 Aers, *Community, gender, and individual identity*, p. 59.

and homonyms, techniques well explicated by Mary Clemente Davlin in her study, *A game of heuene*. Perhaps the most illuminating pun in helping us grasp what Langland understands of poverty is in the name of the allegorical figure who propounds its worth. Patience, as well as denoting forbearance, tolerance and acceptance is also semantically inseparable from suffering (Latin *patiens*). The poverty of which Patience speaks so eloquently is unmistakeably that of those who are poor by necessity, and only at the end of the passus (B.14.261–72) is there a mention of those who have chosen voluntary poverty.

The crux of the passage lies in two texts, one at the start and the other towards its close. The first states, with some precision, where Charity is to be found:

> There parfit truþe and poore herte is, and pacience of tonge. (B.14.99)

The second describes unequivocally the terms of true pardon:

> Ac þe parchemyn of þis patente of pouerte be moste,
> And of pure pacience and parfit bileue. (B.14.192–3)

'Parfit truþe' which, as Davlin has illustrated (pp 30–4), is a synonym for faith, is echoed in 'parfit bileue'. 'Poore herte', is paralleled by 'of pouerte be moste'; and 'pacience of tonge' parallels 'of pure pacience', with the punning of 'poore' and 'pure' stressing the moral worth of poverty. The importance of poverty for justification is unambiguous, and the rest of the argument fits within the parameters of poverty, patience and faith established by the two texts.

Haukyn pursues his enquiry with a carefully worded question:

> 'Wheiþer paciente pouerte,' quod Haukyn, 'be moore plesaunt to Oure Driȝte
> Than richesse *riȝtfulliche wonne* and *resonably yspended*?'
> (B.14.101–2; my emphasis)

'Riȝtfulliche' and 'resonably' are key words here. In his *Glossary of legal diction,* Alford points to the identification of reason and justice as reflecting

> the basic premise of natural law theory that the rules governing human conduct should be in conformity with the natural order. Reason is the name given both to that order [Lat. Ratio] and to the faculty that apprehends it.[68]

'Right and Reason' are regularly linked in medieval texts to express justice, equity, law; the phrase is especially associated with equitable law.[69] Haukyn is

---

68 Alford, *Piers Plowman: A glossary of legal diction*, p. 134.
69 Ibid. p. 134.

interested in the lawful acquisition of wealth and its expenditure in accordance with natural law. Patience will respond to him in terms of natural law, 'kynde', that will not only surprise Haukyn, but will reduce him to tears of near despair. There is a somewhat sarcastic note to Patience's response:

> Ye – *quis est ille?... quik – laudabimus eum!'* (B.14.103)

as he refers to a verse from Ecclesiasticus. For a person to achieve wealth with right and reason is rare indeed:

> Beatus dives qui inventus est sine macula et qui post aurum non abiit nec speravit in pecunia et thesauris. Quis est hic et laudabimus eum? Fecit enim mirabilia in vita sua. (Ecclesiasticus 31. 8–9)
>
> (Blessed is the rich man that is found without blemish: and that hath not gone after gold nor put his trust in money nor in treasures. Who is he, and we will praise him? For he hath done wonderful things in his life.)

Word association, from 'reason' to 'reckon', leads him then to discuss the reckoning every person must make at death; the recurring association of reason and reckon is a pun illustrated by the *MED* definition 6a, 'an account, reckoning.' In lines 104–10, rich and poor are placed in antithesis, both facing justice. The rich man is in fear ('dredde hym soore'), while the poor person is confident ('þe poore dar plede'). The rich man is embroiled in money matters ('arrerage', 'dette'), while the poor brings a suit. The poor person appeals to 'reson', law, justice or the principle of right order ('by þe lawe he it cleymeþ'), making a legal claim and declaring his title to 'allowaunce of his lord'. This allowance is a technical term in manorial accounting and represents credit or reimbursement for expenses, especially those incurred in the service of another.[70] The source of all this confidence comes from natural justice; the poor man knows that God is a 'riʒtful iugge' from whom he can expect an equitable judgment.

The basis of the poor man's claim to his title of joy is that he has not yet had it, and an analogy drawn from the natural world proves his title (B.14.111–15). God, who is the God of all nature, uses the harshness of winter to afflict and chasten the animals, causing them to be docile ('wel neiʒ meke and mylde for defaute'). Summer, by contrast, is 'souereyn ioye' for the animals, and 'blisse' to all, 'boþe wilde and tame'. Even the wild, those who have not become docile, have endured the suffering. In terms of the natural world, it is the pain, the 'defaute', that deserves the reward; natural justice is enshrined in the natural cycle of the seasons. As the passage progresses winter and summer become significant symbols of natural order and right.

The poetry then moves to press home the analogy (B.14.116–20). Beggars can be compared – at the lowest level – with beasts, and with the angels of hell. Even

[70] Ibid. p. 4.

at the bare minimum justice has to be done. Drawing upon two meanings, as Langland often does, beggars may both wait for and expect 'boote'. (They have been waiting for it all their lives; there is a suggestion here of an expectation of a certainty). The 'boote', in legal terms, is amends or compensation for an injury or wrongdoing (sense A). 'Boote' in this case, is the beggars' compensation for their suffering, an injury done to them by God. Calling on sense B, 'boote' is amends or compensation for the worse part of a bargain, something to make up the difference: 'to boot'.[71] The beggars, whose whole life has been 'langour' and 'defaute', pain and want, have as much right to expect recompense for enduring the bad part of the bargain in their lives on earth as animals have to expect summer after winter; 'defaute' has to be balanced by 'boote'. It would be against God's nature for them not have joy either in this world or the next: 'kynde wolde it nere'. The unnatural idea that someone could be created never to have any joy is expressed by the antitheses: 'wroþerhele ... wro3t'/'ioye shapen' and highlights a dreadful irony which can be paralleled only by the experience of the damned angels who were, indeed, created for joy, but created their own evil destiny. Misery on earth and in the hereafter is hell indeed. If even the angels of hell experienced joy at first, God would not destine a human being to misery both here and hereafter.

The corollary of this idea makes the situation of the rich look bleak. Lines 121–4 link the rich with the fallen angels who had 'ioye som tyme'. Dives had 'deyntees' and *'douce vie'*, rich men and their wives lived in 'murþe'. Playing on the term 'mercymonye' which derives from Latin *mercimonium* meaning 'merchandise' or 'reward' and in Middle English carries the additional connotations of salary or hire, Patience stresses the precarious situation of the rich to whom God gives reward in advance. In the course of the next twenty-nine lines (B.14.125–53), Patience makes a measured and detailed analogy in which man's life under God is likened to the relationship between employer and employee. The notions of labour, hire, reward and wages interweave; rich and poor each have a responsibility to earn their heavenly wage.

Patience feels 'ruþe' for some of the rich who have been paid their 'hire', 'withoute labour of bodye'. This mismatch is 'disalowed' when they come to the judgment; they are refused credit in their final account because they have not done the work. The second meaning of 'disalowe', to annul, cancel, or invalidate, adds the depth of a pun to the first. Whereas the poor were earlier said to claim 'allowaunce', the rich are 'disalowed'; poverty validates, wealth invalidates. Patience laments the ironic fact that, in the context of the end of life, 'at his laste ende', the time when the reckoning is being made, riches behave like a thief to 'reue and robbe', rather than being the object of theft as they were in the worldly situation. The treasure now is not riches but 'þe loue of Oure Lord'. Riches rob the soul of this, its true treasure.

In an extended image drawn from current labour practices Patience compares life to the work of a day-labourer, pointing up the link between work and

---

71 Ibid. p. 18.

worth, 'devoir' and deserving. Variant terms for labourers ('hewen' and 'werkman'), synonyms of labour ('werk', 'deuoir' and 'dayes journee'), and variants of earning ('wroʒt', 'worþi for his werk', 'deserved', 'deserve'), create an extended metaphor of life as hired labour in which the rich must earn their wages equally with the poor. Advance payment is said to be a dangerous practice which can lead a person into debt, the debt already attributed to the rich (B.14.107), and reflected again here (B.14.139–40). In the world of justice, labour attracts payment,[72] but taking wages in advance leads to the likelihood of running out of credit ('drede of disalowyng'), a phrase which echoes the dread mentioned earlier experienced by the rich man as he draws close to his Judgment (B.14.106). Emphatically, Patience drives home the point that the life of the wealthy is heaven 'for youre here-beyng' which God will treat as wages in advance. God's justice is stressed in this contemporary application of the parable of the labourers in the vineyard. The prepaid servant – the rich – cannot 'clayme' wages over and above those paid to the other workers ('he þat noon hadde') – the poor – at the end of the day.

Thus far the logic of law, nature, right reason and equity is clear: summer must follow winter, comfort replaces pain, bliss is compensation for suffering, wages are paid for work done. Conversely bliss in advance must be paid for by subsequent pain; wages in advance cause later need. And, unlike the earthly economy in which there is only a limited amount of goods to go round, in the heavenly economy justice decrees that the happiness of one does not detract from that of others. All who earn will obtain their reward. This is one of the clearest statements made in the poem of how the involuntarily poor earn heaven as of right, and I know of no other contemporary statement about the poor that carries such force.

From this halfway mark the passage moves into compassion both for rich and poor who are inextricably linked in that the damnation suggested as inevitable for the rich can be averted if they give help to the poor. Two words, 'rewarde' and 'ruþe' weave through the imagery, defining reciprocal responsibilities of rich and poor. Earlier, the wealth of the rich had been called 'mercymonye', which Alford glosses as 'reward, salary, hire'.[73] Now the rich are expected to 'rewarde' the poor so that they will themselves, in turn, be rewarded by Christ 'of his curteisie'. The implication of the term 'reward' is that the poor have actually earned this attention, and that it is not an arbitrary requirement; the rich are not being requested to donate something to the poor as if of their own accord; they are bound to pay the hire of the poor who have earned it by their suffering lives. Moreover, this is an obligation according to the law and the demands of 'leaute', justice (B.14.144–5). If the rich act with compassion they will be granted a 'bountee' (B.14.150), something over and above their contractual rights, out of the goodness of the lord – Christ – 'of his curteisie' (B.14.147). Then, in one of

---

[72] 'Dignus enim est operarius mercede sua.' (The labourer is worthy of his hire), (Luke 10. 7).
[73] Alford, *Glossary*, p. 99.

'Marchaunt3 in þe margyne': how can the non-poor be saved

those shifts of application so common in *Piers*, Langland deftly places rich and poor on an unmistakably equal footing. To live 'rewfulliche' and to do 'deuoir wel' is to receive 'double hire' which he finally defines as, not riches on earth, but forgiveness of sin and 'heuene blisse after' (150–3).

The mention of heavenly bliss for the compassionate rich and the suffering poor is not a way of dismissing indigence as if to be tolerated in view of a future recompense. The poem stresses immediately that the poor who must be relieved are paupers, the indigent who suffer physical hardships. It places them in stark contrast with the wealthy whose life of plenty parallels the summertime comfort of wild animals (157–8). The poor must endure starvation in the summer, trudging with no shoes in the winter,[74] and to their hunger and thirst are added maltreatment from the wealthy:

> Ac beggeris aboute midsomer bredlees þei soupe,
> And yet is wynter for hem worse, for weetshoed þei gange,
> Afurst soore and afyngred, and foule yrebuked
> And arated of riche men, þat ruþe is to here. (B.14.160–3)

The only 'ruþe' in question is the pity evoked by their harsh treatment *by* the rich (162); contrary to earlier hopes, they are not getting any pity *from* the rich. With cutting irony, the poetry juxtaposes rich people's protection from the tribulations that afflict the poor. Of the rich it is said:

> For may no derþe be hem deere, droghte ne weet*e*,
> Ne neiþer hete ne hayll, haue þei hir heele;
> Of þat þei wilne and wolde wanteþ hem no3t here. (B.14.171–3)

These lines are repeated almost verbatim within the space of two lines, now applied to the poor:

> Thoru3 derþe, þoru3 droghte, alle hir dayes here,
> Wo in wynter tyme for wantynge of cloþes,
> And in somer tyme selde soupen to þe fulle. (B.14.176–8)

Such tribulations echo words of Patience in B.13, spoken when he first launches into his defence of charity:

> For, by hym þat me made, my3te neuere pouerte,
> Misese, ne mischief, ne man wiþ his tonge,
> Coold, ne care, ne compaignye of þeues,
> Ne neiþer hete, ne hayl, ne noon helle pouke,
> Ne neiþer fuyr, ne flood, ne feere of þyn enemy

---

74 'Weetshoed' is possibly a kenning for no shoes at all.

> Tene þee any tyme, and þow take it wiþ þe:
> *Caritas nichil timet.* (B.13.159–64a)

This, in turn, is Langland's paraphrase of Romans 8. 38–9:

> Certus sum enim quia neque mors neque vita neque angeli neque principatus neque instantia neque futura neque fortitudines neque altitudo neque profundum neque creatura alia poterit nos separare a caritate Dei quae est in Christo Iesu Domino nostro.
>
> (For I am sure that neither death, nor life, nor angels, nor principalities, nor powers, nor things present, nor things to come, nor might, nor height, nor depth, nor any other creature will be able to separate us from the love of God which is in Christ Jesus our Lord.)

Langland, as Alford says, substitutes more concrete phenomena which correspond with the six tribulations of Job 5. 19 and the six tribulations of Matthew 25. 35–6.[75] The abbreviated versions of B.14 quote from Langland's own quotation, carrying within themselves, rather like the *etc.* in his Latin quotations, the sense of the original. The point behind all these related texts is that God's charity is directed towards those who suffer earthly trials, and that the only way the protected rich can share in this charity is to care for those in need. If they do this, they will be acting like God by shielding the poor from tribulation, as God shields them.

Lest it should appear that the poem is acquiescent, accepting that conditions cannot be improved, Langland here reiterates the specific kinds of suffering that the rich must relieve. The poor endure the same tribulations from which the rich are protected, so if the rich are to participate in God's charity which is awarded to the suffering poor, they must be the channels of that love to the poor, using their goods to do so. This is reminiscent of Holy Church's words in the first passus when she makes it a condition of salvation that goods are shared 'goodliche' – as God shares, without expectation of return. The irony for the rich is that these recall the conditions laid out in Matthew's parable of the Last Judgment, the tribulations of Christ in his poor followers (Matthew 25. 35–6). Scripture endorses practical acts of poor relief as the condition for salvation, and the poem is explicit that care for the poor will make up for the sins of the rich (B.14.144). There is no abatement of passion, for the poetry appeals with equal fervour for God to have mercy on the poor who suffer and the rich who are in danger of damnation, having demonstrated in precise terms what the rich must do to be saved. The whole tenor of this passage makes poverty the evil to be endured and wealth to be the reward. Yet the ironic paradox is that the pain of

---

75 Alford has demonstrated Langland's indebtedness to commentaries and concordances for his quotations; he has also pointed out clearly how Langland uses the material he found in the concordances for his own poetic ends: 'The role of the quotations', p. 97.

poverty earns the heavenly kingdom, the 'riche', while the comfort of riches earns the pain of hell.

Finally, Patience describes the nature of Jesus Christ to be 'of his gentries', a nobility of spirit that includes rather than excludes. Christ extends his salvation to all, sinners on a par with rich and with poor. Baptism first purifies sinners, confession repeats forgiveness. And to seal the legality of this forgiveness Patience returns to the legal imagery with which the passage started, making the discussion intimately personal by shifting to 'we' and 'us' (B.14.188–200). Gone are the distinctions between rich and poor; in the sacramental life all souls are equal before God. If the devil wants to 'plede' – to bring a suit – as, at the start of this section, the poor man dared to plead, all the sinner needs to do is take his 'acquitaunce', his deed of release,[76] and show it to the evil one, the devil. In doing so he shows the documentation that confirms he is under a pledge, 'borwe'. Someone else, Christ, has undertaken to be surety and to guarantee the repayment of the loan or debt. But the parchment of this deed – the 'patente', the letter patent, possibly the indulgence,[77] – has to be made of poverty, pure patience and perfect faith. Unless a person is 'poore of herte', every good practice is invalidated. This includes repetition of the *Paternoster*, penance, and pilgrimage to Rome, all three being activities which could provoke an indulgence, the 'patente' issued by the pope, as contrasted with the 'patente' made of poverty. Unless expenditure and expenses – 'spences' and 'spendynge' – another nice bit of word-play – are from a 'trewe welle', or the well-spring of truth which is faith, spending money or effort on gaining indulgences is no use.

Throughout the poem, but especially in Passus B.6–7 and B.13–14, Langland wrestles with the ideology of *ne soliciti sitis*, trying to find some practical application of it in his fourteenth-century environment. His destitute beggars wear the same garb as pilgrims – 'barefoot and wolleward'. They are to be regarded as having the same potential sanctity as pilgrims with the same lack of care about their material needs which the community of their Christian brethren is supposed to attend to. Haukyn expresses the deep need for spiritual understanding that those people experience whose lives are caught up with the economics of this world's affairs. To him, not to the suffering poor, Patience unfolds the beauties of poverty. After the severe punishment which he has predicated for the rich, some consolation is required, and this comes in the praise of poverty which counteracts all the sins, and protects the person who embraces it voluntarily. Such praise of poverty is not unique to Patience, who draws upon traditional constructs of the ideal. Nor is it unique to this section of the poem; the character of Rechelesnesse, particularly in the C-text, advances strong arguments drawn from lives of saints, Scripture and exempla in praise of poverty. After Patience has taken Haukyn through the study of the seven sins showing how poverty is

---

[76] Alford, *Glossary*, p. 8.
[77] Ibid., p. 111.

an antidote to them, and after he has glossed Vincent of Beauvais showing poverty as a good, not an evil, Haukyn is ready to become a penitent, shirtless and shoeless like the pilgrims who emulate the poorest:

> 'I were noȝt worþi, woot God,' quod Haukyn, 'to werien any cloþes,
> Ne neiþer sherte ne shoon.' (B.14.329–30)

Much later in the poem, Will, too, accepts the starkest poverty when he has undergone his spiritual odyssey:

> Wolleward and weetshoed wente I forþ after
> As a recchelees renk þat of no wo reccheþ. (B.18.1–2)

For Haukyn, Will, and the involuntarily poor, poverty puts them under the protection of Christ, who is their good lord. The 'sute' of poverty is called the 'sute' that Jesus wore; and poverty is the 'signe', the badge that shows:

> That God is his grettest help and no gome ellis,
> And he is seruaunt, as he seiþ, and of his sute boþe.
> And wher he be or be noȝt, he bereþ þe signe of pouerte,
> And in þat secte Oure Saueour saued al mankynde. (B.14.256–9)

Anna Baldwin has recently suggested that Langland's ideal society is one in which charity becomes the norm and the rich scale down their wealth, giving to the poor and becoming poor themselves. Langland, she argues, will change the world by eliminating not poverty, but riches.[78] This is a further development of her earlier premise that:

> if justice is the crying need of society (as appears from the Visio), it might be better to teach all men to desire poverty, rather than to try to prevent the unrepentant rich from oppressing the poor.[79]

Charity is, undoubtedly, the underlying virtue of Langland's ideal society, and the one without which all is disaster. But I cannot agree that Langland wants to scale down society. His poetry subtly reconstitutes the ideal Christian society as one in which every estate has its place, while recognizing that in essence all are blood brothers and equal in the sight of God, in the charnel house, and in the final journey:

> And euery man helpe ooþer – for hennes shul we alle:
> Alter alterius onera portate. (B.11.210–a)

---

[78] 'Patient politics in *Piers Plowman*', p. 100.
[79] 'The triumph of patience', p. 83.

'Marchaunt3 in þe margyne': how can the non-poor be saved

The context of this quotation in Galatians, which Langland uses as a kind of refrain for the brotherhood of all men, is that of accepting earthly life as a crucifixion, so that in earthly suffering the Christian is united with Christ. Charity and poverty come together in this celebration of Christ's redemptive and loving sacrifice. The C-text at the same point recognizes the Last Judgment connotations of this message by quoting the words of Piers' pardon:

> Forthy loue we as leue childerne, and lene hem þat nedeth,
> And euery man helpe other – for hennes shal we alle
> To haue as we haen serued, as Holy Chirche witnesseth:
> *Et qui bona egerunt, ibunt in vitam eternam ...*   (C.12.118–20a)

The poor form the best class, the one that is going to redeem society, but only when it is treated with justice. Poverty is best, and the rich must be just stewards towards their poor brethren if they are to be poor in heart; but there is no call for all Christians to become needy. The rich are supposed to relieve the needs of the poor, but not to make themselves indigent. Neither are they supposed to make the poor rich; what they must do is satisfy their needs. The poem acknowledges that, as Shepherd says, there is a mystery about the creation of some rich and some poor:

> Almi3ty God [my3te haue maad riche alle] men, if he wolde,
> Ac for þe beste ben som riche and some beggeres and pouere.
>   (B.11.196–7)

This is repeated in B.14 and, with a slight variation, in C.16:

> For al myhtest þou haue ymad men of grete welthe,
> And yliche witty and wys, and lyue withoute nede –
> Ac for þe beste, as Y hope, aren som pore and ryche.   (C.16.19–21)

As Langland presents it, however, the relationship between rich and poor is far stronger than that proposed by formulas of mutual benefit such as those described in the first part of this chapter. The rich are to accept the suffering of imitating God's poverty in their own lives, giving away their surplus without anxiety or solicitude – not an easy proposition, as the discussion from Gutiérrez and Ignatieff in Chapter One suggests, but essential for salvation. To act in this way is to accept God's will, his *voluntas*, which causes suffering to all, if they accept it fully, as Christ in Gethsemane, and Mary at the Annunciation both knew.

At the very end of his uncompromising response to Haukyn's question Patience makes a categorical statement:

> Forþi Cristene sholde be in commune riche, noon coueitous for hymselue.
>   (B.14.201)

Perhaps 'in commune' refers to the common body of the people, as a collective entity. In Acts, it is said, all things were held in common:

> Multitudinis autem credentium erat cor et anima una nec quisquam eorum quae possidebant aliquid suum esse dicebat sed erant illis omnia communia.
> (Acts 4. 32)

> (And the multitude of believers had but one heart and one soul. Neither did any one say that aught of the things which he possessed was his own: but all things were common unto them.)

This returns to the idea of *dominium* and the conflict between the patristic argument, (represented by my earlier reference to St Ambrose) which holds that private property has no place in the ideal society, and later moralists' views that private property is a necessary instrument of the good life and an orderly society.[80] Although Langland does not enter the debate as such, the poem breaks down the differences between rich and poor. Its whole tenor is that the rich hold their property as lent by God, as if in trust for the poor for whose needs they are responsible. All through Patience's disquisition there has been mirroring as well as antithesis between rich and poor. Many times, as I have illustrated, the same words are used with reverse significance – reward, hire, ruth, allowance, disallowance, the list of tribulations from which the rich are saved but the poor must endure. A symbiosis is in operation. God's grace and forgiveness are available for all, and if the rich take care of the poor they will not fall into arrears at the final reckoning, neither will the poor be in 'defaute' during life. Patience has several times expressed compassion for the rich. His regret at their difficulties in performing the charity that is necessary can be taken to suggest convincingly that only a sharing in common, like that of the early Christians, can effectively save them. This may not be a blueprint for social justice; it is poetry, and the speaker is Patience, not a social legislator. But it is an attempt to make a coherent statement about the value of poverty, the social responsibilities of the rich and the straight road to salvation for poor and rich alike. In this attempt, Langland is responding to his cultural ideology, revealing its gaps and inconsistencies, making the text articulate the deep-seated needs of his society for justice.

Where some scholars, such as Aers, Hewett-Smith and Pearsall, whose views I have considered in an earlier chapter, consider that Langland looks at the material problems of the poor and advocates transcending those problems by embracing a belief in spiritual reward, I argue that the poetry maintains but inverts contemporary notions of value, reversing the ideals that associate personal value with goods. Not goods but poverty is to be the measure of a person's worth. The principal locus for this reversal of values is in B.13 and B.14. Here, Patience inducts both Will and Haukyn into the understanding of the practice of poverty, particularly within the philosophy of *ne soliciti sitis*. This is done without any hint

---

80 Little, p. 176.

'Marchaunt3 in þe margyne': how can the non-poor be saved

that the indigent should ignore their sufferings. On the contrary, the intensity with which Langland records them suggests that they are so great as to deserve both the justice of relief in this world and the reward of justification in heaven.

For Marxist thinkers, such an emphasis on the value of poverty is a betrayal of the sufferings of poor people who look to a better life hereafter. For Langland, the life of poverty *is* the better life here and now. This is not to deny that the indigent are the weakest members of society and the most vulnerable. Langland has no difficulty in recognizing this and in representing their vulnerability as the occasion both for the best of good works and for the worst deeds of unkindness and injustice. He cannot ignore the sufferings of poor people and, in the C-text, as Pearsall says, his preception is more acute even than in B.[81] The truly indigent are a deep scandal, one which the poetry faces in graphic detail without offering any solution that would satisfy a modern social reformer. Langland is not attempting to suggest ways of reducing the numbers of the poor, nor is he offering ways of abolishing poverty. This would be out of accord with his important premise that poverty is part of the straight road that leads to heaven. He is, however, making the forceful proposition that no amount of conventional 'charity' can substitute for direct assistance to the indigent. The next chapter will examine how the character, Will, has to learn the practice of poverty and endure the physical suffering and moral opprobrium that his contemporary society metes out to the poor. In doing so Will achieves an integrity that depends, not on the opinion of others, nor on identification with any group, but on his identification with Christ.

---

[81] 'Poverty and poor people', p. 167.

CHAPTER 4

Voluntary poverty and involuntary need: Will's experience of being a poor man

There already exists an almost bewildering wealth of scholarly exposition on the character of Will.[1] My reason for adding to it in a study on poverty is that Will comes closest in medieval literature to representing a truly poor man, and his voice comes closest to recording the voice of the medieval poor. Of the many other reasons for including a chapter on Will, three stand out. Firstly, his life demonstrates very clearly why poverty is an essential of Christian living. Secondly, Will suffers the privations and loss of dignity that a fourteenth-century poor man experiences. Thirdly, the poetic expression of his poverty engages with what Anne Middleton calls 'intertextualities'[2] – of Scripture, statute and church regulation – in such a way as to make visible the gaps in pieties and social structures that express (rather than describe) his culture. Althusser's description of the way in which art makes visible the ideology of a culture is particularly pertinent to the role of Will:

> What art makes us *see*, and therefore gives to us in the form of *'seeing'*, *'perceiving'* and *'feeling'* (which is not the form of *knowing*), is the *ideology* from which it is born, in which it bathes, from which it detaches itself as art, and to which it *alludes*.[3]

My assertion that a medieval writer's representation of poverty and the poor becomes a touchstone of faith, of moral probity and of identity[4] is nowhere more clearly exemplified than in the character of Will, a poor man through whose eyes and voice the poem, *Piers Plowman,* conducts a dialogue with its culture.

This chapter is structured around Will's waking moments because, for the purposes of relating Will's experience of poverty to that of his indigent contemporaries, the waking moments demonstrate his life in the world of 'nowadaies'. The underlying argument of the chapter is that a life of poverty

---

1 Full studies of Will and his visionary learning are found in Simpson, *Piers Plowman: an introduction*; G. Rudd, *Managing language in 'Piers Plowman'*; Bowers, *The crisis of Will in 'Piers Plowman'*; J. Wittig, 'The dramatic and rhetorical development of Long Will's pilgrimage'; and '*Piers Plowman* B, passus IX–XII.'
2 See Middleton, 'Acts of vagrancy', pp 246–7.
3 Althusser, 'A letter on art in reply to André Daspré', p. 204.
4 Introduction, p. 13.

156

Voluntary poverty and involuntary need: Will's experience of being a poor man 157

brings Will close to Christ and gives him both the authority to fight against forces that oppose Christ's kingdom and the insight to promote the gospel standards of justice and love. The discussion follows Will's progression through various stages of poverty which relate to the 'five meanings' with which I opened my study. Initially he seems like Juvenal's carefree traveller, wandering the world, but during close analysis of what many scholars call Will's 'apologia' in the C-text (C.5.1–108) it emerges that he has actually made a choice of voluntary poverty in his youth. I elaborate on how, with the passage of time, Will comes to experience the various aspects of material need, the scandalous privation of the involuntarily poor: hunger, thirst, cold, and the marginalization that comes from being regarded, at times, as not only poor but insane. My argument is that by showing Will suffering the privations of poverty Langland not only portrays a poor man 'from the ground up' so to speak, but offers a concrete representation of what it means to choose a life of poverty in order to follow Christ in fourteenth-century England. We have already seen how the poem draws distinctions between instances of deserving and undeserving poor. This chapter considers its sharpest satire of a third group, those voluntarily poor who adopt the religious life but exploit their condition in idleness and sin.

First, I suggest that, in portraying Will as a religious itinerant who behaves like the fake mendicants of its satire, the poem demonstrates how possible it is for a sincere person to abandon the initial fervour of voluntary poverty and how hard it is to accept material poverty as a way of life. The rest of the chapter examines how Will learns that the poverty which imitates Christ is indistinguishable from the material need of the involuntarily poor. In this, the poem presents a view of voluntary poverty radically different from that of the established religious orders for whom ownership, not need, is the test of Christian poverty.[5] I argue that Will embodies all the facets of poverty as it was understood, practised and endured in the fourteenth century and that, by the end of the poem, his varied experiences of poverty and need lead him to participate in the reform of the Church within the barn of Unity (B.20.204–11). In stripping away all that seems essential in worldly terms, Will discovers his identity with Christ in ultimate indigence. To study Will as a poor man is to question the meaning and practice of voluntary poverty, the position of the indigent, and moral responsibility, both individual and collective, within his contemporary medieval society.

SOME POOR MEN IN LITERATURE

In the previous chapter I discussed Langland's vision of poverty, and how necessary it is for everyone to understand and live a life of poverty, both to achieve

---

[5] The view put forward by Clopper is that Langland uses the persona of Will (and, at other times in the poem, Rechelesnesse and Lyf) to call the friars, particularly the Franciscans, to attention for offences against their rule of 'perfect poverty'. This does not conflict with my point, but relates it more specifically to one form of religious and clerical life than I wish to do. See *Rechelesnesse*, p. 315.

personal salvation and to further the kingdom of God's justice. This was explored in the light of prescriptions for care of the poor, and the practice of poverty for the non-poor. Previous chapters have suggested that there is more than one way of living poverty. This one elaborates on Will's quest for salvation and his understanding of the role poverty plays in helping him towards his goal. Before looking closely at Will's life, brief reference to a few 'poor men' of medieval literature will show how Langland's view that the non-poor must adopt Christian ideals of poverty seems to go against society's prevailing trend. Hoccleve's old man, a beggar, has already been mentioned, and Chaucer gives an eccentric portrait of a poor man in his Canon's Yeoman.[6] Thomas Chester's Sir Launfal is a poor knight fallen on hard times,[7] and Hoccleve, the poet, is a man in prosperity who fears himself to be teetering on the brink of falling into poverty (*Regement*, ll.820–61).[8] For them, poverty is a state to be avoided, and even the old man, who has resigned himself to accepting it as a penance for past sins, still prays for deliverance, likening himself to Job whose material prosperity was restored (*Regement*, ll.729–42).[9] To appreciate their revulsion against poverty is to understand more clearly the power of Langland's social demands on the non-poor.

For all these men, poverty is an alien condition, an ill from which deliverance is necessary – in the case of the Canon's Yeoman, at an ironic cost. The Yeoman has fallen from prosperity, not by an accident of fortune, but deliberately, spending his fortune by slow degrees in an attempt to win the big prize – the ability to turn dross into gold. He demonstrates the addict's ability to endure a life of privation in the hope of gaining fabulous wealth. He is not one of the 'shamefaced poor' for whom the fraternities looked out, nor is he an 'honest' pauper, though he is probably equally needy, living, as he does,

> In the suburbes of a toun ...
> Lurkynge in hernes and in lanes blynde,
> Wheras thise robbours and thise theves by kynde
> Holden hir pryvee fereful residence.   (ll.657–60)

The account of the physical privations he endures in the worst part of the town puts him in the category of the poorest; his poverty is indeed voluntary, but the reward he seeks is material, not heavenly. The horrors of his poverty suggest Chaucer's authorial rejection of greed for gold in itself rather than as a commodity for trade and use, but demonstrate, too, all that the non-poor detest about the poor and the moral evils of their life.

The story of *Sir Launfal* exemplifies the social value of wealth in establishing a person's reputation, giving and receiving honour and maintaining a place within

---

6 'The Canon's Yeoman's prologue and tale', in *Chaucer*, pp 270–5 (ll.554–971).
7 *Sir Launfal*, ed. A.J. Bliss.
8 *Hoccleve's works: the regiment of princes*, ed. F.J. Furnivall.
9 A pictorial detail illustrating St Gregory's *Moralia in Job* shows Job re-established in his former state, crowned, enjoying a banquet: Paris, Bibliothèque Nationale, MS lat.15675, fol. 8v.

society. At the core of Thomas Chester's story is the issue of how poverty disables and wealth enables. With wealth Launfal is a full person able to act freely in love, war, and Christian charity; without it, he counts for nothing. Other people treat him with contempt; the mayor reluctantly gives him lodging in a small orchard room, he is not invited to the Trinity Sunday feast in the town and a boy in the market disparages him as a wretch of no account. Launfal derives his identity from wealth. Without it he has no standing and is disregarded by society, but when Triamour endows him with fine clothes, a horse, rich armour and a purse that magically refills, Launfal is restored to his former state as the most noble knight of them all.

This definition of a person's intrinsic moral worth by his perceived social value is most feelingly played out by the poet Hoccleve. From his vantage point in the office of the Privy Seal, Hoccleve regards the prospect of a fall into poverty with intense dismay. Philosophically he can accept the spiritual value of poverty but, having lived within the purlieus of government, he contemplates his own potential old-age indigence as a fall on a par with that of Richard II (*Regement*, ll.22–8). He recognizes that, as Launfal discovered, money is the sign of belonging:

> Who no good hath, is fer his frendes fro;
> In muk is al þis worldes frendlyhede.   (*Regement*, ll.957–8)

In his writings, an expressed fear of poverty becomes the touchstone of all that he values: not material possessions, but the identification and sense of purpose that come from having a role and function within a group. The *Complaint*[10] describes how a period of mental illness set him apart from the life and world of Westminster which was not only his whole world, as a liveried servant of the Crown, but that which gave him status, value and a purpose for living. In the prologue to *The regement of princes* the worst of his fears had been that he would cease to have a place among his old acquaintance, and would lose the identity he clung to if he did not have enough money to maintain himself in their company. Now, in 1419, he describes feelingly how he lost not only their good opinion but their perception of him as the person he knew himself to be and to have been. The *Complaint* shows that the social dislocation which he had anticipated from falling into poverty became a reality when he suffered from a bout of insanity. Hoccleve's begging poems express poverty as an evil to be avoided, because the poor are outsiders, 'other'; the *Complaint* and *Dialogue* explore the personal hell of being an outcast through insanity.

Reading these 'poor men' of literature side-by-side with Will illuminates the social gulf between poor and non-poor in the medieval mind. None of these men is morally bad. Launfal, once he regains wealth, sets about his Christian duty of performing conventional works of charity and almsgiving by the fifty, a poetic way of saying 'with liberality':

10 *Thomas Hoccleve's complaint and dialogue*, ed. J.A. Burrow.

> Fyfty fedde pouere gestes,
> Þat in myschef wer ...
> Fyfty rewardede relygyons,
> Fyfty delyuerede pouere prysouns.   (ll.422–3; 427–9)

The Canon's Yeoman, apparently sinful, makes a bid for integrity by exposing his master's swindle and offering himself as a living exemplum of greed's perils. Yet all these figures, including the devout Hoccleve and his aged interlocutor, find their lives defined by material goods, and the Yeoman has allowed lust for possessions to destroy his life. These men exhibit no understanding of Christ's call to place love of spiritual goods above earthly ones, nor do they regard the indigent as entitled to the human dignity they value for themselves. Even Launfal, who has known what it is to be penniless, does not translate this experience into any sense of brotherhood with the poor. When he is rich he returns to his knightly role and adopts traditional practices, donating to the poor as anonymous 'others', fixed in their condition. Will's exploration of identity in Christ is, in comparison to these 'poor men', revolutionary.

Piers Plowman is not alone among late medieval devotional and didactic works in promoting the value of poverty in the spiritual life. There are many others, but they differ from the approach of *Piers* in polarizing material and spiritual as irreconcilable opposites. Rolle's *Ego dormio* and *Form of living* give practical advice to a non-poor lady on retreating from all that is worldly so that her soul may concentrate on the spiritual.[11] Rolle's practical good sense makes allowance for bodily needs, and warns against excess in fasting, lest bodily hunger should prevent the soul from concentrating on contemplation of the divine, but the poverty experience he recommends requires disengagement from all worldly concerns.[12] *The castle of perseverance*[13] is an example of a text which condemns everything in 'the world' as ranged with the devil, in direct opposition to God and his heavenly kingdom. This kingdom is one in which the seven deadly sins are combated by the contrary virtues and the soul is ultimately saved by the mercy of God. It is an abstraction, far removed from the everyday world of the fourteenth century in which Will operates. For the devout nobleman Henry of Lancaster, the only way of achieving a truly poor following of Christ is to embrace the religious life. For him, holiness and the active life are irreconcilable opposites, as Ann Warren explains:

> His career was an example of the active life played to its ultimate perfection: he was a good man by every definition. Yet his literary work was an expression of the inherent sinfulness of that life, a sinfulness from which there seemed no escape, save perhaps for the religious and certainly for

---

[11] *English writings of Richard Rolle*, pp 61–72; 85–119.
[12] Ibid. pp 64–7; 86–7.
[13] *The macro plays*, ed. Mark Eccles, pp 1–111.

Voluntary poverty and involuntary need: Will's experience of being a poor man 161

the recluse. Henry's endowments of religious institutions were not the attempts of a wicked man to redeem his way into heaven but vicarious acts completing his life.[14]

In comparison to such texts it becomes clear that Will is an outstandingly important medieval literary figure because he gives textual expression to an experience of Christian poverty in the active life that goes beyond devotional formulas. Study of his waking experiences will demonstrate without doubt that Langland portrays the hard life of the poor not as a mystery, still less as a condition that must be transcended by thoughts of heavenly reward, but as state to be embraced willingly as defining the true Christian's identity.

Will is the unifying force within the poem, a personification of the human faculty, will, *voluntas*. Choice, responsibility and intention are guiding forces in a life which is full of failures and renewals.[15] Will lives a life of poverty in his waking moments, and a life of spiritual quest during his visions. The visions take us into the deepest recesses of his mind and emotions; the waking moments show him suffering the practical effects of striving to renew his intention. Will *chooses* a life of poverty (B.Prol.2–4); by definition this is voluntary poverty. Yet he experiences, in the course of the poem, all the aspects of basic need which the involuntarily poor have to endure; he goes hungry, thirsty and barefoot (B.20.3; C.22.3; B.18.1; C.20.1), begs for the basic necessities of life (C.5.51–2), is treated as though he is an idle vagrant (C.5.12–34; B.12.16–17), sometimes as a madman (B.15.1–10), scorned as an outsider (B.15.4), and left to drink from the ditch in utter destitution (B.20.19). These experiences lead him to come to terms in his own life with the fact of poverty as a scandal and a condition calling for reform, while all the time wrestling with the concepts of it as a religious virtue, and a philosophical good. He eventually accepts that his life in poverty has value because it identifies him with Christ (B.20.48–50).

Although such conditions of involuntary poverty are also regarded by the non-poor as a terrible fate, something in the nature of poverty seems to have held an attraction for people throughout the centuries. Juvenal's carefree traveller assumed an almost symbolic character in medieval commentaries, and Langland recreates it in Rechelesnesse's exemplum of the swift-footed messenger (C.13.32–63). In Bosch's painting of the Wanderer, peasants dance while a wealthy traveller who has been robbed is being tied against a tree. The Wanderer himself walks safely, though his poverty is emphasized by the snarling dogs generally associated with beggars.[16] The concept of the carefree poor man is closely

---

14 Warren, p. 173.
15 Wittig defines the controlling argument of the poem as being 'that all reform is rooted in the reform of the individual human will': 'The dramatic and rhetorical development of Long Will's pilgrimage', p. 53. Simpson points out that the name of Will, linked as it is to the Latin *voluntas*, sums up Will's nature as his 'kynde name', and fits within a medieval commonplace scheme in which the affective part of the soul works with the cognitive part, represented by Thought, Wit and Imaginatif: *Piers Plowman: an introduction,* pp 95–6.
16 Here I draw on Graziani's, 'Bosch's *Wanderer* and a poverty commonplace from Juvenal'.

allied in the medieval mind with Christ's *Beati pauperes*, the first of the Beatitudes (Luke 6. 20). It is essentially a single person's maxim which glorifies the single, non-conjugal way of life; as such, it fits with Christ's call to his disciples to leave all family ties, parents, children and spouse, to have treasure in heaven. As a wanderer, Will subscribes to this aspect of poverty, an ideal for anyone in search of a happiness that comes, not from the accretion of property and personal relationships, but from the stripping away of anxieties associated with worldly life. He is in the tradition of those medieval people who, time after time, sought ways to attain detachment from material things in order to concentrate on those of heaven. Following Christ, St Paul established it:

> Mind the things that are above, not the things that are upon the earth. For you are dead: and your life is hid with Christ in God.
> (Colossians 3. 2–3)

The visionary Francis of Assisi fled from material wealth so that he could move unencumbered from place to place preaching to those whose spiritual need was greater than his material indigence. Those who embraced the mendicant or the eremitical life as an ideal saw Christ and his apostles as prototypes who had sublimated the poverty of the vagrant, raising its spiritual status to that of the itinerant preacher, an ideal that would attract men and women throughout the succeeding centuries. In the lives of these wanderers material goods are a hindrance to the true business of their lives – the search for perfection and the preaching of this to others. The ideal is alluring, whether embodied in the secular *viator* of Juvenal or the religious vagrant, Francis. For medieval people the ascetic life is the practical manifestation of this ideal, the profoundly attractive yet disturbingly hard way of perfection. Its attractions lie in the spiritual liberation promised to its faithful devotees; the penalty is a hard life of penance, solitude and self-denial. Hermits, anchorites and friars act as representative poor within the community, contemporary embodiments of Christ. All medieval society, from kings to poor widows, contributed to their support in varying degrees, depending on the regularity and generosity of benefactions.[17] In this, as in so many other manifestations of poverty, inconsistency in medieval attitudes leads to moral judgments about the poor. Those who hear and answer the call to perfection are respected and valued, whereas the tramp, the vagabond and the beggar are mistrusted by their contemporaries. Will expresses this duality in his own life, for it is by no means clear whether he is a true hermit or a feigning mendicant. Nevertheless, whatever ambivalence there may be in Will's initial choice of poverty, clothed as he is 'in habite as an heremite vnholy of werkes' (B.Prol.3), the poem shows him sharing in and developing an understanding of the material want experienced by the indigent.

---

17 See Warren on the differential support of various anchorholds, pp 50–1.

Will, the seeker, has to come to terms, in his own life, with the conflicts inherent in embracing poverty voluntarily. This does not happen in the initial instant of donning the hermit's habit for the life of an apparently prayerful mendicant; it is worked on repeatedly throughout his quest, refined in response to visionary circumstances and ideas debated with his allegorical interlocutors. Will's extreme poverty positions him firmly in the *saeculum*, the earthly and tangible world. Even though the whole poem is concerned with Will's quest for truth and for heavenly treasure, the poverty he achieves, which Holy Church (B.1.175–9), Trajan (B.11.230–318), Rechelesnesse (C.13.1–97), Patience (B.14 passim) and Anima (B.15.268–317) elevate to a state of spiritual good, is a corporeal experience. In the process of definition and redefinition, Will chips away at the accretions of philosophy that propose a concept of poverty far removed from that which is lived and perceived by the indigent. By the end of the poem, Will's poverty, voluntarily assumed at the outset, becomes absolute, physical need. I argue that his experience of need is a challenge to the interpretation of poverty practised by religious orders, a legal detachment from the goods of this world which allows a person to enjoy material goods without actually owning them. By persistently reassessing his mode of poor living and its social and moral significance, he reaches the uneasy understanding, shared by modern thinkers, that to follow Christ is willingly to accept a life of solidarity with involuntarily poor people. Will's voluntarily accepted poverty has the goal, simultaneously both spiritual and socio-political, of achieving for them access to the justice and charity of God's kingdom on earth. The poem demonstrates this most clearly when Will joins the struggle against the forces of Antichrist.

Much of the poem, especially the *Vita*, relates spiritual encounters and explores the scriptural and theological world of salvation history, yet with all its renewed starts and disappointments the poem returns repeatedly to the earth, to the world. Study of the poor man, Will, brings out the importance of choice in the life of the Christian. Will makes choices all through life – he chooses the life of a poor wanderer but not the monastic life of perfection. Though Will chooses voluntary poverty it becomes clear that his motives are suspect. By his association with lollers (C.5.1–108) he lays himself open to charges of idleness and fraud; he chooses to be a clerk, perhaps, initially, because he does not want to do manual labour. What separates him from being a waster? It is the distinction that he begs 'withoute bagge or botel but my wombe one' (C.5.52)[18] and the return his work gives to those who support him; he is a labourer worthy of his hire. Will works on his intention throughout the poem, always being taught that charity must underlie all his actions. During the course of the *Vita*, in particular, we see him progressively defining and redefining the terms of his search which starts

---

18 This phrase is widely used in contemporary polemical writings to refer to evangelical poverty, based on texts where Christ sent forth his apostles without purse or bag, e.g. Luke 10. 4. By using this term Will claims that his poverty is purposeful and accredited by the Gospel. Scase (pp 136–60) examines the full anticlerical implications of the concept.

as an aimless quest for 'wondres' (Prol.4) before becoming focused on a search for Truth (B.1.83–4). In the course of his dreams the visionary learns, among many other things, about the spiritual value of poverty and about trust in God, putting into practice Christ's counsel: *Ne soliciti sitis* (B.14.29–80). He also learns about the scandal of poverty, the need for Christians to relieve the poverty of their fellow human beings, to recognize that the poor are their brothers, and to accord the poor the dignity of their human condition as brothers of Christ: *Alter alterius onera portate* (C.13.77a).[19]

Poverty is a significant aspect of Will's life, probably because, to the medieval clerical mind, the practice of poverty is a *sine qua non* of the sincere Christian who seeks personal reform. Gordon Leff points to the significance of the concept of poverty in medieval reform movements, calling it 'the most universal and venerable of all the impulses to religious reform'.[20] Will's quest for Truth throughout the poem brings him into contact with all the competing philosophies and rationales of poverty that characterize the late middle ages. Although the poem is written about the journey of one man, it concerns itself with the practicalities of the spiritual life within the Christian community, an earthly phenomenon with a heavenly justification. The modern theologian Régamey enumerates five ways in which poverty is essential to the following of Christ. These have already been enumerated in Chapter One, but I regard the repetition as important because Will exemplifies them in his life. They are: an awareness of the human being's indigence in the sight of the heavenly Father; a practical acceptance of God's solicitude for each creature; detachment from one's personal will and abandonment to the will of God; a recognition that the poor person is a sacrament of Christ; and finally, an understanding that to be a member of Christ is to be drawn actively into his work. Will's life is an illustration of how these five ways can affect the life of one man. The poetry examines the implications of poverty as an experience of this world with repercussions for the next and shows how Will negotiates the demands of the mundane world of material consumption and those of the spiritual world of justice and charity.

WILL'S ENCOUNTER WITH REASON AND CONSCIENCE

A full study of Will would include commentary on all his visions, but the argument of this chapter is based mainly on the waking moments of Will because they demonstrate sufficiently the fundamentals of choice, charity, justice and solidarity that characterize the life of a faithful Christian, though Will is dependent on his visionary experiences for the knowledge that helps him to make his

---

19 This quotation from Galatians 6. 2 recurs almost like a refrain. It is quoted by Hunger to Piers (B.6.221a), by Rechelesnesse as above, and by Trajan in his disquisition on the relationship between rich and poor, (B.11.196–210a).
20 *Heresy in the later middle ages*, p. 8.

Voluntary poverty and involuntary need: Will's experience of being a poor man

choices.[21] In response to Middleton who says that the arrangement of Langland's episodes 'seems somewhat reiterative rather than progressive',[22] I suggest that Will, within the repetitiveness of the episodes, works out the scriptural truism that he quotes in his waking encounter with two friars (B.8.20–9): the just man falls seven times a day (Proverbs 24:16).[23] The poem moves forward through repeated failures of Will and of his contemporary society to the last three passus which demonstrate the necessity of redemption. Even after the harrowing of hell, the resurrection, the descent of the Holy Spirit and the formation of the church, the poem narrates how human beings continue to sin and society continues to experience problems. Will's falling reflects the human condition, and though it provides the occasion for sorrow and repentance, it also gives Christ scope to show his love and mercy:

> I may do mercy þoruȝ rightwisnessse, and alle my wordes trewe.
> And þouȝ Holy Writ wole þat I be wroke of hem þat diden ille
> (*Nullum malum impunitum* ...)
> Thei shul be clensed clerliche and [clene] wasshen of hir synnes
> In my prisone Purgatorie, til *parce* it hote.   (B.18.390–3)

Christ's redemption is a continuous act, liturgically repeated in the eucharist and applied to human beings in the sacrament of penance.

Choice of a poor life, a tendency to fall into sin, and a striving to align his will with the Will of God are dominant features of Will, whose quest for Truth brings him up sharply against the problem of which Gutiérrez speaks: how to distinguish and deal with the scandal of poor people's need while at the same time living a life devoted to prayer, meditation, and love of God in the practice of voluntary poverty. I consider first a section of the poem that appears only in the C-text, (C.5.1–108), because it portrays clearly the problems of a person who embraces voluntary poverty and then has to work out how to live it with fidelity and justify its purpose to others.[24] The argument of this passage proceeds by a series of *distinctiones* played out in the dialogue of a waking interlude in which

---

[21] I am conscious that the visions contain much material that is relevant to Will's experience of poverty; most of this is dealt with elsewhere in the study. I am not attempting to write a chronological account of Will's descent into poverty; this has been attempted by Clopper in his interesting biographical study of Will: 'The life of the dreamer, the dreams of the wanderer in *Piers Plowman*'. My concern is to relate Will's experience of poverty to that of his indigent contemporaries.

[22] 'Narration and the invention of experience', p. 92.

[23] Christ expresses repeated repentance and forgiveness to be a mark of his followers. 'Take heed to yourselves. If thy brother sin against thee, reprove him, and if he do penance, forgive him. And if he sin against thee seven times in a day, and seven times in a day be converted unto thee saying: I repent: forgive him': Luke 17. 3–4.

[24] There are compelling reasons, adduced eloquently by Middleton, for believing that this was the last insertion made in the C-text revision. As such it represents the poet's mature understanding of the key issues it faces: 'Acts of vagrancy', pp 266–77.

Will encounters Reason and Conscience. It follows the vision in which the King adopts Reason and Conscience as his officers (C.4) and precedes the vision of the communal act of repentance, when Conscience and Reason conduct the sacrament of penance in a foreshadowing of the Last Judgment (C.5.109–7.151).[25] As such it is placed strategically to emphasize the importance of Will, the individual sinner, who has responsibilities in temporal and spiritual contexts, yet must take personal responsibility for his own life in order to perform his role in each.

There are two main points of intersection with his contemporary ideology that affect Will at this juncture. One is that elucidated by Middleton in her analysis of the poem's intertextual relationship to the 1388 Statute, to gospel paradigms and to the rest of the poem in its different versions.[26] The other is that of Scase who inserts the poem into the mode of anticlerical criticism, the successor to antifraternalism as an impulse towards ecclesiastical reform.[27] Middleton's article is important in establishing Will's relationship to contemporary text and situation, the terms of the various statutes of labourers and the actuality of late medieval vagrancy. It is also very important in situating Will's poetry-writing in the context of what she presents as a mature review of his writing career, the C.5 'apologia'. In tracing how he debates his own practice of poetry in the current political and social environment I agree with Middleton's proposition, that

> specifically literary self-awareness offers a distinctive kind of social intervention, through which other kinds become the more richly legible. A poem can anatomize and demystify, as well as participate in, the social mythologies and ideological constructions in which political and ethical imperatives are invariably framed, and which provide the conditions and much of the language with which poets imaginatively 'play'. (p. 209)

To read Will's 'apologia' is to witness a character coming to terms with his life of dedication and his impulse to write poetry in his own historical moment. We see him acted upon by the forces of his culture, but we also see him and others acting upon their moment of history. In this respect, Will is an agent who participates in activities (idle begging) that cause reactionary legislation. Yet in Will, also, the poem holds up for scrutiny the effects of that legislation in his individual circumstances. My initial survey of Will as the Cornhill 'lollare' takes account of many of Middleton's findings in this context.

My main argument, however, is more precisely directed towards Will's life of poverty rather than his vocation of poetry, so my discussion fits, probably more relevantly, with Scase's argument about anticlericalism in the poem. Will

---

25 Conscience and Reason conduct the service but it is Repentance who hears the confessions and gives or withholds absolution. The whole scene has liturgical links with Good Friday's redemptive act and intimations of the Last Judgment in the sounding of the horn of Hope, and the song of the assembled saints in heaven (C.7.130–5; 151–3a).
26 'Acts of vagrancy'.
27 *Piers Plowman and the new anticlericalism*.

Voluntary poverty and involuntary need: Will's experience of being a poor man 167

uses anticlerical terminology, and demonstrates how, in the course of a long life, a person can purify the intention of practising evangelical poverty. At first he is like the false mendicants whose faults he knows and pillories in detail, but his experience of poverty demonstrates to him, by the end of the poem, that the way to follow Christ in poverty is to accept the suffering of the indigent. I think it is important to stress, at this point, that the poverty the poem portrays in Will is essentially voluntary poverty, even though he comes to experience need. The ideal proposed to him is, therefore, the ideal for the person dedicated to the following of Christ, not a generalized rationale of poverty as a good thing in itself.

The passage presents Will as a 'lollare', living in Cornhill, an unsavoury part of London, traditionally a haunt of vagabonds and thieves[28] and, as Clopper has pointed out, the abode of the very poor.[29] As a loller Will admits to writing satirical pieces on the other 'lollares of Londone and lewede ermytes' (C.5.4) and to avoiding manual labour, even though he is in good health and sound mind: 'In hele and in inwitt' (C.5.10). Will lives among the poor, dresses like one of the lollers whom he satirizes, and depends on benefactions for his living. Some of the phraseology at this point echoes the account of those idlers and wasters who appear in Passus B.6./C.8. Will speaks of the season as being a hot harvest time when, instead of labouring with his hands, he prefers to sleep, exhibiting characteristics of sloth, as Bowers points out.[30] What the wasters have to say when they refuse to work in Piers' harvest field corresponds with his present admission of youth, health and strength:

WILL
In an hot heruest whenne Y hadde myn hele
And lymes to labory with, and louede wel fare
And no dede to do but to drynke and to slepe.   (C.5.7-9)

WASTERS
We may nother swynke ne swete, suche sekenes vs ayleth,
Ne [haue] none lymes to labory with, Lord God we thonketh.
                                                        (C.8.134-5)

This verbal echo links Will unmistakably with the wasters whom the poet portrays as parasites on society. They make false claims to being weak and ill, pretending to be blind and lame:

Tho were faytours aferd, and fayned hem blynde,
And leyde here legges alery, as suche lorelles conneth.   (C.8.128-9)

---

28 Pearsall, *C-text*, p. 97 n.1.
29 'The friars had chosen the area for their friary when they first came to England because it was the poorest section of the town and the place where the abject lived': Clopper, *Rechelesnesse*, p. 303.
30 Bowers, *The crisis of Will*. Bowers develops the thesis that sloth is Will's besetting sin, particularly in Chapters Six and Seven, pp 129–89.

The poet recognizes the falsity of their position and deliberately allies Will with it; the only apparent difference between him and these frauds is that he admits to being in good health. This leads easily into a discussion of Will's vocation of mendicancy, a debate already coloured by the suggestion that he is slothful, wanting to drink and sleep like the wasters of Piers' harvest who only want to sit around 'at the ale' and sing 'hey trollilolly' (C.8.122–3).

Reason interrogates Will in terms of the 1388 Statutes of Cambridge as to why he is not performing manual labour. As Middleton has shown, Will's response draws upon the provisions of the same statutes to assert his right to consider clerkly work sufficient to fulfil his obligation of labour under the statute.[31] Apart from his writings, Will claims to be a wandering mendicant who travels the land praying for his benefactors, both those who provided for his youthful education and those who give him food and shelter on his journeys. The terms in which Reason interrogates him suggest that he is a parasite upon society:

> For an ydel man þow semest,
> A spendour þat spene mot, or a spille-tyme,
> Or beggest thy bylyue aboute at men hacches,
> Or faytest vppon Frydayes or feste-dayes in churches,
> The which is lollarne lyf, þat lytel is preysed.   (C.5.27–31)

Underlying Reason's accusations is the view that Will's stance as a poor man may be a fraud; he may have undertaken the clerical life in his youth, but is now living unproductively. Reason's words carry overtones of the mordant satire in a subsequent passage (C.9.98–281) where Will exposes the slothful, parasitical nature of false hermits. By dressing in the habit of a hermit they believe themselves entitled to live 'in idelnesse and in ese and by otheres trauayle' (C.9.152). Reason's extremely serious accusation, and Will's own admission of idleness, place Will in the position of the undeserving poor who are strong enough to work but will not do so, and, worse, who pretend to a holy vocation which implies a life of self-denial and reliance on God to provide. Will has chosen voluntary poverty as a permanent way of life, yet his interview with Reason and Conscience suggests that, whereas he may have initially answered the call to the ideal of poverty, he has deviated from the ideal to the point where he is now little different from those he satirizes.[32] The ensuing encounter will help Will, and the reader, to discern the difference between adopting poverty as a way of life in itself, and accepting it as a means to serve God and fellow human beings. False hermits and lazy friars are open to two charges. Either they are 'sturdy beg-

---

[31] Middleton analyses how close the terminology of Reason is to the provisions of the statute in consideration of what type of work is required of able-bodied men. In particular, she takes Will's claim of having been a scholar since his youth to be his defence against having to do other forms of labour: 'Acts of vagrancy', pp 232–3.

[32] Clopper, 'Need men and women labour?' pp 119–21.

gars' who offend against the statute or they fulfil the legal minimum for a life of clerisy, yet neglect the spiritual dedication that makes sense of their poverty. As Middleton has pointed out, sloth has developed from being one of the deadly sins to becoming an offence under the 1388 statute.[33] Yet Will's experience will be that reliance on God to provide can, in practice, plunge a person into the same need as the material poverty endured by the involuntarily poor and widely regarded as an evil. For Will's poverty to be spiritually beneficial, he has to accept it as God's will for him. This encounter makes an early statement of an issue that continues throughout the poem: the potential danger of infidelity to the religious ideal of poverty and its risky interface with contemporary legislation against idle begging.

Reason is explicit in his view that Will's poverty is a scandal because it is unnecessary; Will is strong and healthy, and, according to the statute, should be performing some kind of productive labour. Initially, Will's responses to Reason strain one's credulity; his poverty seems like that denounced in the Cistercian rule written in reaction to those religious orders whose members have more ease and comfort than they would have known in the world:[34]

> 'Sertes,' Y sayde, 'and so me God helpe,
> Y am to wayke to worche with sykel or with sythe
> And to long, lef me, lowe to stoupe,
> To wurche as a werkeman, eny while to duyren.' (C.5.23–5)

Implicitly, Will is contrasted with those who have no choice but to beg, since they are involuntarily poor by circumstances beyond their control:

> Or thow art broke, so may be, in body or in membre,
> Or ymaymed thorw som myshap, whereby thow myhte be excused?
> (C.5.33–4)

Yet he works through the arguments in a self-conscious debate in which he tests the traditional understanding that those who are called to serve God in the clerical life do not have to labour with their hands:

> For by þe lawe of *Levyticy* þat Oure Lord ordeynede,
> Clerkes ycrouned, of kynde vnderstondynge,
> Sholde nother swynke, ne swete, ne swerien at enquestes,
> Ne fyhte in no faumewarde ne his foe greue. (C.5.55–8)

Will claims to have undertaken the life of voluntary poverty as a mendicant in order to be free to write and to serve others through prayer. Such a claim puts

---

33 'Acts of Vagrancy', pp 24–44.
34 Quoted by Régamey in the article 'Religious poverty' in the *New Catholic encyclopedia*, p. 650.

him under the protection of the 1388 statute which, in prescribing the duty of labour for all able-bodied beggars, makes an exception of 'people of religion and hermits approved'.[35] Middleton takes this legal protection a stage further than most readers, pointing out that Will claims to have had the status of *literatus* from early childhood, thus proving that he was not engaged in husbandry before the age of twelve, 'a childhood condition which could, under the statute (c.5), invalidate whatever occupation he now claims against Reason's implicit efforts to draft him into harvest work'.[36] To confirm that this is no specious claim, he outlines the work he does and the tools – 'lomes' – he uses for his craft:[37]

> The lomes þat Y labore with and lyflode deserue
> Is *Pater-noster* and my prymer, *Placebo* and *Dirige*,
> And my Sauter som tyme and my seuene psalmes.   (C.5.45–7)

This important passage places great stress on the personal responsibility of Will, the dreamer, the wanderer, the one who prays but does not labour with his hands. The strong implication is that Will could very easily labour, but chooses not to do so. Reason has no time for excuses that show reluctance to work, for, in a society governed by Reason and Conscience, the poverty which is material evil, lack of necessities, can be kept at bay. Under their rule everyone is expected to turn to and cultivate the land for food in order to ensure survival. To labour for the sustenance of the community is both reasonable and right, for all are entitled to basic necessities, as Will's debate with Reason and Conscience emphasizes. Piers (B.6) also stresses the value of manual labour for the good of the community. It is clear that Langland is using Will's stubborn adherence to voluntary poverty to emphasize the equal importance of his personal vocation as poet and one who prays.[38]

Will claims that he has, in his youth, embraced the other poverty, the gospel ideal, and debates with Reason and Conscience his exemption from the labour laws. Both Conscience and Will are concerned with legitimacy. For Conscience

---

35 12 Ric. II. c. 7, *Statutes of the realm* vol. 2, p. 58. Members of the mendicant orders and other disabled persons were routinely exempted from the labour statutes and mendicants were exempted from poll taxes. Clopper gives a clear discussion of this in 'The life of the dreamer', p. 274.
36 'Acts of vagrancy', p. 252.
37 Hanna quotes from an *ordo* for hermits that specifies the primer and the Book of Hours as the source for the prayers required of literate hermits who are expected to recite the canonical hours, the hours of the Virgin from the primer, a considerable portion of the Psalter and interspersed Paternosters: 'Will's Work', p. 37.
38 Galloway makes the convincing point that Will's problem lies in 'the lack of specific or steady social or professional commitment for his learning': '*Piers Plowman* and the schools', (p. 95). This endorses my feeling that Will's poverty is nearer to that of the involuntarily poor than that of a member of, say, an established religious order. Will is secular, yet has adopted a life of learning rather than ambition. Poverty becomes, for Will, an adjunct to this life, and one he has to accept willingly, even though it does not help him fit into any niche.

Voluntary poverty and involuntary need: Will's experience of being a poor man 171

mendicancy is allowed only under obedience to a religious superior; for Will, legitimacy stems from his youthful clerical calling. A tradition of scholarship whose strongest exponent is Scase (pp 137–60) identifies the Cornhill loller with those he satirizes in a complete and detailed expression of anticlerical satire. I do not dispute the satirical intention of the passage, but am more interested in its portrayal of the loller as coming to terms with the practical aspects of poverty which he has undertaken as a voluntary response to a clerical vocation. At the start of the debate this looks like a career of idleness, taking the path of least resistance like the false hermits he so castigates. This is a real temptation for Will. The issue of his voluntary poverty becomes the debating ground for his divided self and will be the basis of his act of penance.[39]

Ostensibly, Will is one of the virtuous because he has chosen poverty, but his examination by Reason clearly shows that voluntary poverty, in itself, is not enough. Will has to state unambiguously that he is consciously choosing a life of poverty, not to escape work, but because work in the field is not the only way of achieving a just society. He adapts the words Christ used when tempted to turn stones into bread:

> 'Non de solo,' Y sayde, 'for sothe *viuit homo*,
> Nec in pane et in pabulo, the *Pater-noster* wittenesseth;
> Fiat voluntas Dei – þat fynt vs alle thynges.' (C.5.86–8)

Burrow, in his commentary on this passage, aptly calls this modification of Scripture clerkly wit:

> He recasts the first text (Matthew 4. 4) in such a way that the word *solo*, instead of its Vulgate use as an adjective agreeing with *pane* ('bread alone'), stands apart as a noun – the noun *solum* meaning soil. So the quotation now glances back, with a kind of exultant irony, at Reason's earlier talk of field-work: 'Not from the soil does man live, not by bread and by food.'[40]

Will claims that he is prepared to live out the fact of poverty in accepting a life lacking solicitude, a life far from the harvest-field. *Fiat voluntas tua*, perhaps often repeated mechanically as Will prays *Paternosters* for his benefactors, now gives way to meaningful prayer, *Fiat voluntas Dei*. The slight change to the prayer suggests that Will is really thinking about the words rather than repeating the prayer as a formula. He aligns his will with God's: 'let God's will be done'. At this point, Will indulges in a little word-play, but the irony turns against himself. He has

---

39 Galloway discusses the creation of a divided self in the works of Thomas and Adam Usk who seek to distance themselves from the intention of being ambitious while enjoying involvement in professional labours: 'Private selves and the intellectual marketplace', pp 309–14. The ambivalent penitence of these writers can be paralleled by Will's dubious repentance.

40 J. Burrow, *Langland's fictions*, p. 104.

glibly suggested prayer and penance as the labour that Christ demands of him, repeating formulas to confirm his clerical exemption from productive labour which would provide food for himself and the needy. Conscience denies him the right to beg without due accreditation, implying that this is a practice allowable only for the powerless indigent. Now Will prays that God's will may be done, and, in so doing, initiates a movement of surrender to the will of God, and an implicit acceptance of the philosophy: *ne soliciti sitis*. He does not give up the work of seeking, studying, praying, and writing; rather, he renews his commitment, recognizing them to be an expression of God's will for him. Langland makes it clear, through Will's debate, that the philosophy of not being solicitous demands hard work within the terms of his vocation. The lengthy justification dispels any idea that to be poor for the sake of Christ is to retreat from cares and responsibilities in the world. On the contrary, Will's prayers and writings are directly concerned with the lives of his fellow human beings and express his responsibility of care towards their moral welfare.

Many critics argue that Will's responses in the debate with Reason and Conscience are suspect, cloaking a self-deception that devalues Will's practice of voluntary poverty. Burrow shows how Conscience pinpoints this ambivalence with a *double entendre* in 'lyeth', a word which means both 'lies, is untrue' and 'is admissable, sustainable, in law'.[41] Will has pressed both statute and Scripture into service to bolster his right to be excused from labour,[42] and to give authority for not being tangibly productive.[43] But Scripture is the living word of God, and *fiat*, the word of creation, brings into being true repentance as Will, almost in spite of himself, aligns his will with God's will. He admits having wasted time throughout his life as a sinner who has wasted opportunities but is now ready to surrender all for the sake of the kingdom of heaven:

> ... Y haue ytynt tyme, and tyme myspened;
> Ac ȝut, I hope – as he þat ofte hath ychaffared
> And ay loste and loste, and at þe laste hym happed
> A bouhte suche a bargayn he was þe bet euere,
> And sette al his lost at a leef at the laste ende.   (C.5.93–7)

The image of selling all to buy a great bargain is both worldly and scriptural. Will lives in the world, the *saeculum*, where merchants venture all for the hope of profit. The scriptural context of the treasure hidden in a field – '*simile est*

---

41 Ibid. pp 104–5. Donaldson also sees self-deception here: 'Conscience's *double entendre* characterizes Long Will's apology as at once specious and heart-felt, false and true': 'Long Will's apology', p. 32.
42 Leviticus 21 on the priesthood prescribes that priests should keep themselves from all forms of ritual uncleanness. Will's appeal to Leviticus is somewhat ironic in view of his life in Cornhill, which must have provided a lifestyle far removed from the segregation envisaged in Leviticus.
43 'Not in bread alone doth man live, but in every word that proceedeth from the mouth of God': Matthew. 4. 4.

Voluntary poverty and involuntary need: Will's experience of being a poor man 173

regnum celorum thesauro abscondito in agro' (C.5.98a) — and its associated parable of the pearl of great price[44] sets him in the mode of purposeful self-denial. The gospel story of the lost drachma sits between that of the lost sheep and the prodigal son (Luke 15. 4–32), three parables that demonstrate God's great desire to seek out and save sinners. Will admits to sinfulness in having let his ideals slide, living a life that looks like that of false hermits, but he never considers denying his clerical vocation:

> So hope Y to haue of Hym þat is almyghty
> A gobet of his grace, and bigynne a tyme
> That alle tymes of my tyme to profit shal turne.   (C.5.99–101)

This section of the poem stresses the importance of renewed choice for the person who has embraced voluntary poverty. In the Prologue, Will sets off, in poverty, to wander in search of some unspecified 'wondres', some of which have the quality of adventure and even seem like fairy encounters.[45] At the present point of review he admits having been dilatory and accepts the need for purpose; his intention is different, but his choice is the same, and he makes it in humility and repentance.

The brusque response of Reason counterpoises the necessary urgency of repentance with Will's dilatory former life: 'rape the to bigynne'. Conscience adds the rider: 'ȝe, and contynue!' It is worth remarking here that the *Paternoster*, as well as being a most frequently repeated prayer was, in patristic commentaries, considered to be the prayer of the neophytes:

> In *Baptism* and *Confirmation*, the handing on (*traditio*) of the Lord's Prayer signifies new birth into the divine life ... This is why most of the patristic commentaries on the *Our Father* are addressed to catechumens and neophytes. When the Church prays the Lord's Prayer, it is always the people made up of the 'new-born' who pray and obtain mercy.[46]

Will, at this point, is in the right frame of mind to make his confession and regain his innocence, purchased by detachment from his personal will and abandonment to the will of God, one of the five conditions of Christian poverty.[47] The process of self-examination and repentance have been conducted in terms of Will's life within the community and in relation to his observance of laws both

---

44 'Simile est regnum caelorum thesauro abscondito in agro quem qui invenit homo abscondit et prae gaudio illius vadit et vendit universa quae habet et emit agrum illum. Iterum simile est regnum caelorum homini negotiatori quaerenti bonas margaritas; inventa autem una pretiosa margarita abiit et vendidit omnia quae habuit et emit eam': Matthew 13. 44–6.
45 Each of the three prologues, A, B and C uses terms suggestive of romance: 'Me bifel a ferly, of fairye me þoȝte' (A/B.Prol.6); 'and say many sellies and selkouthe thynges' (C.Prol.6).
46 *Catechism of the Catholic Church*, pp 588–9.
47 See p. 50 above.

of church and state, demonstrating how fundamentally earthly the following of Christ must be. The false mendicants behave as though poverty is an end in itself. In Will, Langland makes it clear that poverty has no spiritual value other than as a means to aligning his will with God's:

> And to þe kyrke Y gan go, God to honoure;
> Byfore þe cross on my knees knokked Y my brest*e*,
> Sy3ing for my synnes, seggyng my *Pater-noster*,
> Wepyng and waylyng til Y was aslepe.   (C.5.105–8)

Will has made no overt criticism of society, yet textually he is in dialogue with his contemporary ideologies. In the self-satire that casts himself as sinful and idle he has demonstrated the sinfulness of parasitical hermits who take from society but contribute nothing, damaging the vulnerable involuntarily poor who are incapable of providing for themselves.[48] He shares by association their lack of moral probity which diminishes society's ethical stature. Their deceit exposes the inadequacies of statutes which, on the one hand, allow such deceivers to prey on society under the name of religion, and on the other punish all non-religious able-bodied vagrants as uniformly guilty. Will is examined under the statute as a sturdy beggar, under church law as an itinerant religious, and in terms of scripture as one of Christ's original seventy-two disciples.[49] In all three cases, he may be a guilty exponent of his contemporary culture. In moving from the debate immediately to the Church to make his confession, Will asserts the liturgically repeatable power of the sacrament to purify and renew his intention. He embodies the questions that must be asked of his society and of himself, and in his answers, the only quality that justifies him is his adherence to a life of apostolic poverty in order to do the will of God.

WILL'S CHOICE OF THE WANDERING LIFE

The C-text 'apologia' makes it clear that Will has chosen poverty willingly for the love of God. The rest of this chapter will examine Will's reactions to the experience of poverty in further episodes of his waking life[50] in which the poem represents some of the most testing dilemmas and conflicts a follower of Christ must resolve. Returning to the start of the poem, I explore the way Will regards voluntary poverty in his youth, and trace how his ideas develop in the light of experience when he suffers cold, hunger, inadequate clothing, the pain of being

---

48 Full discussion of the anticlerical implications of Will's self-satire is to be found in Scase, pp 64–5, 137–49.
49 Middleton has drawn attention to the conflation of two scriptural passages concerning Christ's sending out of his disciples: Luke 10 2. 11 and Matthew 10 5–42: 'Acts of vagrancy', pp 264–5.
50 For this purpose I concentrate on the B-text except where otherwise stated.

Voluntary poverty and involuntary need: Will's experience of being a poor man 175

thought mad and the final indignity of growing old. All these are marginalizing experiences of the involuntarily poor, not what he bargained for when embarking on voluntary poverty in his youth. However, they are part of God's will for him, and in accepting them as such, Will aligns his will with God's. I argue that the basic and inescapable need described in the final passus shows more clearly than any other aspect of the poem that Langland does not sublimate involuntary poverty. Will, who suffers like Christ, finds his identity in Christ, and transfers this dignity, by association, to all the involuntarily poor, yet his fight against Antichrist is a fight against injustice and for charity.

Utter need is Will's plight at the end of the poem. At its start he embarks on a life of poverty akin to that of Juvenal's traveller in which he is free from the cares associated with property:

> In a somer seson, whan softe was þe sonne,
> I shoop me into shroudes as I a sheep were,
> In habite as an heremite vnholy of werkes,
> Wente wide in þis world wondres to here.   (B.Prol.1–4)

Within four lines Will has established himself as a poor man outside the mainstream of both religious and secular life. The opening lines suggest that his poverty is voluntary and, by implication, secular. In donning the habit of a hermit 'vnholy of werkes' he presents himself as an irritant who will antagonize society and be treated with all the hostility reserved for those whom society has decided are frauds. Hermits are marginal to society, and an unholy hermit is marginal to hermits. As such Will is in a position to observe and comment on the workings of the society upon whose margin he has placed himself – for his clothing conceals and reveals, as clothing does in the portraits drawn by Chaucer in his Prologue to the *Canterbury Tales*. Will wears the habit of a sinful hermit, and this is an opportunity for an ironic self-representation that recurs throughout the poem.

Will's association with poverty is made from the first; his clothing is rough – 'I shoop me into shroudes as I a sheep were' – he is wearing rough wool, probably russet, a simple garment such as that worn by many a poor shepherd or hermit.[51] Ostensibly he is very poor, but the word 'as' raises a query; is the man beneath the clothing as poor in intention as his garments suggest? He identifies himself as wearing the habit of hermit 'vnholy of werkes'. Equally he is like a shepherd. Shepherds were among the lowest of the low, mistrusted because they might be thieves, shunned because of their solitary life in the wild. Michel Mollat comments:

---

[51] 'But some hermits, harkening back to Cassian's instructions on dress, sought to imitate the desert fathers by wearing the skins of goats and sheep. This may explain why Will says "I shoop me into a shroud as I a sheep were" (B.Prol.2). When a hermit assumed his habit, moreover, he was made to understand that it must be worn day and night for the rest of his life, and that it would become his shroud at burial': Bowers, p. 102. See also Hanna, 'Will's work', pp 34–6.

The shepherd was hardly a sacred figure. Like the forest workers, his presence was troubling. Working alone, he communicated only with his animals, whose bestiality he shared. He was thought to possess evil powers. Many shepherds were odd or mentally retarded and therefore despised. No-one would marry his daughter to a shepherd. People looked upon shepherds as lazy, because their work required little physical effort. They were badly paid. Thus shepherds were poor mentally, socially, and economically – and their filthy appearance only confirmed this general perception.[52]

Hermits, though by profession men of religion, were just as likely to be disreputable characters, subject to no discipline. The *Concordia regularum*, a collection of monastic rules made by Benedict of Aniane around the end of the eighth century, identifies a tradition of false monks who were unfaithful to their rule and became the *gyrovagi* and the *sarabaites*, both apostates from their monastic life, living under no rule, according to their own pleasure. Idleness, reluctance to do manual labour and aimless wandering are recurring features of the satire on the gyrovague.[53] The self-satire implied in Will's association with the gyrovague reflects a certain ambivalence in the poem about poverty such as Will's. As argued by Scase it is part of a late medieval anticlericalism that satirizes secular clerics, extra-regular hermits and friars who avoid manual labour and claim the right to beg for their sustenance.[54] Such identification makes an unprepossessing start for Will, calling into question the irresponsibility of the poor person who chooses to wander and beg rather than work. In the fourteenth century, the secular mobile poor were commonly accused of idleness, and the legislation that criminalized out-of-work labourers voiced society's feeling that the poor, instead of being an estate within society, had become a problem that tested the legal framework and needed to be punished, not protected.[55] In the eyes of late fourteenth-century regulators, the person who could not find work was already deemed to be the person who would not look for work.[56] In portraying Will's vocation as potentially illegal, irregular or even sinful, Langland sets up an ideological dialogue on troubling issues within his contemporary culture.

Will has the potential to become a corrupt man, slothful and venal like the 'lollars' he satirizes,[57] or a force for good through his prayer and writing. His poverty at the moment of initial choice makes no connection with the ideal of Christ. He is in the world but not of it, an observer, not a participant, ready to

[52] Mollat, pp 239–40.
[53] Scase gives a useful synopsis of the different types of aberrant monks, pp 125–6.
[54] Scase, pp 137–49. Hanna, too, in his illuminating article on Will's work, discusses at length the informality of rules for late medieval hermits: 'Will's work', pp 25–44.
[55] Moisa, 'Fourteenth-century preachers', pp 168–72; Middleton, 'Acts of vagrancy', pp 229–44.
[56] Statutes of Labourers, 1351, 1356; Commons Complaint 1376, Statute of Cambridge 1388.
[57] In the C-text, the discussion of hermits is extended by severe criticism of false hermits who live by begging (C.9.188–254).

encounter whatever wonders may be about to happen. It is therefore with a double sense of freedom, from a conventional religious rule and from the restrictions of conformity to the organization of the world, that Will sinks into the slumber that evokes his first vision, the microcosm of society on the 'fair feeld ful of folke'. Yet his poverty is shot through with the potential for sin. The carefree traveller of Juvenal may, in some situations, become a parasite, accused of the besetting sin of sloth to which one critic attributes the initial aimless wandering, the *curiositas* which sends Will seeking after wonders.[58] One thing is certain; like people who are involuntarily poor, Will is on the margins of society. As a poor man in the active life he is indistinguishable from any other beggar, and his interview with Reason and Conscience shows that to sin is not the prerogative of the rich. Poor people sin too, yet even if he is a sinner, sin is not the end; to sin and to repent is in the nature of man. The poem warns about accepting traditional constructs of poverty uncritically as it holds up for scrutiny in the wanderer, Will, the philosophical ideal that rejects possessions and travels the road free of care.[59]

WILL'S VOLUNTARY POVERTY AS SPIRITUAL SEARCH

In the B-text's brief waking interlude between the first and the second dreams (B.5.2–8), Will appears to have gained some sense of direction, for he occupies himself with his prayers – his Creed and, presumably, the Paternosters that were supposed to be interspersed between the recitals of canonical hours, the Hours of the Virgin and the Psalter:[60]

> [I] sat softely adoun and seide my bileue;
> And so I bablede on my bedes, þei brouȝte me aslepe.   (B.5.7–8)

Between the initial aimless wandering and this waking moment, Will has encountered Holy Church and received a lesson in charity which expresses itself in care for the needy (B.1.148–201). Prayer is Will's work, his justification for living on the alms of others, as Imaginatif reminds him:

---

58 Bowers, p. 135.
59 Rechelesnesse, too, is held up for critical scrutiny for similar reasons.
60 The Hours of the Office were substituted by repetition of *Paters* and *Aves* when a member of a religious order, or an anchorhold, was unable to read. Hanna quotes from rules for non-literate hermits: 'The bishop should give him the charge that for whatever canonical hour of the day established by the church he should say a stipulated number of prayers devoutly asking for the salvation of his own soul, and those of all his benefactors, to wit first for vespers twenty Pater nosters with as many Ave Marias, for compline thirteen Paternosters with the same number of Aves': 'Will's work', p. 37. In C.5, and later in the B-text, it is clear that Will is literate, so at this point he may be simply fulfilling the normal injunction for those dedicated to a life of prayer, to fill every spare moment with vocal prayer.

> And þow medlest þee with makynge – and myȝtest go seye þi Sauter,
> And bidde for hem that ȝyueþ thee breed. (B.12.16–17)

and as he claims in his 'apologia' (C.5.40–52). The effect of the brief interlude is not so much to suggest Will's sloth, which, according to Bowers, causes him to fall asleep in prayer, as to emphasize the nature of Will's occupation. He has, in vision, encountered Holy Church and already defined himself as a seeker:

> Teche me to no tresor, but tel me þis ilke –
> How I may saue my soule, þat seint art yholden. (B.1.83–4)

At this point in his waking life personal poverty is not an issue to be debated; he has accepted the life of a mendicant who prays, and he is performing his duty. The fact that he falls asleep in the course of it may be taken as adding to the ironic self-representation of Will as a sinner; he tries and he fails. The repetitious prayers which he 'bablede' may be soporific, yet his sleep is no mere self-indulgent slumber, but the hard work of visionary seeking and learning. He regrets in his waking disappointment 'that I ne hadde slept sadder and yseiȝen moore' (B.5.4). As such, his sleep is not a break in his prayer but a deepening of it; visions during prayer are likely to be propitious and blessed, as we may infer from portraits in late medieval Books of Hours. The celebrated verse from the Canticle, *Ego dormio et cor meum vigilat*, becomes the theme for Richard Rolle's exposition of the contemplative life:

> þis degre es called contemplatife lyfe, þat lufes to be anely, withowten ryngyng or dyn or syngyng or criyng. At þe begynyng, when þou comes þartil, þi gastly egh es taken up intil þe blysse of heven, and þar lyghtned with grace and kyndelde with fyre of Cristes lufe, sa þat þou sal verraly fele þe bernyng of lufe in þi hert ever mare and mare.[61]

In this context the sleep suggested in the scriptural quotation represents a quietening of the body's activities so that the eye of the spirit can take over and lift the visionary to great heights of spiritual understanding. For Will at this point, the medium of dream vision is a foray into mystical, non-corporeal learning. This takes the form of silently witnessing scenes that play out the philosophy behind ownership and consumption in the Meed episodes, sin and repentance in the course of the great confession, and a complex examination of human need in the ploughing of the half-acre. The dreams of Will are a metaphor for his act of writing.

Initially an observer with no axe to grind, Will is drawn gradually into the action of the poem through his visions, and his wandering becomes a quest once he has met Piers the Plowman. The virtue of voluntary poverty is a hard one to acquire and to practise; by the end of the poem he will know physically, intellectually and morally exactly what it means and, like many genuinely poor people,

---

61 *English writings of Richard Rolle*, p. 69.

Voluntary poverty and involuntary need: Will's experience of being a poor man 179

will endure his poverty more than embracing it. In his next waking moment in the *Visio* (B.8.1–66) Will remains a wanderer who has not yet grasped fully what it will mean. He maintains the russet garb of a hermit and the homelessness of the wanderer, though not yet suffering the full seasonal force of practical poverty (the first dream had befallen 'in a somer seson whan softe was the sonne', and his awakening after the *Visio* is still set 'al in a somer seson'). Bowers brings a wealth of evidence to illustrate his reading of Will as slothful in his waking life,[62] yet I feel that sloth is only part of Will's character. It may seem irresponsible, even self-indulgent, to choose to be clear of worldly ties as Will is. Yet to be despised within society gives him precisely the freedom from interference or distraction that he needs if he is to hear, unimpeded, the messages of his mind. Far from appearing to indulge in the sin of sloth as he embarks on his quest, Will walks great distances and asks repeated questions in his search for Dowel:

> And frayned ful ofte of folke þat I mette
> If any wiȝt wiste wher Dowel was at inne,
> And what man he myȝte be of many man I asked.   (B.8.3–5)

Will puts standard questions to the two friars he meets, for as Simpson demonstrates, at this early stage in his scholastic development Will is relying on ready-made materials which he has read.[63] Neither the friars' replies nor his own pat quotation satisfy him, and the ensuing visions take him through the painful process of acquiring spiritual knowledge, not as an escape from the world, but in order to learn how to live in the world. Simpson's comment on his encounter with the two friars implies Will's reliance on his own rational powers:

> Will expresses dissatisfaction at their reply, and, with this brief resort to standard sources of theological charity briefly exhausted, he sleeps and turns instead to his own reason for answers.[64]

In the course of the third sleeping vision he works hard intellectually in his encounter with Thought, Wit, and Imaginatif, all actants which are the constituent parts of the rational soul. Further, as Simpson clearly argues, Will represents the *voluntas*, that part of the soul which feels and desires good:

> Common Latin terms for these two basic parts of the soul are *ratio* for the thinking part of the soul, and *voluntas* for the desiring part. When these terms are translated into the vernacular, there are different words used for both of them, but 'will' is the term most often used in Middle English for *voluntas*.[65]

---

62 Bowers, pp 143–6.
63 This interpretation of Will as quoting from his reading is taken from Simpson, whose article on Will as reader stresses both the moral purpose and effect of Will's reading in its power to educate the will: 'Desire and the scriptural text', pp 222–3.
64 Simpson, *Piers Plowman: an introduction*, p. 94.
65 Ibid. p. 95. Bowers devotes a fully documented chapter to the poem's relationship to contem-

Will is pursuing Dowel willingly and purposefully, with mind and heart. His cloak of slothfulness is, as I have said above, his admission of personal sinfulness, but the intellectual energy of his quest reflects the sincerity and insistence of his repentance. The material poverty of his life at this time is matched by a spiritual sense of what Simpson calls depression in his inability to put his reading to the moral end of ensuring salvation:

> Moral improvement through reading will not, according to the doctrine of predestination, affect Will's chances of being written into the Book of Life one way or the other. And neither will it help him to read the Book of Life itself.[66]

It is essential for him to be homeless and without property if he is to deepen his understanding of himself as indigent in the sight of the heavenly Father and, as such, to work to establish charity and justice by deepening his understanding of the needs, both moral and material, of the world in which he lives. In respect of this aspect of Christian poverty, Will has to keep confronting the purpose of his search, as he does within each succeeding vision, for poverty is not his aim, but an adjunct to his search. The study in which he is relentlessly engaged is the purpose of his life at this point. Were he to concentrate only on his state of poverty he would become like the false practitioners, the mendicants who beg idly, but do not pursue the spiritual aspect of their vocation, deceiving themselves that external poverty is enough to justify and fulfil their lives.

WILL'S EMPOWERMENT IN FOLLY

Each waking interlude shows Will enduring a new and deeper form of poverty, steadily learning, through painful practice, detachment from his personal will and abandonment to the will of God, another fundamental aspect of Christian poverty. The third vision is, in some respects, like an ideological voyage in which he meets the constituent components of his mind as active debating partners in his intellectual quest. By the end of the third vision Will no longer speaks of himself as belonging to a state, whether regulated or unregulated; he is experiencing the deeper impoverishment of incipient madness:

> ... witlees nerhande,
> And as a freke þat fey were. (B.13.1–2)

He is probably suffering from melancholy, the same form of 'madness' that afflicted the poet Hoccleve, the sickness bred of thought[67] that can displace people

---

porary interest in matters of the will, pp 41–60.
66 Simpson, 'Desire and the scriptural text', p. 224.
67 Thomas Hoccleve, *The regement of princes*, ll. 99–105, p. 5.

Voluntary poverty and involuntary need: Will's experience of being a poor man 181

from the rest of society. Even after his first vision he experiences the 'wo' that betokens melancholy:

> Thanne waked I of my wynkyng and wo was withalle
> That I ne hadde slept sadder and yseiȝen moore. (B.5.3–4)

Like Hoccleve, Will lives in his mind; whatever he does in his waking life to gain a living is unimportant now; what matters to Will is the wisdom he has learned in his visions. After the fourth dream he emerges as deranged:

> And so my wit weex and wanyed til I a fool weere;
> And some lakkede my lif – allowed it fewe –
> And leten me for a lorel and looþ to reuerencen
> Lordes or ladies or any lif ellis ...
>   ne loutede faire,
> That folk helden me a fool; and in þat folie I raued,
> Til Reson hadde ruþe on me and rokked me aslepe. (B.15.3–6; 9–11)

Without wishing to imply that Will's tendency to madness is a major issue in the poem, I would like to suggest that it is significant for the consideration of two features of his poverty: the nature of his work as a 'maker' and his life on the margins of society. As a poet, it is Will's responsibility to confront the ills of his society in such a way as to move the will of his readers.[68] He is a poor man, and the powerlessness poverty implies is in conflict with the moral power he displays in his writing, informed as it is by deep visionary thought. As someone who displays tendencies to madness he is socially outcast, yet folly, ironically, gives him a certain immunity from the constraints of social convention, and freedom to speak out against the community's ills. Apart from the terminology Will uses to associate his mental state with lunacy, 'my wit weex and wanyed', we know from a treatise such as Bartholomeus's *De proprietatibus rerum* that madness is a predictable effect proceeding from melancholy, and melancholy is a common affliction of those who spend much time in study:[69]

> Thyse passyons come somtyme of malencoly meetes, & somtyme of drynke of stronge wyne that brenneth the humours & torneth theym into asshes; sometyme of passyons of the soule, as of besynes & grete thouȝtes, of sorowe & of to grete studye & of drede.

The relentless education of the will that takes place in the course of his visions becomes the material of which Will, the maker, writes. His intensive reading, of

---

68 Simpson explains with considerable clarity the different modes of writing and their intended moral effects, particularly as employed in *Piers Plowman*, in 'Desire and the scriptural text', pp 218–19.
69 Bartholomeus Anglicus, *De proprietatibus rerum*, p. 350.

Scripture particularly, is an important part of that education and, at more than one point in the poem, leads him into anxiety.[70] As a poet, Will at times adopts the mantle of a *vates* or an Old Testament-style prophet. He experiences the pain of the poet/prophet who lives in this world, loves it for its wonders – of nature, of mind and of spirit – and understands the distance between the demands of eternity and the failures of the *saeculum*. He is the embodiment of that irony spoken of by Howard in his assessment of the fourteenth-century's view of man's dignity:

> In each poem the ideal is disappointed by events which the poet must, as an observer, report. Were the authors to state explicitly that men are weak or men's ideals unrealistic, the ironic effect would be lost; by maintaining a distance they succeed in saying both ... We know that the figures in *Piers Plowman* – Mede, Waster, Hawkyn, and for that matter Will himself – are sinners; but we also know that a Christianized *mundus* is not for this World.[71]

Haukyn's lament, which immediately precedes the first intimation of madness in Will, expresses as much:

> 'So hard it is,' quod Haukyn, 'to lyue and to do synne.
> Synne seweþ vs euere,' quod he, and sory gan wexe ...
> Swouned and sobbed and siked ful ofte
> That euere he hadde lond or lordshipe, lasse oþer moore,
> Or maistrie ouer any man mo þan of hymselue. (B.14.322–3; 326–8)

Haukyn has been led by Patience to self-knowledge; he is essentially a good man but, like Coveitise in the parade of the sins, he cannot let go the desire for material possessions. His tears express clear-sighted sorrow because he cannot reconcile the demands of charity with a life devoted to worldly affairs. Will awakens from the vision overwhelmed, as Haukyn is, by the consciousness of sin in himself and in society. He recognizes the irony of which Howard speaks, but knows too, in contrast to the view expressed by Howard, that a Christianized *mundus* is Christ's kingdom, and his whole life is engaged in the apparently unequal struggle of the poor to make this come about.

Complaint, prophetic riddle, satire, baldly stated truth are all forms of prophecy which often cause their creator to be imprisoned or cast out from society.[72] The garb of a fool might afford some protection, as Wenzel illustrates in his account of domestic fools in late medieval great houses,[73] who speak out, often on the

---

70 See Simpson, 'Desire and the scriptural text', pp 225; 229–34.
71 D.R. Howard, *The three temptations*, p. 286.
72 Jeremiah, Amos, Elijah, Isaiah all suffered for speaking out against the evils of their times. A useful commentary on the prophet's role is found in B. Anderson, *The living world of the Old Testament*, pp 231, 253–5, 270–95, 380–3.
73 Siegfried Wenzel, 'The wisdom of the fool', pp 225–40.

Voluntary poverty and involuntary need: Will's experience of being a poor man 183

matter of the priority of the spiritual over the temporal, without being impugned. Langland himself, in the C-text, inserts a plea for 'lynatyk lollares' to be given alms on the grounds that they are the poorest and truest of all followers of the Gospel teachings. But in general terms the condition or even the suspicion of lunacy removes a person from the company of society, as Hoccleve describes with utmost feeling in his *Complaint*.[74] Quite clearly, Will is permanently on the fringes of society, driving himself into melancholy pondering the visionary truths which he contemplates from all sides of the debates, yet knowing that his responsibility is to combat the uncharitable, the untruthful and the unjust.

Folly polarizes those who encounter it. It is an aberration; a fool does not fit social norms, so how can Will's folly help him to reform his society? The answer can be found in Will's similarity to the folly recorded in Scripture. Old Testament fools are most frequently those who reject God, so the term carries a connotation of viciousness. The biblical fool who chooses wealth over integrity is only a few steps away from losing all he gained and being equally rejected with the madman who has to live on the fringes of normal society:

> As the partridge hath hatched eggs which she did not lay: so is he that hath gathered riches, and not by right. In the midst of his days he shall leave them: and in his latter end he shall be a fool. (Jeremiah 17. 11)

This fool chooses improbity and earns ultimate loss. Conversely, God's fool, his prophet, has to be prepared for rejection by those who set the norms for life in the world, as the Old Testament prophets knew only too well:

> The days of visitation are come, the days of repaying are come: know ye, O Israel, that the prophet was foolish, the spiritual man was mad, for the multitude of thy iniquity and the multitude of thy madness. (Hosea 9. 7)

Particularly in the New Testament, fools are those who challenge the accepted standards of a society immersed in the *saeculum*, and replace them with opposing standards based on the rules of the spiritual world. Paul develops a politics of folly which is to sustain the Corinthians against the accepted wisdom of their philosophical opponents:

> Has not God made foolish the wisdom of this world? (1 Corinthians 1. 20)

> But the foolish things of the world hath God chosen, that he may confound the wise: and the weak things of the world hath God chosen, that he may confound the strong. (1 Corinthians 1. 27)

> Let no man deceive himself. If any man among you seem to be wise in this world, let him become a fool, that he may be wise.
> (1 Corinthians 3. 18)

74 *Thomas Hoccleve's Complaint and Dialogue*, pp 2–33.

184   Piers Plowman *and the poor*

In the second letter to the Corinthians, Paul ironically sets himself up in the guise of a fool to show the sophisticated Corinthians the contrast between God's messenger who is used as a vessel by God, and the specious false teachers who indulge in their own virtuosity:

> If I must needs glory, I will glory of the things that concern my infirmity
> (2 Corinthians 11.30)

Will's folly is a particularly profound form of poverty, not of his choosing, unlike the poverty he chose as a hermit 'vnholy of werkes' when he originally placed himself on the margins of society. The rejection that Will experiences in his bouts of melancholy intensifies the social stigma he already experiences as a poor man. Medieval madmen and beggars are equally disenfranchised; a medieval lunatic could not own property, and by the late fourteenth century beggars, even religious ones, were socially unacceptable. The elements of Hoccleve's rejection by society are present most compellingly in Will's account of how other people take him for a madman. He experiences the insecurity of the fine line between sanity and madness – 'my wit weex and wanyed til I a fool weere' – and the keen distinction between himself and those who have warm clothes, status and money – 'persons in pelure wiþ pendaunt3 of siluer'. Yet just when his condition might be expected to make him powerless he turns his folly to advantage in the Pauline sense. He translates into action Patience's recent lessons in the value of poverty and begins to accept his marginal state as one of power. Under this new 'cloak' of madness Will is plainly outspoken, refusing to use the *ye* address and assuming a voice of authority that has no respect for the outward trappings of institutional dignity:[76]

> To sergeaunt3 ne to swiche seide no3t ones,
> 'God loke yow, lordes!' – ne loutede faire.   (B.15.8–9)

This is the kind of authority that the C-text specifically attributes to demented lunatic lollers, which it calls the true apostles of Christ (C.9.105–27):[77]

> Ac 3ut ar ther oþere beggares, in hele, as hit semeth,
> Ac hem wanteth wyt, men and women bothe,

---

75 See the complete chapter for Paul's ironic representation of himself as a fool.
76 David Burnley, in discussing the grammatical usage of *ye* and *you* as the polite plural form of address to a singular person, points out that clerics avoided such usage, preferring the singular as a form that emphasized their clerical authority. 'Clerks had for generations resisted the use of *ye* as a symbol of their disdain of materialism and secular status': 'Langland's clergial lunatic', p. 38.
77 Clopper points out that these people follow the apostolic counsels and are God's fools. 'The Dreamer claims to be one of them when he says that he dresses in long "lollares" clothes and lives among the "lollares" of Cornhill': 'The life of the dreamer', p. 276. Pearsall gives a comprehensive account of the role of lunatics in *Piers Plowman* and other works of literature in his article: ' "Lunatyk lollares" in *Piers Plowman*', pp 168–78.

Voluntary poverty and involuntary need: Will's experience of being a poor man 185

> The whiche aren lynatyk lollares and lepares aboute, ...
> Hit aren as his postles, suche peple, or as his priué disciples.
> For a sent hem forth seluerles in a somur garnement
> Withoute bagge and bred, as þe Book telleth:
> *Quando misi vos sine pane et pera* ...
> Barfoot and bredles, beggeth they of no man.
> And thauh a mete with the mayre ameddes þe strete,
> A reuerenseth hym ryht nauht, no rather then another:
> *Neminem salutaueritis per viam.* (C.9.105–7; 118–23)

In context this C-text passage contrasts genuinely poor and needy people with false mendicants in a fully developed anticlerical statement, all the more pointed in its verbal echo of St Francis who called the first brothers 'idiotae', fools of God.[78] In an analysis of this section of the poem, Clopper teases out the opposition of true and false 'lollares', attributing evangelical lack of solicitude to the 'lunatik lollares' and emphasizing how they contrast with 'friars and faitours' who have forgotten their original ideal of poverty:

> The 'lunatyk lollares' are sapiential men and women who prophesy apparently as much through their absence of solicitude as through any words they may utter: *Si quis videtur sapiens, fiet stultus vt sit sapiens* (C.9.127).[79]

Taken together, the range of associated meanings attributed to 'fools' presents an image of Will as a man who, though rejected by society, is morally superior, particularly in his power to oppose injustice without fear. This will be the ultimate role of the fools in the siege of Antichrist.

Will makes the political statement of an individual man on society's fringes who, like the biblical fools, does not respect people for their external trappings, but lives by a practical acceptance of God's solicitude for each creature, another of the identifying signs of Christian poverty. Langland has earlier made an ironic link between paupers and the type of entertainers employed and rewarded by the aristocracy and prelacy:

> Forþi I rede yow riche [þ]at reueles whan ye makeþ,
> For to solace youre soules, swiche minstrales to haue –
> The pouere for a fool sage sittynge at þ[i] table,
> And a lered man to lere þee what Oure Lord suffred
> For to saue þi soule fram Sathan þyn enemy,
> And fiþele þee, wiþoute flaterynge, of Good Friday þe storye,
> And a blynd man for a bourdeour, or a bedrede womman
> To crie a largesse tofore Oure Lord, your good loos to shewe.
> (B.13.442–9)

---

78 Clopper, 'The life of the dreamer', p. 270.
79 Clopper, *Rechelesnesse*, p. 207.

In this context, the poor man and the learned man are the equivalent of the 'fool sage', gaining authority before the rich by such association. Will is by no means mad but is regarded as such because of his poverty and lack of solicitude. His attitude of disrespect towards those who marginalize him is a political statement which associates itself with the dignity of God's poor who, he has said, are neglected by the powerful in favour of sinful entertainers.[80] Will identifies with those who are involuntarily poor as well as with those voluntarily poor, such as Chaucer's poor Parson and Ploughman, who experience true hardship and need. They are powerless and foolish in the eyes of the world but, in the final battle against the forces of Antichrist, they are ranged with Conscience.[81] As part of the anticlerical polemic, Will's actions in solidarity with the poor highlight the injustice towards them practised by hypocritical and avaricious clerics.[82]

Will has moved through several stages of understanding poverty. He has indulged in it as a carefree wanderer and learned the potential for sins of sloth and harm to the needy when one neglects the spiritual end of choosing voluntary poverty. He has accepted it as a concomitant to his search as thinker, reader and writer with a responsibility to communicate what he has learned. Now he has reached a point where he understands it as an experience of the needy, and is actively involved in establishing justice for the poor. The ultimate vindication of fools comes in the final battle against Antichrist, Will's vision which immediately follows his encounter with Need. While Antichrist summons all his forces from the official ranks of the church and the state, Conscience gathers the fools together. In the Pauline sense they are foolish in the sight of the world. Need has left Will destitute; in their foolishness, like Will they, too, are stripped down to bare essentials, the prospect of death, as they choose Christ over Antichrist:

> And al þe couent cam to welcome a tyraunt,
> And alle hise as wel as hym – saue oonly fooles;
> Whiche fooles were wel gladdere to deye
> Than to lyue lenger siþ Leute was so rebuked.   (B.20.60–3)

The fools are allied with gentle, holy men full of integrity, 'mylde men and holye, þat no meschief dradden' (B.20.65), who are ready to defy the powerful, the king and council, 'were it clerk or lewed' (B.20.68). Once more in the poem, the poor, the powerless and the foolish are ranged in political opposition to the rich, the powerful and the institutional. Conscience is the guardian of the fools and brings them into Unity:

---

80 The poor, blind and bedridden are the traditionally quoted poor of the Gospel. Hanna has an interesting gloss on this section in which he surmises that Will constructs himself as one of the worthy entertainers, a quasi-minstrel who recites his poem for the edification of the banqueters. 'Langland is, after all, the only contemporary who fiddles up "of god Friday þe geste"': 'Will's work', pp 47–8.

81 Clopper draws attention to the 'new fools' which the Franciscans are urged to be, *Rechelesnesse*, p. 226. He also equates 'foles' with *sapientia*, p. 248–9.

82 Scase, pp 64–78.

> 'I conseille,' quod Conscience þo, 'comeþ wiþ me, ye fooles,
> Into Vnite Holy Chirche, and holde we vs þere.'   (B.20.74–5)

The term 'fooles' echoes the condition of Will in his wandering poverty. The world marginalizes in folly those who are outside its norms; but at this point in the history of salvation the fools whose conscience opposes worldly standards form the core of Christ's church, while the false churchmen are outside the Barn of Unity, attempting its ruin. The poem at this point is making a profoundly political statement about the power of the poor not only to discern right values but to oppose false ones. The poor, the powerless and the fools are no longer passive sufferers but active witnesses to God's truth like the biblical *anawim* whose ideals are spiritual rather than material.[83] The poor now become powerful as they uphold the supremacy of spiritual values and are deeply concerned both to establish those values in the earthly kingdom and to combat the contrary worldly values which have become systemic in church and state. Like the fools, Will at last becomes active within his society, responding to Conscience's call to learn some craft for the common good of those in Unity. Unlike Conscience's former demand that Will should work, the craft suggested is not labour in the fields to provide food, but the fundamental one of love. At the moment of his deepest poverty, Will learns to take an active part in furthering God's kingdom of justice on earth.

WILL'S EXPERIENCE OF NEED

At the end of the poem, the quality which gives Will authority as a player in the final conflict is precisely his experience of need. Unlike the other aspects of his poverty which are mentioned as part of Will's conscious experience in his waking moments, Need comes to him personified at the start of the final passus. Like Reason and Conscience in the C-text apologia, Need is not part of a dream, but of Will's waking self. At this point Will is as poor as any pauper: 'For I ne wiste wher to ete ne at what place' (B.20.3). In Passus B.18 he is said to be without proper clothing, wearing the apparel of a pauper or a pilgrim, 'wolleward and weetshoed'. Will has clearly not taken advantage of the canonically legitimate exercise of theft to satisfy his fundamental requirements which are reiterated in their starkest form: food, drink and clothing. Need, like an aggressive alter ego, challenges Will for giving himself up to this destitution. There is no question here of the pauper waiting for charitable relief; Need contends that Will should have resorted to theft. In the depths of poverty Need undertakes to act as his lord, his legal support: 'Nede anoonrighte nymeþ hym vnder maynprise' (B.20.17), in the same way that other 'maintainers' endorse criminal actions of their household when they fall within agreed limits. Indeed, theologians agree that it is pre-

---

83 The *anawim* were the faithful remnant of Israel, the small group of poor and humble Jews in the Babylonian exile who retained strict adherence to the faith, and preserved it amidst a people that had given itself over to the worship of idols.

cisely at the point when other people refuse the pauper food that stealing is allowed;[84] no-one will go surety for him, and he has nothing to pawn; charity has failed. When he takes clothing, it must be because he cannot organize a loan:

> And nede ne haþ no lawe, ne neuere shal falle in dette
> For þre þynges þat he takeþ his lif for to saue –
> That is, mete whan men hym werneþ, and he no moneye weldeþ,
> Ne wight noon wol ben his boruȝ, ne no wed haþ to legge …
> And þouȝ he come so to a clooþ, and kan no bettre cheuyssaunce,
> Nede anoonrighte nymeþ hym vnder maynprise.   (B.20.10–13; 16–17)

But there must be no question of excess in what the pauper takes: 'So þat he sewe and saue *Spiritus Temperancie.*' Margaret Kim writes persuasively of the human being's requirement to consume:

> It may seem obvious to us that Langland sees worldly consumption in its excesses as inimical to the Christian enterprise of moral purity and spiritual transcendence, but from the discourses of Hunger and Nede in *Piers Plowman* we also see that the desire and appetite that drive consumption in this world are inescapable. As Langland explores the simultaneous inescapability and limits of Hunger and Nede for Christians seeking transcendence and salvation, we are reminded again and again that the material deprivation we see in involuntary poverty evokes a confluence of political anxieties and Christian interests because human beings must consume and often desire to consume.[85]

Here, in the encounter with Need, the necessity of consuming is seen at its most basic, forcing Will to recognize the full extent of what he undertook when he originally chose the life of a poor seeker after Truth. This is the role of Need – familiar, not wholly unwelcome, and an image of the most basic form of human poverty which, with a voice of authority, Need attributes to the incarnate Christ, 'he þat wroȝte al þe world' (B.20.48–50).

Need is, then, the overriding consideration. The cardinal virtues have nothing to say to someone in need, apart from Temperance which, commentators

---

84 'Nede hath no law' had reached proverbial status, and it is reiterated and discussed by all major theologians of the time, basing their arguments on the premise that those in need have a right to the superfluities of others. Tierney quotes a number of canonists on this point: 'Joannes Teutonicus, *Gl. ord. ad* C.12 q.2 c.11: "Some say that a man ought rather to die than to steal. It is more humane to say that very great necessity excuses." Bernardus Parmensis, *Gl. ord. ad* X. 5.18.3: "From the fact that penance is imposed [for a theft] it is gathered that the need was only slight, for if it had been great a penance would not have been imposed … because in necessity all things are common." Bernardus went on to explain that no degree of want could justify a sin. But that theft in these circumstances was not a sin since the thief had a right to what he took. Similarly, Innocent IV, *Commentaria ad* X. 5.18.3, p. 615, and Hostiensis, *Commentaria ad* X. 5.18.3, fol. 55r': *Medieval poor law*, p. 38. See also Hewett-Smith, 'Nede', pp 247–9.
85 Kim, 'Vision of theocratics', p. 98. See also Kim, 'Hunger, need', pp 162–6.

agree, is equivalent to 'mesure'. Bloomfield quotes extensively to show how temperance equates with humility,[86] and the poem, too, makes this parallel. Need echoes here the virtues of poverty enumerated by Patience (B.14.202–61), which make poverty an antidote to all the seven deadly sins. A practical self-interest rules the truly poor who are powerless in worldly terms. They have to adopt a humble demeanour because they have no power to do otherwise. The naturally poor are in this position by default, but philosophers and Christ have chosen this kind of need. Therefore people should not feel shame at having to wait – bide – be patient, passive, because the most powerful and the most active, the Creator of the world, 'was wilfulliche nedy' (B.20.49). Indeed, Need has just declared himself to be next to God:

> And Nede is next hym, for anoon he mekeþ,
> And as lowe as a lomb, for lakkyng þat hym nedeþ.   (B.20.35–6)

The allusion to a lamb links with the mention of the Lamb of God who, in his incarnation, became the sacrificial lamb. Need allies the pauper to this saving redeemer whose sorrow 'shal to ioye torne.' This is an echo of John 16. 20, when, in his farewell discourse to the disciples, Jesus foretells the sorrow the disciples are to experience before the resurrection. Need is once more given an eschatological meaning. Will, biologically identified with Need, incontrovertibly shares the identification of Need with Christ.

In his note on this passage, Pearsall suggests that Need may at this point be voicing aspects of the poverty debate:

> The authority of Need as a witness in the episode is in fact throughout debatable. Even his use of the life of Christ as a model of Need is suspect, being based on similar arguments falsely used by the friars in the controversy about poverty.[87]

Burrow reminds us that Need's arguments were commonly used by friars to justify a life of 'idleness and self-indulgent mendicancy'.[88] Once again there is ambivalence in Will's life of poverty; his real, physical need to consume becomes overshadowed by the potentially deceptive words of a friar. Is he a sufferer from involuntary poverty, and as such allied with those poor who are a sacrament of Christ, or is he a self-deceiving practitioner of voluntary poverty? Need does sound like a glosing friar, but this serves to emphasize even more starkly the basic quality of Need; it exists in painfully material form both for the voluntarily and involuntarily poor, philosophers and Will, glosing friars and beggars who have no alternative for survival. Need arrives unbidden, as Kim points out, and leaves without a serious engagement of Will in debate. There is no debate except with himself;

---

86 M.W. Bloomfield, *Piers Plowman as a fourteenth-century apocalypse*, pp 133–51.
87 Pearsall, *C-text*, p. 363 37n.
88 *Langland's fictions*, p. 99.

and, as Kim points out again, he speaks of himself in the third person.[89] He speaks like a glosing friar but relates to the essential poverty of man, 'the thing itself' as Lear observes. Certainly it is impossible to overlook the pervasively anticlerical elements that Scase has identified in the poem.[90] Will receives advice at the end of his life from a character who quotes texts used to justify clerical mendicancy. Is this another of those moments when an aspect of poverty is held up for scrutiny? In terms of the anticlerical debate, I think the answer must be 'yes'. Langland's pervasive concern for the involuntarily poor of society expresses itself here as exposing hypocrisy in consecrated religious who give poverty a bad name. But Need's arguments can be taken in more than one way. Will's need shows him how to act in solidarity with the poor as he disregards Need's invitation to steal or beg. He requires no external justification for his life of poverty which, in its destitution, is as distant from the venal Frere Flatterer as it is close to the needy Christ.

The poem's imagery here conveys a powerful argument: voluntarily poor people must be prepared to accept real need such as that suffered by paupers. At this point in the poem, the two poverties, voluntary and involuntary, converge in the figure of Need, an aggressive intellectual concept given uncomfortable incarnation in the body of the starving protagonist. The visual image is of a starving man who has to endure the shame of being considered a fraud, refused even a loan, who has tried everything until he is at his wit's end and finally resorts to stealing some food and a bit of cloth to cover himself. Then he skulks in the hedgerows, drinking from the ditches, an uncompromising picture of genuine indigence which, once again, is identified with Christ, not in transcendent majesty, but in practical earthly need. At this juncture, Will has achieved complete identification with the destitute, and Need has put into clear words the reciprocal relationship between the destitute pauper and the Son of God – 'Nede is next hym'; a recognition that the poor person is a sacrament of Christ and that Christ has taken on the identity of the poor:

> And God al his grete ioye goostliche he lefte,
> And cam and took mankynde and bicam nedy. (B.20.40–1)

Need's final function for Will is to lead him to understand that to be a member of Christ is to be drawn into his work. This identification in poverty gives Will the power to join forces with Conscience against the forces of Antichrist.

There are certain moments when the poem, in describing patient poverty, appears to present a model of poverty akin to that of the great saints and apostles who fled from the world in order to become truly poor followers of Christ (e.g. B.15.268–97). Will, it is true, has tried to follow the ideal of patient poverty, but in his involvement with the active life in the world he is more akin to the incarnate Christ who lived, worked and died in the world, involved with the concerns of the *saeculum* while rejecting its perverse values. In searching for the

---

89 Kim, pp 79–86. See also Hewett-Smith, 'Nede', pp 244–53.
90 See her analysis of the language of what she terms the new polemic, pp 64–78.

truth as handed to the pristine church, represented by Piers in the Barn of Unity, Will chooses to range himself against the administrative machine of the institutional fourteenth-century church, condemning, rejecting and fighting against its ruling ideology of avarice. His only choice in this fight is to embrace poverty. This is action. Patient he may be, passive he is not. At the end of the poem, Need and Christ are associated, and Need becomes Will's alter ego, a familiar spirit, one who sums up his existence:

> Siþ he þat wroȝte al þe world was wilfulliche nedy,
> Ne neuere noon so nedy ne pouerer deide.   (B.20.49–50)

Does the identification with Christ mean that the poet regards the condition of utter need as acceptable? I think not. Will's need is an evil, an aberration, something that belongs to the rule of Antichrist. Need, morally neutral, is nonetheless the forerunner of Antichrist, both in *Piers Plowman* and in Gregory's *Moralia in Job* which, as Robert Adams has convincingly demonstrated, is the ultimate, though not the only source for the Need episode.[91] As such need is to be resisted, not, perhaps, by methods which modern readers might expect – political revolution, systematic schemes of social welfare – but in ways available to a poet for whom salvation is the aim of all living. 'Lerne to loue' is the command Kynde gives to Will. As Holy Church says at the start of the poem, love, which achieves 'mesure' by taking steps to ensure that all have enough, is the only solution to need (B.1.175–8). At the end of the poem, Will experiences the fulfilment of his youthful choice with its uncomfortable consequences – starvation and destitution, compounded by the devastatingly earthly decay of old age. Such inescapable need fuses the experiences of voluntary and involuntary poverty into one, a poverty which he is invited not to transcend, but to suffer in imitation of Christ. Aligning his will with that of God makes him open to the leadership of Conscience and prepared to work at whatever craft the commune needs from him:

> 'If þow wolt be wroken, wend into Vnitee ...
> And loke þow konne som craft er þow come þennes.'
> 'Conseilleþ me, Kynde,' quod I, 'what craft be best to lerne?'
> 'Lerne to loue,' quod Kynde, 'and leef alle oþere.'   (B.20.204; 206–8)

Love is the work required of Will, and the poem has demonstrated thoroughly how love, in the guise of practical charity, helps to bring about justice for the poor. Will's acceptance of poverty with patience demonstrates the conversion of his will which, in itself, qualifies him to join the fight against injustice. The poem is Langland's weapon in effecting reform.

Will's vocation in poverty is textually bound up with multiple concerns of the poem's historical moment, making its ideology visible to the modern reader. At times it expresses itself through the terms of anticlerical and antimendicant

---

91 R. Adams, 'The nature of need in *Piers Plowman* XX', pp 283–9.

satire. Will has to keep his intention constantly under review as he tries to maintain focus on searching for Truth, rather than slipping into the behaviour and thought patterns of the contemporary religious failures he satirizes, whether specifically Franciscan, as Clopper argues, or clerics in general, as Scase suggests. Equally he has to justify to himself his choice of a clerical vocation in the face of society's need for food and for spiritual guidance, negotiating statutory obligations and confronting the terms of apostolic mission. Having chosen a way of life that exempts him from manual labour under the 1388 statute, he is faced with the uncompromising obligation to pray, learn and communicate as a follower of the poor Christ. In this, Will's poverty becomes a unique expression of the this-world/next-world quality of Christian life as experienced in the context of his contemporary world. It is also a profoundly imagined expression of the dilemmas that the Christian life, whether sincerely lived or minimally accepted, throws up for its devotees in whatever context or age they live. It makes an unmistakable statement that the way of poverty is the way of perfection even when it is lived by people who are sinful.

If Langland in his writing is attempting to move the will of his readers, and I firmly agree with Simpson that he is doing so, then what Will learns is what the reader needs to learn.[92] When Will learns that the human value of poor people is confirmed by their identification with the needy Christ, this is what readers should also take from the poem. Through the poor man, Will, Langland makes a powerful statement both for the modern reader and for his medieval audience – which might, conceivably, have included the poet, Hoccleve, who writes so feelingly about the fear of poverty.[93] It is that the poverty of fourteenth-century England cannot be ignored and must not be belittled by being considered only as a state leading to spiritual justification. In following the life of Will, whom I have categorized as a contemporary poor man, readers of the poem see that to live the life of patient poverty involves material suffering, not just verbal commitment. Moreover, those who do choose the poverty of Christ are committed, as Will eventually becomes, to fighting against involuntary poverty when it is caused by the forces of injustice. When these forces deprive poor people of material necessities and human dignity, plunging them into conditions such as Will experiences in his encounter with Need, Will joins to fight against them on behalf of the poor as Christ himself did from within a state of poverty. The poetic representation of Will's poverty gives fictive embodiment to the real opposition that Langland's poem expresses towards all who pervert the church's teaching, all who oppress the poor and all who, like Launfal and Hoccleve, unwittingly negate the simple common humanity of poor human beings. My final chapter will suggest that all these may, in some ways, be the same people.

---

92 Simpson, 'Desire and the scriptural text', p. 219.
93 For this suggestion, see the illuminating article by K. Kerby-Fulton, 'Langland and the bibliographic ego', especially Part VI (pp 110–22). This section of the article discusses possible coterie readership of Langland's poem, and considers that Chaucer, Hoccleve and Usk may have been among its many early readers.

CHAPTER 5

Food of life and heavenly reward: a question of justice

More than any other of my chapters, this concluding one argues that Langland's poetic expression of human needs shows how they exceed the basics of food, shelter and clothing, which many medieval writings, including the decretals, say are enough. The assumption that the needs of the poor can be satisfied by the non-poor providing food, clothing and shelter for them is typical of a 'top-down' approach and implies that these material necessities are the only ones worth considering. This chapter examines the poem's approach to need as seen by the poor who are entitled, not only to food, but to human dignity. Starting from a recapitulation of modern poor people's experience, the discussion moves into analysis of *Piers Plowman's* representation of what the medieval poor require. I argue that, contrary to opinions suggesting satisfaction for the poor will come in the next life, the poem insists they must, in this life, receive dignity, charity and justice. These are all elements of the kingdom of God on earth, and only those who have participated in God's kingdom by acting with justice towards their fellow human beings on earth will qualify for its eternal continuation in heaven. My discussion concentrates on the poem's images of food and commerce through which Langland gives powerful linguistic form to that which all people consider needful and due to them. Both are scriptural as well as fundamental, earthly tropes, and Langland plays on their material and spiritual connotations. The first section of the chapter examines how the poem presents images of banquets from the viewpoint of the poor whose entitlement to food and to human dignity is squandered by those who feast to excess and pervert God's word. Dame Study, Trajan and Will speak for the poor in the context of banquets where over-consumption and waste are allied to perversion of truth. The second part reviews the poem's images of treasure, redemption and reward, and considers how they help to articulate the needs of the poor for dignity, justice and charity. I demonstrate how the poem shows that Christ, by assuming human nature, associates himself with the needs of human beings, and, in achieving the redemption, establishes justice and charity on earth as primary requirements of his kingdom.

In his book, *The needs of strangers*, Ignatieff points to the importance of language in addressing human needs.[1] He implies that, unless needs can be articu-

---

1 Ignatieff, p. 142.

lated in words, they cannot be realized and will eventually die away, leaving human beings without that which elevates them above animal dependency. He talks about fraternity, love, belonging, dignity and respect as essentials, in this echoing the words of three representative poor people of the modern world.[2] A poor older woman in Ethiopia speaks about the importance of love:

> A better life for me is to be healthy, peaceful and live in love without hunger. Love is more than anything. Money has no value in the absence of love.

A woman from Uganda connects poverty with loss of respect and hope:

> When one is poor, she has no say in public, she feels inferior. She has no food, so there is famine in her house; no clothing, and no progress in her family.

For a blind woman from Tiraspol, Moldova, poverty causes complete loss of human dignity:

> For a poor person everything is terrible – illness, humiliation, shame. We are cripples; we are afraid of everything; we depend on everyone. No one needs us. We are like garbage that everyone wants to get rid of.

These few words express a yearning in poor people for things of the spirit, a sense that hope for the future, justice and respect are an essential part of human life, yet denied them by virtue of their material destitution. When modern poor people speak of their need for dignity, they enumerate things like education, health care, and access to justice as equally important with food, decent housing and clothing. This translates, in Langland's terms, into similar requirements for teaching, justice, and access to the kind of love that treats people as equal human beings, not as indigent animals.

'PIERS PLOWMAN', BANQUETS AND THE POOR

Piers Plowman takes the elementary necessity of food and, through imagery of feasting, expresses the human being's need for more than material food. I examine how images of banquets as Langland uses them focus directly on the issue of what people need and how language can either conceal or reveal such need. To understand the poem's use of the banquet in its cultural context, it will be useful, first, to survey late medieval banqueting practice and the scriptural connotations of the banquet image, giving particular attention to ways in which medieval

---

2 Povertynet, *Voices of the poor* (online).

people included the poor in their feasting, whether by ritual or effective provision of food. Provision of food is fundamental to the poem, the image of the banquet a focus for satirical conjunctions. By showing the aberrations of those who feast to excess, Langland does more than add to an already large library of medieval imagery for gluttons. He emphasizes the sinful arrogance that makes them disregard the poor as not needing to be thought of as human; when the feasters cast out the poor they ignore even their basic, animal need for sustenance. This is the greatest sin one human being can commit against another, and the wealth of imagery in the poem ensures that we do not miss the point. Prelates feast with all the pomp of their lay counterparts, and in an ironic reversal give food to the jesters who tell sinful tales, but send away God's representatives, the poor. A magisterial doctor attends a banquet at which Scripture is the main fare, but he rejects the scriptural fare in favour of real food, on which he gorges gluttonously. The spectacle of responsible people over-indulging themselves with food while the poor go hungry produces some of the most animated and repellent metaphors in the poem. Bestial gluttony, arrogance in attitude and downright cruelty of neglect are all sins described in the context of banquets. In striking allegory, Langland sets such neglect of the poor in the larger context of moral decrepitude as feasters turn banquets into parodies of the word. Langland's concern that the poor should be fed is presented as more than a pious, poetic or even personal hope; the poem makes authoritative statements that show without doubt that society is injured when gluttons deprive the poor, and that unless the non-poor feed the hungry they will not be saved.

LATE MEDIEVAL BANQUETING PRACTICE

Langland's reforming satire draws upon material found in late medieval analyses of the seven deadly sins.[3] In this respect it is conventional, yet its vehemence suggests that it reaches beyond the context of the poem to comment upon contemporary practice. The poetry does not dwell on the details of real food and drink at banquets; its language, indeed, seems to make the enjoyment of material food for its own sake into something disgusting, associated with sin. Banquet imagery of excess reflects the waste of spiritual food. Yet, while it is true that Langland uses images of excess in food as satirical weapons, it is also clear that he is alert to the full tropological significance of the banquet, as becomes very clear in the scene of Patience's banquet with Conscience and Trajan's commentary on Luke's all-inclusive banquet. As I have already suggested, the poem's

---

[3] As an example of such writings, *Handlyng synne* under 'Glotonye' has a full account of gluttonous practices at feasts which uses much the same material as this section of *Piers Plowman*, especially its commentary on the Dives parable, *Handlyng synne*, pp 162–72 (ll. 6517–822). Chaucer's *Parson's tale* under 'Gula' links aberrations of speech with impairment of reason induced by drink, *Chaucer*, p. 316.

yardstick for measuring the moral standing of feasters is the seriousness of their commitment to feeding the poor. In order to appreciate the environment of food and feasting that is adumbrated in Langland's imagery, it is worth examining contemporary attitudes to feasting, to feeding and, particularly, to feeding the poor.

Part of our understanding of the way the wealthy and powerful approached food can be gleaned from extant accounts of certain late medieval banquets which were undoubtedly ostentatious affairs at which vast quantities of food were prepared. The Great Feast for the installation of George Neville as Archbishop of York has assumed almost legendary status among antiquaries and modern food historians for the range of its menus and the huge roll of guests:

> To give some idea of the scale of catering, the ingredients include 300 quarters of wheat, 104 oxen, 1000 muttons, 304 'Porkes' and 2000 pigs, and thousands of geese, capons, mallards, cranes, chickens and other birds. Baked dishes of pasties, tarts and custards are similarly counted by the thousand. The diners, ranging from the Archbishop, other clerics and nobles to numerous knights and gentry, franklins, yeomen and servants, not forgetting sixty-two Cooks and over one hundred broche turners, add up to about 3000 people.[4]

Such menus are signs of power and opulence and suggest that the food was meant to impress rather than to be consumed all at one sitting, even though huge numbers of animals and pies would be required to supply the very large number of guests, in itself a visible sign of the lord's ability to provide for and protect his own people:

> It was politic for the host to appear generous, because the lavishness of his table gave the clue to his resources; it was wise to be both hospitable to dependents and discriminating in the choice of guests of honour, because the number and caliber of diners in the hall revealed his importance and his power ... Just as the host needed his guests, so they needed his invitation. They wished to show themselves to be a part of his family, and safely under the umbrella of his protection.[5]

Ceremonial feasts were exceptional, designed for unique occasions. Infrequent, too, were the gargantuan meals that took place in monasteries or halls before or after periods of fasting. Historians of food suggest that such binges reflect society's response to insecurity both natural and political, with plague, famine, rapine and dearth never too distant threats.[6] One historian comments on 'the ever-pre-

---

4 E. White, 'The great feast', p. 404.
5 B.A. Henisch, *Fast and feast*, pp 56, 103, 191. See also M.P. Cosner, *Fabulous feasts*, pp 37, 45.
6 S. Mennell, *All manners of food*, p. 23.

Food of life and heavenly reward: a question of justice 197

sent dangers threatening the granary; what was the good of laying up large stocks if brigands or soldiers might come along the next day and carry them off?'[7]

Yet even when the feast was lavish, the poor were remembered; the office of Almoner, and the custom of beginning a feast by placing a loaf, or a piece of whatever was being served to the lord, in the almsdish 'to serve god fyrst' are testimony to an ongoing consideration for the poor that was built into the structure of the household and the meal.[8] This symbolic act was followed up at the end of the meal with the practical gathering of leftovers, which in many households were given to the poor. Robert Grosseteste's rules, translated in three languages and still being reproduced in the fifteenth century, state the underlying principle:

> Comandetz ke voster aumoyne seyt loyaument cuilla e garde ne pas enuee de la table as garsons ne pas hors de sale porte ne a sopers ne a dyners de garsons uuastroille mes fraunchement sagement e atemprement sanz tenser e batre parti a poures malades e mendinans.
>
> (Command that your alms be faithfully gathered and kept, nor sent from the table to the grooms, nor carried out of the hall, either at supper or dinner, by good-for-nothing grooms; but freely, discreetly, and orderly, without dispute and strife, divided among the poor, sick, and beggars.)[9]

That such attention to alms was not a dead letter in the later middle ages can be seen from arrangements made by the Duke of Clarence:

> In the household of the Duke of Clarence (brother of Edward IV), the almoner was given 12*d*. (5*p*.) a month to give to poor people at his discretion, while every day at dinner and supper he was allowed to take every dish that the Duke had finished with (unless he had given it to one of his guests) and give it to the needy, which could include the Duke's own servants if they fulfilled this criterion. In addition, on four or five days every week the almoner distributed other food to the poor at the gate: one 'cheete' (lower quality) loaf between two people, a gallon of ale between eight and a mess of meat for four. He was instructed to see that the food was carefully kept from 'devouringe of dogges'.[10]

---

7 Mandrou, quoted by Mennell, p. 23.
8 For a clear discussion of the rules drawn up by Bishop Grosseteste for the Countess of Lincoln in the thirteenth century and those in the British Library, Harleian MS, 6815 for a fifteenth-century earl, see M. Girouard, *Life in the English country house*, p. 30.
9 Robert Grosseteste, *Les reules Seynt Roberd*, in *Walter of Henley's husbandry*, p. 134. A Middle English version of the rules quotes the same rule as follows: 'The viii. [C]ommaunde ʒe that ʒoure almys be kepyd & not sende not to boys and knafis nother in the alle nothe outh of the halle ne be wasted in soperys ne dyners of gromys but wisely, temperatly with oute bate or betyng be hit distribute and the[n] departyd to powre menn beggers, sykefolke and febulle.' *Supplement to Les reules Seynt Roberd*, British Museum, Sloane MS, 1986, printed in *Walter of Henley's husbandry*, pp 147–50 (p. 148).
10 P.W. Hammond, *Food and feast in medieval England*, p. 115.

We learn from the accounts of a medieval household such as that of Alice de Bryene, gentry widow of Acton, Suffolk, that, as a matter of course, Alice attended to the needs of the poor and entertained family, servants and guests at table in her hall. Paupers from Alice's estate were occasionally granted corn, given loaves each Maundy Thursday and, in one year, were actually named, which, according to Alice's brief biography, 'makes it easy to identify with their needs and indicates furthermore that they may have been destitute rather than just needy.'[11] Elizabeth de Burgh's accounts reveal that she entertained widely and regularly, for family affairs, business, duty, and charity, and that, towards the end of her life, her gifts to the poor were specific and generous:

> In the summers of 1356, 1358 and 1359 there were regular monthly entries in the accounts of £2 12s. od given to 540 poor people in London and eighty-four at Standon at the rate of one penny each. As the accounting month comprised four weeks Elizabeth was giving alms to 135 poor people in London a week, or nineteen or twenty a day.[12]

The same people who indulged in luxury and apparent excess could be the ones who gave regularly to the poor. Archbishop Neville who held the Great Feast, quoted above as a legendary example of medieval ostentation, used the offices of an Almoner whose duty it was to distribute food to the poor.[13]

Yet such alms were determined by the giver, not necessarily by the requirements of the needy. The danger for the modern reader, as well as for the medieval diner, is to assume that the sharing out of leftovers is adequate for the needs of the poor, and that it covers all the needy. In fact we know that it is selective. In such records as exist, for example the Harleian rules for an earl, the leftovers are to be distributed to seven specified 'poor householders, a different seven for each day of the week'.[14] Henry of Lancaster, writing in 1354 as a sincere great lord who recognized that his efforts fell short, admitted his dual tendency: to indulge his senses in the enjoyment of fine foods and wines at the risk of gluttony, and to be more niggardly than he ought in sharing his food with the poor:

> Et si nul die: – 'Il y a trop, il le convenera doner pur Dieux,' cel la me entre si envys en l'oraille qe trop; et ausi qi me dirroit: – 'Muez ou desportés ceste bone viande pur l'amour de Dieux,' certs ceo n'entroit mye par mon gree.[15]

> (If any one says: There's too much, it will be right to give it away for God's sake', that is something I am most reluctant to hear. And also, if

---

11 Swabey, 'The household of Alice de Bryene, 1412–13', p. 142.
12 J.C. Ward, 'Elizabeth de Burgh, Lady of Clare (d. 1360)', p. 43.
13 Hammond, p. 115.
14 Girouard, p. 50.
15 *Le livre des seintes medicines* (my translation), p. 48.

someone said to me, 'Either shift this good food or distribute it for the love of God', certainly this would not be a welcome sound to me.)

All these practices, however charitable, treat the poor as 'other', as people outside the banqueting hall and its comforts, and Langland sums up this aspect of their condition in his pointed lament for their exclusion from the hall:

> Now haþ ech riche a rule – to eten by hymselue
> In a pryuee parlour for pouere mennes sake,
> Or in a chambre wiþ a chymenee, and leue þe chief halle.(B.10.98–100)

The poem is not dealing with specific historical incidents, but establishing a vision for society that includes the poor in every sphere of life. This inclusion is symbolized by their being admitted to the hall, to be fed as part of the community by right. The sin of gluttony, which might seem to be encouraged by the eating habits of the wealthy, and which Langland interprets as a direct affront to the poor, was condemned not only by church writers. Medieval sumptuary laws, with an emphasis more on the preservation of rank than charity to the poor, sought to control the eating and provision of too luxurious foods with an air of carping restriction similar to that of Dame Study.[16] Perhaps, as Mennell suggests, enormous banquets were acceptable when given by feudal lords 'sharing their viands by custom and obligation with their followers and distributing remains to the poor' but unacceptable when practised by 'rising strata whose social obligations were ill-defined and dependents few'.[17]

Such an analysis would correspond with Dame Study's criticisms of banquets where philosophy and theology become the table talk, not of clerks, but of a rising generation of laity who pretend to knowledge without scholarship. Handbooks of the *ars convivatoria* propose the very kind of discourse that is rejected in Langland's banquets; philosophy 'accepts the company of the anecdote and the practical joke'. The perfect guest is said to be an amateur who can talk about everything, moving freely from one register to another and from one topic to another.[18] In discussing the banquet symposium Bahktin points to the materialistic significance of the banquet speech which accompanies man's celebration of his domination of the material world:

> Man is not afraid of the world, he has defeated it and eats of it ... The banquet speech is universal and materialistic at the same time. This is why the grotesque symposium travesties and debases the purely idealistic, mystic

16 e.g. 'Statutum de cibariis utendis' passed in 1336, which prohibited people of any state from having more than two courses at dinner meals. A law determining more detailed dietary and clothing regulations for different ranks in society was passed in response to a Commons Petition in 1363: F. Baldwin, *Sumptuary legislation*, pp 29, 47.
17 Mennell, p. 30.
18 M. Jeanneret, *A feast of words*, p.95.

and ascetic victory over the world (that is, the victory of the abstract spirit).[19]

More fully documented in texts from the sixteenth and seventeenth centuries, the banquet symposium is a cultural phenomenon with its roots in classical antiquity.

> History teaches us that from the dawn of Greek civilization the banquet has an essential role as a social institution; it is a meeting place where the ties of the community are strengthened. Documentary evidence also proves that in the context of the *symposion* wine and the poetic word are closely linked. In the megaron of Homeric princes, bards recite their epics while *kraters* of wine are being emptied.[20]

The thirteenth-century *Mensa philosophica*, a handbook widely circulated in schools of the later middle ages and the Renaissance, codifies the link between good food, wine and speech by providing an anthology of reference material on diet, health, manners and table discourse.[21] However, as moralists from Plutarch through Langland's allegorical figures to Erasmus and beyond recognize, the banquet can easily become the grotesque symposium:

> Since time immemorial moralists have recognized (if only to exorcise it) the latent power of subversion generated by the pleasures of eating. Discourse, which also has a dual nature, moves from sobriety into delirium, from social polish into wild impulse. At any moment, drunken and deranged speech can invade the disciplined discourse of the diners. Plutarch, in his treatise on banquets, speaks for many other writers: Bacchus is 'the Looser and the Liberator of all things, and ... especially he unbridles the tongue and grants the utmost freedom to speech'
> (*Table Talk*, vol. 8, p. 11).[22]

Excess in food, wine and speech at the grotesque symposium is either celebrated as liberation or lamented as abuse. *Piers Plowman*'s Dame Study sets her ideal banquet symposium against what the poetry presents as a perversion of the ideal – the grotesque banquet symposium.[23] Rabelais celebrates plenty and exuberance but Langland cannot rid his poetry of poor people, impoverished, as he sees it, by waste.[24] Glutton wastes his regurgitated food (B.5.297–385); and the ban-

---

19 M. Bakhtin, *Rabelais and his world*, p. 296.
20 Jeanneret, p. 149.
21 Ibid. p. 96.
22 Ibid. p. 98, and see also his note (p. 99 n. 11): 'The liberation of the power of words in literature goes directly against the condemnation of the abuse of language and the denunciation of the dangers of speech in the moral tradition. See for example Erasmus, *Lingua*'.
23 There is considerable similarity between Dame Study's criticisms of banqueting excess and the dramatizing of the banquet in Conscience's hall (B.13.31–215).
24 Frank makes the point (p. 98) that there is nothing Rabelaisian about Langland's banquets, but

Food of life and heavenly reward: a question of justice

queters' theological discourse degenerates into meaningless, artificially constructed arguments, food for the deadly sin of pride (B.10.72; 81). In one respect, the literary virtuosity of Glutton's portrait, Study's grotesque symposium and the Great Doctor's performance at Conscience's banquet is a celebration of the grotesque. Yet in *Piers*, excess in food and word leads to waste; the grotesque banquet becomes the Dives banquet, food for deadly sin.

BANQUETS IN SCRIPTURE

While the banquet scenes of the poem reflect medieval feasting practice, they are also scripturally based, and read like commentaries on the scriptural texts from which they derive. The scriptural associations reinforce my contention that, when he writes about feasting, Langland foregrounds non-material needs of the poor as well as their material hunger. An initial review of some of these texts will help point up the irony of Langland's satirical representations. When Jesus, in the New Testament, uses the image of the banquet it is deeply resonant with Old Testament usages which come together to foreshadow the messianic banquet. In the Judaeo-Christian tradition the ideal of heavenly bliss is a material place of reward. It is at the same time both the locus and the event of the King-Messiah's glorious return, solemn enthronement and future reign over God's people in fulfilment of God's promise made to David.[25] At the banquet, the poor of Yahweh, the *anawim*, will be fed. Scripturally, the banquet is symbolic of the coming of God's kingdom on earth and Jesus emphasizes its extension to the whole of mankind:

> And I say to you that many shall come from the east and the west, and shall sit down with Abraham and Isaac and Jacob in the kingdom of heaven: but the children of the kingdom shall be cast out into the exterior darkness. There, shall be weeping and gnashing of teeth.   (Matthew 8. 11–12)

Significant banquets in the parables of Jesus are the various versions of the wedding feast to which all are called, expanding on the all-inclusiveness of those who come 'from east and west', to make specific mention of the poor:

> Then the master of the house being angry, said to his servant: Go out quickly into the streets and lanes of the city; and bring in hither the poor and the feeble and the blind and the lame. And the servant said: Lord, it is done as thou hast commanded; and yet there is room. And the Lord said to the servant: Go out into highways and hedges, and compel them

---

rather 'a joyless voraciousness'. I take this to be another aspect of Langland's awareness of how often the poor are near to starvation.

25 *Jerusalem Bible*, p. 431 note g.

> to come in, that my house may be filled. But I say to you that not one
> of those who were invited shall taste of my supper. (Luke 14. 21–4)

These four categories of the needy: the poor, the crippled, the blind and the lame, become standard, to be repeated in medieval sermon and even statute as defining those who are to be considered as poor. There is no ambiguity about their status; they are included at the messianic banquet. Some banquets which are recorded as gospel incidents achieve the status of exempla in subsequent commentary and sermon, such as the marriage feast at Cana (John 2. 1–10), the feast at which the sinful woman pours ointment over Jesus' feet (Luke 7. 36–50), and, most significant feast of all, the Last Supper, where Jesus not only institutes the eucharist but looks forward to the eschatological banquet:

> And I say to you, I will not drink from henceforth of this fruit of the vine until that day when I shall drink it with you new in the kingdom of my Father. (Matthew 26. 29)

Other important feast images are of the banquet at which the disciples are urged to take the lowest place (Luke 14. 7–11) and the banquet of Dives who denied even the scraps to the leper, Lazarus, begging at his gates. This parable is so frequently used in medieval sermon literature and scriptural gloss that it is often alluded to only briefly in works whose authors assume familiarity with the Gospel text.[26] These banquets derive their own resonances from the Old Testament, where eating and drinking carry a redemptive significance by association with the Passover and an eschatological one by association with the Judgment. The New Testament banquets equally range themselves around these themes. The wedding banquet to which all are called is election to salvation;[27] Dives's banquet from which Lazarus is excluded brings him damnation. These two scriptural banquets underlie scenes in *Piers Plowman* and Langland plays on their multiple meanings in a way which highlights the eschatological significance of the poor as well as the moral obligations of society towards them.

26 In a sermon *De contemptu mundi* of St Augustine, the poor man dreams of wealth but the rich man's anxious dreams become his damnation: 'Nam ille dives, qui induebatur purpura et bysso, nec nominatus, nec nominandus, contemptor pauperis ante januam jacentis, epulabatur quotidie splendide; postea mortuus est, et sepultus: evigilavit, et se in flamma invenit (Luke 16. 19–24). Dormivit somnum suum, et post somnum nihil invenit; quia nihil operatus est de manibus suis, id est, de divitiis suis.' (For that rich man who was clothed in purple and fine linen, not called to high office or likely to be, contemptuous of the poor man lying before his gate, feasted sumptuously every day. Later he died, and was buried: he awoke to find himself in the fire (Luke 16. 19–24). He slept his sleep, and after his sleep had no reward; because he had achieved nothing with his own efforts, that is, with his wealth.) *PL* 39, col. 1518.
27 'Multi autem sunt vocati pauci vero electi' (For many are called, but few are chosen). Matthew 22. 14. Will, in old age and poverty, learns from Scripture about election in the context of the banquet; subsequently, in the course of the passus, he is shown that baptism which makes a person one of God's chosen must be followed by good works in charity (B.11.111–318).

I want, now, to consider the implications of the Gospel story of Dives and Pauper – the begging leper, Lazarus, – as Langland uses it. In the Gospel parable, the beggar is not said to be virtuous in any way; he is taken into the bosom of Abraham by virtue of having suffered need on earth; poverty brings its own compensation. Dives is said to be a sinner in no other way than in the fundamental one of denying food to the beggar at his gates. This touches the heart of Christ's message: denying food to one who is in need is a denial of love and leads unerringly to damnation. The parable underlies two important episodes in the poem, the criticism Dame Study makes of prelates who dine to excess and ignore the poor (B.10.30–136), and the banquet of Conscience to which the doctor of Divinity is invited with Clergy, Scripture, Patience and Will (B.13.22–215). In setting up both scenes, Langland points out that excess in food and words is linked to moral failings; greed is portrayed as bestial, and in their loss of human dignity his gluttonous diners fail also to recognize the humanity of others. Such lack of humanity in rulers and teachers, the clergy and lords, underlines a corrosion of values within society as a whole.

THE BANQUET AND STUDY

Dame Study is the custodian of the word. When Will encounters her he is about to embark on his intellectual training, and must learn to distinguish genuine searching for truth from vainglorious display of specious arguments. Study links the dissipation of such empty scholarship with a profound lack of charity; lack of respect for the word becomes lack of respect for the Word who is to be recognized in Christ's poor. She condemns wealthy and powerful lords for destroying truth with sophistry; perversion of words leads to perversion of charity (B.10.29). Her pointed criticism singles out practices that deny justice to the poor when clever words pervert truth at legal hearings (B.10.19–22). The C-text is specific: fallacious arguments rob the people (C.11.19–20). Her principal diatribe against false banquets (B.10.30–136) has two major points. Gluttony and false verbosity are allied, both are sins of the mouth and both lead their perpetrators astray; moreover, both have a direct social effect on the physically and the morally needy. Gluttony makes the wealthy ignore the poor, and love of empty words deprives the ignorant of the teaching they need for salvation.

The rich diners, a gloss on the Dives figure, indulge in a grotesque banquet where perverters of the word, 'iaperis and iogelours and iangleris of gestes' (B.10.31), are entertained instead of true teachers, and where the true word is manipulated by those who wish only to speak clever words, not to hear truth. For Dame Study, such a treatment of theology is an inexcusable travesty, the more so when prelates are associated with it. While the clergy are drunk and sated, their discussion of holy matters is specious and blasphemous, directed not at seeking truth but at putting forward a clever argument (B.10.51–5). The excess of the body perverts the workings of the mind and of the spirit. Far from treating God's word as spiritual nourishment, the banqueters gnaw on it like a bone they have stripped. Langland's use of the word 'dryvele' is a salient pun on the overfed diners dribbling as they gnaw on the bones, talking drivel about sacred things:

> Thus þei dryuele at hir deys þe deitee to knowe,
> And gnawen God wiþ the gorge whanne hir guttes fullen. (B.10.56–7)

They need no further nourishment because their guts are full; they have eaten to excess and have no room for spiritual things. In this vignette of a banquet Study reveals the banqueters to be like hogs drivelling over the words of truth, as baffled by them as hogs with pearls.[28] Inability to recognize the pearl leads the rich and learned diners to materialize truth and to misunderstand it. Small wonder that they fail to see the poor, much less to admit their need to be cherished as brethren, since they replace the gospel message of charity with sophistry.

At this point in Dame Study's satire, Pauper figures in the poor and the distressed who are suffering at the gate. Like the Gospel character who was licked by the dogs, these beggars are hounded from the gate, even while crying out in their cold, hunger and thirst (B.10.58–9). Their sufferings are as material as the gluttony of the clerics whose hearts are closed to the sound of the poor, and whose ears are occupied with excess verbiage, the sound of their own cleverness. The word of God sticks in the gullet of these doctors who cannot get beyond the letter to understand the attributes of humility or charity. The satire of Dame Study is more about intellectual perversion than about gluttony; nonetheless, the poor at the gate are there as a constant reminder of the world to come, just as they are present in Grosseteste's rules or the lord's almsgiving rituals. The virtuous banquet is conducted with the poor provided for as God's representatives. Study satirizes the ill-regulated banquet where, instead of the poor being given food and protected from the dogs, the only 'parcell' (B.10.63) they receive as their share of the leftovers is abuse. This is a direct denial of their need to be treated with human dignity:

> ... hoen on hym as an hound and hoten hym go þennes. (B.10.61)

The message is driven home in unfolding clarity as Study repeatedly glosses the meaning. Humility is set against pride; 'Meene men' are contrasted with the 'grete maistres' and mercy and God's works are contrasted with words which gorge but do not nourish. The measure of the sin is the neglect of the poor who become, in their turn, the practitioners of good:

> God is muche in þe gorge of þise grete maistres,
> Ac amonges meene men his mercy and hise werkes. (B.10.66–7)

The 'gorge' is opposed to the heart:

---

28 Study's first words on encountering Will were to warn against casting pearls to hogs (B.10.9–12).

> Clerkes and othere kynnes men carpen of God faste,
> And haue hym muche in hire mouþ, ac meene men in herte.
>
> (B.10.69–70)

Study pointedly recognizes the humanity of the starving poor who have God in their hearts, though no food in their belly, in contrast with the clerks who are overfed but have neither room for the Word of God nor respect for his poor.

Further, the banqueters' condition is pride, with sophistical friars encouraging the laity to commit the sin of intellectual pride, which Study identifies as the cause of that very corporeal disease, the pestilence. Which is cause and which effect? Fleshly sin is punished by bodily suffering in the plague. Concentration on the flesh leaves no room for charity, so the poor are left languishing in hunger and the rich are condemned to languish from moral and physical pestilence (B.10.78–84). Pride and pestilence are linked as sin and punishment. Disease was considered to be caused by sin,[29] and sinners under the influence of pride become unable to repent, hardened in their intention to indulge the flesh. Intellectual pride links with sins of the flesh, just as over-indulgence in vain words and gluttony in food and drink become one activity in the grotesque banquet.[30]

The use of the intensifier *for*-glutten expresses a sense of perversion in the excess. It is almost as if the gluttonous rich are consuming themselves, feeding upon their own good, thus turning goods into waste, rather than breaking bread with beggars, recognizing their equality as brethren in a eucharistic action:

> But in gaynesse and in glotonye forglutten hir good hemselue,
> And brekeþ noȝt to þe beggere as þe Book techeþ:
> *Frange esurienti panem tuum* ...
>
> (B.10.83–4a)

This type of consumption is self-destructive, as the story of Dives illustrates. Rich wasters and poor beggars are united in a grotesque banquet at which waste, not sustenance, and division, not unity are the themes. Instead of being the banquet of the heavenly kingdom where all are raised to one level of common humanity, this banquet is like that of Dives – it destroys social order and leads to damnation. Through Study's diatribe, Langland forcibly makes the point that, when the needs of the poor for food and for dignity are ignored, society is destroyed. Margaret Kim makes the point well:

---

29 P. Doob, *Nebuchadnezzar's children*, pp 1–10.
30 The connection between gluttony and perversion of knowledge has been made persuasively by G. Rudd who writes: 'Over-indulgence in food is clearly linked with abuse of knowledge as these diners fill in the lulls between minstrels with irrelevant and irreverent quips and displays of clever argument. They have the right information but they put it to the wrong use, just as they have enough food to feed themselves and the poor outside, but choose to gorge themselves and hound the deprived. The knowledge they have does them no good, in fact it does them actual harm, as their amusements lead them into blasphemy and away from the practice of the doctrine they bandy about': *Managing language in 'Piers Plowman'*, pp 104–5.

> By attacking the wasteful and immoral lifestyles of obsequious jesters, clerics and retainers to great lords ... [Langland] satirizes the social magnate of his time as cultivating, with private self-interest in mind, a personal following of grasping and unproductive flatterers and cronies. The author's account of 'waste' manifest in these characters and their ways epitomizes the venality and degeneration of society.[31]

The quotation from Tobias, '*Si tibi sit copia*', another commonplace of writing on charity, complements the Dives parable with its uncertainty of when the end of life will come, and the judgment which will be made on how we have shared our goods, whether we have much or little (B.10.89–91). Dame Study makes the significant gloss that the injunction to share is placed on all, not just on the rich. This leads her to lament the passing of the communal meal, a symbol of familial hospitality and solidarity. The self-centredness of the gluttony practised by clerical banqueters is matched by the inward-looking lord and lady who eat in a private chamber instead of the hall, the traditional place of hospitality where the poor were included (B.10.96–102). The poetry has an elegiac tone, a lament for the death of open-handedness and charity which is matched by a parody of intellectual discussion:

> I haue yherd heiȝe men etynge at þe table
> Carpen as þei clerkes were of Crist and of hise myȝtes,
> And leyden fautes vpon þe fader þat formede vs alle,
> And carpen ayein clerkes crabbede wordes. (B.10.103–6)

In both instances true charity is dead because mutual social obligations are severed; the words are empty and the practitioners will never attain the practice of Dobest (B.10.135–6).

The allegorical figure, Dame Study, gives voice to severe social criticism, and the truth she proclaims is far from allegorical; it is eminently practical. As custodian of the word, she has a duty to give spiritual guidance, and she situates her message about moderation and compassion for the poor in the context of wasted food and over-consumption. Literal and figural meanings are joined as, in condemning the excesses of the banquet symposium, she declares that no amount of subtle discussion can bring a person to Dowel; the reverse is true. She concludes her long speech by linking faith with good works. People should not want to taste and know (*sapere*) more than is needful for them.[32] Simpson draws attention to the scholastic use of knowing by tasting which produces *sapientia*.[33] Study, aware of the connection, has been criticizing those who are gluttonous both in food and in the way they delve into theology. The scriptural quotation is from Romans:

---

31 Kim, p. 149.
32 Schmidt, *B-text* (p. 331) notes the attribution to Augustine who uses *sapere* meaning 'know', with its cognate, 'taste'.
33 'Modes of thought and poetic form in *Piers Plowman*', pp 4–9.

Food of life and heavenly reward: a question of justice 207

> dico enim per gratiam quae data est mihi omnibus qui sunt inter vos non plus sapere quam oportet sapere sed sapere ad sobrietatem unicuique sicut Deus divisit mensuram fidei. (Romans 12. 3)

> (For I say, by the grace that is given to me, to all that are among you, not to be more wise than it behoveth to be wise, but to be wise unto sobriety and according as God hath divided to every one the measure of faith.)

The spiritual truth which the debaters miss is that charity is crucial. Romans goes on to speak of the unity of the body, and of the mystical body of Christ:

> sicut enim in uno corpore multa membra habemus omnia autem membra non eundem actum habent; ita multi unum corpus sumus in Christo singuli autem alter alterius membra. (Romans 12. 4–5)

> (For as in one body we have many members, but all the members have not the same office: so we, being many, are one body in Christ; and every one members one of another.)

Study calls down the curse of blindness and deafness on all who take specious words for truth at the symposium of falsehood; only practical good works can lead a person to Dowel:

> For alle þat wilneþ to wite þe whyes of God almyȝty,
> I wolde his eiȝe were in his ers and his fynger after …
> And þo þat vseþ þise hauylons to [a]blende mennes wittes
> What is Dowel fro Dobet, now deef mote he worþe –
> Siþþe he wilneþ to wite whiche þei ben alle –
> But if he lyue in þe lif þat longeþ to Dowel!   (B.10.124–5; 131–4)

Disregard for the spirit of the letter discussed, vainglorious use of the word, of truth, of knowledge, are linked with lack of love which exemplifies itself in blindness and deafness to the innate human value and concomitant needs of the poor at the gate. In characterizing prelates' banquets as Dives's feasts the imagery demands real food for real paupers, because this is their human right, on pain of damnation. This is not a threat of what will happen, it is a description of what does happen, and what it means for the good order of society. Study's feast is an illustration of Langland's urgent argument that treatment of the poor is society's touchstone of moral probity.

CONSCIENCE'S BANQUET

The meal at Conscience's court (B.13.21–215) is a dramatic representation that shows how it is possible for what starts out as a *convivium* of learned and even holy men to turn into a Dives's damnation. Conducted with all the customary etiquette of a formal meal with Conscience as the host giving the place of honour to the Master 'as for þe mooste worþi' (B.13.33), the banquet seems to be well-regulated. The traveller, Patience the hermit-pilgrim, is given hospitality, and the impoverished travelling student, Will, has been invited into the hall; here they become companions sharing a mess at a side table. Scripture brings in the large dishes of food which, according to custom, are shared in messes by three or more diners, different food given to each group according to rank. The Master and his man, as the most important, receive the most costly foods that take time to prepare and require expensive sauces: 'mortrews and puddynges, wombe cloutes and wilde brawen and egges' (B.13.62–3), while Clergy, Conscience and Scripture share dishes of 'sondry metes manye', selections from the Fathers of the Church and the four evangelists. Patience and Will, as befits their low position, receive a loaf of sour bread and a simple drink followed by another dish of mixed foods, the penitential psalms and 'derne shrifte', confession of the heart. Additionally, Conscience, like a Prior or Abbot, sends an extra pittance for Patience,[34] a psalm for forgiveness. In keeping with his status as the honoured guest, the Master drinks wine, since at a medieval meal wine was reserved for the lord and favoured guests with whom he chose to share it; others drank ale.[35]

The good order of the meal is, however, only on the surface. The food marks deep divisions between the Master, who chooses dishes made from the profits of sin, and the rest of the diners who feed selectively on the true learning of the Fathers and the Scriptures, and on the psalms of repentance. The Master's sauce is a bitter one that reminds him of punishment after death for feasting on sins, 'of þat men myswonne' (B.13.42), an allusion to the frequent accusation that friars indiscriminately accepted monetary donations from ill-gotten gains. It is clear from the start that this friar keeps to the letter of the prescription to eat and drink what is set before them, by eating the most expensive food on the table. Patience, the voluntarily poor man, also accepts what is set before him, as the exemplary hermit-pilgrim for whom simple fare is food fit for a prince (B.13.51). The role of Patience at this point is to demonstrate for Will that needs are more than material; his food may be less elaborate than that of the Master, but it satisfies his need for spiritual health in a spirit of penitence. Patience is like one of Dame Study's 'meene men' who have God in their hearts.

Will is the opposite of Patience; he is one of the impatient poor resenting the hypocrisy he detects in the Master who preached on penance but practises self-indulgence. Will has been fed with plain but nourishing food, as befits the rank of poor student courteously invited to the hall by the host; yet he is envious of the Master's more savoury fare, regardless of its indigestibility and its association with sin. Will clearly feels that he should have had some share in what

---

[34] A bonus portion occasionally given to monks by permission of the Superior, as a supplement to their standard fare.
[35] Girouard, pp 47–50.

the Master ate. It was customary for the lord or those at the high table to send titbits from their dishes to those lower down the hall, and, because the lord was served more than he could eat, leftovers from his dishes were passed to the less well-fed at the end of the meal, and then distributed among the poor outside the gates.[36] This Master seems to have eaten everything, not sharing with anyone else; as guest of honour he behaves gluttonously and with no thought for others' needs, but that is no reason for the poor man to sin in envy. Will correctly challenges him by pointing out the discrepancy between his words, 'Do noon yuel to þyn euencristen', and his gluttony which, taken to its conclusion, will harm the sick and the weak whom the friar should support, directly denying charity. Will's vengeful envy is strongly in contrast with Patience's meek acceptance, and although it is couched in the form of antifraternal satire, says much about Will's discontent with his stratified place in society, where what he eats is determined by his superiors. In this grumbling of Will's we can hear social rumblings similar to those expressed at the end of the harvest scene, when the wasters and beggars demand similar food to their betters. It is a movement towards material improvement reflected in the resistance of a society that enacted sumptuary laws for food,[37] but it conflicts with a view that poverty is to be accepted as a positive way of life. Will's is the voice of the poor who want to become rich because material consumption appears to be the ideal pursued by their spiritual leaders. Yet in expressing the material need of the poor for food he simultaneously demonstrates that food alone will not do anything to lift them above mere animal necessities, for the Master has lost both dignity and authority by indulging in gluttony and venality. This is one of the occasions in the poem when Langland differentiates between the basic need of the poor for food which is their right and the Christian's voluntary acceptance of poverty as a virtue leading to salvation. The Master sins by not recognizing the human dignity of his poor guests, but Will, too, sins in envy of material goods and disregard of what is spiritual.

The banquet demonstrates three interpretations of a life of poverty: the friar who professes poverty but behaves like a glutton, Patience who embraces the life of patient poverty voluntarily and Will who is poor but does not want to be so. Will is the only representative of the poor throughout the poem who takes on an identity. In his indignant reaction to the Master's refusal to share with them, Will expresses the reaction of a sentient and intelligent human being who is poor and who suffers the indignity and injustice of need in the face of plenty. The words of the friar are brief and shallow, contemptuously dismissive of Patience's heartfelt disquisition on charity. His indulgence in food and drink is symptomatic of his philosophy and theology which go no further than textbook

---

36 'The iiij. commaunde ȝe that youre dysshe be well fyllyd and hepid and namely of entremes and of pitance with oute fat carkynge that ye may parte coureteysly to thos thatt sitte beside bothe of the ryght hande and the left throw alle the hie tabulle and to other as plesythe you thowȝt they haue of the same that ye haue': Grosseteste, p. 149.

37 10 Edward III. c. 3 (1336).

debate, instead of reaching to the depths of his spirit. Will, still searching for higher meaning, uses logic to prove that the doctor fails to practise what he preaches. Much later in the poem, Will comes to accept poverty in a state of material need (B.20.1–50) at a point when he is very near to living like Christ.

The whole tenor of Dame Study's satire on banquets and the scene of the banquet in Conscience's court is that two things prevent the practice of Dowel: physical greed which forestalls the generous impulse to charity, and intellectual pride which vitiates understanding of the truth of God's word.[38] For clergy and prelates to indulge in the grotesque banquet identifies them with profanity, vanity, and self-indulgence, the fool's banquet.

THE BANQUET AND TRAJAN

The third banquet scene under discussion relates to the scriptural parable of the all-inclusive banquet (Luke 14. 12–14). In its commentary on this parable, the poem makes an explicit identification of the poor with Christ and, in doing so, moves towards a clear statement that the poor have a dignity which transcends their economic status. This idea is made explicit to Will during his deep inner vision at the heart of the poem, the eleventh passus in which he is plunged into a search for self-knowledge. Here, in the words of the pagan emperor Trajan, the incarnation is linked to God's love of the poor (B.11.175–210a). Trajan who, legend states, was saved because of his kindness, moves from the two most obvious and practical ways of showing love, giving to those in need and to enemies (B.11.181), to the urgency of God's love for his fellow human beings. The incarnation has clothed God in the russet of 'a pouere mannes apparaille' (B.11.185). From within a position of poverty he can look out at the way people treat him and his fellow poor, detecting the extent of their understanding of brotherhood, the 'kynde herte', by their bearing towards the poor, 'castynge of oure ei3en' (B.11.187), as well as by their actions.[39] His urgent love for humanity is reflected in the insistence with which the incarnate 'Iesu Crist of heuene ... pursueþ vs euere' (B.11.184–5), stimulating people to care for the poor without discrimination.

Fusing images of the banquet and of payment, Trajan refers to the all-inclusive banquet of Luke, the classic source for the categories of the poor used by medieval commentators (Luke 14. 12–14).[40] Trajan's gloss on this banquet emphasizes the redemptive potential of really feeding the poor. The conviviality of a banquet is challenged by the suggestion that the poor should take the place of one's friends; what might become the vain talk and vainglory of a

---

[38] Rudd, p. 104.
[39] Elsewhere in the poem, Anima condemns the aloof and scornful bearing that many powerful people adopt towards the poor: 'And to poore peple han pepir in þe nose' (B.15.201–4).
[40] M. Aston, 'Caim's castles', pp 102–3.

grotesque banquet is translated into something which will lead directly to heavenly reward. Friends who are invited to a banquet will, by custom, match meals and gifts in a reciprocal arrangement. For those who invite the poor God will make the repayment, throw the return banquet, the word 'quyte' being used as payment for work done – 'quyte hir trauaille' (B.11.194) – but carrying, too, the concept of making amends.[41] The promise of payment is not reliant on the mediation of the poor, for at this point the poem makes no mention of their being asked to pray for the benefactors; it is a direct act of exchange between God and the giver. Material provision is undoubtedly in question here; such reciprocity gives an unmistakably heavenly dimension to an earthly act. God takes the place of the poor person, so that a gift which the wealthy might have given reluctantly, thinking there would be no reward, is repaid with generosity by God's redemptive recompense. A unequal equation is being made here: food given to the poor will be matched by redemption.

Trajan's argument presses home the notion of reciprocity by unfolding his understanding of human dignity. He chooses the emotive term 'beggere' to drive home the shockingly inclusive nature of God's love:

> Almyȝty God [myȝte haue maad riche alle] men, if he wolde,
> Ac for þe beste ben som riche and some beggeres and pouere.
> For alle are we Cristes creatures, and of his cofres riche,
> And breþeren as of oo blood, as wel beggeres as erles. (B.11.196–9)

In three different ways the equal dignity of all is stressed. Whether beggars are associated with the poor (B.11.197), with earls (B.11.199), or with a 'boye' (B.11.203) – a scoundrel or knave – all have been made rich from Christ's coffers. The blood which makes 'blody breþeren' (B.11.201) is the same blood which makes God human, and the same blood which gave birth to the infant church on Calvary. The poor at the feast are true kin – all brothers of one blood. When Trajan quotes the text *quasi modo geniti* he echoes the mass of the first Sunday after Easter, whose introit refers to 'newborn infants', the new church which is the body of Christ; this is followed, in the liturgical readings, by an extract from John's epistles which speaks of the redeeming blood of the incarnate Christ.[42] As members of the church, feeding on Christ, redeemed by his blood, all are 'gentil men echone' (B.11.202). The discrimination which was a problem to Piers in the harvest episode is no problem here, for the only discrimination is made by sin: 'No beggere ne boye amonges vs but if it synne made' (B.11.203). At this point in the poem the order of society is looked at from what Trajan presents as a heav-

---

41 Alford, *Glossary*, 'QUITEN **I.** To satisfy (a claim); repay (a debt); **II.** To pay for, make amends, ransom', p. 125.
42 'Quis est qui vincit mundum nisi qui credit quoniam Iesus est Filius Dei? Hic est qui venit per aquam et sanguinem, Iesus Christus: non in aqua solum sed in aqua et sanguine': 1 John 5. 5–6. (Who is he that overcometh the world, but he that believeth that Jesus is the Son of God? This is he that came by water and blood, Jesus Christ: not by water only, but by water and blood.)

enly viewpoint, where all are equally 'gentil', but beggars are the point of reference. Gentle blood is derived from the blood of Christ which makes all brothers. Wealth, as the Fathers and the decretists teach, comes from God and is available for all (B.11.198). Trajan goes on to talk of the sharing of knowledge as well as goods; his banquet is indeed a true one with nourishment at which all are open to the word of God, but its truth comes from the inclusion of rich and poor on an equal footing, whether they appear to be sinners or not. Christ was prepared to share a feast even with public sinners:

> Crist to a commune womman seide in commune at a feste
> That *Fides sua* sholde sauen hire and saluen hire of alle synnes.
> (B.11.216–17).

The poem as a whole makes some scathing condemnations of beggars who, as Scase has clearly demonstrated, are frequently to be equated with clerical mendicants. The C-text makes unmistakable reference to these latter in considerable and circumstantial detail, giving their origins, their practices and their hypocrisy (C.9.203–54). The poem also repeats the social stereotypes of beggars who live on the margins of society (B.7.88–97) and, as such, '[threaten] social authority and [violate] the exalted dignity of the collective system'.[43] Nevertheless, beggars, undifferentiated at this point, are made the test of God's kindness towards man, and man's kindness towards his fellow man which, by the reciprocal arrangement of God's mercy, will be rewarded as the kindness of man towards God. Pearsall considers that Langland's use of 'gentil' at this point reveals attitudes ingrained in traditional social and economic relationships:

> Langland really thinks it means something to say that all men will become gentle through the redemption.[44]

I take Langland to be making a more radical statement than Pearsall does. I believe he is speaking about the present state of the poor who are already redeemed and entitled to be treated with the justice that belongs to God's kingdom on earth, already enjoyed by the other estates. Langland does subscribe to the traditional orders in society, but not to the oppression or lack of justice that denies human dignity. Each class is equal in the eyes of God, and the poor are closest to him.

Later in the poem Langland appeals again for a social reversal, one in which the fools of the grotesque banquet are replaced by the poor of the gospel:

> Forþi I rede yow riche [þ]at reueles whan ye makeþ,
> For to solace youre soules, swiche minstrales to haue –

---

[43] Geremek, *The margins of society*, p. 8.
[44] 'Langland's London', p. 199.

> The pouere for a fool sage sittynge at þ[i] table,
> And a lered man to lere þee what Oure Lord suffred
> For to saue þi soule fram Sathan þyn enemy,
> And fiþele þee, wiþoute flaterynge, of Good Friday þe storye,
> And a blynd man for a bourdeour, or a bedrede womman
> To crie a largesse tofore Oure Lord, youre good loos to shewe.
>
> (B.13.442–9)

These are the same categories of poor who are compelled to attend the Lord's wedding banquet (Luke 14. 15–24), not because they have earned the invitation but because they are available in their poverty. They have nothing else to do except to subsist, and to rely on others to provide, 'find' them. They are brought into God's banquet because they are the only ones available to God, unencumbered and therefore open to God's invitation. This is the wisdom they bring to the banquet of the rich who should both feast them as invited guests and learn true spirituality from them; in this way, by a double irony the rich can have their banquets redeemed by the poor, but only if they respect them and deal with the full human range of their needs. Until the poor are taken care of, materially and spiritually, all thoughts and words are empty and even self-destructive.

THE PAYMENT OF HEAVENLY REWARD

Where human judgments declare the powerful and wealthy to be blessed, judgments made in the light of divine justice recognize the equal value and interdependence of all as created by God. It remains now to consider how Langland interprets heavenly reward for the poor. In addressing myself to this question I consider the poem's imagery of redemption and reward, commercial imagery applied to the economy of salvation, as central to any understanding of Langland's poor. I argue that when we read the poem's dramatization of the doctrine of redemption three things become clear. Firstly, redemption is for all human beings regardless of their material condition. Secondly, redemption has been achieved once for all, so the people of fourteenth-century England must consider themselves to be living in a world redeemed by Christ. Thirdly, the reward for the poor is justice and charity to which they are entitled, and the poem relentlessly insists that all members of society are obliged to ensure they receive it. To appreciate this is to understand that what may look like the poem's retreat into spiritual explanations of poverty is, in fact, a statement about establishing the justice and love that characterize God's kingdom on earth.

First, a brief survey of some medieval notions of heaven will help set Langland's ideas within his own culture. The poem challenges the easy acceptance of an order in which some are rich and some are poor. Historically, the presence of the poor was accepted in the middle ages as part of the divine order of things much as the slavery of the Byzantine world was regarded as part of the status quo by the Church Fathers.[45] Close reading of Langland's text shows that it reassesses that order in terms available within contemporary ideology. It attributes to divine wisdom the fact that there are different states within the established order as well as different and complementary gifts of nature and grace (B.11.196–9; B.11.380–1; B.19.253–9). Within these differences, the poem insists that all must treat others with love and justice, since it is against God's will for the poor to be oppressed:

> For vnkyndenesse quencheþ hym, þat he kan noȝt shyne,
> Ne brenne ne blase clere, for blowynge of vnkyndenesse. (B.17.256–7)

Heavenly reward is available for all; the poem subscribes to the same notion of human equality as that proposed in Bede's gloss to Proverbs 22. 2, quoted in the early fifteenth-century *Dives and Pauper*:

> a ryche man is not to be worschiped for þis cause oonli þat he is riche, ne a pore man is for to be dispised bicause of his pouertee, but þe werk of God is to be worschiped in hem boþe, for þei boþe ben maad to þe ymage & to þe licknesse of God.[46]

In many late medieval writings, the imagery used for eternal reward is derived from Scripture and focuses on sensory bliss and a notion of elevation in rank and wealth. The dominant image in *Pearl* is of heaven as a medieval court where the blessed live as monarchs in a palace:

> The court of þe kyngdom of God alyue
> Hatȝ a property in hytself beyng:
> Alle þat may þerinne aryue
> Of alle þe reme is quen oþer kyng.[47]

This poem examines the notion of heavenly reward, especially as it affects those who die in childhood and have not had time to 'earn' heaven by enduring the trials of life. The strong message of the poem is that 'þe grace of God is gret innogh' (l.661). Heaven is given by the gift of God first, and as a reward second. Innocence, however, wins heaven by right: 'þe innocent is ay saf by ryȝt' (l.720). *The castle of perseverance* uses an integrated image of the rewards of heaven as pertaining to a kingdom where Christ reigns in bliss:

> But heueryche is good and trye,
> Þer Criste sytteth bryth as blode,
>   Wythoutyn any dystresse.   (ll.355–7)

---

45 Constantelos, *Poverty, society and philanthropy*, pp 103–4.
46 *Dives and Pauper*, ed. P.H. Barnum, p. 70.
47 *Pearl*, ed. E. V. Gordon, p. 16 (ll.445–8).

Food of life and heavenly reward: a question of justice

The central image is of a palace, 'heuene halle', with thrones from which the good angel comes (ll.317–18; 1334). Here the just enjoy endless happiness, the reward of heaven after a life of penance:

> 'to brynge hys sowle into blis bryth,' (l.1271)

> I schal hym stere to gamyn and gle
> In joye þat euere schal last. (ll.1332–33)

Julian of Norwich presents the same type of image in the sixth revelation where Christ reigns like a royal lord and contemplation of his face brings bliss:

> And in this myn understonding was lifted up into Hevyn, where I saw our Lord as a lord in his owne house, which hath clepid all his derworthy servants and freinds to a solemne feste. Then I saw the Lord take no place in His owne house, but I saw Him rialy regne in His hous, and fulfillid it with joy and mirth, Hymselfe endlesly to gladen and to solacyn His derworthy frends, full homely and ful curtesly, with mervelous melody of endles love in His owen faire blissid chere, which glorious chere of the godhede fulfillith the Hevyns of joy and bliss.[48]

To a certain extent, *Piers Plowman* subscribes to such imagery. For the poorest beggars, Langland envisages heaven as summer after winter, bringing 'som manere ioye' (B.14.118); for the Good Thief heaven is pictured as a great hall where he has been admitted, albeit only to be treated as a beggar, since he has not served God for long and therefore is not equal in 'worshipe' to the great saints:

> So it fareþ by þat felon þat a Good Friday was saued:
> He sit neiþer wiþ Seint Johan, ne Symond ne Iude,
> Ne wiþ maydenes ne with martires ne [mid] confessours ne wydewes,
> But by hymself as a soleyn, and serued on þe erþe. (B.12.201–4)

At other times the poem draws on the scriptural image of heaven as the banquet where guests are ranked according to virtue:

> Thouȝ he be þyn vnderlyng here, wel may happe in heuene
> That he worþ worþier set and wiþ moore blisse. (B.6.46–7)

Such imagery is nuanced and relative to the condition of the person to whom it is applied, not absolute, like the other medieval examples I have quoted. Langland's heaven does not convert beggars into royalty but retains an earthly sense of social order. This in itself suggests that Langland's social vision does not

---

48 *The shewings of Julian of Norwich*, p. 57.

demand the eradication of poverty as a state, but recognition in justice of the needs and the value of poor people. In the remaining part of this chapter I elaborate on how, for Langland, the reward of heaven is less materially imagined than a palace of bliss and delight. With ideas grounded in theology, *Piers Plowman* dramatizes the reward for all, rich and poor alike, as redemption by the Son of God.

LANGLAND'S CHRIST AND THE CONCEPT OF 'BLODY BREÞREN'

As a prelude to presenting the poem's portrayal of redemption, I consider how Langland develops the theme of Christ's assuming human nature and, thus, his identification with the poor. Scripture says that Christ, the second person of the Blessed Trinity, emptied himself of his godhead, becoming a man. Langland portrays Christ as humbling himself, not only by adopting human nature, but by becoming incarnate as one of the socio-economically lowest, even to the extent of wearing the 'sute' of a poor man as if it were a livery in which Christ can be recognized as sharing humanity.[49] Faced with the question of why one should care for the poor, it was common for medieval teachers to give two reasons. One is that giving to the poor secures redemption for the giver. The other is that Christ identified himself with the poor, and that in giving to them one is giving to Christ, thereby earning eternal merit. It will become evident that Langland takes each of these answers far beyond traditional medieval formulas, explaining with the full force of theological argument that all are brothers, and demonstrating practical application of the doctrine in his contemporary world of rich and poor.

Undoubtedly the poor present a paradox within the Christian social order. For Langland, the theological concept of *kenosis*[50] goes a long way towards explaining the existence of suffering for the poor without explaining it away. The main Scriptural text for the understanding of *kenosis*, the occluding of the Godhead in Christ who became man, is Philippians 2. 6–11:

> Who, being in the form of God, thought it not robbery to be equal with God: but emptied himself, taking the form of a servant, being made in the likeness of men, and in habit found as a man. He humbled himself, becoming obedient unto death, even to the death of the cross. For which cause, God also hath exalted him and hath given him a name which is

[49] Elsewhere the poem refers to Christ as wearing a poor man's apparel which, according to the 1363 sumptuary law, had to be a simple robe of russet or blanket: Baldwin, *Sumptuary legislation*, pp 50–1.

[50] 'According to Catholic theology, the abasement of the Word consists in the assumption of humanity and the simultaneous occultation of the Divinity. Christ's abasement is seen first in His subjecting Himself to the laws of human birth and growth and to the lowliness of fallen human nature. His likeness, in His abasement, to the fallen nature does not compromise the actual loss of justice and sanctity, but only the pains and penalties attached to the loss. These fall partly on the body, partly on the soul, and consist in liability to suffering from internal and external causes': *The Catholic encyclopedia*, 'Kenosis'.

> above all names: that in the name of Jesus every knee should bow, of those that are in heaven, on earth, and under the earth: and that every tongue should confess that the Lord Jesus Christ is in the glory of God the Father. (Philippians 2. 6–11)

Langland develops this theological concept as the foundation of his approach to poverty, representing the poor as a commentary on Christ's *kenosis* while also taking part in it. Christ chose to be poor and, ipso facto, to be powerless; his human experience was therefore as different from that of the almighty godhead as it could possibly be. The only mitigation for Christ's earthly poverty was that, after his passion and death, he would return as King with all the power of a Judge. Nevertheless, as man he lived, suffered and died without benefit of divine intervention. Early in Passus B.1 Holy Church portrays love as longing to become earthly in order to fulfil its nature:

> For heuene myȝte nat holden it, so was it heuy of hymselue,
> Til it hadde of þe erþe eten his fille.
> And whan it hadde of þis fold flessh and blood taken,
> Was neuere leef vpon lynde lighter þerafter. (B.1.153–6)

Love *could not be contained in heaven* until it had eaten its fill of this earth. In a foreshadowing of the eucharist, God takes on the form of man by eating of 'þe erþe' and assumes flesh and blood, in reverse action from that of man who eats the flesh and blood of the Son of God and partakes of the divinity. The reciprocal movement between God and man is fundamental to the structure of the poem. Will, in his quest for Dowel, Dobet and Dobest, strives for a way of life that will lead him to heavenly reward; Christ moves from heaven to earth, the Son of God becoming a man. The precise purpose of this incarnation is demonstrated when Christ meets Satan in his duel at the harrowing of hell:

> *Ergo* soule shal soule quyte and synne to synne wende.
> And al þat man haþ mysdo, I, man, wole amende it. (B.18.341–2)

Christ, as man, makes amends to God in an act of atonement on behalf of mankind.

In an important article, Nicholas Watson explores the way several late medieval English writers, including Langland, apply the theological concept of *kenosis* to their understanding of the incarnation and its influence on the spiritual life of the lay and the unlearned.[51] Watson argues that, particularly in connection with texts on the incarnation, several late medieval theologians, many of them women, develop the idea of reciprocal love between God and human beings, which shows God as driven by a passion which becomes 'a revelation of

---

51 N. Watson, 'Conceptions of the word'.

God's essential nature, as love drives him from heaven into the lowest places of the earth'.[52] In Watson's view, Langland represents Christ/Love as needing the incarnation to complete his understanding of his own nature.[53] Watson's interest is in the writings themselves as 'conceptions of the Word'; mine is in the concept of *kenosis* in its application within *Piers Plowman* to that lowest and least educated of all groups, the fourteenth-century poor, particularly with the light shed by the text on the status of the poor with whom the incarnate Son of God identifies. I argue that Langland portrays the incarnation, not as an ordeal, but as Christ's desire to identify with man, and that this gives a sound theological basis to the poem's representation of poor people's dignity.

The climax of Christ's incarnate life is described in the poem's account of the crucifixion, a fate which is regarded in the debate between the Four Daughters of God, Truth, Mercy, Justice and Peace, as necessary for God to understand humanity. Peace, who has the last word in their debate, establishes that only by experiencing the pain of life and death as a man can God appreciate how human beings have suffered for Adam's sin which, itself, was part of God's plan:

> Forþi God, of his goodnesse, þe firste gome Adam,
> Sette hym in solace and in souereyn murþe;
> And siþþe he suffred hym synne, sorwe to feele –
> To wite what wele was, kyndeliche to knowe it.   (B.18.217–20)

God needs to experience the full spectrum of man's suffering in life and death in order to know what pain is, and what mankind will suffer if condemned to eternal punishment for Adam's sin. Christ as man has endured the poverty of taking on human nature and the utter poverty of apparent defeat in death:

> And after, God auntrede hymself and took Adames kynde
> To wite what he haþ suffred in þre sondry places,
> Boþe in heuene and in erþe – and now til helle he þenkeþ,
> To wite what alle wo is, þat woot of alle ioye.   (B.18.221–4)

Being poor is Christ's *kenosis*, the practical means by which the Godhead understands man. If humankind is to be saved from hell, if it is to achieve heavenly reward, incarnation is the only way to achieve redemption.

---

52 Watson, p. 104.
53 'God needed humanity to fall so that *both* could understand "kyndeliche" the reality of suffering and joy: in part, that is, so that God, by becoming something less than himself, might understand his own fullness. This is why, at the harrowing, Christ can argue that he has now attained such intimacy with his "brethren of blood" that it is almost impossible for him to damn even the unbaptized to eternal punishment. In this transformation of the theme of reciprocity between God and the soul common to texts in the "violent love" tradition, Langland makes the quest for mutual knowledge the basic building-block both of the history of the universe and of his poem': Watson, p. 117.

Langland's understanding of this doctrine informs his philosophy of the value of poverty and the place of the poor in a society which he envisages as a theocracy.[54] The notion of power embedded in the Christian 'myth' defined by *kenosis* is based on a reversal technique; the almighty becomes poor, and in reward for the act of self-emptying, the poor one becomes the powerful.[55] Langland interrogates this idea of reward in its relationship to the materially poor, as he does the ideas of reciprocity and redemption. There is, in the doctrine of *kenosis* as expressed by Paul, an explicit understanding that, after emptying himself and gaining the experience of being human, Christ will return to his state of glorification and power. Langland makes sure that the glorified Christ is not a remote deity, but has total concern for humankind, his 'blood brothers' (B.18.327–404). He takes them back from Satan and, pursuing the concept of being *kynde* as being true to the human nature which is hypostatically united with the nature of God, makes it clear that his mercy can be exercised only towards those sinners who have been *kynde* to fellow human beings on earth.[56] Holy Church intimates this affinity between the divine and human natures when she calls the charitable person 'a god by þe Gospel' (B.1.90).

A clear theme develops within the poem from Holy Church's words about the incarnation of love in the first passus (B.1.153–8) to Will's experience of need in the final passus (B.20.1–50). The unfolding poem shows how Christ as man identifies himself with the limitations of human nature; at the same time it shows how Will comes to understand his own human nature and find his identity when he becomes utterly needy in a self-emptying which imitates that of Christ (B.20.199–211). The term 'redemption' is a rendering of Hebrew *kopher* and Greek *lytron*, which in the Old Testament means generally a ransom-price.[57] Medieval semantics stressed the Latin sense of the word: to buy back. Langland, throughout the poem, draws upon the theology of Christ's incarnation which he portrays as an act of insatiable love (B.1.153–4) that drives him to buy back mankind from the power of the devil (B.18.350–4). As God-made-man he takes upon himself the task of protecting the poor by identifying with them specifically as his blood brothers (B.11.198–201).

---

[54] See Kim, p. 148: '*Piers Plowman* is a "theocratic" critique, in terms of deadly sin and fallen nature, of the pragmatics of lordly feudal consumption and its destructive combination with the development of market capitalism in the later middle ages.'

[55] I use the term 'myth' in the sense used by Watson, p. 87: 'So runs the myth of divine kenosis, Fortune's wheel in reverse, as told by Paul (with additions from John and James) to the first generation of Christians'.

[56] Langland's Christ, in the harrowing of hell, confounds Satan by freely granting his mercy to all sinners. However, the Samaritan has already made it clear that unkindness is an obstacle that makes a sinner incapable of receiving God's mercy (B.17.255–6).

[57] 'The word *redemptio* is the Latin Vulgate rendering of Hebrew *kopher* and Greek *lytron* which, in the Old Testament means generally a ransom-price. In the New Testament, it is the classic term designating the "great price" (1 Corinthians 6. 20) which the Redeemer paid for our liberation': *Catholic encyclopedia*, vol. 12, p. 677, 'Redemption'.

Kenosis and redemption are the theological concepts underpinning the representation of poverty in the poem, especially the images of commerce, exchange, wages and reward that characterize God's espousal of poor people. Holy Church, in Passus B.1, describes how, in contrast to his damning treatment of Lucifer and his fallen angels, God exercised mercy by inserting himself into the human situation. The 'mercyment' of God, the fine exacted for man's 'mysdedes' (B.1.162), shows him to be at the same time 'myȝtful and meke', for he both demands and pays the tax in a reciprocal action that corresponds to love as consuming the earth and assuming it (B.1.154–5); eating makes us one with what we eat. As God, because he is man, can give mercy to his killers, so the rich should have 'ruþe' (pity) on the poor; 'mercy', 'pite' and 'ruþe' are all used within a few lines of each other. Langland parallels the redemptive mercy of God and his incarnation with that of man towards man. If God could be 'myȝtful and meke', the wealthy, who in earthly terms are 'myȝty to mote', can also be 'meke in youre werkes' (B.1.176). The verbal correspondences suggest that the wealthy have potentially godlike powers; by giving to the poor they parallel the incarnation, the strong impulse that required God to become man. Sharing goods with the poor is not merely a good action, it is the defining action; the sharing is to be 'goodliche', like God. Honesty and chastity, masses and 'hours', the singing of office, are inadequate without practical charity. The measure that Holy Church commended in her earliest words to Will now becomes another saving measure, the measurement of good works, the balancing of heavenly reward against earthly generosity:[58]

> For þe same mesure þat ye mete, amys ouþer ellis,
> Ye shulle ben weyen þerwiþ whan ye wenden hennes. (B.1.177–8)

At this early stage in the poem, the *kenosis* of the Son of God is locked into treatment of the poor in the understanding of love. Where the Son of God needed to fulfil his godhead by experiencing what only a human being could experience, 'of þe erþe eten his fille', the covetous parson consumes (eats) the charity offered for the poor by being 'vnkynde', repudiating his human nature, which, through the incarnation, is allied to God's nature. The poem describes how Lucifer set himself against the Trinity (B.1.111–27); so too, the covetous cleric, by being 'vnkynde', negates all he knows of truth and not only condemns himself but those whom he teaches, by 'tricherie of helle' (B.1.198). Langland makes it clear from the start that the poem proposes a theological basis for traditional charitable practices, giving a deadly seriousness to acts of unkindness. To behave with charity towards the poor is to lock oneself into the redeeming actions of

---

58 The scales of good deeds are hinted at here. Mannyng recounts the exemplum of Pers Tollere, a rich usurer who threw a loaf at a beggar because he could not find a stone to get rid of him. In a dream Pers had a vision of his death and judgment, where the scales of justice were weighed down with multiple evil deeds on the one side, and a single loaf, representing his one, questionable, good deed on the other. That loaf outweighed all his misdeeds because it had relieved the poor beggar's need: *Handlyng synne*, pp 140–2 (ll. 5571–674).

Christ; to neglect them is to be relegated to hell. If Langland can be said to have a social programme for the poor, its rationale begins here.

The weakness and sinfulness of human nature which Christ explores in his incarnation emerges in the poem's portrayal of society where Meed has powerful influence. Hope for the apparently hopeless deadly sinners comes through Repentance's sermon at the end of the Great Confession of Passus B.5. Repentance concludes the Great Confession with a declaration that mercy will be given to sinners precisely because God first made man like himself, and then, after Adam's fall, reversed the process and made himself like sinful man:

> And madest Þiself wiþ Þi sone vs synfulle yliche ...
> And siþþe wiþ Þi selue sone in oure sute deidest.   (B.5.487; 488.)

At this moment of acknowledging the all-pervasive sinfulness of mankind, represented by the personifications of the seven deadly sins, Repentance links incarnation and redemption to God's personal experience of human nature. The image of the 'sute' or 'secte', which characterizes the flesh, *caro*, as the clothing in which God has dressed himself is prominent here. The *MED* defines 'secte' in sense 1c as: 'a bodily form, likeness; **in oure ~**, in our likeness, in human flesh', and the references for this sense are all from *Piers Plowman*. Langland plays on the implications of this word, developing the idea from its usual reference to a liveried retinue. Christ's human nature becomes his 'sute', or livery, and he goes in the company of the poor as if this is an honour. Later, the poem will identify that 'sute' or livery as being a poor person's distinctive garb (B.14.257–9). The sermon emphasizes that the suffering of the crucifixion is not suffering for God in his divine nature, but God-made-man suffers the effects of sin when Jesus experiences death, the captivity of sin which leads to his descent into hell, the place of sin (B.5.490–1). Here the first redemptive act of Christ is to feed those in darkness with his blood – redemptive blood which has been spilled, and nourishing, eucharistic blood which revives the forefathers and enables them to emerge into the light of paradise:

> Feddest þo wiþ Þi fresshe blood oure forefadres in derknesse.   (B.5.494)

Mercy comes about because God has extended his Godhead and understands manhood. Reward or punishment is now changed into mercy (B.5.496).

Repentance makes the point that on the third day, when Jesus again appeared in mankind's 'sute', the first greeting was not for his sinless mother, but for the sinner, Mary, re-emphasizing the truth that he died a human death in order to solace the sinful. This, too, is part of the experience of becoming man; only in man's 'sute' can God experience the sorrow and the effect of sin. The final, powerful point is made at the end of the sermon, that the most brave and knightly deeds of God were done in the 'armes', or, as the C-text says (C.7.140), the 'sekte' of mankind. The triumphant imagery reinforces the conception of God glorying in the experience of being man, and expresses the sure and certain reason for believing that God who is simultaneously our Father and our brother will:

> be merciable to vs,
> And haue ruþe on þise ribaudes þat repenten hem soore
> That euere þei wraþed Þee in þis world, in word, þouȝt or dede!
>
> (B.5.504–6)

This aspect of the *kenosis* is most important when we consider Langland's notion of heavenly reward. Christ emptied himself, not in order to return to his Godhead having shed his manhood, but for his Godhead to be fulfilled by the experience of manhood. The suffering, the sin and the poor human 'sute' are what he brings to the Trinity. Heavenly reward, then, does not negate earthly experience, nor sublimate it, but accepts it for what it is, sin and weakness, requiring mercy. The C-text emphasizes this still further when it stresses that Christ is 'of flesch oure broþer' (C.7.143). This is an important element in the theology behind Langland's social programme for the poor. Such a clear statement of God's identification with humankind in all its weakness and sin lays the foundation for the theme of God paying for the poor, a pointed and precise application of the idea of redemption, and one which will lead the non-poor to understand the equal value of the poor as human beings.

Langland makes it clear that the poor are the exemplars of redeemed mankind. Their needy circumstances are not necessarily a result of their sinfulness, as so many practitioners of poor relief suggest, but their entitlement to redemption. Even the sinful poor are eligible for God's special protection. Piers, outlining the terms of the pardon (B.7.76–81), recognizes the human tendency to expect some return on money spent. He promises that money given to poor beggars, even if they appear to be undeserving, will be a good investment, bringing a return on the loan as a commercial transaction. The one who gives pays; the one who begs takes what is given and 'borweþ' – pledges something in return. What he pledges in return is taken care of by God, who goes surety for the amount given. God will repay those who have given, and with interest on the loan. While the word 'borwen' has the primary meaning of 'pledge' here, it has the additional overtone of 'save, save a life, redeem, redeem from sin' (*MED*, 'borwen', sense 3). This additional sense represents the 'vsure moore' (B.7.81); the interest on the loan is redemption from sin.[59]

I have already commented on similar ideas expressed in Trajan's commentary on the banquet where, if the poor are entertained as equals, God will repay – 'quyte' – the giver:

---

[59] I agree with Simpson that Langland goes further than the parable of the talents on which this passage is based. Simpson makes the point that 'the passage as a whole suggests a strict contradiction between earthly and heavenly profit in a way that the parable itself does not: for the statement here is that one receives a profit from one's "investment" in God precisely by giving away one's money in alms': Simpson, 'Spirituality and economics', p. 90.

> Ac for þe pouere I shal paie, and pure wel quyte hir trauaille
> That ȝyueþ hem mete or moneie and loueþ hem for my sake.
>
> (B.11.194–5)

A remarkable extension of Trajan's concept that beggars have the same human value as the noblest of people comes in Will's vision of the leper in Abraham's bosom (B.16.254–69). Medieval lepers were invariably considered sinners, their contagious illness regarded as a direct result of a lecherous life. They were banished to the outskirts of the town and, of all marginals, were probably the most feared. To call a 'lazare' a precious gift fit for a prince is another shocking reversal; no-one would touch a leper, still less offer him as a gift to a prince, yet Abraham does so, in direct allusion to the Gospel parable of Dives and Lazarus. The person least valued in human society is raised to the level of prophets and patriarchs with whom he plays as an equal (B.16.256). The leper in Abraham's bosom seems like an embryo awaiting birth,[60] which, indeed, the poem endorses, as the preceding account of the Trinity suggests that the engendering of children of God had to wait until the incarnation, and conversely, Christ had to wait until Christians were born so that he could act in his guise as son and saviour (B.16.194–7).

The image of a debtor's pledge, already used to identify God's pledge to repay any goods given to the poor (B.7.76–81), now becomes associated specifically with the theology of redemption. Abraham, the prophets and the leper, all the just who died before Christ, are prisoners waiting for the strict accounting which will ransom them from the devil's power. This is a hard legal and commercial transaction. A 'wed' is a monetary pledge; the 'buyrn' is the person who goes surety; 'mainprise' is bail money. In this case there is only one who can lay a satisfactory 'wed', God-made-man, who pledges his life for mankind's life. Only God will come up with the bail money which is a reciprocal act seen by Abraham to be far in excess of the original value. Christ's life is given in exchange for the life of the poor leper who, by virtue of his suffering in poverty, is himself assimilated into Abraham's bosom. At this point in the poem, the incarnation of the Son of God is linked with the redeeming of the pledge given for the poorest of mankind. *Kenosis* is about to enact the notion of reward which has nothing to do with being earned by mankind, but everything to do with God's free gift of mercy.[61] This is a soundly theological foundation for Langland's forceful argument that the poor have value in their own right.

---

60 Kane, commenting on Langland's language, identifies the 'lollynge' of Lazarus as exemplifying the helpless and vulnerable state of humanity waiting for the redemption: *Chaucer and Langland*, p. 100.
61 Simpson draws attention to the two kinds of reward: condign, a wage strictly deserved; and congruent, a gift given out of God's generosity: 'Spirituality and economics', p. 97.

PASSUS B.17 AND B.18: CHRIST'S REDEMPTIVE LOVE IN ACTION

The quality inherent in all the foregoing representations of the incarnation is love, variously called love, charity, 'leaute' and kindness. Passus B.17 and B.18 deal at length, in poetry of compelling power, with how human kindness relates man to the nature of God. The Samaritan, paradigm of brotherly love from the gospel parable and an unmistakable Christ-figure, appears in Passus B.17 to teach Will about the essential nature of the Trinity, source and exemplar of divine and human love (B.17.48–352). The Samaritan's message centres itself on the understanding of *kynde* as being in accord with one's nature and *unkynde* as against nature.[62] With great clarity, he unpacks the doctrine of the Trinity, showing how Father, Son and Holy Spirit act as one, though with distinctive roles. He teaches that human ills can be healed only by the blood of the child 'born of a mayde' in Bethlehem.[63] Blood makes for brotherhood, and the practical application of the Samaritan's explanation of the Trinity leads to a reiteration of God the Son's position as brother to all mankind. Christ shares in the nature of man while retaining the nature of God; this, in itself, is the reason for people to treat each other with love.

Man is made in the image of God but sins; God assumes the nature of man in order to redeem by atoning for that sin.[64] Throughout these two passus which deal with salvation history, humanity is considered as divided into kind and unkind, all sinners and all to be redeemed by God. Earthly rank is irrelevant; the two passus dramatize the proverbial saying of Passus B.6:

> For in a charnel at chirche cherles ben yuel to knowe,
> Or a knyȝt from a knaue þere – knowe þis in þyn herte.   (B.6.48–9)

God repays kindness with kindness. Anyone who is kind can be redeemed; anyone who is unkind cannot be redeemed because unkindness acts as an obsta-

---

[62] Several works deal with this terminology as applied to *Piers Plowman*. Among those I have found most helpful are: Davlin's two articles, '*Kynde knowynge* as a major theme in *Piers Plowman B*', and '*Kynde knowynge* as a Middle English equivalent for "wisdom" in *Piers Plowman B*'; and her full-length book, *A game of heuene*, especially pp 50–4, 57–8. Hugh White devotes a complete volume to Langland's use of the varying nuances of 'kynde': *Nature and salvation in 'Piers Plowman'*. Andrew Galloway adds the sense of 'gratitude' as one of Langland's meanings of 'kynde', 'From *gratitudo* to "kyndenesse"'.

[63] The Samaritan describes how the blood must bathe the victim as in baptism; penance, the plaster which will heal the wound, depends on the 'passion' (B.17.96), the death of the baby; and the victim needs to eat the child and drink the baby's blood. This literal reference to the body and blood is entirely in accordance with the literalness of medieval writings about the eucharist which frequently relate incidents in which the consecrated host is transformed into the figure of a child; such writings, among them this section of *Piers Plowman*, acknowledge the full humanity of the Christ-child and show the depths of Christ's *kenosis* in the immolation of the child's body and blood. Such a painful reminder of incarnation and redemption emphasizes that, in the sacraments, salvation and redemption have been made part of everyday human existence.

[64] See discussion of Repentance's sermon above, pp 221–2, and the argument of Peace, p. 218.

Food of life and heavenly reward: a question of justice 225

cle to the action of the Holy Spirit. The Samaritan relates the Holy Spirit to practical human love in the apt metaphor of the taper which, with its three components of wax, wick and flame represents the Trinity. The one thing that can quench the flame is unkindness, and the only way of reviving the flame is for 'lele loue' to blow on the smouldering wick.

Such love is not only true to nature, but denotes a social relationship, as Galloway has pointed out, of cultural cohesion.[65] The duty of the rich and the powerful is to give to the needy who represent God, and the C-text adds that, in a redemptive act of reciprocity, even those who sin in getting may be saved by giving (C.19.231–53). Once love has acted, the flame of the Holy Spirit sets the Father and the Son into action, stimulating them to show mercy at the time of the particular judgment[66] to those who try to make restitution for their sins (B.17.230–9). Such restitution is the responsibility of all sinners, regardless of their earthly rank:

> For þer nys sik ne sory, ne noon so muche wrecche
> That he ne may louye, and hym like, and lene of his herte
> Good wille, good word – boþe wisshen and wilnen
> Alle manere men mercy and forʒifnesse,
> And louye hem lik hymself, and his lif amende.   (B.17.346–50)

The kindness the Samaritan promotes is practical human behaviour which, according to the nature of God's creatures, includes the possibility of sin and repentance in both rich and poor. It takes account of late medieval commercial activities which are not always free from sin – 'That wykkidliche is wonne, to wasten it and make frendis' (C.19.248) – and sets itself within a culture that includes, as Galloway says,[67] both 'werkmen' and 'ye wise men þat with þe world deleþ' (B.17.260). In being kind, the human person behaves in a manner true to nature, able to be redeemed and eligible for heavenly reward which starts already on earth when God's principles of justice and kindness govern social relationships.

The redemption of mankind from the power of Satan can be achieved because Jesus is man as well as God and therefore eligible to buy back the souls taken by Satan. He does so in two duels, first with Death and then with Satan, thus satisfying legal requirements for redemption. But it is more than a cold legal action; he has wanted to do this for humankind whom he loves as his brothers.[68] As I have suggested earlier, in contrast to many late medieval religious writings, the reward promoted in *Piers Plowman* is not primarily residence in the heavenly

---

65 'From *gratitudo* to "kyndenesse"', pp 379–83.
66 The particular judgment is the individual's meeting with God at the hour of death.
67 'From *gratitudo* to "kyndenesse"', p. 383.
68 The language of law gives a grim seriousness to the encounter which A. Baldwin explicates with considerable subtlety as a double duel, of civil law and of chivalry: 'The double duel in *Piers Plowman* B XVIII and C XXI'. The analogues for the lover-knight aspect of Jesus as Jouster have been well analysed by L. Warner, 'Jesus the jouster'.

mansion, though the notion of this appears at times. The poem's reward is redemption, played out with stirring drama in Passus B.18. Christ's victory, when it comes, is a restoration of his kingly rights and is conducted as ransom, literally the release of a prisoner by the payment of a certain sum.[69] The payment is, however, not made to the Devil who, according to the theology developed by Anselm and later writers, did not hold humanity by any kind of right, and, in Langland's imagery, had imprisoned mankind through treachery. Christ's death is a payment made to God, making amends, satisfaction for man's sin.[70]

Christ undertakes such ransom 'by right and by reson' (B.18.350), because he has a title to mankind and they are his in justice;[71] redemption occurs on a finely balanced gauge in which Christ's life is an exact exchange, compensation, a payment of debts and an acquittal. Beguilers are beguiled; what sinful man has wrongly done, the God-man will compensate, sacrificing limb for limb and life for life, following the Old Law. The death of the God-man will undo the damage that Death caused to Adam's issue, and, in an act of exact recompense, restore to life that which was killed by sin:

> Þe Olde Lawe grauntep
> That gilours be bigiled – and þat is good reson:
> *Dentem pro dente et oculum pro oculo.*
> *Ergo* soule shal soule quyte and synne to synne wende.
> And al þat man haþ mysdo, I, man, wole amende it.
> Membre for membre [was amendes by þe Olde Lawe],
> And lif for lif also – and by þat lawe I clayme
> Adam and al his issue at my wille herafter.
> And þat Deeþ in hem fordide, my deeþ shal releue,
> And boþe quyke and quyte þat queynte was þoruȝ synne;
> And þat grace gile destruye, good feiþ it askeþ. (B.18.339–49)

So that there shall be no mistaken interpretation, Christ reiterates the reason for his mercy, not so that the devil shall be tricked, but because Christ is man and, as such, must show mercy to those who became his blood brothers at his incarnation and whom he has won legally by both ransom and right of kingship (B.18.401). This double right of king and brother gives him the right to pardon even sinners, in a mercy that leads him to create Purgatory as a place of purification:

> And my mercy shal be shewed to manye of my breþeren;
> For blood may suffre blood boþe hungry and acale,
> Ac blood may noȝt se blood blede, but hym rewe. (B.18.394–6)

69 Alford, *Glossary*, p. 126.
70 A full appraisal of critical writings on Langland's representation of redemption and other medieval literary portrayals of the ransoming of mankind from hell is given by C.W. Marx on whose findings I draw here: *The devil's rights and the redemption in the literature of medieval England*.
71 Alford defines the phrase 'by right and by reson' as meaning 'justice, equity, law ... The phrase is especially associated with equitable law': *Glossary*, p. 137.

His longing to show this mercy to all mankind is expressed in his pledge not to drink until the Last Judgment, when he will drink the new vintage of the Valley of Jehosaphat, an allusion that echoes the words of Jesus to the disciples the night before his crucifixion:

> And I say to you, I will not drink from henceforth of this fruit of the vine until that day when I shall drink it with you new in the kingdom of my Father. (Matthew 26. 29)

Such an exercise of mercy is an expression of Christ's kindness to those whose nature he shares and an activity belonging to his heavenly nature as ruler of heaven and hell. It echoes the words of Holy Church when she contrasts God's reactions to the sin of Lucifer and his angels with his response to Adam's sin; God damned the devils, but took upon himself the nature of man. Now, whereas Lucifer and the inhabitants of hell receive strict justice, Christ stresses his kinship with man which demands that he be 'kynde':

> Ac my rightwisnesse and right shal rulen al helle,
> And mercy al mankynde bifore me in heuene.
> For I were an vnkynde kyng but I my kyn holpe –
> And nameliche at swich a nede þer nedes help bihoueþ. (B.18.397–400)

The redemption or ransom of mankind from Satan by the legal processes of duels with Death and with Satan is the archetype of all other ransoms, pledges and promises of recompense which, as the poem has stated so often, God has made on behalf of the poor. Here, in hell, all are equally poor as prisoners, awaiting the exercise of God's mercy to bring them relief, restore them to 'wele'. By association, the mercy that Christ extends to all sinners at this moment in his capacity as Christ the King is the paradigm of the mercy which the poem has been demanding on behalf of the poor. In these two passus, Langland clinches the argument that God's promised reward for the poor must take place on earth. He has demonstrated, through the words of the Samaritan, and through Christ's crucifixion, death, and harrowing of hell, that human beings who thwart God's design by being unkind put themselves in direct opposition to God's plan. That is why the Holy Ghost cannot work through them, and why they are damned.

PASSUS B.19 AND B.20: GOD'S KINGDOM ON EARTH

The final two passus of the poem return the reader to the temporal world in which Christ is indubitably a real man who, nonetheless, is simultaneously God.[72]

---

72 The *Vita Christi* of B.19.69–199 lays considerable stress on the undoubted human nature of Jesus which is united with the divine nature, typified as the miracle-working and redeeming Christ.

They are a strong endorsement of the continuing process of redemption through the incarnation of Christ in the church, which is structured by Grace and given into the care and guidance of Piers, the human representative of Christ. At the descent of the Holy Spirit the role and dignity of all Christians are established without discrimination, for the Holy Spirit is the gift of Grace distributed to each person as a distinctive skill according to the will of the Spirit:[73]

> 'Thouȝ some be clenner þan some, ye se wel,' quod Grace,
> 'That he þat vseþ þe fairest craft, to þe fouleste I kouþe haue put hym.
> Thynkeþ [þat alle craftes,' quod Grace], 'comeþ of my ȝifte;
> Loke þat noon lakke ooþer, but loueþ alle as breþeren.
> And who þat moost maistries kan, be myldest of berynge;
> And crouneþ Conscience kyng, and makeþ Craft youre stiward,
> And after Craftes conseil cloþeþ yow and fede.'   (B.19.253–9)

Although this doctrine relates to the proper organization of society, it does not endorse political oppression.[74] As a paraphrase of the Pauline injunction (1 Corinthians 12. 4–11) to recognize the equal brotherhood of all, the passage helps to confirm the poem's strong case against discrimination, even in those texts which might, at first reading, appear to condone it:

> Almyȝty God [myȝte haue maad riche alle] men, if he wolde,
> Ac for þe beste ben som riche and some beggeres and pouere.
>   (B.11.196–7)

> For all myȝtestow haue maad noon mener þan ooþer,
> And yliche witty and wise, if þee wel hadde liked.   (B.14.166–7)

> For al myhtest þou haue ymad men of grete welthe,
> And yliche witty and wys, and lyue withoute nede –
> Ac for þe beste, as Y hope, aren som pore and ryche. (C.16.19–21)

The passage in 1 Corinthians immediately following the account of the Spirit's varied gifts is the analogy of the body in which all members are of equal value (1 Cor. 12–30). Far from demonstrating a fatalistic acceptance that there will always be poor, the poem insists that the poor be accepted as of equal value with all other human beings, whatever their station or role in society.

Piers is given the task of procurator and reeve, harking back to Passus B.5, B.6 and B.7 when he took charge of the harvesting. His role is to keep good

---

73 1 Corinthians 12. 4. See also Hewett-Smith, 'Nede', pp 239–42.
74 It is worth noting that patient poverty is mentioned as but one of the gifts, for a specially talented few: 'And som he lered to lyue in longynge to ben hennes, / In pouerte and in pacience to preie for alle Cristene.' (B.19.249–50) This is voluntary poverty, one of the gifts of the Holy Spirit, a gift of grace and not imposed as an obligation for all.

order, and particularly, to make sure that debts are paid; *redde quod debes* becomes a leitmotif of the two passus, stressing the need for social justice. The end of the poem is the beginning of the church and the background to the role of Piers fourteen centuries later. We have seen how the story progresses in the ploughing of the half-acre, and now we see how it started; we see how the church and society are intended to be, knowing from the early passus what they have become. Grace establishes the structure, starting with the four evangelists, ending with the priesthood. Then Grace goes

> as wide as þe world is, wiþ Piers to tilie truþe
> And þe lo[nd] of bileue, þe lawe of Holy Chirche. (B.19.336–7)

As has happened so many times before in the poem, once the order is established for society, in this case the structure of the church, and all is set to operate efficiently according to the rule of Christ, the good order is disturbed by human sin, expressed in the reluctance of some of the crowd to cooperate.

The disruption centres on the Easter duties; according to the Fourth Lateran Council, confession must be made and communion received at least once an year and that at Easter or thereabouts. Restitution sticks in the gullet of the commons. The brewer rejects the whole ideology out of hand, addressing Conscience in very similar language to that used in Passus B.6 by the Waster and the Bretoner. As Haukyn said, with tears, 'Synne seweth vs euere' (B.14.323). Restitution is the sticking point; and most people are happier in their sin which they know than in self-denial which they fear. The ignorant vicar understands little about theology or even the basics of religious instruction, confusing cardinal virtues with worldly cardinals. However, he has grasped the central plank of Christ's teaching on salvation: it is available to all providing they repent. Moreover, the sinners are Piers' people whom he cares for without discrimination:

> A[c] wel worþe Piers þe Plowman, þat pursueþ God in doynge,
> *Qui pluit super iustos et iniustos* at ones,
> And sent þe sonne to saue a cursed mannes tilþe
> As brighte as to þe beste man or to þe beste womman.
> Right so Piers þe Plowman peyneþ hym to tilye
> As wel for a wastour and wenches of þe stewes
> As for hymself and hise seruaunt3, saue he is first yserued.
> [So blessed be Piers þe Plowman, þat peyneþ hym to tilye],
> And trauailleþ and tilieþ for a tretour also soore
> As for a trewe tidy man, alle tymes ylike.
> And worshiped be He þat wro3te al, boþe good and wikke,
> And suffreþ þat synfulle be til som tyme þat þei repente. (B.19.434–45)

This, then, is Piers' order – a society full of sinners at every level, but human beings, Piers' kind, all capable of being saved.

The poem presents the redemption of humankind and the establishment of God's kingdom as needs of the human being that must be articulated and addressed. In spending so much of his poem on these issues, Langland does not retreat into a realm of spiritual escape, but stresses the entitlement of all human beings to a reward which is simultaneously spiritual and temporal. It takes the form of justice, charity, and respect for human dignity, and it must take place here and now, on earth, in the kingdom of God's justice, a world which the poem shows to be redeemed by Christ. As Christ's words about the criteria for Judgment declare (Matthew 25. 34–45), this is not something that will only happen at the end of time, but is inextricably bound up with human concerns, to be enacted on the earth. The reward for the poor is treasure on earth in the form of spiritual ideals which make for the temporal good order proposed by Christ: honesty, integrity, justice, fortitude, temperance – the virtues that combat vices which make a person less than human, and which poor people have to combat in themselves as well as in others.

For Langland the good society is the theocracy, and practical justice is built on theological foundations. To invoke heavenly reward is not to opt out of earthly action; on the contrary, it is to insist on the urgency of such action, and its intimate relevance to each individual. The poem as text elucidates what is required to make Christ's kingdom come, and provides a solid theological basis for the doctrine of giving to the poor. When God pays for the poor he is performing redemption; a human being who pays for the poor is entitled to share God's redemption with them. God becomes human to fulfil his divine nature with full experiential knowledge. He experiences poverty when he wears mankind's 'sute' and the 'apparaille' of the poor. God's return in power at the harrowing of hell effects the redemption, life for life, which is constantly to be re-enacted under the livery of Piers, for the incarnation is a continuing process and Christ is continuously made present in the world through the poor. Similarly, the text of *Piers Plowman* is a continuing process; in the poem the word is being made incarnate for the poor, the ignorant, the non-poor and the learned, all of whom are in equal need of redemption.

Conclusion

One of the problems a modern reader has to negotiate in *Piers Plowman* is the troubling suspicion, adumbrated in the *lewed vicory's* words about the social distribution of functions, that Langland condones the existence of poverty, for the poem recognizes poverty to be an accepted fact of the contemporary social order and offers no suggestions for the elimination of the poor as a class. A 'poor reading' of the poem makes it obvious that, for Langland, poverty in itself is not an evil, but a state that leads straight to God. A life of ever-increasing indigence leads a character like Will to cease being solicitous about material needs so that he can concentrate on his goal of finding Truth. Patience claims that those who are poor have no opportunity to commit the deadly sins. The two images of feast and reward which relate directly to heavenly bliss place the poor in the forefront of God's kingdom. The association of Jesus 'our iuele' with the poor in a poor man's 'apparaille' elevates the poor to the status of the Son of God. All these factors might suggest that the poem can only understand poverty by giving it a value as leading people to spiritual fulfilment with God.

I have argued that Langland's attitude towards the poor should be understood differently. The poem is an expression of late medieval political and social order; it does not propose a levelling of the estates, for such a lack of order, to the medieval mind, is a characteristic of hell where there is no order.[1] What it does promote is the just organization of political and social order, in which 'mesure' is the principle and waste is eliminated. Langland has a clearly expressed sympathy for the sufferings of the involuntarily poor whose indigence is a sign of injustice and exploitation. The very words of Patience (B.14.202–61) to which I have just referred are, in context, a wry acknowledgement of the deprivation suffered by the poor. The poem's equation of Christ with the suffering poor reminds the reader that to be unkind to the poor violates humankind in the same

---

[1] Wimbledon's sermon at Paul's Cross, 1388, is one contemporary expression of this concept: 'so he shal be put þanne "in þat place þat noon ordre is inne, but euerelastynge horrour" and sorwe þat is in helle' (p. 66). It derives from a passage in Job: 'antequam vadam et non revertar ad terram tenebrosam et opertam mortis caligine terram miseriae et tenebrarum ubi umbra mortis et nullus ordo et sempiternus horror inhabitans.' (Before I go whence I shall not return, even to the land of darkness and the shadow of death; a land of darkness, as darkness itself; and of the shadow of death, without any order, and where the light is as darkness), (Job 10. 21–22).

way that to crucify Jesus violates God-made-man. Langland uses the same expression to comment on each of these issues. Repentance, exclaiming about Adam's *felix culpa*, named in the Holy Saturday liturgy as the sin which occasioned the blessed act of redemption, speaks of God as having allowed Adam to sin, 'And al for þe beste' (B.5.484). Trajan says that God, in his almighty power, could have made everyone rich, 'Ac for þe beste ben som riche and some beggeres and pouere' (B.11.197). The crucifixion can be accepted as part of God's overall plan for the redemption of humanity, but the act of those who carry out the crucifixion is, for all eternity, an act of evil. The historical crucifixion came about by the evil of human injustice; mystically Christ is crucified again every time a person sins. So, too, it is a sinful evil for people to mistreat the poor and leave them in unrelieved need, regardless of the fact that God will recompense the poor for their earthly sufferings by granting them heavenly bliss. God's love, 'kyndenesse' and mercy are freely available for the repentant sinner; the message of the Samaritan, however, is that charity is the fundamental impulse of humanity towards fellow human beings as well as towards God. Without 'kyndenesse' a person has lost the quality that makes him the image of God; there is only one alternative for the medieval mind – despair which leads directly to hell:

> Drede of desperacion þanne dryueþ awey grace,
> That mercy in hir mynde may noȝt þanne falle;
> Good hope, þat helpe sholde, to wanhope torneþ.   (B.17.309–11)

Throughout the poem Langland works through such mysteries of human existence by making distinctions, and this technique enables him to keep sight of the material and the spiritual nature of human life. The expression of this in two scriptural images, of banquets and of the heavenly economics of redemption, food of life and treasure in heaven, makes not only a powerful poetic statement, but also a soundly theological one. The poem's spirituality emerges as an expression of the active life in which Will, the poor man, learns that spiritual fulfilment comes from right living within the world of secular life. Such right living relates directly to treatment of the poor and is expressed as 'mesure' and charity, the moderation which defines itself in opposition to waste, and the open-handedness that unites the giver with God, the redeemer. By grounding itself in Scripture, the imagery underlines the fundamental oneness of this world and the next world, the inseparability of the secular and the sacred, the interrelatedness of the earthly and the spiritual life of mankind.

The poem interrogates seriously the idea that, just as Christ received his reward by being restored to the power of his Godhead, those who endure earthly poverty will be rewarded by being given a place in God's heavenly kingdom. In terms of the involuntarily poor, this is emphasized as an expression of justice which will not allow someone to be punished or rewarded both in this life and the next, as Patience clearly explains to Haukyn and Will (B.14.140–54). Those who voluntarily embrace poverty in imitation of Christ are guaranteed such a reward if they are faithful to their chosen poverty (B.19.67–8). But Conscience reminds Will that the reward of heaven is for all the just, not merely for the poor:

> His herte blood he shadde
> To maken alle folk free þat folwen his lawe.
> And siþ he yeueþ largeliche al his lele liges
> Places in paradis at hir partynge hennes,
> He may wel be called conquerour – and þat is 'Crist' to mene.
> (B.19.58–61)

The emphasis is on the redemptive nature of that reward, gained by Christ in shedding his blood. To a modern reader this 'promise of payment' may appear hollow words, an excuse for society to tolerate evil conditions on earth for the powerless and credulous poor whose spirits may be lifted by belief in a better hereafter. But in the fourteenth-century context the poem's teaching on the essential dignity of the poor is a striking rejection of the discrimination which was institutionalized in contemporary social structures.

It is common to find scholars commenting on the pessimism of Langland's vision of humanity, suggesting that he has no earthly solution for its ills. Helen Barr writes well on Langland's use of quotations, yet comes to the conclusion that

> no matter how many texts are turned up, quoted, and commented upon, the contemporary world fails to match up. In Passus B.18, the use of the quotations represents almost a withdrawal from the intricacies of a real human struggle.[2]

Aers calls Langland's vision for society doomed and anachronistic because his return to traditional ideas about the poor and about community 'continually dissolves the drastic social and economic problems his poem continually returns to'.[3]

I feel that my 'poor reading' of the poem has given me three main insights that go some way to counter such reactions. First, I return to my introductory warning that we cannot expect medieval ways of dealing with poverty to be the same as modern ones because 'we seek ways of dealing with poverty that seem real to us but for which the medieval writer had no vocabulary, partly because the language lagged behind the reality'.[4] Galloway has shown that, in his use of the term 'kyndenesse', Langland was moving towards a new expression of social cohesion and making 'an important contribution to secular cultural identity'.[5]

---

2 'The use of Latin quotations in *Piers Plowman* with special reference to passus XVIII of the B Text', p. 488.
3 *Community, gender, and individual identity*, p. 67.
4 Introduction, p. 21.
5 'From *gratitudo* to "kyndenesse"', p. 381.

The discussions in my second and third chapters have outlined Langland's clear portrayal of society as dependent upon the reciprocal functioning of all orders. They have also stressed the poem's call for justice in portraying the sufferings of the poor as injustices needing to be relieved. Langland's notion of reward for the poor moves towards a modern understanding that surplus must be shared. This does not require a levelling down of the social order, but a respect for common humanity, and a positive response to human need.

In the second place, my final chapter shows the poem as an attempt to restore a theological rationale for human activity, not by retreating from the world of material productivity, but by imagining it in all its complexity. The theological interpretation of the concepts of justice and 'kyndenesse', far from being a withdrawal from 'the tumultuous world of the 1380s and 1390s',[6] is a revitalizing of that world's moral foundation. The poem portrays fourteenth-century English culture within which such concepts have practical meaning for precisely imagined poor women with crying babies, labourers who work for a wage, starving beggars who are unable to work, and a whole array of dubious claimants and outright sinners who test the community's commitment to charity. Theological solutions are not apolitical. In Langland's world, the moral and ethical foundation required for the good society comes from an understanding of religion. His poem injects new life into the terminology of charity and fraternity, taking account of trade and commerce, wages, labour, and the laws of equity. This is what I mean by repeatedly denying critics' suggestions that the poem's destitute can only raise their eyes to reward in the world to come. Langland's theological solution is for society to put into practice God's justice and charity towards the poor here and now. His arguments for the eradication of poverty are grounded in the theology of charity and redemption because the language available to discuss socio-economic issues in the late fourteenth century derives from the language of religion.

Finally, I believe that the act of writing *Piers Plowman* is part of Langland's solution for the eradication of poverty. Simpson has shown how medieval modes of thought and reading accepted the importance of writing which appeals to the will and 'persuade[s] through emotional experience rather than rational argument'.[7] *Piers Plowman* is an imaginative and moral text whose intention is clearly to effect change by heightening the consciousness of contemporary culture in its late medieval audience. Elizabeth Kirk has written about the literary newness of its image of the ploughman as moral leader, yet suggests that the soil was already fertile for its reception. She uses the image of a spark falling into a powder keg to describe the effect of the poem on its contemporaries.[8] Wendy Scase speaks about the power of the poem as 'an energy-source for new anticlerical making', having shown how it responds to the conflicting manifestations of late

---

6 Ibid. p. 381.
7 'Modes of thought and poetic form', pp 1–9.
8 'Langland's plowman and the recreation of fourteenth-century metaphor', p.11.

medieval anticlericalism.[9] I believe that, in its portrayal of the poor, the poem's language moves beyond traditional formulas to reflect the socio-economic circumstances of fourteenth-century England. Langland creates a new vocabulary of compassion and realism to portray the complex interrelationship of social ills and forces of development within his culture. His reforming purpose is the rationale for the whole poem, and there can be no doubt that *Piers Plowman* influenced later writings and thought.[10]

Literature has the power to engage the mind and to move the will, and Langland engages his readers, whether medieval or modern, in dialogue with his culture and theirs. He and Ignatieff are remarkably similar in their ultimate intention, as the modern writer expresses it:[11]

> We need justice, we need liberty, and we need as much solidarity as can be reconciled with justice and liberty. But we also need, as much as anything else, language adequate to the times we live in. We need to see how we live now and we can only see with words and images which leave us no escape into nostalgia for some other time and place.

The words and images of *Piers Plowman* are embedded in Langland's culture, and express, in language for his time, understanding of the poor and their importance to the fourteenth-century world. Both Langland's times and modern times participate in the ever-present kingdom of Christ's justice. His poem demands that we engage with it as a questioning of our own faith, moral probity and identity.

---

9 *Piers Plowman and the new anti-clericalism*, p. 173.
10 See A. Hudson, 'The legacy of *Piers Plowman*'. There is also a brief but useful survey of literature influenced by the poem in Kerby-Fulton's article on *Piers Plowman* in *The Cambridge history of medieval English literature*, pp 534–38.
11 Ignatieff, p. 141.

Bibliography

EDITIONS

Langland, William, *Piers Plowman: a parallel-text edition of the A, B, C and Z versions*, ed. A.V.C. Schmidt (London and New York: Longman, 1995)

The Holy Bible, Douay: (1609); Rheims: (1582) (London: Washbourne, 1914)

Biblia sacra vulgata (online). Available from: http://bible.gospelcom.net/ bible?language=latin

WORKS CONSULTED

Adams, Robert, 'The nature of need in *Piers Plowman* XX', *Traditio*, 34 (1978), 273–301

Aers, David, *Chaucer, Langland, and the creative imagination* (London: Routledge and Kegan Paul, 1980)

——*Community, gender, and individual identity: English writing 1360–1430*, (London: Routledge, 1988)

——'Justice and wagelabor after the Black Death: some perplexities for William Langland', in *The work of work: servitude, slavery, and labor in medieval England* (Glasgow: Cruithne Press, 1994), pp 169–90

——'*Piers Plowman* and problems in the perception of poverty: a culture in transition', *Leeds Studies in English* n.s. 14 (1983), 5–25

Alford, John A., 'Literature and law in medieval England', *PMLA*, 92 (1977), 941–51

——ed., *A companion to Piers Plowman* (Berkeley: University of California Press, 1988)

——'Haukyn's coat: some observations on *Piers Plowman* B XVI: 22–7', *Medium ævum*, 43 (1974), 133–8

——'*Piers Plowman': A glossary of legal diction* (Cambridge: Brewer, 1988)

——'The role of the quotations in *Piers Plowman*', *Speculum*, 52 (1977), 80–99

Allen, Judson, 'Langland's reading and writing: *Detractor* and the pardon passus', *Speculum*, 59 (1984), 342–62

——*The ethical poetic of the later middle ages: a decorum of convenient distinction* (Toronto: University of Toronto Press, 1982)

Althusser, Louis, 'A letter on art in reply to André Daspré', in *Lenin and philosophy and other essays*, trans. Ben Brewster (London: New Left Books, 1971)

Anderson, Bernhardt, *The living world of the Old Testament*, 3rd edn (Harlow: Longman, 1978)

Aristotle, *The Nicomachean ethics*, trans. J.A.K. Thompson (London: Penguin, 1976)

Aston, Margaret, '"Caim's castles": poverty, politics and disendowment' in *Faith and fire: popular and unpopular religion 1350–1600* (London: Hambledon, 1993), pp 95–131

——'Popular religious movements in the middle ages', in *The Christian world: a social and cultural history of Christianity*, ed. Geoffrey Barraclough (London: Thames and Hudson, 1981), pp 15–70

Bakhtin, Mikhail, *Rabelais and his world*, trans. H. Iswolsky (Bloomington: Indiana UP, 1984)

Baldwin, Anna P., 'The double duel in *Piers Plowman* B XVIII and C XXI', *Medium ævum*, 50 (1981), 64–78

——'The triumph of patience in Julian of Norwich and Langland', in *Langland, the mystics and the medieval English religious tradition*, ed. Helen Phillips (Cambridge: Brewer, 1990), pp 71–83

Baldwin, Frances Elizabeth, *Sumptuary legislation and personal regulation in England* (Baltimore: Johns Hopkins Press, 1926)

Barr, Helen, 'The use of Latin quotations in *Piers Plowman* with special reference to passus XVIII of the B text', *Notes and queries*, n.s. 33 (December 1986), 440–8

Barron, Caroline M., 'The parish fraternities of medieval London', in *The Church in pre-Reformation society*, ed. Caroline Barron and Christopher Harper-Bill (Woodbridge: Boydell, 1985), pp 13–37

——'William Langland: a London poet', in *Chaucer's England: literature in historical context* ed. Barbara Hanawalt (Minneapolis: University of Minnesota Press, 1992), pp 91–109

Bartholomeus Anglicus, *De proprietatibus rerum*, trans. John of Trevisa, ed. Michael Seymour and others (Oxford: Clarendon Press, 1975)

Bennett, Judith M., 'Conviviality and charity in medieval and early modern England', *Past & present*, 134 (1992), 19–41

Benson, Larry D. and Siegfried Wenzel, eds., *The wisdom of poetry* (Kalamazoo: Medieval Institute Publications, 1982)

Bloomfield, Morton W., *'Piers Plowman' as a fourteenth-century apocalypse* (New Brunswick: Rutgers UP, 1962)

Boethius, *The consolation of philosophy*, trans. V.E. Watts (London: Penguin, 1969)

Bolton, J.L., The medieval English economy 1150–1500 (London: Dent, 1980)

Bowers, John. M., *The crisis of Will in 'Piers Plowman'* (Washington D.C.: The Catholic University of America Press, 1986)

Brinton, Thomas, *The sermons of Thomas Brinton, bishop of Rochester (1373–1389)*, ed. Mary Aquinas Devlin, Camden third series, 85–86 (London: offices of the Royal Historical Society, 1954)

Burgess, Clive, 'Strategies for eternity: perpetual chantry foundation in late medieval Bristol', in *Religious belief and ecclesiastical careers in late medieval England*, ed. Christopher Harper-Bill (Woodbridge: Boydell, 1991), pp 1–32

——' "By quick and by dead": wills and pious provision in late medieval Bristol', *English historical review*, 405 (October 1987), 837–58

——'Late medieval wills and pious convention: testamentary evidence reconsidered', in *Profit, piety and the professions in later medieval England*, ed. Michael A. Hicks (Gloucester: Alan Sutton, 1990), pp 14–33

Burnley, David, 'Langland's clergial lunatic', in *Langland; the mystics and the medieval English religious tradition*, ed. Helen Phillips (Cambridge: Brewer, 1990), pp 31–8

Burrow, John, *Medieval writers and their work: Middle English literature and its background 1100–1500* (London: Oxford UP, 1982)

——*Langland's fictions* (Oxford: Clarendon Press, 1993)

Bynum, Caroline Walker, *Holy feast and holy fast: the religious significance of food to medieval*

women (Berkeley: University of California Press, 1987)
Campbell, Bruce, 'Land, labour, livestock and productivity trends in English seigneurial agriculture, 1208–1450', in *Land, labour and livestock: historical studies in European agricultural productivity*, ed. B.M.S. Campbell and M. Overton (Manchester: Manchester UP, 1991), pp 144–82
Carlin, Martha, and Joel T. Rosenthal, eds, *Food and eating in medieval Europe* (London: Hambledon, 1998)
Carlin, Martha, 'Fast food and urban living standards in medieval England', in *Food and eating in medieval Europe*, ed. Martha Carlin and Joel T. Rosenthal (London: Hambledon, 1998), pp 27–51
Catechism of the Catholic Church (London: Geoffrey Chapman, 1994)
Catholic encyclopedia: an international work of reference on the constitution, doctrine, discipline, and history of the Catholic Church, ed. Charles G. Herbermann and others, 17 vols (New York: The universal knowledge foundation, 1913–1922)
Chaucer, Geoffrey, *The Riverside Chaucer*, ed. Larry D. Benson and others, 3rd edn (Oxford: Oxford UP, 1987)
Chester, Thomas, *Sir Launfal*, ed. A. J. Bliss (London: Thomas Nelson, 1960)
Clark, Elaine, 'Social welfare and mutual aid in the medieval countryside', *Journal of British studies*, 33 (1994), 381–406
——'Some aspects of social security in medieval England', *Journal of family history*, 7. 4 (1982), 307–20
Clopper, Lawrence, 'Need men and women labor? Langland's wanderer and the labor ordinances', in *Chaucer's England: literature in historical context*, ed. Barbara Hanawalt (Minneapolis: University of Minnesota Press, 1992), pp 110–29
——'Songes of Rechelesnesse': Langland and the Franciscans* (Ann Arbor: University of Michigan Press, 1997)
——'The life of the dreamer, the dreams of the wanderer in *Piers Plowman*', *Studies in Philology*, 86 (1989), 261–85
Coleman, Janet, *'Piers Plowman' and the 'Moderni'* (Rome: Edizioni di Storia e Letteratura, 1981)
——*English literature in history, 1350–1400* (London: Hutchinson, 1981)
Constantelos, Demetrios J., *Poverty, society and philanthropy in the late mediaeval Greek world*, Studies in the social and religious history of the mediaeval Greek world, 2 (New Rochelle, NY: A.D. Caratcas, 1992)
Copeland, Rita, ed., *Criticism and dissent in the middle ages* (Cambridge: Cambridge UP, 1996)
Corpus iuris canonici, ed. E. Friedberg, 2 vols (Leipzig: Tauchnitz, 1879–81; repr. 1959)
Cosner, Madeleine Pelner, *Fabulous feasts: medieval cookery and ceremony* (New York: George Braziller, 1979)
Cullum, P.H., and P.J.P. Goldberg, 'Charitable provision in late medieval York: "To the praise of God and the use of the poor"', *Northern history*, 29 (1993), 24–39
Cullum, Patricia H., '"For pore people harberles": what was the function of the maisonsdieu?', in *Trade, devotion and governance; papers in later medieval history*, ed. Dorothy J. Clayton, Richard G. Davies and Peter McNiven (Stroud: Allan Sutton, 1994), pp 36–54
Curtius, E.R., *European literature and the Latin middle ages*, trans. W.R. Trask (London: Routledge and Kegan Paul, 1953)
Davlin, Mary Clemente, '*Kynde knowynge* as a major theme in *Piers Plowman B*', *RES*, 22 (1971), 1–19

———'*Kynde knowynge* as a Middle English equivalent for "wisdom" in *Piers Plowman B*', *Medium ævum*, 50 (1981), 5–17
———*A game of heuene: word play and the meaning of Piers Plowman B* (Cambridge: Brewer, 1989)
dei Segni, Lotario, *De miseria condicionis humane*, ed. Robert E. Lewis (Athens GA: University of Georgia Press, 1978)
de Roover, Raymond, 'The scholastic attitude toward trade and entrepreneurship', in Raymond de Roover, *Business, banking, and economic thought in late medieval and early modern Europe: selected studies of Raymond de Roover*, ed. Julius Kirshner (Chicago: University of Chicago Press, 1974)
de Vitry, Jacques, *The exempla or illustrative stories from the sermones vulgares of Jacques de Vitry*, ed. T.F. Crane (London: Nutt, 1890)
Dives and Pauper, ed. Priscilla Heath Barnum, EETS, o.s. 275 (1976)
Dobson, R.B., ed., *The Peasants' Revolt of 1381*, 2nd edn (London: Macmillan, 1983)
Donaldson, E. Talbot, 'Long Will's apology: a translation', in *Medieval English religious and ethical literature: essays in honour of G.H. Russell*, ed. Gregory Kratzmann and James Simpson (Cambridge: Brewer, 1987), pp 30–4
Doob, Penelope B.R., *Nebuchadnezzar's children: conventions of madness in Middle English literature* (New Haven: Yale UP, 1974)
Du Boulay, F.R.H., *The England of Piers Plowman: William Langland and his vision of the fourteenth century* (Cambridge: Brewer, 1991)
Duby, Georges, *The three orders: feudal society imagined*, trans. Arthur Goldhammer (Chicago: University of Chicago Press, 1980)
Dyer, Christopher, '*Piers Plowman* and plowmen: a historical perspective', *YLS*, 8 (1994), 155–76
———'Did the peasants really starve in medieval England?', in *Food and eating in medieval Europe*, ed. Martha Carlin and Joel T. Rosenthal (London: Hambledon, 1998), pp 53–71
———'The English medieval village community and its decline', *Journal of British studies*, 33 (1994), 407–29
———*Everyday life in medieval England* (London: Hambledon, 1994)
———*Lords and peasants in a changing society* (Cambridge: Cambridge UP, 1980)
———*Standards of living in the later middle ages: social change in England, c.1200–1520* (Cambridge: Cambridge UP, 1989)
Ferguson, W., 'The Church in a changing world', *American historical review*, 59 (1953), 1–18
FitzRalph, Richard, 'Defensio curatorum', in *Dialogus inter militem et clericum* by John Trevisa, ed. Aaron Jenkins Perry, EETS, o.s. 167 (1925)
Fowler, David C., '*Piers Plowman*: "Will's apologia pro vita sua"', *YLS*, 13 (1999), 35–47
Frank, Robert. 'The hungry gap: crop failure, and famine', *YLS*, 4 (1990), 87–104
Freedman, Paul, *Images of the medieval peasant* (Stanford: University of Stanford Press, 1999)
Galloway, Andrew, '*Piers Plowman* and the schools', *YLS*, 6 (1992), 89–107
———'Private selves and the intellectual marketplace in late fourteenth-century England: the case of the two Usks', *New literary history*, 28 (1997), 291–318
———'The making of a social ethic in late medieval England: from *gratitudo* to "kynde-nesse"', *Journal of the history of ideas*, 55 (1994), 365–83
Galloway, James A., 'Driven by drink? Ale consumption and the agrarian economy of

the London region, c.1300–1400', in *Food and eating in medieval Europe*, ed. Martha Carlin and Joel T. Rosenthal (London: Hambledon, 1998), pp 87–100

Geremek, Bronislaw, *Poverty, a history*, trans. Agnieszka Kolakowska (Oxford: Basil Blackwell, 1994)

——*The margins of society in late medieval Paris*, trans. Jean Birrell (Cambridge: Cambridge UP, 1987)

Girouard, Mark, *Life in the English country house* (New Haven: Yale UP, 1978)

Godden, Malcolm, *The making of 'Piers Plowman'* (London: Longman, 1990)

Gower, John, *The complete works of John Gower: the Latin works*, ed. G.C. Macaulay (Oxford: Clarendon Press, 1902)

Graziani, René, 'Bosch's *Wanderer* and a poverty commonplace from Juvenal', *Journal of the Warburg and Courtauld Institutes*, 45 (1982), 211–16

Grosseteste, Robert, *Les reules Seynt Roberd*, in *Walter of Henley's husbandry*, ed. Elizabeth Lamont (London: Longmans Green, 1890), pp 122–45

Gutiérrez, Gustavo, *A theology of liberation*, trans. and ed. Sister Caridad Inda and John Eagleson (London: SCM Press 1974; 1st edn Maryknoll: Orbis Books, 1973)

Hammond, P.W., *Food and feast in medieval England* (Stroud: Alan Sutton, 1993)

Hanawalt, Barbara, and David Wallace, eds, *Bodies and disciplines: intersections of literature and history in fifteenth-century England* (Minneapolis: Minnesota UP, 1996)

——ed., *Chaucer's England: literature in historical context* (Minneapolis: Minnesota UP, 1992)

——*Crime and conflict in English communities, 1300–1348* (Cambridge MA: Harvard UP, 1979)

Hanna, Ralph III, 'William Langland', in *English writers of the later middle ages*, ed. M. C. Seymour (Aldershot: Ashgate, 1994), pp 127–84

——'Will's Work', in *Written work: Langland, labor, and authorship*, ed. Steven Justice and Kathryn Kerby-Fulton (Philadelphia: Pennsylvania UP, 1997), pp 23–66

Haren, Michael J., 'Social ideas in the pastoral literature of fourteenth-century England, in *Religious belief and ecclesiastical careers in late medieval England*, ed. Christopher Harper-Bill (Woodbridge: Boydell, 1991), pp 43–57

Harper-Bill, Christopher, 'The labourer is worthy of his hire?—complaints about diet in late medieval English monasteries', in *The Church in pre-Reformation society*, ed. Caroline Barron and Christopher Harper-Bill (Woodbridge: Boydell, 1985), pp 95–107

Harrison, Frederick, *Medieval man and his notions* (London: Murray, 1947)

Hatcher, John, 'England in the aftermath of the Black Death', *Past & present*, 144 (August 1994), 1–35

——'Labour, leisure and economic thought before the nineteenth century' *Past & present* 160 (August 1998), 64–115

——*Plague, population and the English economy 1348–1530* (London: Macmillan, 1977)

Heath, Peter, 'Urban piety in the later middle ages', in *The Church, politics and patronage in the fifteenth century*, ed. Barrie Dobson (Gloucester: Alan Sutton; New York: St Martin's Press, 1984), pp 209–34

Hebblethwaite, Peter, 'Liberation theology: the option for the poor', in *The Church and wealth*, Studies in Church history, 24 (1987), pp 407–21

Henisch, Bridget Ann, *Fast and feast: food in medieval society* (Philadelphia: Pennsylvania State UP, 1976)

Hewett-Smith, Kathleen, '"Lo, here be lyflode ynow, yf oure beleue be trewe"', *Chaucer yearbook*, 5 (1998), 139–62

——'Allegory on the half-acre: the demands of history', *YLS*, 10 (1996), 1–22
——'Nede ne hath no lawe: poverty and the de-stabilization of allegory in the final visions of *Piers Plowman*', in Kathleed Hewett-Smith ed. *William Langland's 'Piers Plowman': a book of essays* (New York and London: Routledge, 2001), pp 233–5.
Hicks, Michael, 'Chantries, obits and almshouses: the Hungerford foundations 1325–1478', in *The church in pre-Reformation Society*, ed. Caroline Barron and Christopher Harper-Bill (Woodbridge: Boydell, 1985), pp 123–42
Highet, Gilbert, *Juvenal the satirist: a study* (Oxford: Clarendon Press, 1954)
Hilton, Rodney, *The English peasantry in the later middle ages* (Oxford: Clarendon Press, 1975)
Hoccleve, Thomas, *Hoccleve's works: The regement of princes*, ed. F.J. Furnivall, EETS, e.s. 72 (1897)
——*Thomas Hoccleve's Complaint and Dialogue*, ed. J.A. Burrow, EETS, o.s. 313 (1999)
Howard, Donald R., *The three temptations: medieval man in search of the world* (Princeton: Princeton UP, 1966)
Hudson, Anne, 'The legacy of *Piers Ploughman*', in *A companion to 'Piers Ploughman'*, ed. John A. Alford (Berkeley: California UP, 1988), pp 251–66
Ignatieff, Michael, *The needs of strangers* (London: Chatto and Windus, 1984)
Jacob's well, ed. Arthur Brandeis, EETS, o.s. 115 (1900)
Jeanneret, Michel, *A feast of words: banquets and table talk in the renaissance*, trans. Jeremy Whiteley (Chicago: University of Chicago Press, 1991)
Jerusalem Bible (London: Darton, Longman and Todd, 1966)
Julian of Norwich, *The shewings of Julian of Norwich*, ed. Georgia Ronan Crampton (Kalamazoo: Medieval Institute Publications, 1994)
Justice, Steven, and Kathryn Kerby-Fulton, eds, *Written work: Langland, labor, and authorship* (Philadelphia: University of Pennsylvania Press, 1997)
Justice, Steven, *Writing and rebellion: England in 1381* (Berkeley: University of California Press, 1994)
Juvenal, *The satires of Juvenal*, ed. E.G. Hardy, 2nd edn (London: Macmillan, 1963)
Kane, George, 'Langland: labour and "authorship"', *Notes and queries*, n.s. 45 (1998), 420–5
——*Chaucer and Langland: historical and textual approaches* (London: The Athlone Press, 1989)
Kerby-Fulton, Kathryn, 'Langland and the bibliographic ego', in *Written work: Langland, labor, and authorship*, ed. Kathryn Kerby-Fulton and Steven Justice (Philadelphia: University of Pennsylvania Press, 1997), pp 67–143
——'*Piers Plowman*', in *The Cambridge history of medieval English literature*, ed. David Wallace (Cambridge: Cambridge UP, 1999), pp 513–38
Kernan, Alvin, *Shakespeare, the king's playwright* (New Haven: Yale UP, 1995)
Kim, Margaret, 'Vision of theocratics: the discourse of politics and the primacy of religion' (unpublished doctoral dissertation, Harvard University, 2000)
——'Hunger, need and the politics of poverty in *Piers Plowman*', *YLS* 16, 2002, 131–68.
Kirk, Elizabeth, 'Langland's plowman and the recreation of fourteenth-century religious metaphor', *YLS*, 2 (1988), 1–21
Kratzmann, Gregory, and James Simpson, eds., *Medieval English religious and ethical literature: essays in honour of G.H. Russell* (Cambridge: Brewer, 1987)
Lancaster, Henry of, *Le livre des seintes medicines: the unpublished devotional treatise of Henry of Lancaster*, ed. E.J. Arnould, Anglo-Norman Text Society (Oxford: Basil Blackwell, 1940)

Bibliography

Lawton, David A., 'On tearing—and not tearing—the pardon', *Philological quarterly*, 60 (1981), 414–22

le Goff, Jacques, *Your money or your life: economy and religion in the middle ages* (New York: Zone, 1988)

Leff, Gordon, *Heresy in the later middle ages* (Manchester: Manchester UP; New York: Barnes and Noble, 1967)

Lis, Catharina, and Hugo Soly, *Poverty and capitalism in pre-industrial Europe* (Hassocks: Harvester Press, 1979)

Little, Lester K., *Religious poverty and the profit economy in medieval Europe* (London: Paul Elek, 1978)

Lovejoy, Arthur, 'The communism of St Ambrose', in *Essays in the history of ideas* (Baltimore: Johns Hopkins UP, 1948; repr. Westport, CT: Greenwood Press, 1978), pp 296–307

McHardy, A.K., 'Ecclesiastics and economics: poor priests, prosperous laymen, and proud prelates in the reign of Richard II', in *The Church and wealth*, Studies in Church history, 24 (1987), pp 129–37

McIntosh, Marjorie Keniston, *Controlling misbehavior in England, 1370–1600* (Cambridge: Cambridge UP, 1998)

——'Local responses to the poor in late medieval and tudor England', *Continuity and change* 3, 2 (1988), 209–45

——'Finding language for misconduct: jurors in fifteenth-century local courts', in *Bodies and disciplines: intersections of literature and history in fifteenth-century England*, ed. Barbara Hanawalt and David Wallace (Minneapolis: University of Minnesota Press, 1996), pp 87–122

Macherey, Pierre, *A theory of literary production*, trans. Geoffrey Wall (London: Routledge and Kegan Paul, 1978)

Maitland, F.W., *Roman canon law in the Church of England: six essays* (London: Methuen, 1898)

Mann, Jill, *Chaucer and medieval estates satire* (Cambridge: Cambridge UP, 1973)

——'Eating and drinking in *Piers Plowman*', *Essays and Studies*, 32 (1979), 26–43

Mannyng, Robert of Brunne, *Handlyng synne*, ed. Idelle Sullens, Medieval and Renaissance Texts and Studies, 14 (Binghampton, NY: Medieval and Renaissance Texts and Studies, 1983)

Marcus, Leah, *Puzzling Shakespeare* (Berkeley: University of California Press, 1988)

Marx, C.W., *The devil's rights and the redemption in the literature of medieval England* (Cambridge: Brewer, 1995)

Masschaele, James, *Peasants, merchants and markets: inland trade in medieval England, 1150–1350* (New York: St Martin's Press, 1997)

Mennell, Stephen, *All manners of food: eating and taste in England and France from the middle ages to the present* (Oxford: Basil Blackwell, 1985)

Middleton, Anne, 'Acts of vagrancy: the C version "autobiography" and the Statute of 1388', in *Written work: Langland, labor, and authorship*, ed. Steven Justice and Kathryn Kerby-Fulton (Philadelphia: University of Pennsylvania Press, 1997), pp 208–388

——'Narration and the invention of experience: episodic form in *Piers Plowman*', in *The wisdom of poetry* ed. Larry D. Benson and Siegfried Wenzel (Kalamazoo: Medieval Institute Publications, 1982), pp 91–122

——'The critical heritage', in *A companion to Piers Plowman,* ed. John A. Alford (Berkeley: University of California Press, 1988), pp 1–25

Milis, Ludo J.R., *Angelic monks and earthly men: monasticism and its meaning to medieval society* (Woodbridge, Boydell, 1992)

Minnis, Alastair J., *Medieval theory of authorship: scholastic literary attitudes in the later middle ages*, 2nd edn (Aldershot: Scolar Press, 1988)

Moisa, Maria A., 'Fourteenth-century preachers' views of the poor: class or status group?', in *Culture, ideology and politics*, ed. R. Samuel and G. Stedman Jones (London: Routledge and Kegan Paul, 1982), pp 160–75

Mollat, Michel, *The poor in the middle ages: an essay in social history*, trans. Arthur Goldhammer (New Haven: Yale UP, 1986)

Morey, James, 'Plows, laws and sanctuary in medieval England and in the Wakefield *Mactatio Abel*', *Studies in philology*, 95 (1998), 41–55

Murphy, Margaret, 'Feeding medieval cities: some historical approaches', in *Food and eating in medieval Europe* ed. Martha Carlin and Joel T. Rosenthal (London: Hambledon, 1998), pp 117–31

Myrc, John, *Instructions for parish priests*, ed. Edward Peacock, EETS, o.s. 31, 2nd edn (1902)

New Catholic encyclopedia, 17 vols, (New York: McGraw-Hill, 1967–79)

Newhauser, Richard, 'Towards *modus in habendo*: transformations in the idea of avarice', *Zeitschrift der Savigny-stiftung für Rechtsgeschichte*, 106 (1989), 1–22

Nicholas, David, *The later medieval city* (London and New York: Longman, 1997)

Owst, G.R., *Literature and pulpit in medieval England*, 2nd edn (Oxford: Basil Blackwell, 1961)

Ozment, Steven, *The age of reform 1250–1550* (New Haven: Yale UP, 1980)

Patterson, Lee, *Literary practice and social change in Britain 1380–1530* (Berkeley: University of California Press, 1990)

——*Negotiating the past: the historical understanding of medieval literature* (Madison: University of Wisconsin Press, 1987)

Pearl, ed. E.V. Gordon (Oxford: Clarendon Press, 1953)

Pearsall, Derek, 'Langland's London', in *Written work: Langland, labor, and authorship*, ed. Steven Justice and Kathryn Kerby-Fulton (Philadelphia: University of Pennsylvania Press, 1997), pp 185–207

——'"Lunatyk lollares" in *Piers Plowman*', in *Religion in the poetry and drama of the late middle ages in England*, ed. Piero Boitani and Anna Torti (Cambridge: Brewer, 1990), pp 163–78

——*'Piers Plowman' by William Langland: an edition of the C-text* (London: Edward Arnold, 1978)

——'Poverty and poor people in *Piers Plowman*', in *Medieval English studies presented to George Kane*, ed. E. Kennedy, R. Waldron and J. Wittig (Woodbridge: Brewer, 1988), pp 167–85

Pierce the Ploughmans Crede: (about 1394 A.D.), ed. Walter Skeat, EETS, o.s. 30 (1867)

Poos, Lawrence R., *A rural society after the Black Death: Essex 1350–1525* (Cambridge: Cambridge UP, 1991)

Putnam, Bertha H., 'Maximum wage-laws for priests after the Black Death, 1349–1381', *American historical review*, 21 (1913), 12–31

——*The enforcement of the statute of labourers during the first decade after the Black Death, 1349–1359*, Columbia University Studies in History, Economics and Public Law, 32 (New York: Columbia UP, 1908)

Régamey, P.R., 'Religious poverty', in *New Catholic encyclopedia*, 17 vols (New York: McGraw-Hill, 1967–79), 11, pp 648–51

Reynolds, L.D., *The medieval tradition of Seneca's letters* (Oxford: Oxford UP, 1965)

Richmond, Colin, 'The English gentry and religion, c.1500', in *Religious belief and ecclesiastical careers in late medieval England*, ed. Christopher Harper-Bill (Woodbridge: Boydell, 1991), pp 121–50.

Rolle, Richard, *English writings of Richard Rolle: hermit of Hampole*, ed. Hope Emily Allen (Oxford: Clarendon Press, 1931)

Rosenthal, Joel T., *The purchase of paradise* (London: Routledge and Kegan Paul, 1972)

Rosser, Gervase, 'Going to the fraternity feast: commensality and social relations in late medieval England', *Journal of British studies*, 33 (1994), 430–46

Rubin, Miri, *Charity and community in medieval Cambridge* (Cambridge: Cambridge UP, 1987)

—— *Corpus Christi: the eucharist in late medieval culture* (Cambridge: Cambridge UP, 1991)

—— 'The poor', in *Fifteenth-century attitudes*, ed. Rosemary Horrox (Cambridge: Cambridge UP, 1994), pp 169–82

Rudd, Gillian, *Managing language in 'Piers Plowman'*, Piers Plowman Studies, 9 (Cambridge: Brewer, 1994)

Ryan, John A., 'Poverty and pauperism', in *The Catholic encyclopedia: an international work of reference on the constitution, doctrine, discipline, and history of the Catholic Church*, ed. Charles G. Herbermann and others, 17 vols (New York: The Universal Knowledge Foundation, 1913–22), 12, pp 324–30

Salter, Elizabeth, *Piers Plowman: an introduction* (Oxford: Basil Blackwell, 1969)

Sandler, Lucy Freeman, *Omne bonum: a fourteenth-century encyclopedia of universal knowledge* (London: Harvey Miller, 1996)

Scase, Wendy, *'Piers Plowman' and the new anticlericalism* (Cambridge: Cambridge UP, 1989)

Scattergood, V.J., *Politics and poetry in the fifteenth century* (London: Blandford Press, 1971)

Schofield, John, and Alan Vince, *Medieval towns* (London: Leicester UP, 1994)

Sears, Elizabeth, *The ages of man: medieval interpretations of the life cycle* (Princeton: Princeton UP, 1986)

Seneca, *Ad Lucilium epistulae morales*, ed. and trans. R.M. Gummere (London: Heinemann, 1953)

Shepherd, Geoffrey, 'Poverty in *Piers Plowman*', in *Social relations and ideas: essays in honour of R.H. Hilton*, ed. T.H. Aston and others (Cambridge: Cambridge UP, 1983), pp 169–89

Simpson, James, 'Desire and the scriptural text: Will as reader in *Piers Plowman*', in *Criticism and dissent in the middle ages*, ed. Rita Copeland (Cambridge: Cambridge UP, 1996), pp 215–43

—— 'From reason to affective knowledge: modes of thought and poetic form in *Piers Plowman*', *Medium ævum*, 55 (1986), 1–23

—— 'Spirituality and economics in passus 1–7 of the B-Text', *YLS*, 1 (1987), 83–103

—— 'The constraints of satire in *Piers Plowman* and *Mum and the Sothsegger*', in *Langland, the mystics and the medieval English tradition: essays in honour of S. S. Hussey*, ed. Helen Phillips (Cambridge: Brewer, 1990), pp 11–30

—— *Piers Plowman: an introduction to the B-Text* (Harlow: Longman, 1990)

Smalley, Beryl, *The study of the Bible in the middle ages* (Oxford: Basil Blackwell, 1983)

Southern, Richard W., *The making of the middle ages* (London: Hutchinson, 1953)

——Western society and the church in the middle ages (London: Penguin, 1970)
Statutes of the realm (London: Dawsons, 1963)
Stokes, Myra, Justice and mercy in 'Piers Plowman' (London: Croom Helm, 1984)
Strohm, Paul, Hochon's arrow: the social imagination of fourteenth-century texts (Princeton: Princeton UP, 1992)
Swabey, ffiona, 'The household of Alice de Bryene, 1412–13', in Food and eating in medieval Europe, ed. Martha Carlin and Joel T. Rosenthal (London: Hambledon, 1998), pp 133–44
Swanson, Robert N., 'Standards of livings: parochial revenues in pre-reformation England', in Religious belief and ecclesiastical careers in late medieval England, ed. Christopher Harper-Bill (Woodbridge: Boydell, 1991), pp 151–95
Szarmach, Paul E., M. Teresa Tavormina, and Joel T. Rosenthal, eds, Medieval England: an encyclopedia (New York: Garland Publishing, 1998)
Szittya, Penn R., The antifraternal tradition in medieval literature (Princeton: Princeton UP 1986)
The anonimalle chronicle, 1333 to 1381, from a MS. written at St Mary's Abbey, York, ed. V.H. Galbraith (Manchester: Manchester UP; New York: Barnes & Noble, 1970)
The chronicle of Lanercost, 1272–1346, trans. Herbert Maxwell (Glasgow: MacLehose, 1913)
The macro plays, ed. Mark Eccles, EETS, o.s. 262 (1969)
The prymer or layfolks' prayer book, ed. Henry Littlehales, EETS, o.s. 105, 109 (1895)
Thompson, John A.F., 'Piety and charity in late medieval London', Journal of ecclesiastical history, 16 (1965), 178–95
——'Wealth, poverty and mercantile ethics in late medieval London', in La ville, la bourgeoisie et la genèse de l'état moderne (XIIe–XVIIIe siècles) (Paris: Éditions du CNRS, 1988), pp 265–77
Tierney, Brian, 'The decretists and the "deserving poor" ', Comparative studies in society and history, 1 (1958–59), 360–73
——Medieval poor law: a sketch of canonical theory and its application in England (Berkeley: University of California Press, 1959)
Turville-Petre, Thorlac, ed. Alliterative poetry of the later middle ages: an anthology, (London: Routledge, 1989)
Vale, Malcolm A.K., Piety, charity and literacy among the Yorkshire gentry, 1370–1480, Borthwick papers, 50 (York: St Anthony's Press, 1976)
Von Nolcken, Christina, ed., The Middle English translation of the Rosarium theologie (Heidelberg: Carl Winter, 1979)
Wallace, David, Chaucerian polity: absolutist lineages and associational forms in England and Italy (Stanford: Stanford UP, 1997)
——ed.), The Cambridge history of medieval English literature (Cambridge: Cambridge UP, 1999)
Ward, Jennifer C., 'Elizabeth de Burgh, Lady of Clare (d. 1360)', in Medieval London widows 1300–1500, ed. Caroline Barron and Anne F. Sutton (London: Hambledon, 1994), pp 29–45
Warner, Lawrence, 'Jesus the jouster', YLS, 10 (1996), 129–43
Warren, Ann K., Anchorites and their patrons in medieval England (Berkeley: University of California Press, 1985)
Watson, Nicholas, 'Conceptions of the Word', in New medieval literatures 1, ed. Wendy Scase, Rita Copeland and David Lawton (Oxford: Clarendon Press, 1997), pp 85–124

Wenzel, Siegfried, 'The wisdom of the fool', in *The wisdom of poetry*, ed. Larry D. Benson and Siegfried Wenzel (Kalamazoo: Medieval Institute Publications, 1982), pp 225–40
White, Eileen, 'The great feast', *Leeds studies in English*, n.s. 29 (1998), 401–10
White, Hugh, *Nature and salvation in 'Piers Plowman'*, Piers Plowman Studies, 6 (Cambridge: Brewer, 1988)
Wimbledon, Thomas, *Wimbledon's sermon Redde rationem villicationis tue: a Middle English sermon of the fourteenth century*, ed. Ione Kemp, Duquesne Studies, Philological Series, 9 (Pittsburgh: Duquesne UP, 1967)
Wittig, Joseph S., '*Piers Plowman B*, Passus IX–XII: elements in the design of the inward journey', *Traditio*, 28 (1972), 211–80
——'The dramatic and rhetorical development of Long Will's pilgrimage', *Neuphilologische Mitteilungen*, 76 (1975), 52–76
Wogan-Browne, Jocelyn, and others, *The idea of the vernacular: an anthology of Middle English literary theory, 1280–1520* (University Park, PA: The Pennsylvania State UP, 1999)
Wright, Thomas, ed., *Political songs of England from the reign of John to that of Edward II* (Cambridge: Cambridge UP, repr. 1996)
Wynnere and Wastoure, ed. Stephanie Trigg, EETS, o.s. 297 (1990)

ONLINE SOURCES

'Fourth Lateran Council: 1215, *Constitutions*', in *Decrees of the ecumenical councils*, ed. and trans. Norman P. Tanner (online). Available from: http://www.piar.hu/councils/~index.htm (Accessed 19 February 2003).
Biblia sacra vulgata (online). Available from: http://bible.gospelcom.net/ bible?language=latin (Accessed 19 February 2003)
Latin text of the *Consolatio philosophiae*, with links to commentary by J.J. O'Donnell, 1990 (online). Available from: http://ccat.sas.upenn.edu/jod/boethius/boethius.html (Accessed 19 February 2003)
St Ambrose, bishop Of Milan, *Three books on the duties of the clergy*, 1997 (online). New Advent. Available from: http://www.newadvent.org/fathers/34011.htm (Accessed 19 February 2003)
St Thomas Aquinas, *The Summa theologica*, 2000 (online). Available from: http://www.newadvent.org/summa/ (Accessed 19 February 2003)
The World Bank Group, 2003. *World development report 2001/2002: Attacking Poverty* (online). Available from http://www.worldbank.org/poverty/wdrpoverty/report/ (Accessed 19 February 2003)
The World Bank Group, 2003. Povertynet (online). Available from: http://www.worldbank.org/poverty/ (Accessed 19 February 2003)
The World Bank Group, 2003. Povertynet, Income Poverty. Prospects for poverty reduction: Scenarios for the next fifteen years (online). Available from: http://www.worldbank.org/poverty/data/trends/scenario.htm (Accessed 19 February 2003)
The World Bank Group, 2003. Povertynet, *Voices of the poor* (online). Available from: http:// www.worldbank.org/poverty/voices/listen-findings.htm (Accessed 19 February 2003)
The World Bank Group, 2003. Poverty reduction and economic management/ Human development/ Development economics, 2001. Income poverty. The latest global numbers (online). Available from: http://www.worldbank.org/poverty/data/trends/income.htm (Accessed 19 February 2003)

The World Bank Group, 2003. *Poverty trends and voices of the poor*, 4th edn. May 2001, (online). Available from: http://www.worldbank.org/poverty/data/trends/ (Accessed 19 February 2003)

The World Bank Group, 2003. 'What the Poor Say' in *Poverty trends and voices of the poor*, 4th edn. May 2001, pp 40–54, (online). Available from: http://www.worldbank.org/poverty/data/trends/ (Accessed 19 February 2003)

Index

Abraham, 201, 203, 223
  account,
  of the rich with God, 117, 143, 147
  reckoning, 146
  ad status sermons, 81, 94
Adam,
  and Christ's incarnation, 221
  and death, 226
  and his *felix culpa*, 232
  and work as punishment for sin, 107
  his sin as part of God's redemptive plan, 218
  his sin contrasted with Lucifer's, 227
  taught how to work by an angel, 83
Agnes Fylour, 122
Alice de Bryene, 87, 198
almoner, 133, 197–8
alms,
  and remission for sin, 39
  and discrimination, 42, 76, 92, 136
  and Hoccleve's old man, 49
  and *lunatyk lollares*, 183
  and religious, 58, 116, 119
  and the able-bodied, 76, 79, 89, 103
  and the clergy, 56, 58, 124, 129
  and the dependent poor, 89, 92
  and the Gospel injunction, 112
  and Will's prayer, 177
  as spiritual investment, 222
  in aristocratic households, 132, 197–9
  see also charity, wills
almsgiving,
  and church legislation, 40–4
  and discrimination, 41–2, 92–3
  and Hunger's views, 104, 106
  and ostentation, 124
  and Sir Launfal, 159
  and the 1351 Statute, 77
  and the gap between rich and poor, 20
  as day-to-day poor relief, 134
  as reparation/restitution for sin, 122–4
  rituals of, 204
almshouse(s), 45, 46, 128, 132, 133
alter alterius, 91, 96–7, 104–5, 115, 152, 164, 207
anawim, 36, 187, 201
anchorite(s), 49, 92, 130–2, 162
Anima, 119, 129, 140–1, 143, 163, 210n
Anonimalle chronicle, 78n
Antichrist, 59, 67, 163, 175, 185–6
anticlericalism, 55–7, 124, 134, 163n, 166–7, 171, 174n, 176, 185–6, 190, 191, 234
antifraternalism, 29, 55, 124, 166, 209
apologia, Will's, 140, 157, 166, 174, 178, 187
appropriation, 57–8, 128–9
aristocracy, 57, 88, 131–2, 135, 185
artisans, 74, 132
atonement, 217, *see also* redemption
avarice, *see* seven deadly sins

badge of poverty, 114, 152
banquet(s),
  and Trajan, 210–13, 222
  eschatological, 112, 201, 202
  evangelical, 97, 99–100, 195, 201–2, 210
  fool's, 210
  grotesque, 200, 203, 205, 210–12
  ill-regulated, 204
  images of, 193–5
  in psalms, 101
  late medieval, 195–201
  messianic, 138, 201–2
  of Conscience, 203, 207–10
  of Dives, 205, 207
  of the rich, 212–13
  Study's criticism of, 203–7
  symposium, 199–201, 206

banquet(s), *(continued)*
  virtuous, 204
  wedding, 142, 213
baptism, *see* sacraments
Barn of Unity, 66, 124, 157, 186–7, 191
beggar(s),
  able-bodied, 46, 55–6, 76, 77, 89, 91, 92, 109, 114, 170, 209
  and almsgiving, 197
  and anticlericalism, 56
  and Bosch, 161
  and clerical mendicants, 212
  and crime, 32, 69, 76, 78 94, 103
  and discrimination, 205, 211–13, 215, 223
  and Good Thief, 215
  and Haukyn, 136
  and Hoccleve, 158
  and labourers, 81–2, 85
  and Need, 189
  and Piers, 104, 109, 113
  and responsibility, 43, 109, 111
  and reward, 146–7, 215, 222
  and St Francis, 53
  and the Gospel, 94, 97, 103, 203
  and the grotesque banquet, 205
  and Will, 128, 134, 177
  categories of, 44, 92
  destitute, 30, 129, 151, 234
  folklore of, 78
  fraudulent, 79–80, 92–5, 103–4, 106, 110–11, 128
  genuine, 103, 109–10
  idle, 79, 111
  in post-plague England, 14
  Langland's representation of, 69, 79
  rejection of, 32, 58, 78, 93, 204, 205
  stereotypes of, 212
  sturdy, 78, 168, 174
  undeserving, 15, 106, 109
  see also vagrants, vagabonds, wanderers
begging,
  as a crime, 69
  as survival, 46, 73, 88, 93, 98, 107
  more lucrative than working, 32
  of false mendicants, 128, 176n
  of idlers, 92, 107, 166, 169
  with honesty, 43, 136
  see also beggar(s)
Beguines, 52

benefactor(s), 127–9, 168, 171, 211, *see also* alms, almsgiving, donor, charity.
Black Death, 72–3, 76–7, 84, *see also* plague
blind, 71, 92, 95, 99–100, 102–3, 114, 129, 167, 186n, 194, 201–2
bliss/e, 86, 99, 112, 120, 140, 143, 146–9, 201, 214–6, 231–2
blody breþeren, 16, 41, 47, 104, 106, 138, 211, 216
Bosch, 161
bread,
  and beggars, 94, 205
  and grain, 87
  and Haukyn, 136, 138, 143
  and Scripture, 21n, 99, 110, 139, 142n, 171, 172n
  and the *Paternoster*, 135–6, 139, 142
  and toil, 70, 107
  at Conscience's banquet, 134, 208
  at funerals, 129
  barley, 88, 110
  wheaten, 103, 110, 112, 134
Bristol, 122, 123n, 124, 132
brother(s),
  and Christ's mercy, 226
  and forgiveness, 165n
  and Galatians, 96, 152, 163
  and God made man, 222, 224, 226
  and St Francis, 53, 185
  and Trajan, 211
  and Will, 164
  both poor and non-poor, 66, 216
  Chaucer's Ploughman, 126
  in Christ's blood, 211, 219
brotherhood,
  and discrimination, 229
  and *Galatians*, 153
  and the Christian laity, 52
  and treatment of the poor, 210
  in Christ, 47
  made by blood, 224
  with the poor, Launfal's view, 160

Cain, 84
Cambridge, 20, 27n, 46, 168, 176n
chantry/chantries, 124–6
charity,
  allegorical figure of, 141, 145
  and justice, 61, 91–2, 99, 116, 119, 157,

Index

163–4, 175, 180, 191, 193, 213, 234
   as mutual obligation, 17, 62, 68, 79–80, 81, 85, 89, 91–2, 97, 104, 106, 119, 209, 232, 234
   essential for salvation, 66, 68, 107, 114, 121, 127, 142, 234
   God's, 95, 150
   monastic, 129, 133
   towards the poor, 20, 41–4, 46, 51, 54, 79, 90, 92, 97, 98, 106, 111, 116–17, 120, 128–9, 131–2, 134–5, 142–3, 152–5, 159, 177, 188, 198–9, 207, 209–10, 220, 234
   Tree of, 60, 66
   virtue of, 43, 53, 95, 96, 141, 149, 152–3, 159, 179, 182, 203–6, 209, 224
children, 32, 47, 78, 92, 94, 109, 114, 162, 223
Christ,
   and brotherhood, 47, 207, 211–12, 222
   and justice, 192
   and *lunatik lollers*, 184
   and mercy, 165, 226–7
   and Scripture, 97, 100–3, 112, 139, 150, 153, 203, 229
   and siege of Unity, 186
   and the Samaritan, 224
   anger of, 91
   body of, 207, 211
   following of, 13
   identified with the poor, 40, 51, 71, 127, 152, 157, 190, 210, 216, 217, 227, 231
   kingdom of, 157, 182, 213–15, 229–30, 235
   livery/*secte* of, 114, 127, 152, 216, 221
   patrimony of, 59
   poor as sacrament of, 50, 65, 67, 79, 93, 164, 189–90, 230
   poverty in imitation of, 25, 28, 30, 47, 50, 52–6, 60, 67, 112, 122, 135, 157, 160–4, 190–1, 232
   poverty of, 29, 36, 189–90
   reward given by, 148, 151
   Will and, 155, 157, 160–1, 163n, 167, 171–2, 174–5, 176, 190, 192, 210
   see also, *kenosis*, redemption, ransom
Chronicle of Lanercost, 72
church,
   and corruption, 58–9, 67, 186
   and poverty, 27, 32, 40, 46, 58, 91, 135
   and reform, 25, 52, 54, 157, 187
   as institution, 15, 23, 26, 28, 64, 66, 191
   donations to, 121–4, 128, 132
   Eastern, 46
   founding of, 66, 165, 211, 229
   law of, 32, 40, 44, 59, 71, 92, 118, 156, 173–4
   responsible for the poor, 27n, 38, 58–9, 91, 93, 128–9
   see also Holy Church
city, 46, 52, 71n, 74, 99, 131n, 136, 201
Clarence, duke of, 197
clergy, 51, 55–9, 67, 72, 121, 124–5, 128–9, 133, 203, 210
Clergy, 203, 208
cleric/clerk, 32, 34, 56–8, 132, 163, 176, 184n, 186, 192, 196, 199, 204–6, 220
clothworker, 30
commerce, 22, 117, 141, 144, 193, 220, 234
Commons Complaint 1376, 76, 176
Complaint and Dialogue, 159, 183n
Concordia regularum, 176
confession, 57, 67, 94, 124, 151, 166n, 173, 174, 178, 208, 221, 229, *see also* sacraments
Conscience, 67, 82–4, 164–6, 168–73, 177, 186–7, 190–1, 195, 201, 203, 207–10, 228–9, 233
Consolation of Philosophy, 48
consumption, 91, 117, 164, 178, 188, 193, 205–6, 209, 219n
Corinthians, 37, 183, 184, 228
corporal works of mercy, 39, 71, 108, 130
Corpus iuris canonici, 43
coveitise, *see* seven deadly sins
creed,
   as pastoral curriculum, 57
   as Will's prayer, 177
   Athanasian, 110, 112
crime, 32, 67, 69, 77–9, 83
cripple(s), 91–2, 99, 111, 194, 202
criterion/a for salvation, 47, 61, 66, 108, 110, 230
crucifixion, 60, 66, 153, 218, 221, 227, 232
culture,
   and charity, 23
   and the poor, 69, 234
   and Will, 166, 174, 176
   and salvation, 225
   and poverty, 14, 21, 22, 25–6, 35, 38, 50–1
   and *Piers Plowman*, 14, 20–1, 27, 62, 81, 144, 156, 234, 235
   and texts, 13, 14–15, 18, 156

Dame Study, *see* Study
damnation, 58, 112, 148, 150, 202, 203, 205, 107, 108
De miseria condicionis humane, 35
De proprietatibus rerum, 181
dearth, 73, 89, 104, 107, 136, 196
debt(s), 33, 58, 148, 151, 211n, 226, 229
decretals, 34, 43, 58, 93, 109, 193
Defensio curatorum, 29
deprivation, 35, 37, 188, 231
destitution, 29–32, 50, 52, 74, 76, 114, 161, 187, 190, 191, 194
deuoir, 58, 143–9
Deuteronomy, 105, 139, 141–2
discrimination, 21, 38, 41, 68, 91–4, 106, 210–2, 228–9, 233
distinction(s),
  of poverty, 25, 27, 29, 30
  scholastic, 22, 23, 60, 91, 92, 94, 98, 100, 103, 109–10, 114, 128, 165, 232
  among people, 44, 86, 109, 134, 151, 157, 184
Dives, 20, 40, 107, 146, 147, 201, 202, 203, 205–8, 214, 223, *see also* parables
Dives and Pauper, 214
Dobest, 30, 88, 206, 217
Dobet, 30, 88, 207, 217
doctor(s),
  scholastic teacher, 57, 109, 118, 138n, 204
  Great Doctor, 134, 195, 201, 203, 210
Dominic, Saint, 53–4
dominium, 55, 119, 154
donor, 41, 45–6, 53, 92–4, 121, 128, 130, 133–4
Dowel, 30, 88, 126, 134, 136, 179–80, 206, 207, 210, 217
dream(s), 164, 177–9, 181, 187, *see also* vision(s)

Eden, 83
Ego dormio, 160
Elizabeth de Burgh, 198
enemies, 106, 119, 210
estate(s), 34, 38–41, 47, 69, 80, 84, 88, 91, 94, 98, 105, 114, 137, 152, 176, 212, 231
eucharist, *see* sacrament
excess, 49, 56, 59, 132, 160, 188, 193–6, 198, 200, 203–6, 223

faith, 13, 26, 37, 64, 105, 145, 151, 156, 206, 207, 235
faitours, 85, 110, 137, 185
familia, 17, 69
famine, 30, 32, 68, 71, 73, 74, 79–91, 98, 104, 106, 109, 113, 133, 138, 194, 196
fiat, 139–42, 171–2
Florence, 46
food,
  as charity, 132–4, 168, 195, 197–9, 211
  as indulgence, 52, 65, 195–201, 203, 205–10
  production of, 81, 84–9, 91, 97, 103, 107–9, 112–18, 115, 137, 170–2, 187
  spiritual, 96, 110, 112, 136, 137, 141–3, 195, 208, 232
fool(s), 181–7, 210, 212–3
Form of living, 160
Fourth Lateran Council, 229
Francis, Saint, 37, 53–4, 162, 185
fraternity, 23, 62, 194, 234
fraud, 36, 79, 108n, 163, 168, 175, 190
Frere Flatterer, 124, 190
friars,
  against seculars, 55
  and Alice de Bryene, 87
  and begging, 88, 92, 128
  and gluttony, 209
  and money, 55, 88n, 122–4, 128, 208
  and need/Need, 53, 189–90
  and penance, 55, 79, 123
  and Will, 165, 179, 208
  as poor of Christ, 162, 167n
  slothful and deceitful, 50, 112, 168, 176, 185
  sophistical, 205
funerary doles, 129–33

Galatians, 96, 97, 104–5, 153
Genesis, 97, 107
Gethsemane, 139, 153
gluttony, *see* seven deadly sins
good works, 105, 120, 127, 135, 155, 202n, 206, 207, 220
grain, 80, 83, 86–9, 103, 133, 136
greed, 33, 48, 92, 94, 119, 139, 158, 160, 203, 210
gyrovague, 176

half-acre, 30, 62, 69, 73, 80, 84, 85, 88, 90, 92, 96, 97, 104, 109, 178, 229

Index

Handlyng synne, 79, 93, 94n, 195n, 220n
harrowing of hell, 60, 66, 165, 217, 218n, 227, 230
harvest(s), 32, 72, 73–4, 77, 81, 83, 86–9, 91, 95–7, 100, 102, 104, 105, 107, 109–10, 112, 129, 137, 167–8, 170, 171, 209, 211
Haukyn, 60, 64, 65, 114, 116, 120, 135–46, 151–4, 182, 229, 232
heaven,
    and *kenosis*, 217–18, 227
    and Piers, 137
    and poverty, 27, 30, 51, 112, 144, 155
    and the poor, 45, 67, 72, 100, 120–1, 143, 148, 155
    and the rich, 40, 51, 113, 115, 145, 148
    imagery of, 21, 112, 139, 214–15
    kingdom of, 40, 51, 62n, 113, 120, 172, 193, 201
    treasure in, 51, 72, 112, 115, 121, 138, 140n, 162, 232
help-ales, 41, 46, 133
hermits,
    and Patience, 208
    and Will, 179, 184
    faithful, 92, 162–3, 170, 175n, 176n, 177n
    false, 32, 79, 91–2, 112, 128, 168, 171, 173–6
    reforming, 50–52
hire, 70, 109, 143, 147, 148–9, 154, 163
Holy Church, 60, 61, 66, 87, 119, 142, 150, 163, 177–8, 191, 217, 219–20, 227
Holy Spirit, 165, 224, 225, 228
homelessness, 127, 179
hours
    canonical, 170n, 177, 220
    of the Virgin, 170n, 177
Humiliati, 52
humility, 124, 133, 173, 189, 204
hunger, 28, 80, 87, 90, 91, 97, 108, 112, 127, 133, 139, 149, 157, 160, 175, 194, 201, 204, 205, *see also* famine
Hunger, 88–92, 95, 97, 98, 104–10, 113, 138, 164n, 188
hungry gap, 89
hypocrisy, 112, 134, 189, 208, 212

identity,
    cultural, 13, 156, 233, 235
    of Christ and the poor, 127, 161, 190
    of the individual, 36, 49, 159
    of Will in poverty, 134, 157, 160, 175, 209, 219
idleness, 76, 78, 79, 84, 87, 91, 103–5, 136, 157, 163, 168, 171, 176, 189
Imaginatif, 177, 179
incarnation, 37, 189, 190, 210, 217–30
indigence, 49, 50, 61, 66, 76, 81, 84, 149, 157, 159, 162, 164, 190, 231
indigent, the, 30, 33, 38, 44, 46, 66, 75, 116, 121, 149, 155, 157, 160, 162, 163, 167, 172
indulgence(s), 92, 110, 120, 122, 126–7, 151
injustice(s), 30, 34–6, 47, 60, 65, 67, 71, 89, 91–2, 119, 155, 175, 185, 186, 191, 192, 209, 231, 232, 234
Innocent III, 35, 53
Innocent IV, 71
insanity, 159, *see also* lunacy, madness
International Development Goal, 38
itinerant(s), 44, 80, 157, *see also* vagrant, vagabond

Jacob's well, 78
Jerusalem Bible, 36n, 37, 201n
jesters, 32, 58, 93n, 136, 195
John of Gaunt, 132
John the Baptist, 97, 98
justice,
    and charity, *see* charity
    and Christian faith, 26
    and God's kingdom, 187, 193, 212, 213, 226, 230, 232, 235
    and law, 99, 146
    and merchants, 118, 114
    and reason, 145
    and society, 82, 91, 92, 99, 114, 152, 154, 194, 230
    and the Fathers, 33, 93, 119
    and the poor, 26, 30, 32, 47, 59, 61, 65, 80, 116, 121, 153, 186, 191, 193, 203, 212–16, 229, 234
    and the rich, 65, 119, 146, 148
    and work, 87–9, 92, 103, 143–4, 148
    God's, 60, 72, 97, 99, 148, 157, 213, 225, 227, 234
    natural, 146

kenosis, 216–23, 224n
kindness, 43, 62, 210, 212, 224–5, 227

knight(s), 34, 68, 84, 85, 99, 109, 158, 159, 196, 225n
kynde, 146, 147, 158, 169, 218, 224
Kynde, 191
kyndenesse, 21, 232, 233, 234

labourer(s), 68–70, 73, 76–86, 89–91, 95, 97, 102–4, 109, 143, 147–8, 153, 166, 176, 234
lady/ladies, 17, 57, 85, 98, 120, 124, 160, 181, 206
lame, 71n, 99–100, 114, 129, 167, 201–2
language,
    and development of ideas, 21, 190n, 233, 234
    and imagery, 195
    and moral tradition, 200n
    of *Piers Plowman* related to contemporary institutions, 15, 79–80, 89–90, 114, 166, 225n
    of poverty, 21, 27
    of statutes, 77–8
    to express contemporary needs, 14, 193–4, 234–5
Last Judgment, 28, 41, 61, 66, 68, 82, 97–8, 100, 108–13, 126, 129–30, 137–42, 150, 153, 166, 227
Latin America, 27–8, 31
Launfal, 158–60, 192
law,
    canon, 16, 34, 41, 44, 59, 69, 70, 114, 129, 173–4
    civil, 16, 21, 32, 46, 82–3, 85, 89, 98, 99–100, 109, 147, 148–9, 170, 173, 199, 209, 225n
    natural, 43, 144, 145–6, 234
    of charity, 89, 103
    of the Old Testament, 226
lawyer(s), 36, 109, 110, 111
Lazarus, 107, 202–4, 223
leader/ship,
    Conscience, 191
    Piers, 68, 83, 87, 91, 97
    spiritual, 209
    the ploughman, 80, 83, 84, 324
learning, 156n, 170, 178–80, 208
lechery, *see* seven deadly sins
leftovers, 129, 132, 134, 197, 198, 204, 209
Le livre des seintes medicines, 198n
leper(s), 45, 50n, 53, 71, 131, 202–3, 223

Les reules Seynt Roberd, 197n
lewed vicory, 95, 231
Leviticus, 172
Lex Christi, 43, 106
liflode, 39, 80, 81, 84, 87–9, 95, 107, 125, 127, 136, 138–42
literatus, 170
livery, 114, 120, 216, 221, 230
loller(s)/*lollare(s)* 163, 166, 167, 171, 176, 183, 185
lord(s)/*lordes*, 17, 32, 35, 57–8, 65, 69, 74, 84, 85, 93n, 99, 102, 108, 114, 120, 132, 141, 143, 146, 152, 181, 184, 187, 196–99, 203, 204, 206, 208, 215
lunacy, 181, 183, *see also* insanity, madness
lunatic/*lunatik*/*lynatik*, 183, 184, 185

madman, 161, 183, 184
madness, 34, 180–84
maisondieu, 45, 131
margin(s), 52, 118, 120, 129, 175, 177, 181, 184, 212
Mary, 46, 139, 153, 221
Meed/*Mede*, 59, 79, 82, 84, 94, 124, 178, 182, 221
mendicants/mendicancy, 45, 51, 54, 55, 79–80, 95, 123, 127–8, 157, 162–3, 167–71, 174, 178, 180, 185, 189–90, 212
Mensa philosophica, 200
merchant(s), 21, 32, 45, 49, 110–11, 116–20, 128, 131–2, 135, 137n, 138, 140–1, 172
mercy,
    God's, 103, 150, 160, 165, 173, 212, 219–23, 225–27, 232
    works of, 33, 39, 51, 71, 98, 108, 127, 130, 204
Mercy, 218
mercymonye, 147, 148
meritum, 143
mesure, 64, 87, 92, 142, 144, 189, 191, 220, 231, 232
minstrels, 32, 93n, 186n, 205n
monastery/monasteries, 46, 51–3, 58, 83, 128–9, 133, 196
monasticism, 51–2, 133
monk(s)
    and poverty, 50–2, 83, 132
    and the poor, 133
Moralia in Job, 158n, 191

Index

ne soliciti sitis, 54, 112, 116, 135, 136, 139–42, 151, 154, 164, 172
necessities, 35, 74, 86, 87, 94n, 106, 137, 142, 161, 170, 192, 193, 209
Nede/Need, 66, 88, 186, 187–91, 192
Neville, George, 196, 198

order(s),
   divine, 72, 83, 102, 121, 213
   mendicant, 29, 54, 87, 123
   natural, 145–6
   Piers', 228–9
   religious, 54, 116, 119, 157, 163, 169
   social, 13, 28, 34, 37, 39, 40, 46, 62, 68, 78, 80, 83, 85, 89–90, 91, 94–7, 98, 113, 118, 205, 207, 211, 213–14, 215–16, 230, 231, 234
   traditional/three, 41n, 81, 212, 234
Ordinance, 1349 of Labour, 76–77
orphans, 53, 71, 75

parable(s),
   Dives and Pauper/Lazarus, 40, 107, 195n, 202–3, 206, 223
   eschatalogical, 108
   good Samaritan, 224
   labourers in the vineyard, 97, 102, 148
   Last Judgement, 141, 150
   lost drachma, 173
   lost sheep, 173
   pearl of great price, 140n, 173
   prodigal son, 173
   sheep and the goats, 111
   talents, 93, 97, 108
   ten virgins, 108
   treasure in the field, 172
   unjust steward, 97, 106–7
   wedding banquet(s), 71n, 97, 99–100, 138–9, 142, 195, 210
   parasite, 15, 167–8, 177
   pardon, 43, 59, 64, 69, 92, 94–5, 98, 110–13, 118–20, 126–7, 136–8, 139–40, 145, 153, 222
Paris, 31, 55, 78
parody/parodies, 194, 206
Passover, 109, 202
Paternoster, 57, 127, 136, 139–41, 151, 170–1, 173, 177
Patience, 30, 49, 61, 64–6, 116–17, 120, 126, 134–54, 163, 182, 184, 189, 195, 203, 208–9, 231, 232
patience, 47, 116, 145, 151, 191
Paul, Saint, 37, 39, 62, 81, 104–5, 142–3, 162, 183–4, 219
pauper(s), 20, 22, 40, 43, 45–6, 51, 52, 73, 83, 87, 101, 129–30, 131–5, 149, 158, 185–90, 188, 203, 204, 207
pauperes Christi, 50
payment, 57, 74, 127–8, 129, 148, 210, 211, 213, 226, 233
pearl, 140n, 173, 204
Pearl, 214
peasant(s), 31, 34, 39, 68, 70, 73–4, 78, 81, 84, 86, 87–9, 94, 117, 125, 134, 161
penance, 49, 110, 112, 113, 127, 134, 138, 140, 143, 144, 151, 158, 162, 165n, 171, 172, 188n, 208, 215, 224, see also sacraments
Philippians, 37, 216
Philosophy, 48–9
pilgrim, 51, 101, 134, 151, 152, 187, 208
pilgrimage, 67, 85–6, 94, 96, 98, 100, 112, 127, 137, 143, 151
pity, 13, 93, 149, 220
plague, 15, 31, 46, 70, 73, 196, 205, see also Black Death
pledge, 151, 222–3, 227, see also wed
plough, 83, 89, 95
ploughing of the halfacre, 62, 67, 69, 73, 80, 85, 87–92, 98, 102, 109, 128, 137, 178, 229
ploughman/ploughmen, 67, 68, 80, 82–4, 86, 87, 91, 110, 126, 186, 234
poor relief, 21, 26, 27n, 32, 37–8, 41–4, 46, 51, 58, 64, 72, 75, 111, 116, 120–1, 128–35, 150, 155, 187, 222
possession(s), 38, 48, 55–6, 65, 119, 135, 159–60, 177, 182
possessioner(s), 56, 124
poverty,
   and controversy, 28, 51, 55, 124
   and crime, 78–83
   and culture, 14, 21, 22, 25–6, 35, 38, 50–1
   and heaven, 27, 30, 51, 112, 144, 155
   and perfection, 51, 53, 60, 112, 135, 140n, 162, 163, 192
   and reform, 30, 49, 59, 134, 161, 164
   and salvation, 60, 63–4, 117, 139, 158, 209
   and seven deadly sins, 49, 65, 120, 189, 231

poverty *(continued)*
  and the Church, 27n, 32–4, 40–4, 46, 58, 91, 135
  and Will's identity, 134, 157, 160, 175, 209, 219
  as a philosophical good, 30, 49, 60, 161
  as a scandal, 25, 30, 36, 37–8, 40, 60, 67, 69, 135, 155, 161, 164, 175, 169
  as an evil, 25, 30–7
  as imitation of Christ, 25, 28, 30, 47, 50, 52–6, 60, 67, 112, 122, 135, 157, 160–4, 190–1, 232
  as liberation from care, 25
  badge of, 114, 152
  Christ's own, 29, 36, 189–90
  Christian principles of, 50, 164, 173, 180, 185
  compensation/palliative for, 64, 72, 120, 144, 154, 161, 220, 232, 234
  evangelical, 27, 28, 50, 54, 56, 117, 164, 167
  five distinctions of, 25, 27, 28, 30, 60, 79
  hardships of, 28, 31–2, 69–80, 88–9, 187–8
  modern perceptions of, 26–7, 29, 31–2, 34–5, 37–8, 194
  religious/monastic, 29, 51–4,
  Scripture on, 36–7, 115
  voluntary, 25, 28–9, 50–4, 55, 63, 67, 117, 145, 157, 158, 161, 163, 165, 167, 168, 169–75, 177–8, 186, 189–90, 191, 209, 228n
  writing as Langland's solution for, 234
prayer(s),
  and charity, 72, 120, 127
  and good works, 128
  and Will, 127–8, 140, 165, 169–72, 177
  as food, 110
  for the dead, 45, 121–2, 124–7, 129, 131, 134
  of friars, 124
  of hermits, 49
  of the poor, 45, 128, 131
  prescribed, 127, 170n, 177
  purchase of, 45, 121, 123–8, 131
prelate(s), 55, 56, 58, 80, 128, 195, 203, 207, 210
pride, *see* seven deadly sins
priest(s)
  and the Pardon, 110, 137

  appropriating, 57
  debate between secular and regular, 55
  in secular employment, 57
  in *Leviticus* 172n
  parish, 58–9, 69, 129
  stipendiary/chantry, 122, 124
prisoner(s), 53, 71, 72, 92, 101, 128, 131, 223, 226, 227
profit, 21, 52, 61, 80, 82, 87, 89n, 118, 120, 136–8, 140, 172–3, 208, 222n
property, 32–4, 48, 51–6, 58, 70–1, 92, 117, 119, 120, 122, 154, 162, 175, 180, 184, 214
prophet(s), 36, 88n, 112, 113, 182, 182n, 183, 223
providence, 47, 138
purgatory, 99, 121–3, 126–7, 226

quaestiones, 91

rank(s), 21, 102, 186, 199, 208, 214, 224, 225
ransom, 211n, 219, 226–7
Reason, 62, 82, 145, 164, 166, 168–73, 177, 187
Rechelesnesse, 21, 49, 61, 64, 115, 120, 151, 161, 163
reciprocity,
  between donors and recipients, 94
  between God and giver, 211–12
  between God and man, 217–20, 223, 225
  between labourers and non-labouring estates, 68, 181
  between poor and non-poor, 39, 130, 148, 212
  between poor person and Christ, 190
  between rich and rich, 129, 211
  in the duties of society, 68, 94, 98, 234
reckoning, 143, 146, 147, 154, *see also* account
redde quod debes, 229
redeemer, 189, 219n, 232
redemption, 27, 165, 193, 211, 212, 213–30, 232, 234
reform,
  of poverty, 30, 49, 59, 134, 161
religious, 25, 50, 54, 157, 164, 166
  personal reform and poverty, 161n, 164
  social, 47, 62–3, 71
  Will and reform, 30, 157, 191

Index

Regement of princes, 36, 49, 69n, 158, 159, 180n
repentance, 46, 95, 124, 127, 136, 137, 165, 166, 172–3, 178, 180, 208, 225
Repentance, 67, 93n, 124, 166n, 221, 224n, 232
responsibility,
  for actions, 16, 136, 147
  for eradicating poverty, 38
  for the poor, 27, 32, 38, 92, 111, 136
  moral, 41, 43, 94, 111, 136, 147, 157, 161, 166, 170
  of clerics, 32, 128, 129
  of restitution, 225
  of the non-poor, 42
  of Will as writer, 172, 181, 183, 186
  social, 13, 46, 68
restitution, 49, 56, 93, 118, 1120, 123, 128, 225, 229
resurrection, 29, 111, 165, 189
reward,
  and good works, 105, 220
  and incarnation, 218, 222
  and justice/merit, 143, 144, 146, 213, 230
  and mercy, 221, 223
  and poor intention, 93
  and punishment, 87, 107
  and redemption, 193, 211, 213, 216, 225, 233
  and responsibility, 72, 148
  and Scripture, 214
  and wealth, 150
  as compensation/palliative for poverty, 64, 72, 120, 144, 154, 161, 220, 232, 234
  earthly application of heavenly reward, 225, 227, 230, 232
  heavenly, 30, 64, 211, 213, 214, 217, 231, 232
  material, 158, 201
  to be earned, 147–8
rich young man, 115, 135, 139
Roman de la rose, 55
Romans, 97, 105, 106, 108, 150, 207
russet, 21n, 45, 175, 179, 210, 216n
ru_e, 147, 148, 149, 181, 220, 222

sacrament(s),
  baptism, 151, 173, 202n, 224n
  and everyday life, 224n
  eighth, 50n
  eucharist, 67, 138, 143, 165, 202, 217, 224n
  penance, 55, 123, 138, 143, 165, 174, *see also* confession
  poor person sacrament of Christ, 50, 65–7, 164, 189, 190
salvation,
  and charity to the poor, 29, 47, 63, 72, 108, 111, 114, 117, 121, 122, 126–7, 150, 153
  and election, 202
  and Haukyn, 137
  and Hewett-Smith's interpretation, 60, 64, 66
  and identity with Christ, 127
  and medieval society, 23, 117
  and Piers' Pardon, 92, 110, 137
  and poverty, 60, 63–4, 117, 139, 158, 209
  and prayers of the poor, 45
  and repentance, 229
  and sharing goods, 150
  and sinners, 95, 150
  and St Francis, 54
  and teaching, 203
  and the non-poor, 117
  and the poor, 101, 113–4, 117
  as redemption and reward, 213
  Will's search for, 13, 180
Salvation History, 66–7, 163, 187, 224
Samaritan, 66, 219n, 224–7, 232
Satan, 217, 219, 225, 227
scandal of vagrants and beggars, 75, *see also* poverty
scholasticism,
  and distinctions, 22, 94
  and knowledge, 206
  and theologians, 44, 117, 118, 138n
secte/sekte, 114, 127, 152, 221
self-denial, 162, 168, 173, 229
self-indulgence, 208, 210
seven deadly sins,
  and poverty, 49, 65, 120, 189, 231
  and traditional teaching, 195
  and 1388 Statute, 169
  and contrary virtues, 160
  and Haukyn, 136, 142, 151
  avarice, 52, 55, 59, 124, 28, 191
  Coveitise, 124, 182
  envy, 209

seven deadly sins *(continued)*
   Gluttony, 65
   gluttony, 82, 89, 194, 198–9, 203–10
   lechery, 103
   personifications of, 221
   pride, 201, 204–5, 210
   Sloth, 59
   sloth, 83, 94, 103, 104, 107, 112, 167, 169, 177–9, 186
shame, 35, 42n, 60, 189, 190, 194
shepherds, 175–6
sick, the, 53, 71, 92, 99–100, 103, 111, 114, 129, 142, 197, 209
siege, 124, 185
solicitude,
   and *lunatik lolleres*, 185
   and Patience, 116
   and the Gospel, 47
   and the rich, 143, 153
   and Will, 171, 185
   'be not solicitous', 48, 112, 138
   God's, 50, 164, 185
   three types of, 142
   see also ne soliciti sitis
solidarity, 26, 30, 32, 38, 53, 109, 163, 164, 186, 190, 206, 235
sophistry, 203–4
sowing, 87, 96, 97–8, 100, 102, 104–5, 140
stained glass window, 45, 124
status, 21, 25, 35, 41, 71, 78, 81, 83, 100, 159, 162, 170, 184, 208, 210, 218, 231, *see also* estate
statute(s),
   1351 Statute of Labourers, 76–77, 104, 176n
   1356 Statute of Labourers, 176n
   1388 Statute, 77–78, 104, 166, 168–70, 172, 174, 176n, 192
   and the able-bodied, 76–7, 80, 111, 170, 174
   and language of *Piers Plowman*, 79, 80, 89, 90, 91, 111, 114
   and Piers, 106
   and society's ills, 104
   and the poor, 16, 76, 156, 201
   conflicting with charity, 44
   Episcopal, 58
   inadequacies of, 174
   sumptuary, 21, 199, 209, 216n
Study, 119, 193, 199–201, 203–7, 208, 210

subsistence, 70, 84, 88, 89, 91, 137
surety, 21, 93, 151, 188, 222, 223, 224, *see also* pledge
surplus, 38, 62, 74, 80, 89–90, 137–8, 153, 234
sute, 21, 114, 120, 152, 216, 221–2, 230

temperance, 65, 188–9, 230
The castle of perseverance, 66, 160, 214
The shewings of Julian of Norwich, 215n
theocracy, 219, 230
The Seafarer, 70
The Wanderer, 69
'three orders', *see* orders
tithe(s), 41, 56, 58, 74, 129
trade(s), 32, 74, 86, 98, 118, 138, 142, 144, 158, 234
Trajan, 163, 164n, 193, 195, 210–12, 222–3, 232
treasure,
   earthly, 52, 138–9, 146
   imagery of heaven, 21, 172, 193
   spiritual, in heaven, 21, 47, 51, 72, 112, 115, 121, 138–40, 147, 162, 163, 230, 232
tribulations, 141, 149–50, 154
Trinity, 159, 216, 220, 222–5
Truth, 66–7, 85, 92, 98, 136, 164, 165, 188, 192, 218, 231

Unjust Steward, *see* parable
unkindness, 155, 219n, 220, 224–5
unkyndenesse, 65, 142, 214
usurer(s), 58, 93, 108, 141, 220n
usury, 93, 118

vagabond(s), 776–8, 92, 99–100, 162, 167
vagabondage, 74, 76
vagrants, 30, 44, 75, 76, 111, 114, 161–2, 174
viator, 25, 162
vicar(s), 57, 58, 122, 129, 132, 229
vision(s), 60, 64, 161, 164, 166, 177–82, 186, 210, 220n, 223, *see also* dreams
vocation, 30, 60, 79, 136, 166, 168, 170–3, 176, 180, 191–2
Voices of the poor, 26, 34n, 38n, 81n, 194n
voluntas, 139–41, 153, 161, 171, 179

wafers, 135, 138, 142

Index

wage(s), 59, 68, 70–1, 73–6, 83–4, 89–90, 91, 95, 98, 100, 106, 144, 147–8, 220, 223n, 234
wanderer(s), 70n, 89, 162–3, 170, 177, 179, 186
Wanderer, 161, see Bosch
waste, 59, 82, 84, 89, 193, 195, 200–1, 205–6, 231, 232
waster(s), 32, 79, 84–5, 86, 91, 94–5, 98, 104, 106–7, 113, 163, 167–8, 182, 205, 209, 229
wealth,
  and folly, 183
  and Haukyn, 135, 146
  and justice, 148–50, 212
  and monasteries, 52
  and Patience, 137–52
  and purgatory, 123
  and Sir Launfal, 158–60
  and St Francis, 162
  and the Canon's Yeoman, 158
  as image of heaven, 214
  as spiritual reality, 63
  disproportion in, 27, 90
  drawbacks of, 31, 48, 113, 120, 151
  ecclesiastical, 56
  imagery of, 21, 214
  of peasants, 125
wed, 188, 223
wedding,
  banquet, 142, 202, 213
  feast, 99, 138, 201
  garment, 138
widow(s), 45–6, 71, 74, 86–7, 130, 162, 198
Will,
  against Antichrist, 67, 163, 186, 190
  and anticlericalism, 166–7
  and choice, 163, 174
  and contemporary ideologies, 174, 175–85, 191
  and Dame Study, 203
  and folly, 180–7
  and Haukyn, 64, 116, 138–9
  and intention, 163
  and Need, 186–91, 219
  and practical charity, 64, 66, 191
  and the quest for salvation, 13, 29, 30, 165, 177–80, 217
  and solicitude, 154, 171–2, 231
  and spiritual labour, 85, 127–8, 140, 171–2, 177–80
  and the 1388 Statute, 166–72
  and the banquet of Conscience, 134, 207–10
  and the quest for Truth, 164
  and the *sute* of Christ, 152
  and the will, 161, 165, 171–4, 175, 191
  and wasters, 167–8
  and writing, 166, 167, 181–2
  as a poor man, 28, 30, 47, 50, 66, 152, 155, 156–92,
  as a sinner, 30, 173
  as hermit, 175
  as visionary, 163–4, 177–81
  as voice of the poor, 134
  like Christ, 175, 190
  poor in Cornhill, 167
  the poem's unifying character, 13, 161
will
  of God, 50, 54, 136–41, 153, 164–5, 169, 171–4, 180, 191, 214, 226, 228
  Haukyn's, 143,
  the reader's, 63, 143, 181, 235
will(s), testamentary, 45–6, 71, 87, 112, 121–5, 127–32, 137
wisdom, 181, 183, 213, 214
women as poor, 30, 34, 45, 71–5, 77, 128, 130, 133, 162, 184–5, 194, 234
work,
  and the Statute of Labourers, 76–7, 176
  as defining status of the poor, 81
  as labour, 80–3, 85, 87, 92, 93, 95, 103, 168, 171
  as necessary for salvation, 143, 148, 211
  as punishment for sin, 97, 107
  as reciprocal responsibility, 81, 85, 89, 91, 97, 98, 110, 118
  as survival, 85, 108, 133, 147
  in the ideal society, 82, 84–5
  of Christ, 50, 54, 164, 190
  of clerics, 56. 58
  of mercy, *see* mercy
work *(continued)*
  on the half-acre, *see* half-acre
  social, 55
  Will's, 140, 163, 168, 170, 177, 181, 191
works, good, 53, 105, 110, 113, 120, 122, 126, 127, 134, 135, 155, 159, 206, 207, 220, *see also* mercy

World Bank, 26, 31–2, 35, 38
writing,
   and medieval 'conceptions of the Word', 218
   as Langland's solution for poverty, 234
   as the education of the reader's will, 63, 143, 192, 234
   criticized by Imaginatif, 178
   moral power of Will's, 181
   Will's dreams, a metaphor for, 178
   see also Will's work

York, 45–6, 75, 129–31, 196
Yorkshire, 45, 131, 133

Index of authors

Adams, 191
Aers, 14n, 60-3, 73n, 85n, 89, 90, 136n, 144, 154, 233
Alford, 43, 92n, 96, 102n, 101, 102n, 138, 142n, 145, 148, 150, 151n, 211n, 226n
Allen, 43, 60n, 92n, 96
Althusser, 15, 22n, 156
Ambrose, Saint, 33n, 41, 42n, 86, 93, 94n, 119, 154
Anderson, 182n
Aquinas, 34, 42, 70, 118
Aristotle, 34
Aston, 51n, 210n
Augustine, 40, 42, 93, 100, 202n, 206n

Bakhtin, 199, 200n
Baldwin, Anna, 11, 143n, 152, 225n
Baldwin, Frances, 21n, 199n, 216n
Barr, 233
Bartholomeus, 181
Bennett, 41, 46, 133
Bernard, Saint, 53
Bernardino, Saint, 118
Bloomfield, 189
Boethius, 44-5
Bowers, 91n, 156n, 167, 175n, 177n, 178, 179, 204n
Brinton, 39, 81
Burgess, 121-2, 123n, 124, 132
Burnley, 184n
Burrow, 159n, 171-2, 189
Bynum, 14n

Caesarius of Arles, 39
Campbell, 86n
Chaucer, 18, 19, 21, 29, 35, 36, 125, 126n, 158, 175, 186, 195n
Chester, 158-9

Chrysostom, 33, 41-3, 118, 142
Clark, 20, 74, 86n, 87n, 133n, 134
Clopper, 55, 56, 65n, 140n, 157n, 165n, 167, 168n, 170n, 184n, 185, 186n
Coleman, 17n, 19
Constantelos, 30n, 46n, 214n
Cosner, 196n
Cullum, 45, 46n, 130

Davlin, 11, 145, 224n
dei Segni, Lotario, 35, 38
de Meung, 55
de Roover, 118n, 138n
de Vitry, 70
Donaldson, 172n
Doob, 205n
Duby, 41n
Dyer, 20, 39n, 41n, 70n, 72-3, 74n, 77, 78, 80n, 81, 83n, 84, 86, 89n, 125n, 133, 134n

Erasmus, 200

FitzRalph, 29, 55, 100n, 144
Fowler, 22n
Frank, 89n, 91n, 200n
Freedman, 30n, 39n, 83n, 84n, 85n

Galloway, Andrew, 11, 18n, 21, 57, 170n, 171n, 224n, 225, 233
Galloway, James, 86n, 87n
Geremek, 75n, 78n, 212n
Girouard, 197n, 198n, 208n
Goldberg, 130
Gower, 21, 89
Gratian, 34
Graziani, 161n
Gregory, 33, 41, 93, 191

Grosseteste, 58, 197, 204, 209n
Gutiérrez, 26–9, 32n, 37, 40, 50, 53n

Hammond, 197n, 198n
Hanawalt, 20, 77, 72n
Hanna, 170n, 175n 176n, 177n, 186n
Harrison, 132n
Hatcher, 31, 70, 73, 78, 89, 90
Heath, 112n, 137n
Hebblethwaite, 37n, 50n, 53n
Henisch, 196n
Hewett-Smith, 11, 27n, 60, 63–4, 66, 67n, 85n, 90, 91n, 154, 188n, 228n
Highet, 48n
Hilton, 20, 84
Hoccleve, 18, 36, 49, 69n, 158–60, 180–1, 183–4, 192
Howard, 182
Hudson, 255n

Ignatieff, 13, 23, 26, 38, 153, 193, 235

Jeanneret, 199n, 200n
Jerome, 42, 43, 93, 96
Julian of Norwich, 215
Justice, 14
Juvenal, 25n, 48, 79, 157, 161–2, 175, 177

Kane, 223n
Kerby-Fulton, 22, 192n, 235n
Kernan, 14
Kim, 11–12, 16, 28n, 40, 69n, 79n, 90–1, 117n, 188–90, 205, 206n, 219n
Kirk, 84, 234
Lancaster, Henry of, 160, 198

Lawton, 110, 111n
le Goff, 119n, 141n
Leff, 51n, 54n, 164
Lis and Soly, 31, 62n, 70n, 71n, 74n
Little, 51n, 52n, 53n, 54n, 59, 119n, 154n
Lovejoy, 86n, 94n

McHardy, 125
McIntosh, 20, 44, 77
Macherey, 15, 16, 17
Maitland, 28
Mann, 41n, 84

Mannyng, 127, 79n, 220n
Marcus, 14
Marx, 226n
Masschaele, 89n, 117n
Mennell, 196n, 199
Middleton, 14n, 79, 89, 156, 165–70, 174n, 176n
Milis, 39n, 51, 133
Minnis, 18
Moisa, 39n, 40n, 78n, 94n, 176n
Mollat, 20, 30–1, 34, 38–9, 54, 60, 62n, 63, 70n, 74n, 75n, 175, 176n
Morey, 83n
Murphy, 86n, 87n

Nicholas, 20, 74n, 75n

Owst, 94n

Pearsall, 11, 60, 63–4, 66, 71, 127n, 128, 154–5, 167n, 184n, 189, 212
Plutarch, 200
Poos, 20, 31, 45n, 70, 71n, 73, 74n, 77, 78n
Putnam, 76n, 77, 78n

Rabelais, 200
Régamey, 32, 35n, 50, 164, 169n
Reynolds, 48n
Rolle, 160, 178
Rosenthal, 121, 123, 125n, 126, 127n, 128, 131n, 132
Rubin, 20, 27n, 46, 62n, 69n
Rudd, 156n, 205n, 210n
Rufinus, 42
Ryan, 29n

St Amour, William, 55
Sandler, 59n
Scase, 55–6, 124, 163n, 166, 171, 174n, 176, 186n, 190, 192, 212, 234
Schmidt, 22n, 206n
Seneca, 48–9
Shepherd, 60–1, 64, 66, 79n, 153,
Simpson, 11, 86, 112, 113n, 143–4, 156n, 161n, 179–80, 181n, 182n, 192, 206, 222n, 223n, 234
Strohm, 14, 18, 23

Index of authors

Swabey, 87n, 198n
Szittya, 55

Thompson, John A. F. 123
Thompson, J. A. K. 34n
Tierney, 27n, 42n, 43n, 44, 58n, 71n, 93n, 99n, 110n, 129n, 132, 188n

Vale, 131

Wallace, 14, 18, 19, 46n, 90

Ward, 198n
Warner, 225n
Warren, 123, 130–2, 160, 161n, 162n
Watson, 217–18, 219n
Watts, 48n
Wenzel, 182
White, Eileen, 196n
White, Hugh, 224n
Williams, 17, 19
Wimbledon Thomas, 39, 81, 231n
Wittig, 156n, 161n